THE POWER OF CULTURE

THE POWER OF CULTURE

Critical Essays in American History

Edited by Richard Wightman Fox and T. J. Jackson Lears

 The University of Chicago Press · *Chicago and London*

Richard Wightman Fox is professor of history and director of American Studies at Boston University.

T. J. Jackson Lears is professor of history at Rutgers University.

The University of Chicago Press, Chicago 60637
The University of Chicago Press, Ltd., London
© 1993 by The University of Chicago
All rights reserved. Published 1993
Printed in the United States of America

02 01 00 99 98 97 96 95 94 93   5 4 3 2 1

ISBN (cloth): 0-226-25954-4
ISBN (paper): 0-226-25955-2

Library of Congress Cataloging-in-Publication Data

The Power of culture : critical essays in American history / edited by
    Richard Wightman Fox and T.J. Jackson Lears.
         p.   cm.
    Contents: Sherwood Anderson / Jackson Lears — Unlimn'd they
disappear / Christopher P. Wilson — Early American murder
narratives / Karen Halttunen — Intimacy on trial / Richard Wightman
Fox — The class experience of mass consumption / Lizabeth Cohen —
Between culture and consumption / Joan Shelley Rubin — Fighting for
the American family / Robert Westbrook — Making time / Michael L.
Smith — An atmosphere of effrontery / Casey Nelson Blake.
    1. United States—Civilization—20th century. I. Fox, Richard
Wightman, 1945–   . II. Lears, T. J. Jackson, 1947–   .
E169.1.P75   1993
973.9—dc20   92-31011
                                                          CIP

Contents

Introduction

For historians of the United States the 1980s was the decade of the turn toward "cultural" history. There was in fact a good deal of cultural history before that, although much of it was celebratory or anecdotal chronicling of everyday life in the American past. Critically minded historians usually studied politics and diplomacy, society and ideas. The development of vaudeville and film, the rise of the dime novel and literary realism, the spread of a therapeutic mentality in liberal religion—these and a thousand other topics were, when not dismissed outright, relegated to the periphery of the historical enterprise. Analytically minded cultural historians before the 1980s remember being mocked by many of their colleagues, who considered their interest in the alleged ephemera of popular life quirky at best, silly and irrelevant at worst.

Today cultural history has occupied the central terrain of the historical profession, in part because its definition has broadened to include much scholarship that until recently was called "social" or "intellectual" history. But the change is much more than terminological. We are in the midst of a dramatic shift in sensibility, and "cultural" history is the rubric under which a massive doubting and refiguring of our most cherished historical assumptions is being conducted. Many historians are coming to suspect that the idea of culture has the power to restore order to the study of the past. Whatever its potency as an organizing theme, there is no doubt about the power of the term "culture" to evoke and stand for the depth of the reexamination now taking place. At a time of deep intellectual disarray, "culture" offers a provisional, nominalist version of coherence: whatever the fragmentation of knowledge, however centrifugal the spinning of the scholarly wheel, "culture"—which (even etymologically) conveys a sense of safe nurture, warm growth, budding or ever-present wholeness—will shelter us.

Yet hopes for the restoration of order are premature. The cultural history field of the 1990s is not like a well-tended garden with diversified plants waving harmoniously in the breeze. It resembles a staging area in which a number of different and only weakly allied intellectual armies have assem-

1

bled and are warily eyeing one another. The historians of popular culture were there first. Then came a band of emigrating social historians who had tired of the "documentary" effort launched in the 1960s to establish the existence and significance of previously neglected Americans. Social-scientific methods worked well when the goal was to determine, for example, how much social mobility took place in nineteenth-century cities, how many immigrants went back to Europe, which types of people were institutionalized for deviant behavior, or how many women worked outside as well as inside the home. But when social historians began to wonder about the consciousness as well as the behavior of their subjects, to doubt whether the poor or oppressed were really as "inarticulate" as social historians originally assumed them to be, and to throw critical light on the very notions of class, ethnicity, race, deviance, gender, and other "variables" that had previously been taken as quantifiable givens, they had to move toward cultural history.

Meanwhile, intellectual historians, themselves heavily influenced in the 1970s by social-historical assumptions, tended in the 1980s to declare their independence from social history. Rather than continuing in Marxist or "neo-progressive" fashion to see ideas as shaped by such social determinants as class, many intellectual historians returned more or less to the view that ideas could be studied "in themselves." But now doing the history of ideas meant not arranging the "great ideas" in proud procession across the centuries, but considering how all ideas were produced, communicated, and received, and examining the methodological and conceptual dilemmas of present-day scholars who try to communicate the history of those ideas to their own readers. Rhetoric, textuality, and audience became bywords for the cohort of intellectual historians who inched closer and closer to the campfires not only of the popular culture investigators and the social-cultural historians, but of the cultural anthropologists, literary theorists, and semioticians who, increasingly drawn by historical study, had crept into the field under cover of darkness and planted the new banner of "cultural studies."

Semiotics and critical theory have been central to the rapid spread of cultural history. A semiotic approach encourages the historian to recognize that cultural meaning can be carried by a variety of vehicles—that political pageants and advertisements as well as sermons and speeches are texts to be deciphered. An emphasis on the inescapable textuality of all sources, even census rolls and market research reports, has freed historians from a positivist conception of data retrieval and focused their attention on the fundamental task of interpretation.

The rejection of positivist orthodoxy has more than methodological significance. Epistemological challenges to conventional notions of objectivity are also in some instances political challenges to the hegemonic discourse of instrumental reason. Feminist scholars were among the first to realize this, and cultural studies have often come to fullest fruition under the aegis of women's studies. Grasping the contingent character of categories once deemed immutable came easily to feminists eager to dismantle the barriers to women's liberation, as well as to critics of the imperial designs that for so long had been legitimated by the supposed superiority of Western science. The turn toward textuality has coincided with an awakening of feminist and environmentalist consciousness.

At the same time, much new cultural history signals its withdrawal from the world of politics. The emergence of cultural history in our era is linked to the collapse of the consensus that had shaped public discourse in the United States after World War II, and to the subsequent failure of New Left alternatives. A quarter century ago progressive liberalism or radicalism seemed to many Americans (and probably to a majority of historians) to offer a coherent framework for faith in the future. Today it is more likely to be conservatives who proclaim their commitment to progress and growth—a proclamation that seems to require willful denial of ecological devastation and rigid adherence to the allegedly character-building discipline of the market. From Vietnam and Watergate to the fall of the Soviet Union, historians and nonhistorians alike have been shaken in their longstanding belief that history is in principle open to, or even moving toward, greater freedom-in-community for all. Having lost much of their trust in the national state as the ultimate guarantor of justice, and much of their conviction that "community" will some day be national in scope, many have turned to local politics or given up "public" concerns altogether.

Cultural historians may have gravitated to the study of "private" experience for the same reason. In this post-progressive age it has made increasing sense to many historians to tell individual life stories, even of obscure people who had no impact on the course of public events. And to a small group of cultural historians, it has seemed proper to leave individuals behind altogether and tell stories about webs of discourse that have, as it were, a life of their own. If historians continue to follow these trends— pushing pluralism to the extreme of treating each individual experience as separate from every other experience, insisting upon the power of culture to impose its "own" agenda while neglecting the power of culture to spark individuals and communities to deliberation and action—the historical profession will be transformed beyond recognition. It will no longer be primarily about public life or power, about identifying the "causes" and "effects" that allow us to understand "change over time." It will be about private life, webs of cultural discourse, and the elaboration of "meanings" in the encounter between the scholarly "construction"-worker and the ever elusive evidences of the past.

The authors of the following essays occupy different standpoints on these issues. But we all agree that historians must become more "cultural" in attending to private as well as public life, and in paying close attention to the ways in which meaning is layered into the documents (of all kinds) that we use and that we write. We also share the conviction that becoming "cultural" must not lead to the neglect of power. Cultural meanings have social and political origins and consequences, in private and public realms alike. A "good society" would be a democratic order in which everyone shared access to the means of producing meaning in private and public, in which everyone participated in making decisions about the common life while also developing a rich network of personal loyalties. It may in fact be in the arena of the private that metaphors of the good communal life can now best be articulated. Historians—even those who no longer envision their work as a direct contribution to a "progressive" future—have much to contribute to the task of clarifying the basic values by which we live and have lived, in our most intimate as in our most impersonal relations.

We make no claim in this volume to "cover" the field of American cultural history, or even to represent fully the mini-camps of social-cultural, literary-cultural, and intellectual-cultural historians from which we ourselves have come. But comprehensiveness is an illusory goal for anything but a multivolume encyclopedia, and in this era of redefinition even a multivolume work would fall short. The absence here of anything about African-American, Hispanic-American, or Native-American experiences, about Catholics or Jews, about the South or the West, should not be taken as an assertion that northeastern or Euro-Protestant traditions are alone central to the production of American culture. The absence of other issues that are currently sparking much debate in cultural history, such as theoretical discussions of gender and the body, or of colonialism and imperialism, should not be taken as a denial of their importance. We also omit many crucial subfields now flourishing on the periphery of cultural history, but bound soon to become mainstream, such as the environment, medicine, and material culture. And we neglect countless significant topics that are so far beyond the horizon of contemporary scholarly fashion that their absence is not even noticed, such as conservative religious subcultures, black and white, urban and rural.

What this collection lacks in comprehensiveness it intends to make up in careful attention to the actual practice of cultural history. We aim to suggest how historians can, whatever period or group or theme they are studying, attend both to the "textual"—visual as well as verbal—character of our knowing and to the broad structures of power that constitute the "real" social world in which our knowing takes place (though of course that world is known to us only through the social constructions of it that are available to us). We want to promote an open-ended American cultural history in which a multiplicity of voices are heard, new experiments are made, and rigor and depth of description and analysis are demanded.

For heuristic purposes we have grouped the essays into four thematic areas. These rubrics are contingent, not necessary; others might have been chosen, and individual essays could have been rearranged among them. The categories are meant to help raise key questions about the essays and about the field of cultural history. In part 1, "The Representation of Experience," Jackson Lears and Christopher Wilson are centrally concerned with authorship, both of texts and lives. How do writers gain authority in and over their own lives? How do they represent, remember, and re-create their own experience for their readers? Lears is more interested in the *life* of Sherwood Anderson, Wilson in the *text* produced by Tillie Olsen, but both Lears and Wilson stress that these lives are written as they are lived. Their essays signal one of the most basic truths of the new cultural history, that experience is mediated by language, that our access to experience in the past as in the present is decisively shaped by its encoding in particular rhetorical conventions.

Lears's study of Anderson breaks through the usual split between "serious" writing and commercial advertising copy by showing that Anderson's fiction and ad copy were both part of an effort to express his desire for authentic experience. His yearning for unmediated intimacy was, for all its modernist features, quite continuous with earlier liberal Protestant male attempts—such as those of Henry Ward Beecher, discussed in Richard Fox's essay—to represent and achieve a transparent connection to some (gendered female) ground of being. In the writing of Anderson, modernism was intimately tied to mass culture, as he struggled to find an unconventional voice among the traditional idioms marginalized by modern commercial speech.

Christopher Wilson's examination of Tillie Olsen's *Yonnondio* suggests that we need to approach such quests for authenticity cautiously. In Wilson's view, one of our key problems in recovering *Yonnondio's* voice is negotiating the text's resistance to our own act of recuperation. The text operates, as it were, as a brake upon the author's or reader's desire for a fulfilling, reassuring transcendence. The novel suggests that neither language, nor the self, nor culture are reservoirs that can be easily tapped for personal or political restoration. Although recent social history and literary criticism have been prone to emphasize the resisting power of immigrant- and working-class cultures—and our own ability to "recover" that resistance in a gesture of partisanship—Olsen's "arduous partnership" with the earlier "Tillie Lerner" challenges our own recovery practices. Instead, *Yonnondio* depicts a cultural battleground where real damages are inflicted to ways of remembering as well as standards of living. Cultures, for Olsen, are not renewable, anymore than material resources are. Nor are texts themselves, as Wilson reads *Yonnondio,* easily retrievable for the edifying purposes to which readers often put them.

In part 2, "Cultural Sagas of the Moral Life," Karen Halttunen and Richard Fox examine the transformation of moral boundaries in northern Protestant life. Halttunen looks at varied bodies of literature over several generations, Fox at an explosive series of events in a single decade, but both are interested in how people reconfigure the horizons of their culture in the stories they tell about moral transgression. Both essays are about the power of narrative to delimit the available range of peak experiences. The essays are typical of the widespread effort in recent cultural history to explore the many intersections between private experience and communal life.

Just as our own era, thanks to Freud, assumes there to be a permeable boundary between health and neurosis, so the Puritans, in Halttunen's analysis, assumed an easy passage from virtue to vice, even murderous vice. Execution sermons were ritual reaffirmations of the tie binding a confessed murderer to the rest of the community, and reassertions of the diabolical potential in every human being. As northern Protestant culture was liberalized, and as the trial report replaced the execution sermon, the belief in a depraved human nature proved impossible to maintain. Evildoers had to be redefined as inhuman monsters, and good citizens had to become ashamed of their growing fascination in the literature of horror.

The cult of horror, which enforced a stark split between normal and criminal people, led to a pornography of horror, in which evil deeds and even pain and suffering returned to haunt the imagination of a liberal middle class that officially regarded tham as bad form. Halttunen's essay, like several others in this volume and like much recent cultural history, displaces the categories of "high" culture and "low" culture from their previously central interpretive position. If we ask the right questions of it, "mass cultural" horror literature—no less than the canonical writings of Poe or Melville, Howells or Wharton—can take us straight to the heart of the bourgeois experience.

Richard Fox's essay on the Beecher-Tilton affair also attempts to fathom the "experience" of the northern Protestant bourgeoisie. He focuses especially upon Henry Ward Beecher and Elizabeth Tilton, who along with Tilton's husband, Theodore, sought self-consciously to grapple with the problem of how to make peak experience—especially the experience of intimacy—a way of life. The Beecher-Tilton affair offers a crucial case study of the battle within bourgeois culture to define the bounds of legitimate behavior and to publicize or suppress alternative modes of action and belief. It is a story of representation, as the lawyers and the principals, themselves renowned authorities on sentimental fiction, debated the question of which plotting could best clarify a very murky stream of events. And it is at its center a story of gendered opportunities, as Elizabeth Tilton discovered again and again during Beecher's, and by extension her own, trial. Fox's essay tries to resurrect Elizabeth Tilton from the obscurity to which she had been (in part voluntarily) consigned, and to argue that the critical study of "experience" must be one primary goal of cultural history.

In part 3, "Constructing and Contesting 'Mass Culture,'" Lizabeth Cohen and Joan Rubin present two essays that on the surface have little to do with one another. Cohen is investigating working-class consumption; Rubin, middlebrow literary institutions. But both authors strive to reconstruct lived experience—the experience of consuming goods on the one hand, that of producing knowledge on the other. They also aim to complicate our understanding of mass culture. Just as Cohen contests the common view that consumer culture creates a homogeneous populace with undiscriminating tastes, Rubin challenges the standard line that distinguishes "highbrow" art from the "middlebrow" or "lowbrow" work that is alleged to be adulterated by its pandering to hoi polloi.

Cohen's study is careful not to romanticize working-class experience. Working-class culture is not, in her analysis, a warm web of traditional relations which holds the line against cold cosmopolitan modernization. "Modernizing" forces do in fact exercise preponderant power, but not by erasing working-class culture. The working-class does adapt (itself an exercising of power) to the economic power of the chain stores, and to the cultural power of consumption, by surrendering many of its ethnic particularities. But it remains distinctively working class. Indeed, advertisers themselves, far from promoting mass standardization, learn to market goods with class firmly in mind. Cohen shows that cultural power operates in a much more complex fashion than our favorite paradigms have frequently allowed us to grasp.

Joan Rubin's analysis of the production of "middlebrow" knowledge asks us to reexamine our usual assumptions about artistic excellence. Contrary to the long-standing tendency of intellectuals to see middlebrow culture as a sell-out, she argues that the work of such now-forgotten figures as Stuart Sherman and John Erskine had its own aesthetic integrity. They managed to keep alive an interest in great literature and even to witness to inherited ideals of "character" that were being swamped by the flood of "personality." But Rubin, like Cohen, refrains from romanticizing her subjects. The careers of Sherman and Erskine testify not only to their commitment to art and character, but to the countervailing power of the culture of personality—a power all the more pervasive because of its appeal even to those, like Sherman and Erskine, who sought to resist it. Like Cohen, Rubin challenges us to reconfigure the concept of "mass culture" so that it does not permit us a stance of dismissive condescension. We must learn to listen to the actual voices of those homogenized and silenced by the label "mass."

In part 4, "Cultural Power and the Public Life," Robert Westbrook, Michael Smith, and Casey Blake turn their attention to public manifestations of cultural power. Westbrook's analysis of conceptions of "obligation" in World War II, Smith's study of representational strategies at the New York World's Fair in 1964, and Blake's essay on the rise and fall of Richard Serra's *Tilted Arc* all explore the ways in which the public realm has been shaped not only by private interests but by the forced exclusion or voluntary secession of many citizens from public activity itself.

Westbrook's essay investigates popular ideas and feelings about political obligation. Just as Cohen demonstrates the unsuspected complexity of the popular world of consumption, Westbrook shows that obligation to the public—a sentiment that Americans express with particular clarity during wartime—is a more complicated phenomenon than we usually suppose.

Public obligation is inseparable from private loyalty. Indeed, in a society as "liberal" as the United States, it has been difficult to maintain a conception of the public interest that is more than the sum total of private interests. Yet even the longing for civic community, which Westbrook finds in the visual documents of wartime, is a form of participation, however rudimentary, in public life. Westbrook's essay is a contribution, along with Halttunen's and Fox's, to the cultural history of American liberalism.

Michael Smith's study of the 1964 New York World's Fair is, like Westbrook's essay, a case study in the intersection of private and public. Arguing that the expressive role of technologies is inseparable from their design and function, Smith finds that corporate and government sponsors did far more than advertise products; they simulated the multiple and overlapping arenas of identity that postwar mass culture assigned to technology. Visitors to GM's "Futurama II" or GE's "Progressland" encountered technological tableaux that conflated the personal aspirations of consumers, corporate public relations, and national identity itself. Mediating between liberal invocations of progress and Cold War paranoia, the Fair employed elaborate representational strategies to *domesticate* outer space and the atom—to render them as familiar as family vacations and children's playgrounds.

Casey Blake's examination of the *Tilted Arc* affair further nuances the problem of the power of culture. Richard Serra's sculpture was itself a cultural power—an artifact imposed upon a public space by a public authority in alliance with a modern art establishment. Both government and art establishment saw themselves as standing for the people. This was not an implausible assumption at a time when public life had so seriously atrophied that "the people" could not represent themselves. Yet here too, as in Westbrook's account of wartime obligation, the people—the federal government workers who actually used the plaza—found ways of expressing their desire for a voice in deliberations about the public realm. But in the absence of a vigorous communal life, the power of competing cultural interest groups—some private and some public—left the people, for the most part, out of the debate. They streamed out of their glass-walled office buildings wondering why no one, neither artist nor government, asked their opinion about how to ornament their own surroundings.

The work of historical imagination, of evoking and interpreting the private and public consciousness of the past, has always been a vexed and complex process of engagement, selection, and documentation. The documentary style so favored by historians of past generations worked to manage this complexity, render the scholarly enterprise "provable," author-itative. Now, under the influence of literary theory, philosophy, anthropol-ogy and other fields, historical writing has become more open-ended, inter-weaving the personal and the public agendas, bringing both to the surface of inquiry. Of course, we can't all be multidisciplinary theorists and prac-titioners. But we do have to tell much more complicated and multilayered stories than most of us have been accustomed to telling. In all of our work we will have to be much more rigorous in questioning our favorite assumptions, and becoming more self-conscious about our own writing. We must insist that the intellectual choice is not between cultural pluralism on the one hand, and reverence for tradition on the other—as the combat-tants in the current "political correctness" and "canon" debates would have it. Rather, the choices concern matters of candor, explicitness, and our willingness to reappraise our method of historical inquiry, to reassess our public conceptions and private experiences of the power of culture in the American past, present, and future.

1 THE REPRESENTATION OF EXPERIENCE

Sherwood Anderson

He left his factory where he found it—by the side of a stream that flowed under a bridge in a little Ohio town—at a time in his life when most men are saving for a soft berth in old age

1 Sherwood Anderson

Looking for the White Spot

T. J. Jackson Lears

It is now almost impossible to find an intellectual who will use the word "reality" without quotation marks. The ideal of authentic self-expression, of faithfulness to some inwardly felt or outwardly observed sense of the real, has fallen on hard times. Current critical perspectives emphasize the constructed, artificial character of all cultural forms; from the poststructuralist (and more broadly postmodern) view, the effort to touch some core of unmediated experience is a relic of simpler times, before writers and artists recognized that the ideal of authentic expression was itself a cultural construction—that reality was always mediated by representation and interpretation.

The discourse of authenticity has been the target of political as well as philosophical criticism. The quest for authentic self-expression, indeed the very sense of unified personhood on which it depended—these have been identified as elements of patriarchy that pervaded not only the bourgeois culture of the nineteenth and early twentieth centuries, but also the modernist attempts to transcend it. According to some critics, the discourse of authenticity has been at the core of what they claim was the central modernist project: the attempt to disengage the autonomous work of high art from the corrupting embrace of mass culture. As Andreas Huyssen observes, that project rested on "the notion which gained ground during the nineteenth century that mass culture is somehow associated with woman while real, authentic culture remains the prerogative of men." The links between women and mass culture were forged in the overheated atmosphere of fin-de-siècle social thought: "the fear of the masses in this age of declining liberalism [was] always also a fear of woman, a fear of nature out of control, a fear of the unconscious, of sexuality, of the loss of identity and stable ego boundaries in the mass." Gustave Le Bon was merely articulating the conventional wisdom in *The Crowd* (1895) when he wrote that "Crowds are everywhere distinguished by feminine characteristics." Huyssen notes: "We may want to relate Le Bon's social psychology of the masses back to modernism's own fears of being sphinxed. Thus the nightmare of being devoured by mass culture through co-option, commodification, and the 'wrong' kind of success is the constant fear of the modernist artist, who tries to stake out his territory by fortifying the boundaries between genuine art and inauthentic mass culture." Despite the apparently adversary relationship between modernism and modernization the two were intimately linked at the core; mandarin modernist and philistine modernizer shared a belief in progress—though for the modernist (Huyssen cites Clement Greenberg and Theodor Adorno) progress was to be constituted by the evolution of an aesthetic logic rather than by the spread of freeways. The current postmodern critique of modernism, from this view, has much in common with the ecological critique of industrial and postindustrial capitalism and with the feminist critique of bourgeois patriarchy. This is a powerful and important argument.[1]

But one aim of this essay will be to show its limitations, at least with respect to American cultural history. In the United States, the modernist discourse of authenticity was without question rooted in masculine anxieties about the emasculating effects of mass culture, but it had a more complex significance as well. To try to catch that complexity, this essay will look at an American writer, Sherwood Anderson (1876–1941), whose career embodied some of the central tensions between modernism and mass culture. For more than twenty years, from 1900 to 1922, Anderson supported himself by writing advertising copy, yet he was probably among the most tormented and relentless literary critics of advertising during the early twentieth century. Railing against the culture created by the corporations, he was proud of his ability to survive in it. Longing for the vitality of rural life, he was also relieved to be rid of it. Anderson was a modernist in his bohemian rebellion against the prim respectability of the American village and in his flat understated style, a compound of Hemingway and Gertrude Stein that sometimes achieved a certain moving eloquence, at other times slid into bogs of solemnity. Like many of his European predecessors and contemporaries, he was embarrassingly, almost self-parodically obsessed with authentic experience and expression; and he revealed that obsession in flagrantly sexual language. Yet his quest for authenticity was more than the sum of its symptoms; it echoed Anglo-American traditions of social critique and spiritual longing, traditions that encouraged more

---

1. Andreas Huyssen, "Mass Culture As Woman: Modernism's Other," in his *After the Great Divide* (Bloomington: Indiana University Press, 1987), pp. 47, 52–53, 57. For a philosophically acute critique of contemporary historians' use of the discourse of authenticity, see Joan Scott, "The Evidence of Experience," *Critical Inquiry* 17 (Summer, 1991), 773–797.

significant critiques of mass culture than a masculine cry of pain. Anderson's was a modernism in the American grain; it resonated with ecological and perhaps even (albeit obliquely and ambivalently) with feminist critiques of modernity. This essay is an effort to suggest that, as cultural critics cast about for an honorable standpoint in the late twentieth century, they need not automatically discard the discourse of authenticity.

It is also the beginning of an attempt to grapple with the implications of poststructuralist theory for cultural history. For some time now I have been impatient with historians' tendency to dismiss the epistemological challenge posed by antifoundationalist movements in philosophy and literary criticism; that challenge has pointed the way toward a salutary emphasis on the textual character of all historical evidence, toward an appropriate stress on the interpretive tasks the historian faces, and toward a more fruitful, less postivistic and literal approach to "the sources." Yet I have also been impatient with certain characteristics of poststructuralist sensibility: the sweeping and unsupported critiques of modernism, the reflex dismissal of any concern with authentic experience as little more than vestigial "essentialism," the assumption that any notion of coherent selfhood merely masks an agenda for white male domination. Among historians I have felt like an outré theorist; among literary critics, a plodding empiricist. This essay is a preliminary gesture toward a more genial middle ground.

To begin to understand Anderson and other American modernists, one has to acknowledge that for them the category of the authentic had more than aesthetic significance. Some of its roots can only be called religious. Longings for union with the deity, which may be universal and timeless, were gradually reshaped in the crucible of Anglo-American Protestant culture. The spiritual ancestors of Anderson (as well as of Stephen Crane, Frank Norris, Ernest Hemingway, Theodore Dreiser, William Carlos Williams, and countless other devotees of the palpable) were the seventeenth-century Protestants who burned to reestablish a core of authentic religious experience beneath the encrustations of ritual. The tendency to equate display and deceit remained a central psychic reflex in many Protestant cultures even after Puritan theology had dissolved into romantic liberalism. Nineteenth-century political thought politicized the discourse of authenticity, locating public virtue in plain speech and plain living, disdaining the "parasitical" vices of commerce, celebrating the leather-aproned "producer" as the ultimate embodiment of republican reality. The producers were invariably male, the parasites effeminate.

Still, the personal dimension of the discourse could not be collapsed into its gender politics. Women as well as men yearned for sincerity and (as the century drew to a close and the emotional ante was raised) for authenticity as well—for unproblematic immediacy in personal as well as artistic expressions. As orthodox Protestantism became more difficult to sustain, writers and artists resorted to romantic, Victorian, and finally modernist idioms to characterize their fascination with intense, unmediated experience: the romantic veneration of the sublime, the Victorian assumption that the spontaneous emotional outburst was the surest guide to wisdom, the modernist preoccupation with primal irrationality. Though the secular idioms sometimes lacked the clarity and conviction of their Calvinist predecessors, they embodied the same persistent search for some reliable ontological bedrock. By the late nineteenth century it is not merely metaphorical to refer to a religion of reality in American culture. Acolytes of authenticity were often God-haunted souls who longed for what Emerson had called "an original relation with the universe," but who lacked a language to express their longings. And their particular historical circumstances deepened their sense that they were surrounded by a pasteboard world of deceptive artifice.

Among the most prominent of those circumstances was the spread of anonymous economic transactions in the business civilization that matured during the decades after the Civil War. The fear of being cheated out of some fundamental level of experience, the desire to tear away the layers of concealment from the reality beneath them—these emotions flourished in the atmosphere of mistrust that accompanied the shell game of modern market exchange. The manuals advising their readers how to recognize counterfeit notes, and the advice literature explaining how to tell false self-representation from true were the nineteenth-century ancestors of *Consumer Reports*. ("Imagine having a large literary industry called *Consumer Reports*," Lionel Trilling once said, "which has to tell you whether the thing you're buying is authentic.")[2]

During the later decades of the nineteenth century, the rise of national advertising provided critics of fraudulence with an obvious target: here was the virus of inauthenticity institutionalized and made visible. At the same

---

2. "Sincerity and Authenticity: A Symposium," in Robert Boyers, ed., *The Salmagundi Reader* (Bloomington: Indiana University Press, 1983), p. 307. For a wide-ranging account of the discourse of authenticity during the post–Civil War decades, see Miles Orvell, *The Real Thing: Imitation and Authenticity in American Culture, 1880–1940* (Chapel Hill: University of North Carolina Press, 1989).

time, the pursuit of reality had accelerated. By 1900 fears of counterfeit experience had acquired a visceral quality: yearnings for unmediated spiritual life took on palpable physical form, as devotees of the real reacted ambivalently to the comforts released by the mass production measures of the major corporations. Advertising agencies were the servants of those corporations; so to Anderson and his cohort they became not only the masters of misrepresentation but also the sponsors of an ever-thickening insulation between the consuming self and the unpredictabilities of the natural world. For critics like H. G. Wells, who overlooked the driven rationality behind much advertising ideology, advertisers could be blamed for "the philosophy of the loose lip and the lax paunch" that was enveloping modern commercial life—or so Wells implied in his satire of a patent medicine empire, *Tono-Bungay* (1908). In a society characterized by slackness and self-indulgence as well as by systematic deceit, Trilling observed more than sixty years after Wells, "we are put under a diminishing pressure of what we can call duty, we are put under a diminishing pressure of what we can call necessity." If one restricts Trilling's characteristically lofty "we" to the comparatively comfortable managerial and professional classes in the United States, the observation acquires some force. As Trilling said, this "relative ease of material life leaves us confronting areas of choice which require us to look for a hardness somewhere, for a kernel of actuality and experience which perhaps we have to find for ourselves."[3]

By the 1920s the desire to locate that "kernel of actuality and experience" led many literary critics of advertising (often themselves veterans of agency work) to resurrect republican and romantic idioms of authenticity. They found alternatives to the inauthenticity of white-collar culture in an imaginary realm of male camaraderie, honest craftsmanship, and pastoral harmony. From George Babbitt's son Ted to Willy Loman's son Biff, refugees from business imagined (as Biff did) that "we don't belong in this nuthouse of a city. We should be mixing cement on some open plain, or—carpenters. A carpenter is allowed to whistle!" This idyll began to pall a little, if only through repetition, by midcentury.[4]

But for Anderson, writing in the years before and immediately after World War I, the romantic and republican idioms were still fresh. Despite his reputation as a bohemian rebel, Anderson was always powerfully drawn

3. H. G. Wells, *Tono-Bungay* (New York: Duffield and Co., 1909), p. 324; Boyers, "Sincerity and Authenticity," p. 307.

4. Arthur Miller, *Death of A Salesman* [1949] (New York: Viking, 1958), p. 61.

back to green memories of his boyhood. Like his contemporary Dreiser, he was subject to fits of sophomoric solemnity: he used "human" as an honorific and pondered the pulsating "real life" that seemed just beyond his reach. (Though never as moronically as Eugene Witla, the artist/ad man in Dreiser's *The "Genius"* [1915], who constantly poses questions like: "What was this thing, life?") But unlike Dreiser, Anderson located "life" not in the department store but amid the woods and open fields of his native Midwest.[5]

Still, it would be a mistake to categorize Anderson too neatly. It is difficult to sort out his actual beliefs because he so often and so deliberately cultivated an authorial persona. His favorite was the bumbling but thoughtful hayseed, insisting "I want to know why." Intensifying a strain that had always been present in doctrines of plain speech, he assumed that the voice of truth was always halting and inarticulate: the shy farm boy rather than the confident advertiser. Anderson's primitivist leanings led to the self-conscious literary slumming that provoked Hemingway's parody in *The Torrents of Spring* (1926), but they also underwrote a compelling commentary on advertising, from the inside out.

Anderson was born in Camden, Ohio, in 1876. The family were of pious Presbyterian stock, but by the time young Sherwood was coming of age religion seemed to be less a matter of fervent belief than of social habit. Nor was the Protestant ethic a path to success for them. His father was a harness maker and sign painter; but machines were putting the harness makers out of business and, as Sherwood Anderson later observed, "the day of universal advertising had not come." He remembered his father as a windbag and a failure. His mother took in washing to support the struggling family and died of tuberculosis at forty-two. Out of this bleak background Anderson worked his way. He was a newsboy, a farmhand, a factory laborer, and for a brief period after the Spanish-American war, a soldier. When he returned from Cuba he enrolled for a short time at Wittenberg College and was selected as class orator. He delivered an encomium on "the Jews." "I made quite a speech," he recalled. "We story tellers are also, almost without exception, actors. I have always envied actors. Oh how I would love to strut the boards." An advertising man from Chicago heard him speak and offered him a job. Beginning with the advertising department of the *Woman's Home Companion,* by 1900 Anderson was a copywriter

5. Theodore Dreiser, *The "Genius"* [1915] (New York: New American Library, 1967), p. 34.

for the Frank B. White Company, which in 1903 became the Long-Critchfield Company. He worked there, on and off, until 1922.[6]

The men who hired Anderson were no doubt responding to his glib intelligence. "To tell the truth I was pretty slick," he later recalled. "I could bend people to my will. I was plausible, thought faster than most people about me, was always putting others in the wrong." Probably that latter tendency accounted for Anderson's greater success as a copywriter than as a solicitor. Nevertheless he was able to curb his domineering sarcasm sufficiently to attend copy conferences and curry favor with clients—which he astutely recognized was usually more important than currying favor with consumers. ("Many of the most successful advertisements are written, not primarily to sell more of the goods advertised, but rather to flatter, in some subtle way, the maker of the goods.") In the advertisements and trade journal columns he wrote during these years, Anderson allowed his earnest side, and his keen ear for commercial clichés, to work to his advantage. Like many authors in the advertising journal *Printers' Ink,* he celebrated the replacement of the carnivalesque traveling salesman by the "new business man." "Common to the verge of imbecility, dressed as only a fool would dress nowadays, and having as his chief stock of trade a fund of vile and indecent stories," the old-fashioned salesman "went forth with his soap, his cigars, and his ladies' underwear to smear the path of all decent men who must follow him for years to come." But thank God, he's dying out, "and it isn't his fellows who are causing his welcome death. It's the new business man, the new manufacturer, the new buyer—clean, well read clever men who are not going to buy goods of our fellows like our friend above when they can buy of their equals, of men who can be quiet, earnest, and decent, even when away from home and with the eyes of high school girls and waitresses upon them." The last reference gave these progressive platitudes an idiosyncratic twist: Anderson had a lot of trouble resisting "high school girls and waitresses," and his sexual obsessions would play a central role in the commentary on the advertising business. Here, though, in the pages of *Agricultural Advertising* for February 1903, illicit sex was invoked only to be dismissed as a relic of the benighted business past.

6. Sherwood Anderson, *A Story Teller's Story* [1924], (Cleveland: Case Western Reserve University Press, 1968), p. 5; Ray Lewis White, ed., *Sherwood Anderson's Memoirs: A Critical Edition* (Chapel Hill: University of North Carolina Press, 1969), p. 198. See also Kim Townsend, *Sherwood Anderson* (Boston: Houghton Mifflin, 1987), pp. 9–13; Christopher Benfey, "Inconstant Anderson," *New York Review of Books,* 30 January 1986, 16–20; William A. Sutton, *The Road to Winesburg* (Metuchen, N.J.: Scarecrow Press, 1972).

Anderson had quickly mastered the most up-to-date tools in the commercial rhetorician's kit: above all, the connectors that linked cleanliness, decency, and modernity. That was the trinity conventionally evoked by apologists for national advertising when they felt called upon to dignify their calling with some social worth. Anderson's early writings were often indistinguishable from the boilerplate of the trade press.[7]

But even in these early years, there were signs that Anderson was hardly ever at home in the world the advertisers made. Despite his paeans to progress, his vision of life in advertising was distinctly rural rather than suburban or metropolitan. He worked in Chicago, not New York; and his company's clients were men who made plows in southern Illinois or grew tobacco in Kentucky. This was Anderson's account of an advertising man on the road:

You can imagine a fellow who spends his days in the offices and his nights in all sorts of hotels looking forward with no little pleasure to a day on a country road among the farmers who buy the things he helps to advertise. When that fellow is fortunate enough to have for a companion a man who understands the country and is full of love of it and when these two start off at sunrise down a road that follows the winding course of the Mississippi and [have] no more to carry than a stout stick for the chance of knocking down nuts from the trees along the road; when all these things work out in this manner, I say . . . [a] fellow is rather bound to have a good day ahead of him. If you want to take part in a conversation that reaches every sort of business and life and is in a pleasant and happy vein withal, try this sort of walking on this sort of day with this sort of man. The road leads up hill and down, past farm houses and about sharp turns, over bridges and through marshes and along the road are many old companions of the catalogue and farm papers. Here is a wind mill and there a wire fence, here a cultivator and there a plow and up the road rolls the Studebaker wagon in use by the family going to church, and over all the quiet of Sunday and Indian summer.[8]

The narrator begins in offices and hotels, travels through a Whitmanesque idyll of the open road, and ends in a setting that became as much a talisman of childhood for Anderson as it had been for Mark Twain—a "soft, reposeful" landscape along the Mississippi, where it is always Sunday, and always summer. This was also the backdrop used by agricultural advertisers in their catalogues and other promotional circulars.

7. *Sherwood Anderson's Memoirs*, pp. 238, 289; Sherwood Anderson, "The Traveling Man," *Agricultural Advertising*, February, 1903, 15–16; Anderson, "Boost No. 1," *Agricultural Advertising*, June 1903, 56–57. See also William A. Sutton, "Sherwood Anderson: The Advertising Years, 1900–1906," *Northwest Ohio Quarterly* 22 (Summer 1950): 120–57.

8. Sherwood Anderson, "About Country Roads," *Agricultural Advertising*, November 1903, 56.

For Anderson the season was Indian summer; the way of life he longed for was waning. Yet much of his own advertising copy remained rooted in the oral traditions of village entrepreneurship—the world of carnival barkers, itinerant peddlers, and medicine show impresarios. "I want to make you another offer right now," he wrote around 1920 in a piece of mail-order advertising for his friend Pete Moberly, who owned the Green River Tobacco Company of Owensboro, Kentucky. "If you want to win a lady you might as well propose while she's liking you, and while you've got her out in the moonlight, eh?" The bantering question evoked the standard seduction scene of nineteenth-century consumer culture and sought to create a mood of male camaraderie. A similar atmosphere enveloped "A Little Sermon to Smokers," which Anderson wrote for Green River at about the same time.

> I am sending you, free of charge, a fair-sized sample of pure Kentucky tobacco, undoped, unadulterated. Here is a clean, healthy smoke that you will learn to enjoy more and more as you grow away from the doped and doctored smoking tobaccos on the market. . . .
>
> Do you know that the raisers of the finest tobaccos in the world would no more smoke doped and doctored smoking tobacco than they would take a drink out of a half-filled old patent medicine bottle found in a deserted house.
>
> These men are healthy, they haven't nerves, they live to a vigorous old age. They smoke tobacco—lots of it—and they enjoy their smoke. They take it straight and pure . . . [just as "our fathers" took their old Kentucky bourbon]. There was no dope to shred their nerves and ruin their stomachs. . . .
>
> Now look here—don't think that because I'm saving you money I'm putting you in a class with users of cheap tobacco. You ought to see my list of regular smokers, newspaper editors, judges, congressmen, manufacturers.[9]

The earthy idiom, the appeal to the authority of farmers and fathers as well as professional men, the straightforward buttonholing conversational style—all this was a far cry from the tortured folksiness of the Prince Albert ads produced by the N. W. Ayer Agency through the 1910s and 1920s: those were celebrated in the trade press as "smart copy," but they were written in a stilted psuodo-dialect designed to be read rather than spoken. ("Pull the monkey wrench out of your smokegears with a tidy red tin of Prince Albert—*and*—get-down-pat the hang and the happiness of making every puff of a jimmy pipe or home rolled cigarette pay you in smokejoy at the interest rate of ten-per-cent-*per,* Sundays and holidays

---

9. Follow-up copy to Green River Sample, Moberly Folder, Sherwood Anderson Papers, Newberry Library, Chicago; "A Little Sermon to Smokers," copy in Smoker's Health folder, Anderson papers.

included!")[10] The point is not only that Anderson was a better writer than the authors of the Prince Albert copy, or that he had a keener ear for the actual rhythms of speech, but also that he was more attached to an older oral tradition than were the legions of college-educated copywriters at the big metropolitan agencies.

There were signs, even early on, that Anderson felt himself to be an honest bumpkin fallen among thieves. In *Agricultural Advertising,* he told the story of Peter Macveagh, a young Indiana farm boy who "was clean, right down through to his heart . . . like the fields and the woods, sort of kept clean by God and the seasons." Then he went to Chicago, to "stretch his mental muscles," and discovered that "in this world there are many people who are stupid and incompetent, and many more that are unclean pretenders." Disillusioned and toughened, he becomes a successful "man of affairs" by learning how to play on the weaknesses of humanity, "and the blood that hurries through his brain draws warmth from his once big heart." The story could have come from *Godey's Ladies' Book* in the mid-nineteenth century; it suggested not only the tenacity of romantic and Victorian assaults on the amorality of the marketplace, but also Anderson's anxiety about what was happening to him as he grew wise in the ways of deceit. "I was in business for a long time," he told his fellow bohemian Floyd Dell, "and the fact is I was a smooth son of a bitch."[11]

In advertising Anderson learned that "it is always possible, if you have at all a subtle mind, to get around others"—as he concluded toward the end of his life, in an unpublished memoir dated 1941. In Anderson's view, this manipulative skill was what Dale Carnegie had in mind in the "excruciatingly popular" *How to Win Friends and Influence People* (1936): "it was in me, this faculty." He could convince a client that a campaign strategy had been the client's own "when he had said nothing of the sort." "For a moment a puzzled look in the eye and then, usually, he swallowed the bait. 'Oh yes, I remember.'" This was how Anderson operated: feigning self-effacement, feinting and sparring, "never attacking directly. It was a game. I made flattering little remarks, dropped suggestions, hints. . . ." And he experienced "a nasty feeling of triumph" when he got what he wanted.[12]

10. Advertisement, Prince Albert Pipe Tobacco, 1919, in Book 180, N. W. Ayer Collection, National Museum of American History, Smithsonian Institution, Washington, D.C.

11. Sherwood Anderson, "The Man of Affairs," *Agricultural Advertising,* November 1904, 36–37; Anderson to Dell, quoted in Malcolm Cowley, Introduction to *Winesburg, Ohio* [1919] (New York: Viking Press, 1964), p. 3.

12. "American Money," memoir dated 1941 in Anderson papers, Newberry Library, Chicago.

Anderson habitually resorted to words like "nasty" and "unclean" when he characterized his experiences in advertising. He viewed his moral descent as in part a form of sexual corruption. In Anderson's account, the pursuit of success enmeshed the businessman in a web of deception that enveloped his personal life as well as his office affairs. Adultery, for Anderson, became the most prominent and galling form of everyday deceit. He married Cornelia Lane, the attractive and articulate daughter of a Toledo industrialist, in 1904. While he was courting her he was writing *Agricultural Advertising* editorials about the new-model traveling salesman who resisted the wiles of waitresses, and the modern businessman who "loves one woman, and . . . knows that honesty is a solid wall and truth is a shining light." In 1907 he moved his young family to Elyria, Ohio, where he started his own paint-merchandising company. It was only a matter of time before he was mixing business with pleasure in the acceptable ways—chasing golf balls over fields where he had once cut corn, arranging trips to Cleveland as pretexts for picking up a little something on the side, phoning "Ed" to see if he could "manage" some women. "Sure, boys," the generic "Ed" would say when they arrived in town. "Let's have a shot or two. I can see that you boys are several shots to the good." As Anderson recalled the scene in 1933 he wrote: "God, why did we always have to call each other 'boys'?" To Anderson, at least in restrospect, the pose of boyishness epitomized the dirty lie at the heart of American businessmen's social life—the rank hypocrisy, so reflexive it could hardly even be called hyprocrisy, of confidence men feigning earnestness and innocence while they cut crooked deals and consorted with prostitutes.[13]

So what was the alternative? Anderson claimed he saw it one morning from his bedroom window, as he gazed out dazed and bleary after a night of false hilarity and drunken groping. In the yard of the house next door, an Italian man and his wife were laying out a garden with strings and wooden stakes. Their children joined them. "One of the children, a boy of nine or ten, suddenly began to dance. He threw up his arms and began whirling about the pile of dead weeds and vegetable stalks left from another year," while the younger children and eventually the parents stopped their labors, laughed and laughed. "Myself above . . . stale and dry mouthed from my night of so-called 'fun,' American business men's fun." It was this "dance of life," this pastoral celebration of vitality and fecundity, Anderson later claimed, that focused his flight from a life of systematic deceit and

---

13. Anderson, "Boost No. 1," p. 56; *Sherwood Anderson's Memoirs,* pp. 241, 263–64.

self-hate. And in a sense this was true: much of his literary work was animated by a search for what he called a sense of "aliveness"—it seemed present in preindustrial settings (whatever their other limitations) but lacking in the culture promoted by advertising. He began to write in the interstices of a life still dedicated to marketing paint.[14]

By 1912 Anderson had reached a breaking point. He had three children, and he had four novels underway; his paint business, fueled by his clever advertising circulars, was superficially successful but financially overextended; his marriage was a mess of boredom and guilt. He was thirty-six years old. On the afternoon of 27 November 1912 he was dictating a letter in his best promotional idiom: "The goods about which you have inquired are the best of their kind made in the . . ." when suddenly he stopped without completing the phrase. Acting as if in a trance, he stared at his secretary for a long time and finally said: "I have been wading in a river for a long time and my feet are wet." He left the office and trudged toward Cleveland along the railroad tracks.[15]

Anderson retold the story many times, in many forms. In his own mind, his departure from the paint business became an archtypal moment of artistic heroism in the bohemian war on the bourgeoisie. But his actual experience was somewhat more complicated. As Malcolm Cowley observed, "he didn't continue wandering from city to city, trading his tales for bread and preaching against success." Instead Anderson tramped aimlessly around Cleveland for three or four days until some business acquaintances recognized him and took him to a hospital. After recovering from what was diagnosed as "exhaustion and aphasia," he returned to Elyria, tied up the loose ends of his business, then returned to Chicago and managed to get rehired by the Critchfield Agency. He sent for his wife and children, and settled down to writing advertising copy by day and (other forms of) fiction by night. It would be two years before Anderson separated from his wife, and ten before he departed the advertising business.[16]

In many ways the later divorce was harder for him to face. As he recalled in 1933, "only in the advertising place could I make enough to buy a little leisure." The money was easy for a man who was facile with words. "It sometimes amazes me," he wrote his confidante Harriet Finley in 1917, "when I see how I am able to go on here year after year, giving so little for

14. *Memoirs*, pp. 265–66.
15. Cowley, Introduction, p. 9.
16. Ibid., pp. 9–10.

the money I get and each year giving less and less." These were the years when he wrote some of his best work, including *Winesburg, Ohio* (1919), in the evenings, on weekends, and sometimes at his agency desk. Yet for a writer who composed as Anderson did, in erratic bouts of inspiration, office routine could be profoundly frustrating. So at any rate he claimed to Finley.[17]

With me writing has never been in any sense a science. There are days when to save my life I could not write one good sentence. I have really no knowledge of words; no mastery of the art of sentence construction.

And then a mood comes on me. The world is of a sudden alive with meaning. Every gesture, every word of the people about carries significance. . . . If I can get to pencil and paper I write blindly, scarcely seeing the sheets before me. . . .

Now if you can understand what it means at such times to have a man come to my office door and tell me that I am to go into a room with other men and drone for hours over the question of the advisability of advertising a new kind of hose supporters you will understand what I mean by the peculiar difficulties of my position. I go because there are children to be fed, obligations that I have not the courage to face down, but as I go I often feel that I could take a revolver from my pocket and begin shooting the men in the room with the greatest glee. I don't want you to misunderstand me. I don't always feel this way about the hose supporter gentlemen. At times I go with delight and all their words strike on my consciousness as just a part of the inexhaustible drollery of life.[18]

The passage showed the influence of bohemian clichés on Anderson's thought, but also revealed his power to resist them. In the discourse of the avant-garde literati, it was a standard rhetorical move to juxtapose the banality of business conferences against the white-hot ecstasy of artistic inspiration, as Anderson did in this letter. Equally standard was the assumption that it was cowardly to support one's children rather than abandon them to pursue Art; Anderson shared this assumption, too, but he refused to conform to its dictates. He kept at his copywriting until 1922, when the success of *Winesburg* and several lesser books made the break from advertising seem less risky. He announced with characteristic solemnity in a letter to Finley, "The other morning I walked, thought it all out, bowed my head before the gods and took the oath that I would write no more drivel about plows and breakfast foods." Five years later he was considering a return to advertising, thinking it might restore "grace and

17. *Memoirs,* p. 396; Anderson to Marietta D. Finley, 1 February 1917, in William A. Sutton, ed., *Letters to Bab: Sherwood Anderson to Marietta D. Finley, 1916–1933* (Urbana and Chicago: University of Illinois Press, 1985), p. 62.

18. Anderson to Finley, 23 November 1916, in *Letters to Bab,* p. 8.

ease" to his writing and reconnect him with "the labor of the world." This apparent reversal demands some explanation.[19]

Edmund Wilson caught the impulse behind Anderson's reconsideration of advertising when he said that Anderson's "ideal of literature seemed partly to have been derived from his training as a composer of advertising copy. . . ."[20] But this was only at moments of discouragement. More often, the basis of Anderson's ideal of literature—and the source of both its strength and weakness—was his determination that his fiction would be as unlike his ad writing as possible. His ad copy is simply a more conversational version of the hail-fellow-well-met bonhomie that dominated much national advertising (especially male-to-male) before the First World War. The jarringly gritty details in "A Little Sermon to Smokers"—like the half-empty patent medicine bottle in the abandoned house—revealed the provincialism of Anderson's audience; they were vestiges of the era when the vernacular tradition of entrepreneurial advertising had not yet succumbed to the homogenizing logic of corporate rationalization. While Anderson scorned both the earlier and later traditions of advertising, in fact the vernacular version of commercial speech had in his early career helped to loosen up the understated intensity of Anderson's fictional prose; it accounted for some of the strength of *Winesburg*. But at the same time, Anderson was learning the tricks of simplification and understatement from Gertrude Stein, and like hers his prose could slide into self-parody. That had begun to happen by the late 1920s, as Anderson strove to ascend into the reaches of high art. His prose became clotted with globules of profundity.

Anderson's brief yearning to return to advertising embodied a flickering recognition of this problem. But in the end he rejected the idea, for reasons that revealed some of the psychic complexities behind Andreas Huyssen's formulation: "Mass culture has always been the hidden subtext of the modernist project." Anderson assumed that the advertising agency would begin to market his presence as a magnet for clients—"Have your advertising writing done by Sherwood Anderson—the great writer etc. etc." Given the agencies' hostility to copywriters' signing their copy, this was probably a false assumption, an indication of Anderson's inflated self-regard, of his continuing engagement with the world of advertising, and of his continuing

19. Anderson to Finley, August 1922, in *Letters to Bab,* p. 186; and October 1927, in ibid., pp. 297–98.

20. Edmund Wilson, *The American Earthquake* (New York: Farrar, Straus, and Giroux, 1958), p. 127.

need to exorcise its appeal with a gesture of heroic renunciation. Advertising, and the culture it was helping to create, played a crucial contrapuntal role in all of Anderson's literary work.[21]

Anderson presented advertising copywriters as men like himself, tormented by self-hate as they subordinated their literary talents to commercial necessity. "Sometimes, at lunch, in some little saloon, we talked it over among ourselves. 'For God's sake let us keep trying. It may be we can hold on.' There would have been two or three of us who dreamed of someday becoming real writers. This fellow was, in secret, working on a play, that fellow on a novel." Some became drunks, others committed suicide. One fat man among them claimed they were all sinners in another life who were being punished: "We are in the advertising department of hell," he said.[22]

It may be that the hellishness of this picture was partly a result of cultural fashion. Anderson told these anecdotes in the version of his memoirs he published in 1933, when many of his literary contemporaries had embraced a communist variant of the producer ethos. Matthew Josephson, who had celebrated advertising during the 1920s, by 1935 was attacking "the gentlemen who spend their days and nights counterfeiting and misrepresenting, the copy-writers, the knights of press-agentry, the Junior Leaguers and the tennis champions who give lying testimonials," juxtaposing their hypocrisy against the "true, simple human dignity" that could be found in "the most threadbare Soviet student or the grimiest of coal miners."[23]

But Anderson's producerist outlook was never simply tied to prevailing political doctrine. He had always cultivated a notion of writing as a preindustrial craft and ad writing as a betrayal of craftsmanship. Words were tools for expressing "the Real" and to use them deceptively was to defile them. "I am soiling my tools," Anderson complained of his copywriting. "Surely nothing in the modern world has been more destructive than the idea that man can live without the joy of hands and mind combined in craftsmanship, that men can live by the accumulation of monies, by trickery," he wrote in 1924. What was destroyed, in Anderson's view, was manhood itself. True to the republican tradition, he linked the construction

21. Huyssen, "Mass Culture as Woman," p. 47; Anderson to Finley, October 1927, in *Letters to Bab,* pp. 297–98.

22. *Memoirs,* p. 414.

23. Matthew Josephson, "The Consumer Consumed," review of J. B. Matthews and R. E. Shallcross, "*Partners in Plunder,*" *New Masses* 14, 12 March 1935, 22–23.

of masculine identity with productive labor. He told of trying to answer a banker's question about his writing: "'But what do you get out of it?'" What he got, he said, was a feeling understood by "men of the arts" as well as "workmen" and "good farmers"—the feeling of satisfaction that came to a man after he had patiently brought a piece of neglected land back into cultivation.[24] "'You should have seen this field, some five years ago, when I got it.' Just that, man's old inheritance, your own sudden swift love of him, respect for him. 'Here's a man.' Something workmen sometimes know, writers, painters, actors, builders of all sorts sometimes know."[25]

In Anderson's scheme of things, the coming of mass production had undermined and indeed virtually eliminated the possibilities for men to define their identities through craftsmanship. In offices as well as in factories, "the men never having sense of completion of self in work, in these places always, all day long, talk of women." The industrialization of male consciousness, Anderson believed, had brought a new obsession with sex. "Men forever declaring their potency. . . . Why?"

> I thought then and I still think that it is because man has his source of strength, of quiet, of life itself always coming into him through his hands.
> He touches. His hands hold tools. They hold the plow handles, the saw, the hammer, the scythe, the painter's brush, the pen, the hoe.
> Man is a doer. It is his nature to find strength in doing. It is what he does through things in nature, through tools and materials, that feeds his manhood and it is this manhood that is being lost.[26]

Anderson's reinterpretation of producerist ontology reflected his private sexual obsessions. Women were his delight and his downfall. He wrote about them with far greater sympathy and understanding than his male contemporaries did; the portraits of lonely, thwarted women are among the most powerful in *Winesburg,* and in *Perhaps Women* (1932) he argued that women had preserved the humane traits men had lost in "the grim wrestle of modern industrial life." Yet in "His Chest of Drawers," he wrote of a little chicken-chested advertising man, a Spaniard named, incongruously, "Bill," who was crowded out of his home and ultimately reduced to keeping his belongings in a single drawer—all as a result of the domineering behavior of his wife and daughter. Anderson's view of recent history had misogynistic implications: in robbing men of useful work and making them depend on sex for self-expression, he complained, industrial-

24. *Memoirs,* p. 353; Anderson, *Story Teller's Story,* p. 236; *Memoirs,* p. 412.
25. *Memoirs,* p. 412.
26. Ibid., p. 387.

ization had transformed American society into a "matriarchy." Behind his fear of matriarchy was his own panicky incapacity to sustain heterosexual intimacy. "Most women simply frighten me," he confessed to Finley. "I feel hunger within them. It is as though they wished to feed upon me." To keep "clean," he kept leaving them.[27]

Yet he remained intensely, ambivalently engaged with actual and emblematic women. His conceptions of sexuality shaped his attitudes toward advertising and the literary life. He habitually referred to business in general and advertising in particular as prostitution. "Was there a kind of male whoredom, brought on by a certain kind of civilization, inevitable perhaps?" he wondered. His friend Luther, the small town printer who handled the advertising circulars for his paint company, refused to let Anderson off the moral hook with any talk of "inevitability." Luther knew of Anderson's ambitions to write, saw glimmers of his ability in his promotional brochures, and scolded him for soiling his talents in advertising. "'Suppose you were a woman with some beauty of person and went and threw yourself away, going into any kind of dive, lying with any kind of man. How long would you be thought of as any kind of woman at all? You'd be a slut, a whore, wouldn't you?'" Selling one's literary talent was like selling one's "beauty of person," prostituting one's gifts at the altar of cash. Anderson took the equation seriously. He used to call one of his fellow copywriters (the fat man who spoke of the "advertising department of hell") "Little Eva" and the fat man called him "Mable." "It was a kind of mutual recognition of our common whoredom."[28]

It may also have been a way of exorcising ambivalent homoerotic longings. Anderson idealized but also resisted male intimacy. He never went to a psychoanalyst because he was appalled by "some other man attempting to thrust in and in, to search out your very soul, resentment, all kinds of resistance." He described his relationship with Luther as "a growing thing, my being more and more with the man, sensing things in him. Let us think of it as a kind of lovemaking on his part. And I do not mean physical lovemaking. Luther was no fairy." Repeatedly in his memoirs he evoked the aura of homosexuality around his male friendships, only to dismiss it by denying they were "fairies." He seemed to enjoy playing with the idea. He and "Little Eva" deliberately sought out "tough saloons" where they

27. Anderson to Finley, 11 December 1916, in *Letters to Bab*, p. 30; *Memoirs*, pp. 218–22; Benfrey, "Inconstant Anderson," pp. 16–17.

28. *Memoirs*, pp. 285, 289.

ostentatiously called each other by women's names. "There would be down-and-outers hanging about. They leared [sic] at us. 'What have we here, a couple of fairies, eh?' All of this a kind of satisfaction to us." Why? because it seemed to capture something essential about their job—the task of catching and holding a client by watching him "as a man might watch some woman for whom his loins ache." In Anderson's mind, advertising was associated obscurely with homosexuality as well as explicitly with prostitution—both forms of illicit sex were signs of decline from an earlier, solider male identity.[29]

Yet there was more than a vestigial producer ethos and a muddle of male anxieties behind Anderson's commentary on advertising. To be sure, his preoccupation with cleanliness was genuinely obsessive: in the Elyria years, he scrubbed himself and his study down every time he started writing. But it was not only the taint of forbidden pleasure that he was seeking to cleanse: it was a much more diffuse disorder, a feeling that with the rise of national advertising "the time of the wise-crackers" had come, that there was a new tone of "brittle hardness" in the popular magazines, a new smart-ass ethos characterized by the "effort to drag down, always to drag down, even life itself."[30] Anderson suspected that the emergent culture was profoundly hostile to "life itself." For him, that elusive phrase seemed to signify a sense of pure being. It was a feeling he associated with the vanishing rural landscape and with the intimate relationships he courted but rarely consummated.

It was as if Anderson spent his whole writing life looking for what "Sally, the quiet one" had seen from their bed in a fleabag hotel room—"the white spot. . . . [T]he thing lost. . . . [T]he thing that eludes us"—some sign that the two of them had, however fleetingly, formed a genuine union, transcended self-absorbed sensuality. The "white spot" may seem a weak rendition of "life itself," but in spite of its pallor the image has powerful religious resonance that can be traced back to the time of the Transcendentalist movement (perhaps the first collective effort to move the discourse of authenticity outside orthodox Christianity.) In 1850 a Transcendentalist author named George Loring wrote: "Between the individual and his God, there remains a spot, larger or smaller, as the soul has been kept unclouded, where no sin can enter, where no mediation can come, where all the discords of . . . life are resolved into the most delicious harmonies, and his

29. Memoirs, pp. 284, 285, 290, 414–15.
30. Memoirs, p. 387.

whole existence becomes illuminated by a divine intelligence. Sorrow and sin reveal this spot to all men—as, through death, we are born to an immortal life." Anderson was no Transcendentalist; nor is it likely he would have read one as obscure as Loring. But Anderson was a lifelong devotee of Emerson, whose desire to "become a transparent eyeball" was another version of the Transcendental longing for the "spot." According to his best biographer, "Anderson placed himself in the tradition of Emerson and Whitman." Like them, like other romantics influenced by Anglo-American Protestantism, Anderson may have imagined that intense communion with another person might be the way modern people experience authentic spiritual life—now that the question of "immortal life" had become too embarrassing to discuss. The "white spot" was about the closest a self-conscious bohemian could get to admitting he was animated by religious longings.[31]

More commonly Anderson's discourse of authenticity focused on the uses and misuses of language. An unpublished sketch, "Advertising Words," pulled together these preoccupations and their relationship to Anderson's advertising career. Two "word slingers," small-time fellows in advertising, are at a table with some big fellows in a Chicago restaurant. The narrator's mind wanders—sometimes you can get as much as the buyers and sellers, he thinks, just by slinging words. "Oh the word men—the little words with which we make love, greet our friends, worship our gods and our heroes." He pictures a boy with his first girl, walking alone, trying to come up with the words to express his feelings. "This is the sort of thing older men, painters and poets try later to recapture. . . . Oh to tell her. Once I heard a fat advertising man—a bit worse—or God knows perhaps the better! for drink mourning over this matter. 'I was an Illinois farm boy,' he said, 'and I used to go of a Saturday night to an Illinois town. I saw girls there. Oh how I ached. I walked up and down the main street of the town. . . . All of my body ached with desire but I had no words.'" He had become a philandering slob but "he meant I think that there was something in him that remained alive, inspite of the coarseness of suc-

31. *Memoirs,* p. 233; George Bailey Loring, *Massachusetts Quarterly Review* 3 (September 1850): 484–500, as reprinted in Joseph Donald Crowley, ed., *Hawthorne: the Critical Heritage* (New York: Barnes and Noble, 1970), p. 171; Ralph Waldo Emerson, "Nature," [1836], reprinted in Stephen E. Whicher, ed., *Selections from Ralph Waldo Emerson* (Boston: Houghton Mifflin, 1957), p. 24; Townsend, *Anderson,* p. 110. For the nearly religious importance placed on friendship by some of Anderson's bohemian contemporaries, see Christopher Lasch, *The New Radicalism in America: The Intellectual as a Social Type, 1889–1963* (New York: Knopf, 1965), esp. chaps. 1–4.

cess. . . . White [?] boy running still inside fat man. Give me the sound. I still want it—the word.—The advertising man slinging the word around."[32]

The narrator's mind wanders to an ad man named Big Tom, who was always breaking his pencils—awkwardness was a sign of authenticity for Anderson, who nurtured romantic suspicions of polish and efficiency. He and Big Tom go drinking, pick up two whores who take the men to an apartment and demand five dollars. Tom motions Anderson into a bedroom and the two men lock the door. While the "poor bitches" rage outside, Big Tom tells the narrator of his Tennessee boyhood; he was "an innocent enough mountain boy, far from Chicago, far from advertising, far from a bedroom that belonged to a Moll . . . quite innocent yet." "All of us advertising word slingers are at bottom whores and we know it. We have made a whore of the word, let us lead the lives of whores. Let's get drunk." Tom tells of walking with a girl in the moonlight on a mountain road, imagining her "sweet little body." Then the men leave the apartment, Tom throwing a five at the whores: "Get the hell back into the street and at your trade, you cried to her. And you and me back to our whorish trade, you added, taking my arm." Back at the restaurant, the "big man" enters. The narrator reports the reverential conversation at the table. "'But who is he?' 'Why, he is the man who wrote "eventually, why not now,"' 'No!' And in my own voice too."[33]

This truncated, hastily composed sketch summarized the conflicts and confusions at the heart of Anderson's work. Juxtaposing social lies tossed off at a table of "big fellows" against the words of love spoken on a mountain road in Tennessee, Anderson worked the conventional vein of contrast between urban whorishness and pastoral innocence. From his copywriter's desk he looked backward to an earlier mode of commerce, one that recalled his paean to the open road in *Agricultural Advertising.* "I dream of being a wandering pedlar, a man who lives in a tiny frame house at the edge of a small town," he wrote Finley in September 1919. And sometimes his dreams were more complicated. "The inner thing in me is a clean boy running over the hills," he wrote Finley three months later, evoking his characteristic claim that he (like Big Tom) was "quite innocent yet." Yet the process of self-justification quickly grew more tangled. "I turn to women," he wrote, "because men are too concerned with making money and overfeeding their lusts. I am stupid. I forget that women are as much involved in the tangle as men. So much of the time I do not want hands

---

32. "Advertising Words," Undated manuscript in Anderson Papers, Newberry Library, Chicago.
33. Ibid.

on me but want to run clean and alone. I can't have that I know but like a silly fellow I keep asking it."[34]

The problem for Anderson was that like many of his contemporaries he distrusted the capacity of language to represent real life. For Wittgenstein and his intellectual heirs that distrust provoked a major move away from positivist and platonic identifications of word and thing. For Anderson it led to frustration. Words of love, he gloomily concluded, were as flat and inadequate as advertising words. The only expression of self that could truly be trusted was the preverbal ache of longing—a longing for emotional as well as sexual intimacy with other human beings. That is why the characters Anderson meant to be admirable are so often tongue-tied, like the fat advertising man who recalls himself as a boy, thrumming with desire on the streets of an Illinois town. Anderson treated facility with words, the key to his own success in advertising, as the sign of mere glibness. Soon after he quit the Critchfield agency for good, he complained that "There is so much to unlearn. One who has spent so many years as I had just saying words to get a quick surface effect, as we advertising writers are always doing, are paid to do, has later got to whip himself with much scorn." This hyperbolic self-hate may itself have been a performance: the creation of the guilt-ridden plain speaker as a part of Anderson's artistic persona.[35]

The sense of theatrical posturing is inescapable in some of Anderson's other stances as well. His equation of fluency and glibness, for example, led him to sentimental primitivism. Perhaps the best known product of that outlook was *Dark Laughter,* which celebrated the vitality of Negro life in the South and provoked Hemingway's mockery in *The Torrents of Spring.* In 1922, from Kentucky (where he was writing *Dark Laughter*), Anderson wrote "I am myself as I was when I was a boy." The trip South was for him "a kind of pilgrimage back into the realities of life."[36]

Still it is too easy to caricature Anderson's quest for "the realities of life" as either sentimental primitivism or guilt-ridden plain speech. His search had led as well to what Anderson described as "my first authentic tale"—the story "Hands," which recounted the pathetic life of Wing Biddlebaum. Wing was an inspired teacher in a small Midwestern town. He was betrayed by his "nervous expressive fingers" and his ever-mobile hands, which seemed to have lives of their own. Fluttering like birds about the young boys in his charge, his hands provoked their parents to accuse him

34. Anderson to Finley, September 1919, in *Letters to Bab,* p. 111; and December 1919, in ibid., p. 113.
35. Anderson, *Story Teller's Story,* p. 296.
36. Anderson to Finley, 14 June 1922, in *Letters to Bab,* p. 183.

of making homosexual advances to them. Dismissed and disgraced, the teacher (whose name had been Adolph Meyer) flees to Winesburg, Ohio, where he becomes known as Wing Biddlebaum and lives as a fearful recluse—except that he tries to teach young George Willard, who writes for the *Winesburg Eagle,* the same lesson he taught his own students: "You must begin to dream. . . . [Y]ou must shut your ears to the roaring of the voices." The source of this story, Anderson said, was "that strange, more real life into which I have so long been trying to penetrate and that is the only real reality." Whatever that may have meant, the springs of memory released more characters and stories; Anderson assembled them into *Winesburg, Ohio.*[37]

The book was permeated by the assumption that unlike advertising copy, serious fiction could not be content with surface effects. Anderson dedicated the book to his mother, who (he said) "first awoke in me the hunger to see beneath the surface of lives. . . ." The school teacher Kate Swift, who believes that young George Willard may be a writer of genius, tells him that "You must not be a mere peddler of words. The thing to learn is what people are thinking about, not what they say." Anderson posed the contrast repeatedly: the job of copywriters, popular journalists, and other makers of the emergent mass culture was to create "surface effects" by manipulating words; the task of the writer was to plumb the depths of being—to capture the catch in the throat, the yawp of authentic experience.[38]

Winesburg was many personal moments that made up a larger historical moment. Anderson aimed to capture the town when it was being swept up into the standardized patterns set by national advertising, when metropolitan elites were repackaging "the folk" into "the masses." By the 1910s, when Anderson was writing the book, the process was nearly complete. Or so he thought:

In our day a farmer standing by the stove in his village has his mind filled to overflowing with the words of other men. The newspapers and the magazines have pumped him full. Much of the old brutal ignorance that had in it also a kind of beautiful childlike innocence is gone forever. The farmer by the stove is brother to the men of cities, and if you listen you will find him talking as glibly and as senselessly as the best city man of us all.[39]

For Anderson as for many of his contemporaries, the vision of a preindustrial folk culture carried connotations of linguistic transparency—what

37. *Memoirs,* pp. 237–38; Anderson, *Winesburg,* p. 30.
38. Anderson, *Winesburg,* frontispiece, p. 163.
39. Anderson, *Winesburg,* p. 71.

a student of Jurgen Habermas might call an "undistorted speech situation" where people spoke their own words (not "the words of other men") and spoke them truly. Anderson's view of language, perhaps no more naive than that of Habermas (or George Orwell), allowed him to form a coherent critique of developing cultural tendencies. As early as the 1890s, when the action in Winesburg is set, the movement toward a senseless pseudosophis-tication is well underway. "The time of the wise-crackers" has come. Anderson looked for authentic life in the interstices of these developments, among the people he calls "grotesques"—withered Victorian maidens disappointed in love, country doctors with pockets full of paper pills. These people are obsessed by "vague hungers and secret unnameable desires;" as Anderson said, "they have got hold of a single truth and tried to live their lives by it." This refusal to become "sensible" and "well-rounded," to adjust to the demands of a routinized society, makes them failures in the eyes of the smart and up-to-date. Yet to Anderson it was the crux of their appeal. Shunted aside by the forces of progress, they are like "the few gnarled apples" left in the orchard after the pickers have moved on. "One nibbles at them and they are delicious. Into a little round place at the side of the apple has been gathered all of its sweetness. One runs from tree to tree over the frosted ground picking the gnarled, twisted apples and filling his pockets with them. Only the few know the sweetness of the twisted apples."[40]

The twisted apples are abandoned by the new civilization, but some try to catch up with it. Anderson detailed their flailings. Enoch Robinson, a sensitive farm boy who goes to New York to study art, tries his hand for a while in advertising illustration; he marries, rides the streetcar to work everyday, wears the same grey wool overcoat the other men did, pays his taxes. But after a while he takes to telling lies about business engagements, lies that allow him some time to walk the streets alone at night. His marriage falls apart and he withdraws into a single room, which he peoples with imaginary characters. He finds it "warm and friendly" in there; outside, among the swarms of people, he feels "alone."[41]

One does not have to be compulsively reclusive to be shunted aside by the developing culture of chatter; mere reticence is enough to brand one as "queer." Seth Richmond, dubbed "the deep one" by the town wits because of his habitual silence, decides to leave town altogether: Everyone

40. Martin Jay, "Should Intellectual History Take a Linguistic Turn? Reflections on the Habermas-Gadamer Debate" in Dominick LaCapra and Steven Kaplan, eds., *Modern European Intellectual History: Reappraisals and New Directions* (Ithaca: Cornell University Press, 1982), pp. 100, 104; Anderson, *Winesburg*, pp. 25, 36.

41. Anderson, *Winesburg*, pp. 167–78.

talks and talks. . . . I'm sick of it. I'll do something, get into some kind of work where talk don't count. Maybe I'll just be a mechanic in a shop." This was an example of Anderson's strongest prose, its energy intensified by simplification and understatement. He had moved far enough from advertising to rid himself of its self-conscious salesman's bonhomie, but not so far that he had lost his ear for colloquial speech. Seth Richmond's words were an uncommon expression of a common sentiment: as in the literary critique of business from *Babbitt* to *Death of a Salesman,* Anderson invoked the producer ethos to envision the possibility of work more substantial than the peddling of words.[42]

Anderson created a romantic modernist's version of the producer ethos by linking the author with carpenters and cultivators. The writer cultivated inner resources, the throb of youthful naïveté and candor that enabled him to "see beneath the surface of lives," to view the world in the fresh light of day, not the dim dusk of copywriters' clichés. Elizabeth Willard seeks to protect that sense of wonder in her son George by subverting his father's plans to turn the boy into a conventional "wide-awake" success. "'He is not a dull clod, all words and smartness,' she thought," neatly upending urban conventional wisdom about the idiocy of rural life: in Anderson the clods come from the city and are full of metropolitan "pep." Then she endows George with the ultimate Anderson accolade: "Within him there is a secret something that is striving to grow. It is a thing I let be killed in myself." She will not let him be thwarted as she has been, tricked by the cunning of conventionality into a loveless marriage and a dead domestic life. She subtly encourages him to sidestep the "brisk and smart" agenda of his dad, to follow his deepest impulse, which is "to go away and look at people and think." The book concludes with George's departure from Winesburg. What is he running away from? Not the pinched, repressive morality of the old producer culture—Anderson knew the narrowness of that village world, but he located a greater danger in the culture created by advertising.[43]

Though Anderson was attracted to the producerist critique of advertising, he leavened it with his own romantic primitivism: a pastoral fondness for vanishing preindustrial life and a positive fascination with the people who had been left behind by the locomotive of progress, the people—in effect—who had somehow not managed to secure tickets on the Twentieth Century Limited. Anderson's affectionate preoccupation with these "grotesques" was not an isolated trait. Some of the masterpieces of twentieth-

42. Ibid., p. 141.
43. Ibid., pp. 39–48.

century literature have been concerned precisely with people who have been disdained (or even exterminated) by modernizing elites. Faulkner's Yoknapatapha County and Garcia Marquez's Macondo, like Anderson's Winesburg, are populated in part by "twisted apples" trampled underfoot in the rush to development. Yet in all cases the authors stress the toughness and resilience of these despised folk. Their resistance is rooted not in morality but in idiosyncrasy. They are "queer," and in queerness there is strength.

The invocation of "masterpieces" is a risky business. Thanks to the work of Huyssen, Jane Tompkins, and other scholars, we are beginning to see how the category of "masterpiece" has been constructed and reconstructed under particular historical circumstances, how it has been enmeshed in the modernist myth of the autonomous work of art, how it has been implicated in a masculine discourse of authenticity.[44] I do not mean to imply that any of these authors (Anderson, Faulkner, or Garcia Marquez) transcended their time and place; on the contrary it was precisely their immersion in a particular historical situation that accounted for their interpretive power— their capacity to make the discourse of authenticity something more than a male complaint.

To be sure, Anderson's own worldview could be dismissed as merely a bohemian version of romantic and republican mythology. Yet even a writer with an oeuvre as uneven as Anderson's could orchestrate the discourse of authenticity with results worth pondering. His pursuit of the real through craftsmanship suggests that the quest for fulfillment through satisfying labor was more than a sign of patriarchal producerism; it could lead to a hedonistic definition of work as play—an attempt to break down the barriers between gainful employment and sensuous enjoyment. His longing to catch sight of "the white spot," though he rarely satisfied it, suggests his determination to break down other barriers as well, the barriers of self-absorption that kept him unconnected to this world or any other. And finally, his fascination with "the dance of life" in his Italian neighbors' garden suggests the centrality of a biological or ecological dimension to that desire for connectedness. As he stared out from his bedroom window, losing himself in contemplation of the yard next door, Anderson may have glimpsed a fundamental insight: all our cultural constructions—our longings for the white spot of eternal harmony, our dances of life and death— are rooted in the earth, the ground of being. That may be one reality that, try as we might, we cannot contain in quotation marks.

44. Jane Tompkins, *Sensational Designs: The Cultural Work of American Fiction, 1790–1860* (New York: Oxford University Press, 1985).

THE IRON THROAT

Tillie Lerner

THE WHISTLES always woke Marie. They pierced into her sleep like some guttural voiced metal beast, tearing at her; the sound meant, in one way, terror. During the day if the whistle blew, she knew it meant death—somebody's poppa or brother, perhaps her own—in that fearsome place below the ground, the mine.

"Goddam that blowhorn," she heard her father mutter. Creak of him getting out of bed. The door closed, with yellow light from the kerosene lamp making a long crack on the floor. Clatter of dishes. Her mother's tired, grimy voice.

"What'll ya have? Coffee and eggs. There ain't no bacon."

"Don't bother with anything. Haven't time. I gotta stop by Kvaternicks and get the kid. He's starting work today."

"What're they going to give him?"

"Little of everything at first, I guess, trap, throw switches, maybe timberin'."

"Well, he'll be starting one punch ahead of the old man. Chris began as a breaker boy." (Behind both stolid faces the claw claw of a buried thought—and maybe finish like him, buried under slaty roof which an economical company had not bothered to timber.)

"He's thirteen, ain't he?" asked Marie.

"I guess. Nearer to fourteen."

"Marie was tellin me, it would break Chris' heart if he only knew. He wanted the kid to be different. Get an edjiccation."

"Yeah? Them foreigners do have funny ideas."

"Oh, I dunno. Then she says that she wants the girls to become nuns, so they won't have to worry where the next meal is comin' from, or have to have kids."

"Well, what other earthly use can a woman have, I'd like to know."

"She says she doesn't want 'em raising a lot of brats to get their heads blowed off in the mine. I guess she takes Chris's . . . passing away pretty hard. It's kinda affected her mind. She keeps talking about the old country, the fields, and what they thought it would be like here. —'all buried in da bowels of earth," she finishes.

2 Unlimn'd They Disappear

Recollecting *Yonnondio: From the Thirties*

Christopher P. Wilson

Suppose that we could recover the literary texts that have been lost, censored, and suppressed. Suppose, too, that we could figure out why they have been erased from consciousness while other texts had come down to us as cultural legacies. Our discoveries might add up to a new literary and social history, an analogy to the way in which the concept of the black hole has given astrophysicists the premise for a new cosmology.
—Catharine Stimson, in a review of *Yonnondio*

In an otherwise forgettable episode in the *first* generation voyage of the *Starship Enterprise,* entitled "All Our Yesterdays," Captain Kirk, Spock, and McCoy beam down to a planet named Sarpeidon in order to rescue a civilization whose sun—in what amounts to an intergalactic oxymoron—is about to "go nova." How the Federation would effect such a massive evacuation with a single starship is never made clear; before long, however, the issue is moot, since no one is at home. What Kirk and his crew discover is that the populace of Sarpeidon has escaped destruction by travelling into the past. At a series of transfer stations akin to public libraries, each citizen has arrived, consulted the local librarian named Mr. Atoz (A to Z), scanned a card catalog of videotapes ("Verisims"), and then stepped through a portal called an "Atavachron" into the era illuminated on the catalog screen. Unfortunately, it isn't long before this interesting premise degenerates: Kirk, hearing a woman's scream from beyond the portal, gallantly if rashly leaps through, travelling to a seventeenth-century English village; the others, gallantly if rashly following Kirk, travel instead to a prehistoric ice age, where Spock—that angel of objectivity—regresses into a violent, lovelorn, caveman of the dark Vulcan past. At the end, however, the *Star Trek* crew is able to get back to the future, because (we are told) their chromosomes hadn't originally been properly aligned, or "prepared," by Mr. Atoz—who

I would like to thank Casey Blake, Lizabeth Cohen, Richard Fox, Jackson Lears, Joan Shelley Rubin, Judith Smith, Michael Smith, and especially Andrew Von Hendy for their comments on drafts of this essay. Permission to cite the Olsen manuscripts granted by the Henry W. and Albert A. Berg Collection, The New York Public Library, Astor, Lenox and Tilden Foundations.

himself leaps into historical oblivion at the episode's close. Needless to say, the show leaves the viewer with a certain ambivalence about the business of historical time-travel. On the positive side, this episode seems to say, if you are sufficiently *prepared,* you can actually get into the past, share its frame of reference—indeed, your own present can be saved from destruction. But, on the down side, the risks of time-travel are many: sentimental chivalry, imaginative disorientation, even regression (atavism) into your own primitive subject. Worse yet, the show discloses, Sarpeidon time-travel had originally been a form of exile for political dissidents—as if a civilization can bury its discontents in arguments over what it once was.[1]

Admittedly, it may seem light years from this space "western" to the often rarified air of metahistorical anxiety. Yet something like the interpretive turbulence above has been unsettling the traditional federation of literary, intellectual, and cultural history over the last decade. To be sure, the ideas that one can "feel" one's way into a context, understand a text from the past (as it is said) "on its own terms," even recover a past author's original intention—still exercise a strong hold on the historical imagination. Among critics prepared (like myself) in the climate of revisionism in the 1970s, historical interpretation is still often likened to simple anthropological transcription of "informants" from America's past—and in sympathetic reviews, praised as a form of empowering social rapport with the past and its traditions of political resistance. In the discipline of English, meanwhile, a kindred spirit of pluralism has generated a number of new reference volumes, anthologies, and editions of previously lost texts, all of which have reopened the literary canon in invaluable ways.[2] On the other hand, just as these new portals to the past have been opened, the cosmology upon which recovery itself is based seemed to be going nova. Specifically, some basic tools in the revisionist historian's workshop—the language of symbolic anthropology, techniques of formalist interpretation, the "docu-

1. This episode, originally written by Jean Lisett Aroeste, has been adapted by James Blish in *Star Trek 4* (New York, Bantam Books, 1971), pp. 1–22.

2. For the durability of these views, witness the reactions to David Harlan, "Intellectual History and the Return of Literature," *American Historical Review* 94 (June 1989): 581–609; see David Hollinger's reply, "The Return of the Prodigal: The Persistence of Historical Knowing," same issue, 610–21, and Joyce Appleby, "One Good Turn Deserves Another: Moving Beyond the Linguistic: A Response to David Harlan," *American Historical Review* 94 (December 1989): 1326–32. For a recent overview of the impact of the revisionist paradigm on literary study, see Elizabeth Fox-Genovese, "Between Individualism and Fragmentation: American Culture and the New Literary Studies of Race and Gender," *American Quarterly* 42 (March 1990): 7–34.

mentary" style of historical writing—have come under attack. On a variety of fronts, revisionist recovery practices have been faulted as outmoded, "monologic" historical techniques which disguise the relations of dominance and dialogue between interpreter and historical subject. If postmodern critics have complained about psychoanalytic transference between the historian and the past, for instance, sociologists have exposed the intersubjectivity of interviews; contemporary ethnographers, meanwhile, challenge the entire "fable of rapport" of the fieldwork and participant-observer models. On top of that, the "culture concept" itself—in various forms, still the constitutional plank of the American Studies federation—has been criticized as a static, even objectifying tool which often cannot narrate lived experience or behavior, much less encompass fundamentally private affairs like personal grief.[3] These new challenges seem to go beyond the complaints of facile objectivity, presentism, or consensualism that have long populated historical self-criticism; in particular, they unsettle the very core of revisionist (sometimes called "oppositional") partisanship with the past.[4]

One could hardly hope to address all the methodological challenges implied above; nor is the myopic invocation of a postmodern "eternal present" my horizon here. Rather, in this essay, I want merely to explore a few implications of these recent challenges for the practice of recovering "lost" literary texts, focusing particularly on matters of *memory* and *political rapport* that revisionists often overlook. My case study is the rediscovery

3. On the original centrality of the culture concept to American Studies, see Robert Berkhofer, Jr., "Clio and the Culture Concept," in Charles Bonjean and Louis Schneider, eds., *The Idea of Culture in the Social Sciences* (Cambridge: Cambridge University Press, 1973), 77–100. For recent criticism alluded to above, see Dominick LaCapra, *History and Criticism* (Ithaca: Cornell University Press, 1985), esp. pp. 71–94, and the exchange between LaCapra and James Kloppenberg in the *Intellectual History Newsletter* 9 (April 1987): 3–22, and 10 (1988): 3–11; Lynn Hunt, ed. *The New Cultural History* (Berkeley: University of California Press, 1989), esp. Lloyd S. Kramer, "Literature, Criticism, and Historical Imagination: The Literary Challenge of Hayden White and Dominick LaCapra," pp. 97–128. On ethnographic debates, see Louis A. Sass, "Anthropology's Native Problems: Revisionism in the Field," *Harper's*, vol. 272, May 1986, 49–57; Renato Rosaldo, *Culture and Truth* (Boston: Beacon Press, 1989); Aletta Biersack, "Local Knowledge, Local History: Geertz and Beyond," in Hunt, pp. 72–96; and James Clifford, *The Predicament of Culture* (Cambridge: Harvard University Press, 1988), esp. pp. 21–54, 215–51. On sociological transcription across class and ethnic lines during interviews, see Catherine Kohler Riessman, "When Gender Is Not Enough: Women Interviewing Women," from *Gender and Society* 1 (June 1987): 172–207.

4. On another front entirely, one recent challenge to "oppositional" criticism has been put forth by Walter Benn Michaels, *The Gold Standard and the Logic of Naturalism* (Berkeley: University of California Press, 1986), see esp. p. 27. In a similar vein, see Lora Romero on "alterity" and social structure in "Bio-political Resistance in Domestic Ideology and *Uncle Tom's Cabin*," *American Literary History* 1 (Winter 1989): esp. p. 716.

and reception of Tillie Olsen's *Yonnondio: From the Thirties,* a book which Olsen brought to light in 1974–and which was immediately hailed by American Studies critics as a "classic" of 1930s-style proletarian realism.[5] Indeed, Olsen herself, with the work which culminated in *Silences* (1978) and the resuscitation of Rebecca Harding Davis's *Life in the Iron Mills* ([1861] 1972), contributed significantly to the wider revisionist project itself. But rather than delineate that influence, I want instead to examine the critical methods, tools, and guiding assumptions—the genre category "proletarian novel," the desire for an authentic cultural artifact, formalist assumptions about textual wholeness—which affected (and deflected) the process of recovery when *Yonnondio* first appeared. Then, as a way of "reading" back against the grain of those processes, I will examine the book's *own* story, in a sense, its "own say," about texts, voices, and "classics" (and even memory itself). Ultimately, I want to show how *Yonnondio* challenges some of the re-collecting we, as cultural historians, customarily do.

The notion that this particular text may have something to say about how *we* read or regard it may seem like a conventional idea itself, a return to those more familiar notions of textual (cultural) power. In a sense, it is. But however much we revise our fables of rapport with the past, however much we discover our own recovery practices at cross-purposes, we need to be cautious about simply abrogating the text's own power/authority willy-nilly—an authority, I would suggest, which bears comparison to indigenous control over the knowledge gathered in field work itself. This caution has been a common refrain, in fact, among moderate, dialogic historicists who acknowledge their own inventions, yet (in Natalie Zemon Davis's phrase) remain "held tightly in check by the voices of the past." Indeed, my case for attending to *Yonnondio's* own authority derives from a suggestion by ethnographic critic James Clifford. Pausing over an encounter between a French curator and an American Fox Indian, in a review of museum exhibition styles to which I will return, Clifford speculates about what an engaged, respectful, even more *historical* collecting might be. If we can imagine an act of collection, Clifford writes, which "unsettles" the viewer, which speaks back against our collecting practices, we might then be reminded of "our *lack* of self-possession, [and] of the artifices we employ

5. For a good summary of the climate of proletarian criticism, see Richard Pells, *Radical Visions and American Dreams* (New York: Harper and Row, 1973), esp. pp. 169–80. For exemplary reviews, see Catharine Stimson, "Three Women Work It Out," *The Nation,* 30 November 1974, pp. 565–66; Robert Coles in *New York Times Book Review,* 1 December 1984, 72; Jack Salzman in *Book World, Washington Post,* 7 April 1974, 1.

to gather a world around us." More important, by according the text such power, we might see artifacts not only as aesthetic objects or primitive survivals, but part of a *current,* ongoing history. In *Yonnondio*'s case, that is, we might recover a voice which can speak to its own classification as Art and Artifact—remind us that a collected item is also, in a fundamental sense, a contested possession with its own will (and even testament).[6]

In fact, *Yonnondio*'s cultural power is unsettling in just this way. For Olsen and her book imply two rather challenging ideas to our own strategies of rapport in "recovering" its political force: first, that some of her original radical horizons were, in the writing of *Yonnondio* during the thirties, actually disappearing; second, that classic status was a categorization the book was actually designed to resist. In other words, whatever the itinerary of our own imaginary time travel, *Yonnondio* suggests the closing down of some of its own temporal horizons, and may partially resist— albeit in vain—being collected into our present in the forms which we have made our custom.

II

Above all else: in God's name don't think of it as Art. . . . The deadliest blow the enemy of the human soul can strike is to do fury honor.
—James Agee, *Let Us Now Praise Famous Men*

When *Yonnondio* reemerged in the early seventies, the critical acclaim was instantaneous and nearly unanimous. As many readers know, Olsen had begun the book in 1932 at only nineteen; parts had originally appeared in the *Partisan Review,* and then Olsen had received a contract from Bennett Cerf of Random House for a chapter a month. The manuscript began to tell the story of a working-class family named the Holbrooks (Jim and

---

6. The label "moderate historicism" is applied by John Toews, "Intellectual History after the Linguistic Turn: The Autonomy of Meaning and the Irreducibility of Experience," *American Historical Review* 92 (October 1987): 905ff.; Davis in *The Return of Martin Guerre* (Cambridge: Harvard University Press, 1983), p. 5. For other instances of "dialogue" in a non-Bahktinian sense, see also Hans Robert Jauss, "Literary History as a Response to Literary Theory," in *Toward an Aesthetics of Reception,* trans. Timothy Bahti (Minneapolis: University of Minnesota Press, 1982), pp. 3–45, and Jauss's *Question and Answer,* ed. Michael Hays (Minneapolis: University of Minnesota Press, 1989), esp. pp. 197–231. The idea that the past has "voices" that must be "respected" is cited in Dominick LaCapra, *Rethinking Intellectual History: Texts, Contexts, Language* (Ithaca: Cornell University Press, 1983), esp. p. 63ff. For a good reading of the "dialogic" in LaCapra, see Biersack, pp. 72–96, and Kramer, esp. p. 103ff. Text of *Yonnondio* cited throughout is the Dell edition (New York, 1974). "Indigenous control" cited in Clifford, *Predicament of Culture,* p. 45.

Anna, and their children Mazie, Will, Jimmie, Ben, and Baby Bess) physically and psychologically brutalized by life in a mining camp, tenant farm, and packing-town. But the book was left incomplete, until Olsen herself reassembled—with "no new writing," she said—its first eight chapters from surviving notes and drafts in the winter of 1972–73. When the book was published by Delacorte in 1974 with a title alluding to a poem by Walt Whitman, reviewers like Catharine Stimson, Robert Coles, and Jack Salzman greeted *Yonnondio* as a brilliant expression of the working-class consciousness of the 1930s, and beyond that, as a work of art which *transcended* its historical value. To affirm this implicitly dual status as artifact and aesthetic object, the book was frequently labeled, in Coles's enthusiastic phrase, "instantaneously" a "classic."[7] But beneath this justifiable praise of Olsen's heroic act of recovery—let alone the extraordinary beauty of *Yonnondio* itself—several issues went unnoticed.

Naturally, what immediately attracted revisionist readers was the book's apparent historical authenticity as a literary survival—as its title suggests, "from" the thirties. Olsen's own shepherding, in fact, provided an opportunity to supplement critical-historical interpretation with a living author's testimony. Much of Olsen criticism has reconstructed her life experiences, as if to authenticate the book still further. Even formalist readings (which claim to eschew the biographical fallacy) repeatedly compared this "youthful" narrative to the creative act of an actual working-class mother in her early twenties. Meanwhile, the book was categorized as a species of proletarian realism as it was formulated by left-wing writers like Mike Gold, Robert Cantwell, and V. F. Calverton (whom Olsen had read). Deborah Rosenfelt and Erica Duncan, for instance, showed convincingly (by reference to Olsen's private papers) that the book's original plot outline—subsequent sections leading to a strike, more family disintegration, and death, and Will Holbrook's conversion to political organizing and the Communist Party—reiterated 1930s' prescriptions for proletarian realism. Moreover, the book exhibited devices—cinematic cross-cutting, revolutionary prophecy, direct appeals to the audience—venerated by proletarian

7. Aside from the associations of "classic" status with immortality, LaCapra notes that it is "commonplace to observe that a sign of a 'classic' is the fact that its interpretation does not lead to a definitive conclusion and that its history is very much the history of conflicting or divergent interpretations and uses of it." *Rethinking*, p. 38. Salzman declared the book the best of its genre, yet said it could not "be restricted by any particular time or period." On mutability in canon formation, see Jane Tompkins, *Sensational Designs: The Cultural Work of American Fiction, 1790–1860* (New York: Oxford University Press, 1985), pp. 1–5, 186–201.

critics. Rosenfelt argued that *Yonnondio,* a proletarian novel which failed to reach fruition, was part of a feminist socialist tradition. Even in more generally humanistic criticism, Olsen's work has been identified with a "perfectionist" portrayal of a "representative American proletarian family."[8]

On the other hand, in practically the same breath, critics claimed that proletarian realism could not fully account for this text's power. Rosenfelt, Salzman, and Amy Godine all argued that much of the didacticism of Gold's platform ran counter to Olsen's more lyrical and modernist aims. Critics like Elaine Neil Orr and Kathleen McCormack, meanwhile, deployed formalist interpretation to find a case for spiritual "transcendence" in the book's motifs. These critics emphasized an essentially Romantic idiom in the text, cantilevering off children's wonder to invoke political spirituality (from Mazie at the start to Baby Bess's "Neanderthal" [153] confidence at the close), the "heart shaped" leaves (117) the family collects, the butterflies and stars and sparks of intelligence that express stifled creativity. Implicitly, the book has been likened to novels like Charles Dickens's *Hard Times* (1846) which parallels the thwarted imagination of children with the exploitation of workers. Whether these critics saw themselves as "saving" the text from ideology or reclaiming an uplifting account of human potential, implicitly the book was thought to be born again.[9] The book thus came both to represent its era and to transcend it.

Given the heady hyperbole of reviewese, such contradictions are hardly uncommon. But a closer look suggests what was really at stake. It was not only that a book which supposedly captured a historical moment perfectly

8. For a good account of Olsen's "perfectionist" strain, see Bonnie Lyons, "Tillie Olsen: The Writer as Jewish Woman," *Studies in American Jewish Literature* 5 (1986): 89–102; quotes here from pp. 91, 93. See also Elenore Lester, "The Riddle of Tillie Olsen," *Midstream* (January 1975): 77. These critics point out the brief injection of Anna Holbrook's lost ethnicity in her memory of her Jewish grandmother (*Yonnondio,* pp. 38–39).

9. Annie Gottlieb characterized *Yonnondio* as "no less than a saved life: a never-to-be-finished work that nonetheless lives with great depth and vibrancy." *New York Times Book Review,* 31 March 1974, 5; other critics reapply the imagery of orphanage to *Yonnondio's* newly-"found" status. See also Elaine Neil Orr, *Tillie Olsen and a Feminist Spiritual Vision* (Jackson: University Press of Mississippi, 1987), esp. pp. 51–69; Elaine McCormack, "Song as Transcendence in the Works of Tillie Olsen," in *Symposium: Tillie Olsen Week,* as cited in Orr, *Tillie Olsen,* p. 65, and Deborah Rosenfelt, "From the Thirties: Tillie Olsen and the Radical Tradition," *Feminist Studies* 7 (Fall 1981): note p. 496. For biographical information, I have relied on Rosenfelt, "From the Thirties" and Erika Duncan, "Coming of Age in the Thirties: A Portait of Tillie Olsen," *Book Forum* 6 (1982): 207–22. See also Amy Godine, "Notes Towards a Reappraisal of Depression Literature," *Prospects* 5 (1980): 217, and Rose Kamel, "Literary Foremothers and Writers' Silences: Tillie Olsen's Autobiographical Fiction," *MELUS* 12 (Fall 1983): 55–72.

was now said to supersede it. Rather, it was that a work which might well testify to working-class imagination—or provide rapport and power for left-wing critics—suddenly became, implicitly, a case-in-point *against* the narrow premises of Marxist ideology.[10] Even more dramatically reflecting the power of critics' own formalist assumptions, the book (of a radical atheist, no less) was now said to transcend the materialist determinism it so forcefully documented. Revisionst rapport was thus in something of an unacknowledged double bind. By being aestheticized into a (sometimes high-cultural) by-product of individual genius, the text's authenticity—as the voice of a representative cultural informant, a typical working-class woman—now seemed in jeopardy. The tension has been equally apparent in critical treatments of the book's fragmentary, incomplete status. Even avowedly contextual critics have deployed a number of formalist techniques in order to treat the book *not* as a fragment but as an "organic" whole, hence to restore its artistry, help it be reborn; others used its fragmentary status as an example of ideological disagreements with proletarian realism's rigid demands. The resulting explanations often showed the strain. Godine, for instance, said the "absence of a finished, flowing conventional plot"—as if the early Olsen planned never to finish—affirms the "incidental, commonplace, fragmentary detail that really imperils the quality of human life" (217). Duncan said that the "not-yet-grown-up quality of this book" (again, identifying *Yonnondio* with the age of its creator) renders it "if not in realized form and content—the very epic it was meant to be" (218). Even reviewers who acknowledged the book's unfinished status, and yet therefore lamented the absence of catharsis, underlined what even revisionists wanted in texts they recovered.[11]

Nevertheless, a brief look at the novel's manuscripts (in the New York Public Library) suggests how great a role editorial choice and memory, rather than sheer transcription of a 1930s artifact, actually had in Olsen's own recovery of *Yonnondio*. For instance, the young Olsen had often com-

10. Thus another unintentional byproduct of this criticism, despite its contributions to feminist understanding, is that it implicitly reiterates the "God that Failed" hypothesis first formulated by disillusioned Marxists themselves. The original affiliation of American Studies with Popular Front ideology is worthy of further study. But Olsen herself has said of her Communism that "for me it was never a God and it never failed" (Duncan, "Coming of Age," p. 209). Compare Godine or Salzman's reading with Pells, *Radical Visions,* p. 350ff.

11. John Alfred Avant, review of *Yonnondio* in the *New Republic,* vol. 170, 30 March 1974, 28–29. Michael Staub, who emphasizes the self-development theme, dismisses the entire issue of the book's fragmentary state; see his "The Struggle for 'Selfness' Through Speech in Olsen's *Yonnondio: From the Thirties,*" *Studies in American Fiction* 16 (Autumn 1988): 131–40.

posed and revised on the typewriter; sometimes she typed an intention and then tried several times to execute it. Sets of lines are written on stationery from the Common Brick Manufacturers Association, on forms from the Civil Works Administration of San Joaquin County (notifying the recipient of a cut-off in funds), or on the back of bank receipts from the Conservative Savings and Loan Association of Omaha, Nebraska. (One sheet has on its reverse side a "Resolution for a Farmer Labor Party": the sole word "Whereas" appears, and the rest is blank.) Today entire pages are crossed out; words are scratched out in pencil and pen; only a solitary page from "Chapter 12" remains. Nor was this proletarian book unaffected by commercial publishing demands. Because Olsen was working "piecemeal" (her word) under contract to Cerf, she computed composition schedules for chapters in her margins. Meanwhile, the Berg manuscripts are dotted with "How could I have written this?" or "No more of this kind of writing— faltering—," or resolutions about bearing down, "just write thru in the lousiest manner if thats the best you can do," followed by "but I don't think that can work." If anything, some notes suggest Olsen doubted proletarian fiction could surmount her frequently changed circumstances or the erosions of time and memory: "What I don't understand about Cantwell and co.," she writes, "—how do they expect to be working class writers—the way they live. What actual contact with ordinary people does he have now anyway—only memories . . ."[12]

The role of memory was thus quite pivotal in 1972–73. The older Olsen apparently found multiple drafts, literally fragments of torn paper and obscure notes. Coming back to such already-divided fragments and choosing among them must have been baffling; Olsen's statement of "no new writing" understates the choices she of necessity made. By comparison with the published text, one can see that Olsen may well have restored words from drafts from *earlier* in the thirties, in place of ones from later in the decade; mixed early sentences with later; added in some revisions made in the thirties and let others (not equally decipherable) go. If anything Olsen understates how *much* recollection affected the later chapters, which are (to an outsider, even in an organized collection) wholly inchoate. And

---

12. Olsen, Tillie, [Yonnondio: From the Thirties]. Holograph notes and typewritten drafts (incomplete) of novel, Berg Collection, New York Public Library. This collection does not contain any *final* manuscripts sent to Delacorte, and is now roughly organized (presumably by the author) by chapter. Interestingly, "How could I have written this?" refers to the passage when Old Man Caldwell tells Mazie to "rebel" (p. 49). On the Cerf contract, see Rosenfelt, "From the Thirties," pp. 386–87.

finally, I have found no evidence that *Yonnondio* was the title Olsen chose in the thirties; the manuscripts in New York also contain no opening stanza from Walt Whitman.[13]

The matter above may indeed be settled by further empirical research, and the critical ambivalence *Yonnondio* provoked in critics is surely not unusual. But at least in part, this interpretive turbulence, and the problems it creates for a clear path of rapport with the "thirties" or a proletarian author—for us or for Olsen herself—also derive from tensions within the most basic "protocols" around the recovery practice itself.[14] This is not merely a matter of an "artifact" to be restored. As James Clifford has suggested in *The Predicament of Culture,* even the most rudimentary terms and assumptions, labels like "text" or "document" or "classic" or "artifact" itself, can significantly affect the processes of memory, classification, and—most important—interpretation. Within museums, Clifford points out, artifacts are customarily arranged within one of four different semantic "zones": an upper "authentic" tier of (1) cultural "artifacts" versus (2) works of art, or a lower, "inauthentic" tier of (3) tourist art or curios or (4) "not culture" fakes (224). Clifford elaborates:

> The system classifies objects and assigns them relative value. It establishes the "contexts" in which they properly belong and between which they circulate. . . . These movements select artifacts of enduring worth or rarity, their value normally guaranteed by a "vanishing" cultural status or by the selection and pricing mechanisms of the art market. The value of Shaker crafts reflects the fact that Shaker society no longer exists: the stock is limited. (223)

Despite our habitual belief in "intrinsic" meaning, Clifford suggests (as have others) that these zones of cultural classification in fact have open borders; in fact, objects readily circulate *across* such zones. Tribal possessions travel to the Museum of Modern Art, soup cans appear on Warhol

13. Olsen may actually have selected her Whitmanian frame in the 1970s: his "Yonnondio" is mentioned in Olsen's biographical afterword to Rebecca Harding Davis, *Life in the Iron Mills* (New York: Feminist Press, 1972), p. 154.

14. By "protocol" I mean the implied rules, and taboos, of a given interpretive method, especially *preliminary* preparation (not unlike etiquette) in carrying out a given critical procedure. Such protocols are, in effect, the second nature of critical methods, unstated but no less powerful. Compare Robert Scholes, *Protocols of Reading* (New Haven: Yale University Press, 1989), esp. pp. 50–88. Compare also Elizabeth Williams's discussion of the tensions between "universality" and historicity in the collections of "primitive" *ars Americana,* in "Art and Artifact at the Trocadero," in *Objects and Others,* ed. George W. Stocking, Jr. (Madison: University of Wisconsin Press, 1985), esp. p. 161ff. See also in the same volume Ira Jacknis's discussion of "Franz Boaz and Exhibits," esp. the account of Franz Boas's dissatisfaction over the lack of "imaginary transport" in "realistic" life-groupings, p. 101ff.

canvases, once revered paintings are demoted to "period pieces," items of technology are promoted to "design" exhibits, and so on. Conversely, a given zone can decisively affect the act of representation and exhibition. In museum photos of supposedly "primitive" islanders, for instance, wrist-watches are airbrushed away so as to present a supposedly more "authentic" picture of their culture.[15] In other words, how we classify *Yonnondio* will affect what we think its significance is.

Most relevant to *Yonnondio*'s re-collection are the series of covert assumptions governing the distinction between art and artifact. Art objects, on the one hand, are labeled with individual artists' names, identified with their controlling "genius," and, as Raymond Williams once suggested, are often deemed oppositional to their culture's domain. But cultural artifacts, on the other hand, are deemed communal, their artists' presence diminished or removed, said to bear "humility" (and not anger, as James Agee realized). Paradoxically, though such humble "arti-facts" (the word itself cannoting evidence of artisanal workmanship) often appear in fragmentary form, they often are taken to express something like premodern wholeness, the continuity of tradition (rather than originality), and the spiritual essence of a people—often, indeed, a whole way of life fragmented by modernity.[16] In recent times the fragment or shard has become not just a cabinet curio, but both evidence *of* and a figure *for* an implied narrative of historical decay. If an object is designated as a cultural artifact, moreover, it ostensibly speaks on *behalf* of a people who have often been silenced—that is, recovery works as an act of rapport, the work as an informant. Collecting such objects, Clifford points out, "implies a rescue of phenomena from inevitable historical decay or loss. The collection contains what 'deserves' to be kept, remembered, and treasured. Artifacts and customs are saved out of time" (231).

As Clifford acknowledges (235), these processes of categorization are not merely arbitrary. The assumptions governing collecting practices may exist for worthwhile political, pedagogical, and even scientific reasons.

---

15. Compare Stuart Hall, "Notes on Deconstructing 'the Popular,'" *People's History and Socialist Theory,* ed. Raphael Samuel (London: Routledge and Kegan Paul, 1981), esp. pp. 234–36; Lawrence Levine, *Highbrow, Lowbrow* (Cambridge: Harvard University Press, 1988); Michael Denning, *Mechanic Accents* (London, Verso 1987), esp. pp. 9–17, 58–59. See also Edwin L. Wade, "The Ethnic Art Market in the American Southwest," in *Objects and Others,* pp. 167–91.

16. See James Agee and Walker Evans, *Let Us Now Praise Famous Men* (Boston: Houghton Mifflin, 1988), pp. 15–16; Raymond Williams, *Culture and Society* (Edinburgh: R.R. Clark, 1961).

Anthropologists' sense of a primitive culture's fragility, for instance, might retard their own contributions to its decay; films classified by *auteur* resist their colorization. The imputed authenticity of a given artifact—say, a slave narrative—can be a volatile issue for good reasons.[17] Rather, the point is simply to recognize how fluid and contested this system usually is; to demonstrate how recovery practices attribute qualities to the recovered object itself; and perhaps, to help us ward off the unwitting misrepresentation which can occur even in our most honorable desires to preserve. Recovery can be quite mutable, politically ambidextrous (for example, Robert Bork's recovery of the "intentions" putatively shaping the Constitution) and quite unintentionally derogatory. Literary history, for example, is notorious for serving up various labels around the recovery process—"popular" text, "period piece," "minor classic," "political novel"—all of which memorialize in the sense of mummifying, contextualize in such a way as to (in Olsen's own term) silence. (Given the Soviet Union's demise, "proletarian novel" may become vulnerable to just such a risk.) By contrast, Clifford suggests, we might instead use our preserving to invoke "[w]hat is hybrid or 'historical' in an emergent sense"—that is, to recognize that what is often exoticized as an authentic "primitive" artifact can also represent a living historical text for its culture, its creator, its living descendants. Such artifacts may even represent not a static or holistic culture (like proletarian culture) but rather differing paths to modernity—as Olsen's manuscripts suggest, not a transparent window into past consciousness, but a collage of mixed desires, hopes, and mystifications connected to the present.

Furthermore, the interpretive friction *Yonnondio* provokes begins to lend plausibility to those critics—Clifford himself, Natalie Davis, and particularly Hans Robert Jauss and Dominick LaCapra—who have suggested historical recovery might well be reconceived in "dialogic" terms. Although not unilaterally well received by revisionists—LaCapra, in particular, has often been mistaken as a stalking horse for Derrida—these critics have argued for a historical criticism which, in place of documentary realism, exposes the exchange between present and past, its points of friction and insight, its flashes of rapport and its inevitable disjunctures. (We cannot assume, LaCapra has argued, that there is a "pure" meaning which guaran-

17. See esp. Jean Fagan Yellin's introduction to the Harvard University Press edition (Cambridge, 1987) of Harriet Jacobs's *Incidents in the Life of a Slave Girl, Written by Herself* (1861), pp. xii–xxxiv. Contrast Levine on "sacrilized" art, *Highbrow, Lowbrow*, p. 120; compare Wade, "Ethnic Art Market," p. 168.

tees a "fusion of horizons," or "authoritative continuity with the past.")[18] Within recent studies, Jauss and his American extrapolators have challenged the recurring fashions of formalism by resurrecting literary history from the mélange of popular journalism, influence studies, and outlines of Great Authors or genres which occupied chronological pigeonholes. Jauss proposed that literary historians instead reconstruct the "horizons of expectations" around a text's historical reception—in a sense, the concentric rings beginning from the text's own statements about its preferred treatment (e.g., from prefaces or asides to the reader), through the expectations of past readers, through its critical receptions in its own day, to its modern recovery. To Jauss literary history, rather than an unchanging progression of great works with fixed messages, was a question and answer exchange *between* these horizons, a continuing dialogue between the present and a text's "orchestration" of themes and motifs *in* its history.[19]

LaCapra's or Jauss's models are not without their own limitations. We should not merely replace exoticizing the past with exoticizing interpretation, nor treat frictions of recollection as intrinsic, rather than socially produced.[20] Furthermore, both critics employ a notion of textuality—a text as an orchestration of variable meanings endlessly renewable and available to interpretation—not so very different from the New Criticism, and quite alien to *Yonnondio* itself.[21] But for the balance of this essay, I want to distinguish heuristically two horizons in *Yonnondio* by referring to the Olsen "of" the thirties as Tillie *Lerner,* the name she used in print in that decade. Listening to both Olsens—the agent of origination and of

18. "The relativist simply turns objectivist 'logocentrism' upside down. The historian places himself or herself in the position of 'transcendental signifier' that 'produces' or 'makes' the meanings of the past." LaCapra, *History and Criticism,* pp. 137–38ff. On pure horizons, see LaCapra, *Rethinking,* p. 63.

19. Recent elaborations on Jauss's model in American literary history, the new historicism, and *histoire du livre* have refined this basic model. See esp. the work in the issue of *American Quarterly* 40 (1988); see also David Hall, *Worlds of Wonder, Days of Judgment* (New York: Knopf, 1989). Perhaps the best example of the dialogue model in American criticism is Janice Radway, *Reading the Romance* (Chapel Hill: University of North Carolina Press, 1984). On the issue of intrinsic "textual power" and its place in earlier cultural histories, see R. Gordon Kelly, "Literature and the Historian," *American Quarterly* 26 (1974): 144–48.

20. The risks of exoticizing interpretation have been made apparent in Frances E. Mascia-Lees, et. al., "The Postmodernist Turn in Anthropology: Cautions from a Feminist Perspective," *Signs* 15 (1989): 7–33.

21. LaCapra's working definition is helpful here: a text is "a situated use of language marked by a tense interaction between mutually implicated yet at times contesting tendencies." *Rethinking,* p. 26. Jauss, as well, assumes a text's meaning is "inexhaustible." *Question and Answer,* p. 231.

recovery—we may better hear the book's arguments about texts, classics, and even memory itself in a modern industrial society.

III

With the title *Yonnondio*—apparently chosen to compare families like the Holbrooks to virtually extinct American aboriginals (specifically Iroquois)—Tillie Olsen's book begins to orchestrate its own aura of recovery. Indeed, Olsen herself frames the book's recovery in nearly pre-historic figuration. In what is either the preface or afterword (it has been published in both positions), Olsen discusses her recollecting this way:

This book, conceived primarily as a novel of the 1930's, was begun in 1932 in Faribault, Minnesota, when the author was nineteen, and worked on intermittently into 1936 or perhaps 1937 in Omaha, Stockton, Venice (Calif.), Los Angeles and San Francisco. Unfinished, it yet bespeaks the consciousness and roots of that decade, if not its events.

Thought long since lost or destroyed, some of its pages were found intermixed with other old papers last winter, during the process of searching for another manuscript. A later, more thorough, search turned up additional makings: odd tattered pages, lines in yellowed notebooks, scraps. Other parts, evidently once in existence, seem irrevocably lost. (157)

Olsen's initially bold claim here, that the book bespeaks the consciousness of a decade, is easily lost in the tone, the hesitancy, of this passage. The "book" (not in book form) is a surprise discovery, stumbled over in search of another past; like a neglected possession (indeed a lost child), it was thought gone, out of sight, lost in all the traveling from city to city. Moreover, the tone of this passage is quite pointedly occluded, forgetful: "perhaps 1937," "evidently," "seem"—the manuscript's life history expressed merely in terms of a birth date. And the narrative persona of this passage, recessed in the passive voice, says she felt strangely cut off from the author of nineteen as the recovery began. This recessed, restrained, respectful distance is sustained in the note's final claim: "In this sense [having made editorial choices only about what to include and where]—the choices and omissions, the combinings and reconstruction—the book ceased to be solely the work of that long ago young writer and, in arduous partnership, became this older one's as well. But it is all the old manuscripts—no rewriting, no new writing" (157–58).

This is not a voice from the thirties, nor one which finds a text born again. Rather Olsen guardedly walks the line between stressing the collaboration between past and present, and lamenting the loss of connection. But she establishes two essential signals. First, she establishes the book's artifactuality: it is from the "thirties" (the shorthand, diminutive term has always lent affection, an historian's nickname), indeed expressive of that decade's spirit. That is, the book is not merely an *instance* of proletarian writing, but *evidence* of the toll of class warfare upon its own author. And its appearance as artifact—in essence, pieced together from scraps almost as an archaeologist would assemble fragments—is sustained by other features of the book. First, of course, is the book's premature ending ("Reader, it was not to have ended here . . ." [155]); whatever our formalist desire to effect closure, or find continuous patterning in its imagery, Olsen's notes deny wholeness. Moreover, Olsen insists, paradoxically but importantly, that this is a recovery which only enhances the sadness of disappearance. In the prefatory stanza from Whitman, Olsen affirms the archaeological effect further:

> *Lament for the aborigines . . . a song, a poem of*
> *itself—the word itself a dirge . . .*
>
> Race of the woods, the landscapes free and the falls.
> No picture, poem, statement, passing them to the
>   future:
> Yonnondio! Yonnondio!—unlimn'd they disappear;
> To-day gives place, and fades—the cities, farms,
>   factories fade;
> A muffled sonorous sound, a wailing word is borne
>   through the air for a moment,
> Then blank and gone and still, and utterly lost. (7)

In this allusion, Olsen not only compares her recovered Holbrooks to native American tribes (collectively); she also emphasizes the muffled, indistinct cry which, rather than being saved, disappears. At the very moment of memory, the very voice that brings forth such words goes blank, "utterly lost." The book's closing address to the reader reaffirms this sense of loss: "Only fragments, rough drafts, outlines, scraps remain—to tell what might have been, and *never will be now*" (155, my emphasis). "Limning," or re-limning, is a paradoxical process: seeming to evoke what Whitman calls (in a line Olsen deletes) "misty strange tableaux the syllables [were] calling up," but outlining only bubbles, lost words.[22]

Olsen's preface itself delineates two related personae embodying this lost

---

22. The lines deleted reprinted in *Leaves of Grass: A Textual Variorum of the Printed Poems,* ed. Sculley Bradley et. al. (New York: New York University Press, 1980), vol. 3, p. 716.

cry: the editor/preserver/recoverer, and "that long ago young author." The preserver, implicitly paralleling her own forced mobility to the Holbrooks, is ostensibly a not-writer, just an arranger: respectful, recessed, quiet. By contrast, by creating *Yonnondio* as an artifact, Olsen's Tillie Lerner, the original writer, albeit occluded, implicitly speaks collectively. Although both Olsen and her manuscripts suggest these levels are not quite so neat, it is important to respect these provinces of authority. For instance, we can easily miss that *Yonnondio*'s narrator—indeed, even the voice of those passionate inter-passages which moves away from the text and addresses us directly—is consistently that of Tillie *Lerner,* in her twenties, and aligned with the same tribe Olsen aligns her with. We can unconsciously be misled, I think, because certain passages speak in a powerfully retrospective and didactic tone (e.g., "I'm sorry, Jim Tracy, sorry as hell we weren't stronger and could get to you in time. . . ." [79]), so much so, in fact, that some critics believe them to present an *interjected* narrator. Rather, though speaking from the thirties, Lerner's voice is already hardened by time, already recollecting herself, writing *from memory even then.* (The novel is *set,* after all, in the 1920s.)[23]

The province of the Olsen of the 1970s is equally potent. Although some have claimed that it is unfortunate that this proletarian novel is incomplete, and, again, that its fragmentary status denies us the cathartic "release that fulfilled art brings," its incompleteness is actually a source of its testamentary power.[24] As I have said, thanks to its artifactual aura, critics tend to see Lerner's story as *so* authentic that it is simply History itself, experience even in some cases unmediated and unliterary. Lerner's narrator—or Lerner?—in fact addresses characters (like Jim Tracy) as if they are real people she has known. Yet however admirable these critical sentiments are, their rapport seems to be set on unstable (and perhaps unwittingly condescending) grounds. The matter of the narrator's unsettling maturity is only one fact that works against the autobiographical or tribal grain, even the equation of young Olsen and immature text. Additionally, we might note that

23. Compare Godine, "Notes" p. 218, who sees the voice of the Jim Tracy passage as that of a "smug," male "intellectual" who Olsen introduces to contrast with her own, more lyrical voice. In fact, in draft Olsen had taken a "man could be a man for the first time on earth" and changed "man" to "human." Similarly, the setting resists the familiar categorization of this book as "Depression Literature." What is striking about the book is the *absence* of references to those public events—bank closings, the NRA, and so forth—which marked the thirties.

24. Contrast my reading with that of Rosenfelt, "From the Thirties," p. 389; Godine, "Notes" p. 217; and Avant on "release," p. 29.

the plot accompanies an Americanized family (the Holbrooks), and that the allusion to the Jewish background of Anna's grandmother is so brief most readers will overlook it. And what of that nineteen-year-old Lerner herself? We know, thanks to scholars like Duncan and Rosenfelt, that she was raised in a highly literate socialist family; that she read her way rapidly through the Omaha Public Library as a teenager; that she read Coleridge, Nietzsche, Edna St. Vincent Millay, and radical literary journals. We also know that she later spoke of feeling separated from her working-class comrades by virtue of her reading and her literary aspiration, and chafed under the party discipline which assigned her to a typewriter.[25] Finally, *Yonnondio* also has much in common with experimental forms outside of Mike Gold's domain, notably, the less official, thoroughly personal and passional documentary style of simple human endurance William Stott has identified.[26]

That Lerner's contemporary horizons were broader than proletarian realism—and yet, internally at war in her own artistic spirit—is apparent by glancing briefly at the first chapter, which ran in the *Partisan Review* (*PR*) in 1934 as "The Iron Throat." Here, as in the novel form, we find a counterpointing with Joyce that might have been admired by Gold, and a literary self-consciousness anything but aboriginal. Rather, young Mazie Holbrook, in a pointed echo of Stephen Daedalus and the moo-cow, reconstructs a metaphor around her social existence:

"Bowels of earth. It means the mine. Bowels is the stummy. Earth is a stummy and mebbe she eats the men that come down. Men and daddy goin' in like the day, and comin out black. . . . Poppa says the ghosts down in the mine start a fire. That's what blowed Sheen McEvoy's face off so it's red. It made him crazy. Night be comen and everything becomes like under the ground. . . . The whistle blows. Poppa says it is the ghosts laughin 'cause they have hit a man in the stummy, or on the head. Chris, that happenened too. Chris, who sang those funny songs. He was a furriner. Bowels of earth they put him in. Callin it dead. Mebbe it's for coal, more coal." (12–13)

---

25. "I can't put out one of those 800 page tomes," she wrote at the time. Cf. Rosenfelt, "From the Thirties," p. 383ff. and Duncan "Coming of Age," p. 218ff. And this sense of separation is reaffirmed by Olsen's recent comment in a letter to Michael Staub: "The Holbrooks were who I would be *if I had led that life.* You feel such respect when you know them and the agony of their defeats. They never realize what possibilities there could have been" [my emphasis]. See Staub, "The Struggle for 'Selfness,'" p. 140.

26. Olsen in fact later praised James Agee and Walker Evans's work. Compare Pells, *Radical Visions,* p. 199, and William Stott, *Documentary Expression and Thirties America* (New York: Oxford University Press, 1973), p. 7.

Its beauty and pathos notwithstanding, what is striking is how this passage argues *against* its own allusive talent. Metaphor making is removed from school, from literary elites, made part of the sensibility of working people, *in* their lives; bodily construction provides the fusion of nature and capitalism in the world of Mazie's family. Here was a quite literary talent the *PR* editors (and apparently Cerf) recognized. Yet almost as soon as *we* recover this young talent, she resists. The *PR* version ended optimistically, with Mazie using her sense of beauty to rise *above* the pain (the last line, speaking of coal bits which sting her face, says "Somehow it reminded her of the rough hand of her father when he caressed her, hurting her, but not knowing it, hurting with a pleasant hurt.") However, in the manuscript drafts, the text Olsen saved, and book *we* read—we turn to Sheen McEvoy's attempt to sacrifice Mazie *to* the mine, and an ending of Mazie's crazed, hysterical laughter.[27]

Facing the obvious pathos of this loss, which critics naturally extend from Mazie to Lerner herself (in effect, as a portrait of the artist), little wonder that critics have often deployed formalist techniques to restore the book's individuality, the imprint of an authentic genius. The act of rapport extends from character to author—this is such a reflex action it's hard to suppress it. We can see the cumulative effect of this kind of recovery when we visualize the well-wrought urn ostensibly restored from the fragments. In *Yonnondio* itself, there are various motifs which could, in a formalist reading, thus restore the text, make it symmetrical or whole: its movement from the opening of a day to the closing of the day in the final scene; the death in the mine, balanced by Baby Bess's final gesture of "I can do" (153); the motifs of light mentioned earlier. Moreover, the narrative's shifting perspective, interweaving from Mazie to Anna to Jim and others, again seems to affirm the book's collective nature.

Yet much of *Yonnondio* also resists these romantic protocols of formalism. However much symmetry she reimposed, Olsen also retained a pointedly disrupted pastoral pattern: not a retreat, but a ragged movement from mine, to farm, and back to factory. Perhaps more importantly, these positive desires for wholeness, well-intentioned as they are, also contradict the more telling counterforces the book itself documents. A great deal of the book's pathos comes from the sense that the wonder of Mazie has been twisted into near madness, her mind nearly sacrificed to capitalism's stomach. What is collective is also clearly in danger; in the opening, the shifting

27. Originally printed as "The Iron Throat," *Partisan Review,* vol. 1, April/May 1934, 3–9.

narrative positions are likened to worms in a common grave, a collective nightmare. Over time, in turn, workers and family members take on mass individuation which parodies the dream of collectivity: Jim Tracy as a white key in the black and white "piano" (79) of the chain gang; Will as the movie cowboy (126) and thus the "ruggedindividualism" (77) of national ideology; Anna as a mother dictated to by welfare doctors, filling her head with poster banners ("*The Wheel of Nutrition: One Serving: Green Leafy Vegetable Daily*") whose prescriptions she cannot meet. Tellingly, even the motif of song, a combination of romantic wonder and collectivity, appears only as a fleeting bubble in this world: as the forgotten songs of Shenandoah (119), the tunes Jimmie intuitively croons, the songs Anna has given up playing (66–67).

The book's romantic idioms, in other words, are countermanded by more hard-edged instincts and ideas about words and power, texts and lives, memory and making classics. Lerner does not see texts at all in the formalist sense, or even in the senses LaCapra or Jauss propose, as inexhaustible orchestrations, essentially performative in nature. First, she sees texts as traversing all discursive forms (school books, movies, street jargon), thus not specially literary; moreover, she does not see texts as open fields, endlessly renewable (made alive again), any more than human resources are. In a series of quick cuts Lerner instead opens up another version of texts:

Twelve-year-old Jinella's text: the movies, selected. Ones Mazie, the late-come country novice, has never seen. *Sheik of Araby. Broken Blossoms. Slave of Love* . . . (127–28)

On the stoop, evenings Ben imparts his terrible texts to Jimmie:

Skinny, skinny, run for your life
Here comes fatty with a butcher knife. (128)

. . . Pop, tell Ben and Jimmie when you were little. *But the day at Cudahy's has thieved Pop's text*—his mouth open, he sleeps the sleep of exhaustion. (129)

In these moments, texts are constantly traversing the working class family, coming down from the movies, up from the streets. Texts don't just come, in Lerner's view, from authoritative sources: people possess them *to begin with,* and they can be, quite importantly, dispossessed of them as well. Finally, texts are—a crucial nucleus of Lerner and Olsen's idiom—often synonymous with memories themselves. In fact, Lerner invokes a notion of texts as something more akin to an older usage: as pedagogies, lines one learns from and refers to, like a family bible. Consequently even voices are not so much agencies of self-realization, although I doubt we can ever un-see this aspect, as they are testaments of tradition.[28] They need, that is, to be told time and again to be remembered; they are mutable in a people's use; and they can decay—they are, in a nutshell, mortal. Again, we have not only an account of a people being dispossessed of words, but an account of how arduous and ambivalent making *Yonnondio* "live" again must have seemed to Olsen herself.

In *Yonnondio*'s descriptions of Will or Jinella, capitalism's texts take on an unseen, magical and destructive power:

(Already the conjurer is working spells on Anna's children. Subtly into waking and dreaming, into imagination and everyday doings and play, shaping, altering them. Even outwardly: Will's eyes are narrowed now, his mouth drawn up at the corner, his walk—when he remembers—loose; for the rest of his life he will grin crooked: Bill Hart.) (126)

Lerner thus sees texts as intrinsically worded with power: not anonymous discourses, but forces which take on personified agency, author power. As in the "bowels of Earth" passage, even Nature is dictated by capitalism's scripting of consciousness, and this necessarily infuses Mazie's metaphor-making, her political syntax. We have another powerful description of this when one of Jim Holbrook's female coworkers, sitting next to the packing slaughter room in 100-plus degree weather, conjures up the different passive *verbs* that, after the explosion, will be applied to the worker's own bodies: "*steamed boiled broiled fried cooked. Geared, meshed . . . scalded,* I forgot *scalded*" (145–46). Or there is the moment preparing the way for the accident:

Choreographed by Beedo, the B system, speed-up stopwatch, convey. Music by rasp crash screech knock steamhiss thud machinedrum. Abandon self, all ye who enter here. Become component part, geared, meshed, timed, controlled. (133)

Words crashing into one another, here they are established as power relations in a disrupted social sentence; flashed upon us with other scripts, Lerner writes them out quite like screen credits, juxtaposing them wildly with Dante's warning.

That Lerner acknowledges such disruptive discursive power suggests something different than a perfectionist strain at work. Moreover, this power established problems for *Yonnondio* as a work of (whatever you do don't call it) Art. That is, *Yonnondio* itself seems to cast doubt upon what

28. Contrast the theme of intellectual "self-development" *within* proletarian culture of the thirties in Pells, *Radical Visions,* esp. pp. 151–68.

a writer could hope to accomplish against the powers it depicts, especially *with* an aestheticized readerly horizon greeting it. The text, in other words, seems to document the odds against it. At the first level, Olsen and Lerner establish (through their own discursive speed-up) a testament which supplements the overall effect their shards create. The texts and forces created by capitalism gain increasing power, penetrate into the parts of the family, and finally *Yonnondio* itself splits into fragments. Pitted against the choreography of capitalism—"That stench is a reminder—a proclamation—I *rule here*. It speaks for the packing houses (60)"—a work of art seems powerless by comparison.

At another level, Lerner and Olsen choose to engage the horizon of expectations held by readers and potential recoverers. This occurs especially when Lerner pauses while she is recounting the explosion at the mine:

And could you not make a cameo of this and pin it onto your aesthetic hearts? So sharp it is, so clear, so classic. The shattered dusk, the mountain of culm, the tipple; clean lines, bare beauty—and carved against them, dwarfed by the vastness of night and the towering tipple, these black figures with bowed heads, waiting, waiting.

Surely, it is classical enough for you—the Greek marble of the women, the simple, flowing lines of sorrow, carved so rigid and eternal. Surely it is original enough. . . . In the War to Live, the artist, Coal, sculptured them. . . .

(*Dear Company. Your men are imprisoned in a tomb of hunger, of death wages. Your men are strangling for breath—the walls of your company town have clamped out the air of freedom. Please issue a statement; quick, or they start to batter through with the fists of strike, with the pickax of revolution.*) (30–31)

Critics have generally read this passage as a Mike Gold-inspired swipe at the bourgeois reader—here again, the imprint of the proletarian classification.[29] But perhaps more significantly, this is remarkable and creative anger working in several directions. In the second half of this passage, Lerner shifts into a simple letter to the Company: into a form that has no Art value (even little artifactual value), but perhaps more immediate political impact. She challenges the Company directly, mocking its reflex of public relations choreography, almost predicting its textual actions as a knee-jerk reaction to the direct challenge her prose itself can only forecast—the pick-ax of revolution.

But equally interesting is the first half of the quote, where Lerner challenges her reader and recoverer to apply the label "classical" to *Yonnondio*. In part, by "classic" Lerner means formal considerations: she mocks the

---

29. Contrast Godine, "Notes," p. 218.

predilections for Greek balance, a clean and unmessy culture-line, for "limning" which can be made cameo size and thus into what we now call a "collectible." This is, obviously, the antithesis of the form we finally received, over forty years later: shards of which Olsen takes pride in their being fragments rather than balanced forms. (Coal, like other scripting, is quintessentially Artist-as-Destroyer—the text that wins: here, sculpting is a form of breaking into pieces, a negative writing.) By "classic" she also invokes that expectation that the Art form will transcend the temporal, exist eternally and memorialized—and often be drained of its political intentions. It follows, then, that she shifts into that cultural form which is the most temporal of all, most immediate: the letter. But finally, Lerner means to thwart the expectation of *catharsis* which is so customarily linked to the reader's reaction in the classical form. Surely, she says, workers have all the criteria for classical design: their shape is right, the sky is backlit, the outline formed and, most of all, her story "original." Her people—her *own* people—qualify. But as their testifier, Lerner/Olsen seems not to want to leave the reader with that sense of completion, satisfaction, *release* associated with the cathartic moment—or, indeed, with the completed rather than fragmentary form. In a wonderfully minimalized turn on the dynamics of Agitprop, she turns the collectible cameo into a pin that strikes *through* to the aesthetic heart. In this sense the pen becomes analogous to the pickax trying to fight its way out of a premature grave.

IV

Anyone accustomed to the routines of historical scholarship knows the tedium, the excitement, and the absurdities of manuscript research. For every exhilarating discovery of a lost text, there are the moments when an austere librarian sets an archival box on your desk, and you find yourself (as I found myself) facing Jack London's letters to his plumber. A seminar professor insists that the garbage gathering in the yard of an Appalachian family is really folk art. Or, you dutifully transcribe popular magazines for a monograph on American reading habits, and the pulp disintegrates in your hands as you read: you look up, and realize the library is preparing instead, gilt-edged volumes for the papers of Benjamin Franklin. On a more serious front—perhaps, against the grain of these absurdities—many people have also experienced the death of a friend or family member, with funerals that provoke only silence, awkwardness, empty mementos and memorials that seem inadequate next to the memory of the person gone. Any attempt to speak *for* the deceased can seem sacrilegious, even to the radical atheist. When closure is difficult, or a "chapter" remains unfinished, paradoxically it can be because the wound is still fresh, time notwithstanding. (In the preliminary version of "All Our Yesterdays," the library collapsed as the *Enterprise* crew departed—leaving, as the original title went, "A Handful of Dust.")[30]

What I have called Tillie Olsen's recovery of *Yonnondio* (1932/74) seems to me as close to the second set of experiences as the first. Recollecting a text which was, after all, her own, Olsen faced a "lost" manuscript, yet revered it as a record of actual lives she knew had been choreographed by Beedo, un-scripted by Coal, scalded by slaughterhouses. In more than one sense, the proletarian finale was never added. If privately, as Rosenfelt has shown, Tillie Lerner found commitment to the Party exacted only another cost of resisting capitalism, the older Olsen converted her earlier despair over lack of completion into testimony that speaks against capitalism partly by *not* speaking. And whatever ventriloquism inevitably seeps into the process—including my own—Olsen respects *Yonnondio*'s temporality and even mortality, preserving its political kinship to a letter of protest, in its now. Naturally, there are limits even to Olsen's own act of collecting. Her casting of the novel as a recovered "primitive" text may have delimited *Yonnondio*'s highly literate, conflict-ridden, centrifugal aspects— airbrushed, perhaps out of modesty, the ambitious genius of Tillie Lerner so as to emphasize only the child-mother, the collective cry.[31] But as the person returning to a painful gravesite, Olsen's choices seem understandable, because the people the text cast in tableaux were still as real to her as forty years earlier.

Our own recollecting may proceed from less personal connections— ones, perhaps, we only fail to recognize—but Olsen's example is worth considering. Recent postmodern or "mosaic" histories have often taken to comparing themselves to museums which exhibit literary subcultures or ethnic groups as part of a huge American panorama, a more pluralistic canon. Certainly the fuller canon is far better than the restricted zone of the past. But what is surprising is how little our *forms* of recollection, the

30. Allan Asherman, *The Star Trek Compendium* (New York: Pocket Books, 1989), 133–34.

31. For my use of "centrifugal" here, see Scholes, *Protocols,* p. 79.

reference history, the anthology, the specialized library, have changed. In fact what we may still be re-creating—as by sectioning off "the proletarian novel" in our teaching—are dioramas, pacified exhibits of cultural *genuses* behind panes of glass, cut off from each other's tracks.[32] Such static recovery practices in fact run counter to the values a work like *Yonnondio* means to protect: the hybridizing experimentation *of* its own temporal moment; the struggle *among* different texts for official power and recognition; the place of such texts *in* a larger scripting of social life.

Finally, *Yonnondio* may also speak to any fable of rapport created by the sheer act of preserving. We may overlook, for example, that the oppositional text we may mean to recover is fragile, invoking a horizon which may even have been closed down: a "living" artifact, in Clifford's term, because it is still connected to actual people like Olsen herself; yet also lost as people like the Holbrook's are lost. In this respect, re-limning like Olsen's tries to represent the literary power of absence and the historical finality of disappearance. Likewise we may have to be more aware of how, in our academic ritual of denominating classics—for commerce or for classroom—we may tend to gild this arduous partnership, forgetting that some books indeed are not only more intent upon their temporal horizons, but resist transcendence. A period piece may be no less powerful in what it refuses us. The doctrine of the ever-renewable text may have an unconscious resonance in a throwaway society; but it *is* a contradiction if we grant some of Olsen's materialist assumptions. Lerner and Olsen both suggest, on the contrary, that texts and lives have their moments, their scripts and lines, their entrances and exits—that the aura of the classic invokes a privilege remote from the lives of people like the Holbrooks, looking at us *from* the thirties. Witness the line Olsen italicizes from Whitman's *Yonnondio*, "*the very word a dirge.*" In this respect, I for one am drawn to *Yonnondio*'s strategy of anticatharsis, of refashioning a cameo—a term which also implies a brief appearance, a spark of representation which sticks in the aesthetic heart, bringing the pain of mortality, disallowing both simple identification and release or transcendence. Apparently this strategy still applies to Olsen's sense of the performative. In her public readings, Olsen

32. See, for instance, the best volume to date: *The Columbia Literary History of the United States* (New York: Columbia University Press, 1988). Compare Clifford, *Predicament of Culture*, pp. 226–28; Jacknis, "Franz Boaz and Exhibits," pp. 101–107; and George W. Stocking, Jr., *Race, Culture, and Evolution* (Chicago: University of Chicago Press, 1982), pp. 155–60.

customarily reads from her own fragments, pausing to remember how a scene was written; but when her reading is over, "a subtle gesture of Tillie's hand asks for no applause." Instead, her audience is left in silence. Perhaps in *this* roundabout way, what Olsen has to say does recall Dickens after all: in the hard times recollected in *Yonnondio,* some of Time's "Hands are mutes."[33]

in memory my mother
1987–1992

33. Performance at the Radcliffe Institute in Cambridge, Mass., described in Judith W. Steinbergh, "Tillie Olsen Makes Us Shiver," article from *The Patriot Ledger* given to me by Ann Sibley. Rosenfelt describes a similar performance. Charles Dickens, *Hard Times* (New York, Norton, 1966), p. 73.

2 CULTURAL SAGAS OF THE MORAL LIFE

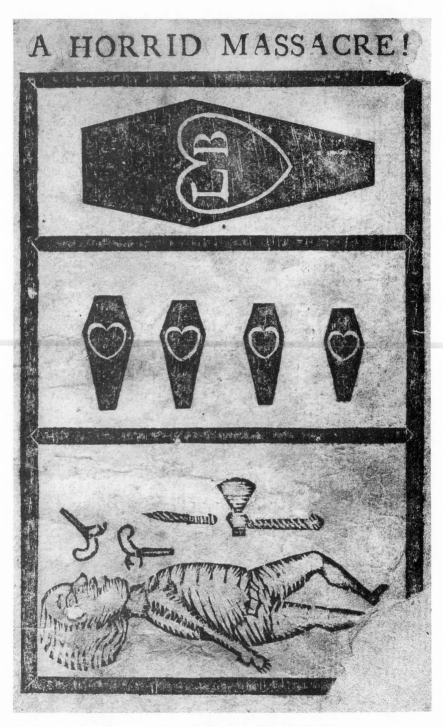

Frontispiece from Stephen Mix Mitchell's *Narrative of the Life of William Beadle* (Hartford, 1783). Courtesy American Antiquarian Society.

3 Early American Murder Narratives

The Birth of Horror

Karen Halttunen

"Other sins only speak; murder shrieks out," wrote John Webster in *The Duchess of Malfi*. The act of murder deeply disrupts and disturbs the community in which it takes place, tearing the social fabric by calling all relationships into question, and posing troubling questions about the moral nature of humankind. Murder thus demands some kind of cultural work through which the community can come to terms with the crime—to confront what has happened and endeavor to explain it, in order to move past the incident to restore order to the world. In literate societies, the cultural work of coming to terms with this violent act takes crucial form in the crafting and reading of written narratives of the murder, stories whose chief purpose is to assign meaning to the incident. As Hayden White has observed, every narrative account—even the allegedly "nonfictional"—is an artificial construct, for the world does not just "present itself to perception in the form of well-made stories, with central subjects, proper beginnings, middles, and ends."[1] Any narrative of murder involves a fictive process which reveals much about the mental and emotional strategies employed within a given historical culture for responding to serious transgression in its midst.

In American culture, the dominant narrative expressing and shaping the popular response to the crime of murder underwent a dramatic transformation in the second half of the eighteenth century. The early American execution sermon, a sacred narrative which focused on the salvation history of the condemned murderer, was gradually replaced by a variety of secular accounts of the crime itself which focused on the *horror* of murder. The cult of horror, which first became a major force in Anglo-American popular fiction during the last decades of the eighteenth century and has since occupied a significant place in modern popular culture, appeared in the "nonfiction" of American murder narratives well before its expression in Gothic horror fiction. This essay examines the transition from salvation

---

1. Hayden White, "The Value of Narrativity in the Representation of Reality," in W. J. T. Mitchell, ed., *On Narrative* (Chicago and London: University of Chicago Press, 1981), p. 23.

history to the horror account in American murder literature, and argues that the historical significance of late eighteenth-century horror rests in its provision of a new way of understanding the problem of evil within an emerging liberal humanitarian culture.

In New England before 1750, the dominant narrative for addressing incidents of murder was the execution sermon, preached in the context of the social ritual of public execution. Execution sermons were delivered on the Sabbath preceding or on the morning of the appointed day of execution, and sometimes on both occasions, with the condemned criminal sitting, guarded and in chains, in the front of the church below the pulpit.[2] They were well-attended events: four or five thousand people gathered for the execution of Esther Rodgers, and at the third and last execution sermon delivered for murderer James Morgan, a crowd of five thousand crowded the gallery of the Second Church until the structure cracked, prompting Increase Mather to adjourn the congregation to the Third Church to finish his sermon.[3] As the hour of execution drew near, the condemned criminal was led from prison to gallows in a solemn processional, sometimes wearing the halter with which he or she was shortly to be hanged. En route, the murderer was accompanied by clergymen who continued their task, begun months earlier with the judicial conviction of the felon, of examining the spiritual state of this soul on the brink of eternity: scanning every step, every breath, for signs of spiritual despair, and relentlessly questioning the prisoner about any grounds for spiritual hope. Once the small party had mounted the gallows, a clergyman or the condemned criminal might read the confession (sometimes read earlier along with the execution sermon), to which the prisoner might add some final remarks: infanticide Esther Rodgers addressed the crowd from the ladder just before receiving the

2. See Ronald A. Bosco, "Lectures at the Pillory: The Early American Execution Sermon," *American Quarterly* 30 (Summer 1978): 156–76; Daniel E. Williams, "'Behold a Tragick Scene Strangely Changed into a Theater of Mercy': Structure and Significance of Criminal Conversion Narratives in Early New England," *American Quarterly* 38 (Winter 1986): 827–47; Daniel E. Williams, "Rogues, Rascals and Scoundrels: The Underworld Literature of Early America," *American Studies* 24, no. 2 (Fall 1983): 5–19; J. A. Sharpe, "'Last Dying Speeches': Religion, Ideology and Public Execution in 17th-Century England," *Past and Present* 107 (May 1985): 144–67; Wayne C. Minnick, "The New England Execution Sermon, 1639–1800," *Speech Monographs* 35 (March 1968): 77–89.

3. [John Rogers], *Death the Certain Wages of Sin to the Impenitent* . . . (Boston: Printed by G. Green and J. Allen for Samuel Phillips, 1701), p. 153; Bosco, "Lectures at the Pillory," p. 160.

halter around her neck; Katherine Garret actually prayed until her breath was stopped, and died with her hands upraised.[4] Final prayers were offered by the clergy and sometimes by the prisoner, and at last, the executioner proceeded with the hanging. The impact of the event on the crowd which had gathered to witness it was reportedly powerful. At the execution of Joseph Quasson, according to the Rev. Moody, "the great Assembly of Spectators, were generally much affected, perhaps almost beyond Example."[5]

The purpose of the execution sermon was not to address the worldly judicial process that had brought the condemned criminal to this solemn end, but to seize the theological opportunity presented by the murder to explore the nature of sin and the promise of redemption. Those sermons preached for condemned murderers were very clear on their view of the offense at hand: "Murder is an exceeding great Sin," "a Sin of a very hainous [sic] and heavy guilt," the gravity of which had been made clear by God's placement of the commandment "Thou shalt not kill" at the head of the second table of Mosaic law.[6] But New England clergymen firmly believed that the underlying cause of even so heinous a crime as murder was the universal condition of postlapsarian humanity: innate and total depravity. "The Venemous Hearts of Men," Cotton Mather explained in 1713, "have in them the Root, which all *Murders* grow upon."[7] The source of murder, as of all human wickedness, was "that *Original Sin,* which the hearts of all

4. [Rogers], *Death the Certain Wages,* p. 147; Eliphalet Adams, *A Sermon Preached on the Occasion of the Execution of Katherine Garret . . .* (New London: T. Green, 1738), p. 40.

5. Samuel Moody, *Summary Account of the Life and Death of Joseph Quasson . . .* (Boston: S. Gerrish, 1726), p. 27. For general discussions of the civil function of public execution ritual, see Michel Foucault, *Discipline and Punish: The Birth of the Prison,* trans. Alan Sheridan (New York: Vintage Books, 1979); Pieter Spierenburg, *The Spectacle of Suffering: Executions and the Evolution of Repression from a Preindustrial Metropolis to the European Experience* (Cambridge: Cambridge University Press, 1984); Randall McGowen, "The Body and Punishment in Eighteenth-Century England," *Journal of Modern History* 59, no. 4 (December 1987): 651–79; J. A. Sharpe, "'Last Dying Speeches': Religion, Ideology, and Public Execution in Seventeenth-Century England," *Past and Present* 107 (May 1985): 144–67.

6. Increase Mather, *Sermon Occasioned by the Execution of a Man found Guilty of Murder . . .* (Boston: Joseph [oblit.], 1686), p. 9; Benjamin Colman, *The Hainous [sic] Nature of the Sin of Murder . . .* (Boston: John Allen, 1713), p. 6. Murder had only recently come to be seen as the most heinous of crimes, gradually displacing the dominant crimes of the Middle Ages and the Renaissance, heresy against God and treason against the state; see Lincoln B. Faller, *Turned to Account: The Forms and Functions of Criminal Biography in Late Seventeenth- and Early Eighteenth-Century England* (Cambridge: Cambridge University Press, 1987), p. 22.

7. Cotton Mather, *The Sad Effects of Sin: A True Relation of the Murder Committed by David Wallis, On his Companion Benjamin Stolwood . . .* (Boston: John Allen, 1713), p. 23.

men are by nature full of, and is a fountain that is always sending forth its bitter streams."[8]

Because the Calvinist doctrine of original sin provided a universally applicable explanation of the roots of murder, it rendered largely unnecessary an attention to what later generations would call "motive." Instead, execution sermons explored the patterns of sinful conduct that paved the way to murder. This heinous crime, according to the preachers of execution sermons, was merely the culmination of a long course of sinfulness whose prevailing pattern was that "Little Sins make way for greater. One Sin allowed, stupifies and makes way for great ones."[9] The life of sin was a slippery slope: the first false step led easily downward to the second, and then another, until at length the hapless sinner arrived at "a great Transgression"[10] such as murder. Many execution sermons offered catalogs of the numerous lesser sins that could lead to murder, such as "your pride, your disobedience to your Parents, your impatience of Family Government, your company keeping, your Whoredoms, and your despising of Christ."[11] Significantly, most execution sermons dwelled at greater length on what they called the "besetting sin" leading to murder than on the final crime of violence: as Cotton Mather exhaustively explained to an infanticide in 1693, "Your *sin* has been *Uncleanness; Repeated Uncleanness,* Impudent *Uncleanness,* Murderous *Uncleanness.*"[12] In Mather's treatment, the crime for which this woman was about to die—killing her newborn twins—was decidedly secondary to those sexual actions which he believed had set her irreversibly down the road to murder.

The effect of the execution sermon's etiology of murder was to encourage a strong moral identification between the assembled congregation (or readership) and the condemned criminal. For the doctrine that the root of murder was innate depravity undercut any notion of the murderer's moral peculiarity, all humankind having shared in that original sin committed by

8. Samuel Willard, *Impenitent Sinners Warned of their Misery and Summoned to Judgment . . .* (Boston: B. Green and J. Allen, 1698), p. 48.

9. John Williams, *Warnings to the Unclean . . .* (Boston: B. Green and J. Allen, 1699), p. 42.

10. Joshua Moodey, *An Exhortation to a Condemned Malefactor. Delivered March 7th. 1685/6,* included in Cotton Mather, *Call of the Gospel Applyed unto All men in general, and unto a Condemned Malefactor in particular . . .* (Boston: R.P., [1686]), p. 87.

11. Willard, *Impenitent Sinners Warned,* p. 26.

12. Cotton Mather, *Warnings from the Dead. or Solemn Admonitions unto All People; but especially unto Young Persons to Beware of such Evils as would bring them to the Dead . . .* (Boston: Bartholomew Green, 1693), p. 73.

the first parents of the race. In the presence of condemned infanticide Rebekah Chamblit in 1733, the Rev. Thomas Foxcroft instructed, "The sorrowful Spectacle before us should make us all reflect most seriously on *our own* vile Nature; which the Falls of others are but a Comment upon: and should excite us to humble ourselves under a sense of the Corruption of *our Hearts,* which are naturally as bad as the worst."[13] The only difference between the condemned murderer and the rest of humanity was "the restraining grace of God, to whose Name alone belongs the Praise, that any of us have been with-held from the grossest and most horrid Acts of Wickedness."[14] The moral identification of the larger community with the condemned murderer was strengthened by the execution sermon's emphasis on the slippery slope of sin, for what unchaste woman could deny that her course might lead to infanticide? What drunken man, what disobedient servant could be certain that he had not placed his foot on the road to murder? Under a New Testament understanding of the law, furthermore, the sixth commandment could be broken quietly in the private heart of the sinner as well as publicly in the flesh: "I would fain have charity, that there is but one in this Assembly, that hath been guilty of Murder in the highest degree of it; yet I fear there are several that have Murdered in their hearts."[15] This collective recognition of a shared criminality generated frequent expressions of sympathy for the condemned murderer within the execution ritual: ministers spoke "With the tenderest Bowels of Compassion" of "the miserable poor Creature" standing before the congregation.[16]

By refusing to treat the condemned criminal as a moral alien, New England clergymen invited members of the congregation to turn their eyes inward to the corruption of their own hearts, and set their thoughts on God. Though the central point of interest in most execution sermons was the salvation drama of the condemned murderer—even such a sinner as this, they emphasized, might close with Christ before his death—their

13. Thomas Foxcroft, *Lessons of Caution to Young Sinners* . . . (Boston: S. Kneeland and T. Green, 1733), p. 60.

14. William Shurtleff, *The Faith and Prayer of a dying Malefactor. A Sermon Preach'd December 27. 1739. On Occasion of the Execution of two Criminals* . . . (Boston: J. Draper for D. Henchman, 1740), p. ii.

15. John Williams, *Warnings to the Unclean* . . . (Boston: B. Green and J. Allen, 1699), p. 21.

16. Shurtleff, *The Faith and Prayer of a dying Malefactor,* p. 17; Arthur Browne, *Religious Education of Children Recommended* . . . (Boston: S. Kneeland and T. Green, 1739), p. 13. For discussions of the essential moral identity of the criminal with the rest of society, see Faller, *Turned to Account,* chap. 3; and Cynthia Herrup, "Law and Morality in Seventeenth-Century England," *Past and Present* 106 (1985): 102–23.

larger goal was the salvation of the entire congregation. Here the convicted criminal was expected to play an important role by delivering a "last dying speech" warning those present to leave their sinful ways, as in Jeremiah Fenwick's last appeal, "I know not how to glorify God more than by solemn warnings unto all people to take heed of such Sins, as have brought me to such a Ruin as is now come upon me."[17] Not only in her great sinfulness, but above all in her own repentance and conversion, was the condemned murderer to offer a saving example to others, like Esther Rodgers, whom John Rogers called "*a* Pillar of Salt *Transformed into a Monument of Free grace.*"[18]

The execution sermon was a major expression of the jeremiad, that predominant literary form of the late seventeenth and early eighteenth century which lamented declension in the Holy Commonwealth and exhorted the people of New England to restore their special relationship with God by returning to moral righteousness and spiritual awakening.[19] The crime of murder was understood as a providential summons to the whole community to repent of their sins. According to the Rev. John Williams, "whensoever God in his just Wrath leaves any to be monuments of shame & ignominy before the world, it is a loud call to all who lye under such guilt, to be speedy and thorough in repentance."[20] The condemned criminal standing before them was intended to serve the congregation as a dramatic reminder that their days too were numbered, that the time would come when they too would be thrust into eternity with no more opportunities for spiritual preparation: "However you now despise instruction, yet you will mourn for it at last," warned Samuel Willard. "It will be a dreadful thing to lose Gods [sic] presence for ever."[21] The message was simple: repent now and be saved.

Early American execution ritual held up the murderer in chains, not to invite the audience to indulge in a collective sense of moral superiority, but to force the people to confront their own common identity with the vilest of sinners, and to acknowledge that there but for the grace of God went every innately depraved sinner in New England. The central thrust of the public execution was thus a ritual of reconciliation between the

17. [Cotton Mather], *The Valley of Hinnom* . . . (Boston: Printed by J. Allen for Robert Starke, 1717), p. 3.

18. [Rogers], *Death The Certain Wages*, p. 118.

19. See Bosco, "Lectures at the Pillory"; and Williams, "'Behold a Tragick Scene.'"

20. Williams, *Warnings to the Unclean*, p. 5.

21. Willard, *Impenitent Sinners Warned*, p. 17.

criminal and the community whose most powerful mores had been violated. The prisoner's part in this reconciliation was to be offered as a moral
exemplum for the congregation and to assume a sacrificial role analogous
to that of Christ by dying publicly and ignominiously for a sinfulness that
was shared by all. The community's part was first to acknowledge that they
shared in the convicted criminal's moral and spiritual condition, crossing
the illusory divide between themselves and the condemned man or woman
standing before them on the gallows. As Nathaniel Clap said, "None of us
all have any reason to despise you, in your present deplorable Circumstances; while we must all own our selves to be miserable Sinners, and the
uncontroleable Soveraignty of the Most High God, is to be acknowledged,
in the differences that are made in our Circumstances: Your Case might
have been my Case or the Case of any other person here, if the Sovereign
Lord of all had so pleased."[22] Having crossed that divide to stand figuratively side-by-side with the criminal at the gallows, the congregation then
hitched their spiritual wagon to this ascending star, in hopes that they,
too, might be saved. In so doing, they succeeded in restoring a sense of
community by symbolically repairing the social fissure opened up by this
murderous assault on another member of the community, and by securing
the criminal's own ideological loyalty to the system that was taking his or
her own life.

Execution sermons thus dealt ritualistically with the problem of evil
within a two-part movement of *acknowledgment* and *transcendence*. They
began by affirming the reality of radical—that is, intrinsic, essential—
human evil, admitting that the crime of murder is heinous, pointing to the
total depravity of the murderer, and asserting the moral identification of
the murderer with every other innately sinful member of the New England
community. But they went on to transcend that evil by putting it to the
service of salvation, setting up the murderers as examples not only of deep
depravity but of spiritual hope, pointing to their spiritual progress and
dying confessions as models for the larger community to emulate.

This two-part movement in execution sermons reflected a larger pattern
at work in early New England culture. Early New Englanders lived in a
world they believed to be pervaded with evil, and devoted great cultural
energy to acknowledging its presence on three different levels: the moral
evil that arose from the innate depravity of humankind, polluted with

22. Nathaniel Clap, *Sinners directed to hear & fear* . . . (Boston: J. Allen for N. Boone,
1715), pp. 36–37.

sinfulness since the Fall of Adam and Eve; the natural evil—disease, death, natural disasters—that had been introduced into the lower creation by that same Fall; and the cosmic evil worked by God's great adversary, Satan, with his legions of demons and witches. But if Puritan culture generated an intense awareness of the problem of evil in the world, it also generated a multitude of techniques for dealing with the problem of evil which participated in the ritual of reconciliation. Such widely diverse practices as private prayer and public church discipline, the care of the sick and dying, covenant renewal and the communal fast day, the witch trial and the clerical exorcism—all evinced the same two-part movement as the execution sermon: first, a full acknowledgment of the evil in which all women and men shared, usually through some combination of private humiliation and public confession; then, the move to transcend that evil by treating it as an occasion for renewed striving for salvation. In the face of such varied evils as epidemic drunkenness, seasons of drought, or outbreaks of witchcraft, the New England community ritually acknowledged that it was the collective sinfulness of the people that had brought down such extraordinary judgments from God, and identified individual transgressors more with an eye to restoring them to membership in the social covenant than to scapegoating them for the community's ills.[23]

The penal system in early New England thus rested fundamentally on the premise that the convicted criminal was not a moral alien. Early American culture offered no place for a hard category of criminality, no fixed sense of the otherness of the social deviant. Charles Dickens's nineteenth-century view that the "criminal intellect" was nothing like "the average intellect of average men" but "a horrible wonder apart"[24] would have made

23. A considerable portion of the secondary literature on New England Puritanism examines Puritan views of evil and the various rituals employed for addressing specific manifestations of evil. Some of the most useful discussions include H. Shelton Smith, *Changing Conceptions of Original Sin: A Study in American Theology since 1750* (New York: Charles Scribner's Sons, 1955); David E. Stannard, *The Puritan Way of Death: A Study in Religion, Culture, and Social Change* (New York: Oxford University Press, 1977); Edmund S. Morgan, *The Puritan Family: Religion and Domestic Relations in Seventeenth-Century New England* (New York: Harper and Row, 1966), and Morgan, *Visible Saints: The History of a Puritan Idea* (New York: New York University Press, 1963); John Putnam Demos, *Entertaining Satan: Witchcraft and the Culture of Early New England* (New York: Oxford University Press, 1982); Charles E. Hambrick-Stowe, *The Practice of Piety: Puritan Devotional Disciplines in Seventeenth-Century New England* (Chapel Hill: The University of North Carolina Press, 1982); Norman Pettit, *The Heart Prepared: Grace and Conversion in Puritan Spiritual Life* (New Haven: Yale University Press, 1966); Emil Oberholzer, Jr., *Delinquent Saints: Disciplinary Action in the Early Congregational Churches of Massachusetts* (New York: Columbia University Press, 1956).

24. Charles Dickens, *Edwin Drood,* quoted in Faller, *Turned to Account,* p. 71.

no sense to early Americans, whose understanding of human depravity instilled in them a powerful sense of the moral precariousness of all women and men, a conviction that anyone could be struck with criminality at any moment should God momentarily suspend his sustaining grace and permit them to act upon their deepest natures. Humankind was not divided into rigid categories of normalcy and deviancy, but strung out along a moral continuum, on which all were equally vulnerable to slippage in the direction of major transgressions such as murder.[25] This view of criminality was shored up by the practice of placing a wide range of social deviants—petty criminals, idlers, debtors, disorderly children, as well as madpersons, the physically and mentally handicapped, the sick, even the unmarried—in orderly households where their conduct might be supervised and corrected by the same social discipline that shaped the lives of all members of the community.[26] This practice placed significant limits on the degree to which criminals were stigmatized by their crime and punishment: when petty criminals were publicly flogged and then sentenced to live in a well-governed household, the social goal of restoring the errant individual as soon as possible into the community was largely realized. And for those criminals publicly executed for a capital crime such as murder, execution ritual aimed at symbolically restoring them to the body of Christ's people before they were ushered into God's presence for a Judgment that the community formally hoped would be merciful.

The execution sermons' central concern for the community's moral identification with the depraved murderer before them helps explain the highly circumscribed nature of their attention to the crime itself. For it was against the interests of the clerical interpreters of murder to dwell at length on the specific crime in question, because such details would have undermined the moral identification of the congregation with the murderer; to dwell on the extraordinary sin of murder, as opposed to the "besetting sins" that all shared with the criminal, was to run the risk of generating a sense of

25. Herein lies a major problem with Kai Erikson's analysis of seventeenth-century New England "crime waves": in applying the theoretical model of the sociology of *deviance* to Puritan society, Erikson is superimposing a modern understanding of the criminal transgressor upon a culture which did not share this concept of the sinner as moral alien. See *Wayward Puritans: A Study in the Sociology of Deviance* (New York, 1966).

26. See Morgan, *Puritan Family*, p. 128; John P. Demos, *A Little Commonwealth: Family Life in Plymouth Colony* (Oxford: Oxford University Press, 1970), pp. 70, 184; David J. Rothman, *The Discovery of the Asylum: Social Order and Disorder in the New Republic* (Boston: Little, Brown and Co., 1971).

moral satisfaction among an audience guiltless at least literally of violating the sixth commandment.

Some execution sermons never referred directly to the murderous action which had brought the condemned criminal to judgment; others were vague on detail. Typically, the execution sermon's account of the crime was short and to the point: "A Man whose Name was Jeremiah Fenwick, was upon a Fair Trial brought in GUILTY of having Murdered his Neighbour with an Axe, which he took up, and Employed a repeted [sic] Blow thereof, at the Person at whom his Anger was enraged."[27] Even the most extensive narratives of murder in this period, the printed confessions offered by the convicted criminals themselves, dwelled at such length on the slippery slope of sinfulness leading to the crime and on the spiritual developments that followed it, as to seem almost interchangeable in their delineation of a morphology of criminal conversion.[28] And virtually no narrators, clerical or criminal, directed much attention to the carnage of murder: the weapons used, the wounds inflicted, the appearance of the scene, the state of the corpse, the circumstances of its discovery—all the staples of a later crime literature. A common rhetorical device was to redirect the congregation's attention from "the blood of Abel"—that is, of the murder victim—to the "blood of sprinkling"—that is, of Christ the Savior. "'Tis true, the innocent Blood cries from the Ground for Vengeance," said Mather Byles in his sermon for a black servant who had poisoned an infant, "But yet, the Blood of Sprinkling speaketh better Things than the Blood of *Abel,* and this lifts up a prevailing cry for Pardon & Forgiveness for you."[29] Byles thus not only urged his listeners to set aside all thoughts of vengeance, he invited them to transcend their worldly interest in the murder by turning to thoughts of salvation.

The execution sermon survived through the end of the eighteenth century. But after 1750, the cultural dominance of the execution sermon came under challenge from a number of alternative literary forms. Descriptive

27. Mather, *Valley of Hinnom,* p. 1.

28. See, e.g., "The Declaration & Confession of Esther Rodgers, of Kittery in the Province of Main [sic], in New England, Single woman," in [Rogers], *Death the Certain Wages,* pp. 121–27; "Rebekah Chamblit's Declaration, Dying Warnings and Advice," in Foxcroft, *Lessons of Caution,* following the sermon; and *A Faithful Narrative of the Wicked Life and Remarkable Conversion of Patience Boston alias Samson. . . , with a Preface by the Reverend Mess. Samuel & Joseph Moody . . .* (Boston: S. Kneeland and T. Green, 1738).

29. Mather Byles, *The Prayer and Plea of David . . .* (Boston: Samuel Kneeland, 1751), p. 18.

accounts of murders, such as *A Curious and Authentic Account of the Re-markable Behaviour of Francis David Stirn* (1761), began to appear, and were sometimes anthologized on the model of the English *Newgate Calen-dar,* as in a collection called *The American Bloody Register* (1784).[30] Some writers cast their accounts in poetic form, in such works as *A Poem on the Execution of Samuel Frost,* convicted of the murder of Captain Elisha Allen, or *A Tribute to the Memory of Catherine Berrenger,* believed to have been poisoned by John Benner, her betrothed.[31] Increasingly popular was the first-person account of the murder by its perpetrator, such as *A Narrative of the Life of John Lewis,* who murdered his wife in 1760, or *An Authentic and Particular Account of the Life of Francis Burdett Personel,* who murdered Robert White in 1773.[32] Such accounts drew on the tradition of the crimi-nal confessions often printed along with the execution sermons of an earlier period, but, freed from the constraints of that theological frame, introduced different narrative dimensions. Most notably, the criminal narrators of these accounts often refused to assume the role of the exemplary sinner. *The Narrative of Whiting Sweeting,* for example, denied his guilt of murder and went on to challenge the predestinarian theology to which he had been subjected in prison, while *The Address of Abraham Johnstone, a Black Man* offered both a dignified denial of his own guilt and a powerful attack on slavery. The single most recalcitrant criminal narrator of the period was one "Ambrose Gwinett," who not only refused to admit his guilt, but also allegedly declined to die at his execution, escaping from his chains after the hangman botched his job, and tracking down his supposed murder victim, alive and well in the West Indies. *The Life and Adventures of Ambrose Gwinett* (whose real author was probably Isaac Bickerstaff) illustrates the new strain of the picaresque at work in late eighteenth-century American murder literature.[33]

30. *A Curious and Authentic Account of the Remarkable Behaviour of Francis David Stirn . . .* (Boston: B. Mecom, 1761); *The American Bloody Register . . . Dying Confession of Alexander White, a murderer and pirate . . .* (Boston: Russell, 1784).

31. *A Poem on the Execution of Samuel Frost . . .* (broadside) (Worcester: Isaiah Thomas[?], 1793); *A Tribute to the Memory of Catherine Berrenger . . .* (broadside) (n.p., 1800).

32. *A Narrative of the Life Together with the Last Speech, Confession, and Solemn Declaration of John Lewis . . .* (New Haven: James Parker and Co., 1762); *An Authentic and Particular Account of the Life of Francis Burdett Personel, written by Himself . . .* (New York, 1773).

33. *The Narrative of Whiting Sweeting, who was executed at Albany . . .* (Lansingburgh: Tiffany, [1791]); *The Address of Abraham Johnstone, a Black Man . . .* (Philadelphia, 1797); [Isaac Bickerstaff,] *The Life and Adventures of Ambrose Gwinett, Apprentice to an Attorney at Law, Who for a Murder which he never committed, was tried, condemned, executed, and hung in chains, in old England . . .* (Philadelphia: Robert Bell, 1784).

Such narratives as these point to a gradual breakup of the clerical mo-
nopoly over the public discourse of murder, occurring in the context of
the larger loss of cultural authority suffered by the American clergy during
and after the Revolutionary period. In the last decades of the eighteenth
century, the cultural authority to interpret murder diffused among a diverse
array of new voices, as printers and hack writers, sentimental poets and
even murderers themselves seized from the ministry the task of assigning
meaning to the crime of murder for the American reading public. But this
buzz of new voices would soon be contained within a new framework
whose cultural dominance would rival that of the early American execution
sermon: the trial report. The first murder trial report printed in America,
in 1741, was an English import, but American cases gradually followed.[34]
By the 1790s, the number of trial reports printed in America was roughly
equal to the number of execution sermons, and in the first decades of the
nineteenth century, their volume swelled, swamping all other forms of
narrative and demonstrating the historical triumph of the legal discourse
of murder over the theological.

Within these new narrative forms, the center of concern shifted from
the salvation drama of the condemned criminal standing on the brink of
eternity, to the worldly action that had brought him to human justice. The
new accounts evinced a growing interest in the exact nature of the violence,
details of time and place, and the larger social narrative in which the
murder was embedded. With a degree of detail unknown in the execution
sermon, readers were told that John Lewis killed his pregnant wife of
twelve years by strangling her on their bed, at 4:00 in the afternoon on
Friday, June 27th, 1762, several hours after she had rejected his midday
sexual advances.[35] Descriptions of the scene of the crime grew increasingly
common, and by the early nineteenth century, some printed trial transcipts
provided readers with maps of the location where the murder had taken
place.[36] Whereas the early American murderer had been represented as

34. The English import is *Some Account of the Trial of Samuel Goodere, Esq., Late Com-
mander of the "Ruby" Man of War* . . . (Boston, 1741). Also see *An Account of the Trial of Joseph
Andrews for Piracy and Murder* . . . (New York, 1769); *The Trial of Alice Clifton, for the Murder
of her Bastard-Child* . . . (Philadelphia, 1787); *Murder, Narrative of the Trial, Conviction and
Execution of Captain William Corran* . . . (Newport, 1794); *A Correct Account of the Trials of
Charles M'Manus, John Hauer, Elizabeth Hauer, Patrick Donagan, Francis Cox, and Others* . . .
(Harrisburgh: John Wyeth, 1798).

35. *Narrative of the Life of John Lewis.*

36. See *Trial of Thomas O. Selfridge, Attorney at Law* . . . (Boston: Russell and Cutler,
Belcher and Armstrong, and Oliver and Munroe, [1807]), p. 170, for a map of the State Street

an archetypal sinner, a bundle of "besetting sins" that explicitly did not distinguish him from any other sinner, the late eighteenth- and early nine-teenth-century murderer was depicted as an individual character with a unique life history: Francis Burdett Personel was an Irishman who emi-grated to America to flee a domineering mother, escaped his indenture in Maryland to become a schoolmaster in Virginia, underwent a superficial conversion under the influence of Baptist New Lights, and eventually landed in New York, where he wed a prostitute who continued to ply her trade after the marriage, until the day he struck and killed one of her clients.[37] Physical descriptions of the murderer grew more common: James Purrinton, who killed his wife, seven children, and himself in 1806, was a man "of the middle size, rather dark complexion, grave countenance, and reserved in company," who "never looked the person in the face he was addressing"; Jason Fairbanks, accused of stabbing Eliza Fales to death in 1801, was an invalid who had lost the use of his right elbow following a smallpox inoculation.[38]

The new murder narratives had much in common with the literary form of the novel that was emerging during the same period; with their close concern for characterization and social reconstruction, physical setting, and the precise sequence of events within worldly time, they adhered to the central novelistic conventions of formal realism. From the mid-eighteenth through the mid-twentieth century, Western societies have evinced an ex-traordinary need for narrative, whose cultural function has been to assign meaning to the chaos of human experience largely by defining its shape in time through attention to plot, "the intelligible whole that governs a succes-sion of events in any story."[39] Peter Brooks explains this historical out-pouring of plotted narrative with reference to "an anxiety at the loss of providential plots: the plotting of the individual or social or institutional life story takes on new urgency when one no longer can look to a sacred masterplot that organizes and explains the world."[40] The secularism of the

---

neighborhood in Boston where he killed Charles Austin; and *Trial of James Graham . . .* (Albany: J. Buel, 1814), for a map of the area where he murdered Hugh Cameron and Alexander M'Gillavrae.

37. *Authentic and Particular Account of the Life of Francis Burdett Personel.*

38. *Horrid Massacre!! Sketches of the Life of Captain James Purrinton . . .* (Augusta: Peter Edes, 1806), p. 4; *Report of the Trial of Jason Fairbanks . . .* (Boston: Russell and Cutler, 1801), p. 7.

39. Paul Ricoeur, quoted in Peter Brooks, *Reading for the Plot: Design and Intention in Narrative* (New York: Vintage Books, 1985), p. 13.

40. Brooks, *Reading for the Plot,* p. 6.

new murder narratives in itself pointed to a weakening of the sacred canopy in late eighteenth-century American culture, while their novelistic realism represented a quest for new ways to assign meaning to human experience.

As the sacred masterplot was yielding ground to secular narrative in American murder literature, the doctrine of innate depravity was slowly losing its intellectual power to explain the etiology of the crime. The combined influence of Lockean psychology, with its assertion of the original moral neutrality of human nature, and eighteenth-century moral sense philosophy, which moved beyond Locke to posit an innate moral sense enabling every man and woman naturally to approve good and abhor evil, made serious inroads against American Calvinism, resulting in various modifications of the doctrine of innate depravity among the orthodox, and encouraging a growing number of believers to move toward an Arminian position.[41] Although the late execution sermons, and some of the new narratives as well, continued to invoke intrinsic human evil as the ultimate cause of murder, popular murder literature increasingly sought a secular understanding of the act, casting about for explanations of the crime more in keeping with an Enlightenment liberal understanding of human nature. Criminal life histories offered environmental explanations of the murderer's action: "The Confession of Winslow Russell" blamed his criminal conduct on parental indulgence, charging that his parents would not make him attend school; Mary Cole recounted how her mother refused her the breast when she was two months old, leaving Mary's father to place the infant with her grandmother until she could eat solid food; Caleb Adams was said to have been damaged in mind and body while still *in utero,* when his father had installed his mistress and her two-year-old child in the Adams home.[42]

41. See, e.g., Basil Willey, *The Eighteenth-Century Background* (New York: Columbia University Press, 1940); Louis Schneider, *The Scottish Moralists on Human Nature and Society* (Chicago: University of Chicago Press, 1967); Joseph Haroutunian, *Piety versus Moralism: The Passing of the New England Theology* (New York: Harper Torchbooks, 1960); D. H. Meyer, *The Instructed Conscience: The Shaping of the American National Ethic* (Philadelphia: University of Pennsylvania Press, 1972); Henry F. May, *The Enlightenment in America* (New York: Oxford University Press, 1976); Douglas Sloan, *The Scottish Enlightenment and the American College Ideal* (New York: Teacher's College Press, Columbia University, 1971); Conrad Wright, *The Beginnings of Unitarianism in America* (Boston: Beacon Press, 1966); Sydney E. Ahlstrom, *A Religious History of the American People* (New Haven: Yale University Press, 1972).

42. *A Brief Account of the Trial of Winslow Russell, for the murder of Michael Bockus. To which is added, the voluntary confession of the said Winslow Russell* . . . (n.p., [1811?]); John W. Kirn, *Sketch of the trial of Mary Cole, for the wilful murder of her mother . . . together with a short account of her life, her farewell letter to her husband, and her dying speech . . .* (Norwich,

Other narratives, reflecting the growing legal orientation of the discourse of murder, attempted to uncover the murderer's immediate motive in committing the crime: although initially this concern was only implicit, as in the explanation that John Lewis killed his wife out of sexual jealousy or that Bathsheba Spooner hired men to kill her husband because her marriage was not agreeable to her, by the early nineteenth century, the term "motive" was expressly invoked in printed trial reports, and the defense attorney for Captain Edward Tinker went so far as to assert that "No crime ever was committed without some motive."[43] One of the most common explanations of the underlying cause of the crime was uncontrolled passion: the Negro youth Bristol had killed out of "cruel Rage and Passion"; the pirate Joseph Andrews had killed because his neglect of religion left him "to be governed by the furious Impulses of his disorderly Passions"; Hannah Ocuish had killed because she had been left "to the uncontrouled influence of the direful passions, malice and revenge."[44] One historically-minded defense attorney explained, with a touch of irony, that the contemporary recourse to human passions had replaced an earlier reliance on demonic intervention as the major cause of crime: since "the Arch Fiend has ceased to walk abroad in his infernal majesty for the purpose of instigating mankind to the commission of crimes; his diabolical purposes are, in *these days* accompanied by the agency of his fell missionaries, the passions of man; by rage, envy, avarice, jealousy, hope and fear. . . ."[45]

Throughout the range of murder accounts printed in America between 1750 and 1820, these three interrelated factors—environmental influences on character, the motive to murder, and the failure to govern the passions—were repeatedly cited in an effort to explain the causes of murder for an age no longer fully satisfied with the execution sermon's formulaic assertion that the source of the crime was universal depravity. But as these

---

Conn.: Israel Brumley, Jr., 1813); Moses C. Welch, *Sketch of the Circumstances of the birth, education and manners of Caleb's life . . .*, bound with execution sermon for Caleb Adams by Elijah Waterman (Springfield, Mass.: Henry Brewer, [1803]).

43. *Narrative of the Life of John Lewis*; Thaddeus Maccarty, *The Guilt of Innocent Blood Put Away . . .* (Worcester: Isaiah Thomas, 1778), p. 36; *Trial of Edward Tinker, Mariner . . .* (Newbern [N.C.]: Hall and Bryan and T. Watson, 1811), p. 59.

44. Sylvanus Conant, *The Blood of Abel, and the Blood of Jesus considered and improved . . .* (Boston: Edes and Gill, 1764), p. 21; *An Account of the Trial of Joseph Andrews for Piracy and Murder . . .* [New York, 1769], p. 6; Henry Channing, *God Admonishing his People of their Duty . . .* (New London: T. Green, 1786), p. 5.

45. *A Sketch of the Proceedings and Trial of William Hardy . . .* (Boston: Oliver and Munroe, 1807), p. 18.

narratives often revealed, none of these factors, whether taken singly or in various combinations, proved as intellectually satisfying as the earlier, universally applicable explanation had been. First, the environmental argument embedded in the life history of the convicted criminal did not always lend itself to a definitive explanation of the crime. Some biographical accounts, such as those of John Joyce and Alexander White, narrated the lives of their subjects without presenting any clearly apparent explanation of why they had eventually come to commit murder; other accounts, such as those of Thomas Starr and Jason Fairbanks, pointed to their subjects' excellent upbringing by upright families, thus suggesting that these men's murderous actions could not be explained environmentally.[46] Some men, it seemed, simply murdered out of character. When William Beadle killed his wife, four children, and himself in 1783, the chronicler of his crimes prodded readers, "'Tis very natural for you to ask, whether it was possible a man could be transformed from an affectionate husband and an indulgent parent to a secret murderer, without some previous alteration, which must have been noticed by the family or acquaintance? Yet this was the case in this instance, there was no visible alteration in his conduct."[47] Beadle fell into a special new category of criminals: the surprise murderer, who showed little or no signs in advance of the danger he posed to his fellow beings.

Just as the environmentalist approach to the causes of murder periodically broke down, so too did efforts to identify the murder motive. Some murderers acted on the basis of seemingly inadequate motives, as when Stephen Arnold brutally beat to death six-year-old Betsey Van Amburgh because the child, whom he was teaching to read, would not or could not pronounce properly the word "gig."[48] Others murdered out of an unexplainable inner compulsion: Henry Halbert confessed that he had murdered the Woolman boy, a victim chosen at random, because "I began to be tired of my Life and I was determined to kill some body"; John Joyce decided first to murder Sarah Cross—"I felt tempted to commit the act"—and only

46. *Confession of John Joyce, alias Davis* . . . (Philadelphia: No. 12 Walnut St., 1808), pp. 12–13; *The American Bloody Register,* pp. 6–8; Enoch Huntington, *A Sermon preached . . . on the day of the execution of Thomas Starr . . . with a sketch of the life and character of said Starr* (Middletown, Conn.: Moses H. Woodward, 1797), pp. 23–24; *Biography of Mr. Jason Fairbanks and Miss Eliza Fales* (broadside) (Boston: Pandamonium Press, 1801).

47. *A Narrative of the Life of William Beadle* . . . (Hartford: Bavil Webster, 1783), p. 14.

48. *The Trial of Stephen Arnold, for the Murder of Betsey Van Amburgh* . . . (Cooperstown [N.Y.]: Phinney, [1805]).

then determined to rob her shop.[49] Nor did all murders prove explainable with reference to the uncontrolled passions of the killer. Some of the era's most notorious murderers, including familicides William Beadle and James Purrinton, murdered dispassionately, on the basis of theological error—"*a systematic calculation from erroneous principles*"[50]—most commonly, an eighteenth-century Rationalist disbelief in human accountability and future punishment. But not all dispassionate murderers were infidels: in the second half of the eighteenth century, the image of the "cold-blooded killer" became a common feature of American murder narratives. "Nor was Pharoah's heart harder than mine," was Barnett Davenport's confessed state while he was killing his benefactor Caleb Mallory, Mallory's wife, and their three grandchildren, merely to rob the house.[51] The hard-hearted murderer of the new accounts committed the crime out of "a cool deliberate wickedness of thought," with a "heart obdurate to all the feelings of nature," and remained an "unfeeling fiend," "insensible" of wrongdoing after the deed was done.[52]

Those men and women who murdered out of character, or out of an inexplicable inner compulsion to kill, or out of cold-blooded insensibility, challenged the prevailing eighteenth-century Enlightenment understanding of human nature, with its liberal attention to character as a developmental product of environmental influences, its emphasis on the powers of human reason, and its reliance on sentiment, the inner moral sense, as the ultimate guarantor of virtue. The many popular accounts of such murderers as these in the late eighteenth- and early nineteenth-century were narratives of noncomprehension, whose thrust was to try *and fail* to come to terms with the crime within an Enlightenment liberal view of human nature. Confronted with this intellectual bind, many narrators, including some murderers writing in the first-person, had recourse to an understanding of the murderer as monster, a terrible aberration from normal human nature. John Battus, who raped and murdered a girl named Salome Talbott, wrote to the victim's parents from his prison cell, saying, "I am fearful you

49. *Last Speech and Confession of Henry Halbert* . . . (Philadelphia: Anthony Ambruster, [1765]), p. 5; *Confession of John Joyce*, p. 14.

50. *Horrid Massacre!!*, p. 18. On Beadle, see James Dana, *Men's Sins not chargeable on God, but on themselves* . . . (New Haven: T. and S. Green, [1783]), p. 21.

51. *A Brief Narrative of the Life and Confession of Barnett Davenport* . . . ([Hartford?], 1780), p. 12.

52. *Trial of James Graham*, p. 17; *Trial of Edward Tinker*, pp. 42–43; *Confession of John Joyce*, p. iii; *A Correct and Concise Account of the Interesting Trial of Jason Fairbanks* . . . (Boston, [1801?]), p. 8.

wil not have hearts to forgive such a wretched creature, such a monster as I have been. . . ."[53] The term sometimes connoted physical ugliness, as in the case of a murderer named Johnson, whom one broadside poet imagined as "a hideous ugly looking monster" in hell; sometimes, it invoked actual physical deformity, most notably in the case of Caleb Adams, whose facial features and physical movements were believed to have been stamped by vicious prenatal influences.[54] Courtroom lawyers were wont to draw on the popular science of physiognomy, which affirmed that character was written into the facial features, and invited jurors to convict if they found the mark of Cain on the prisoner's forehead.[55] But in all cases, the underlying meaning of the image was that physical monstrosity was an outward type of inward moral deformity, the visible marking of the murderer as a moral aberration from nature.

For the earlier clerical interpreters of the crime, it had been sufficient to acknowledge that the murderer had acted upon his deepest intrinsic nature. But for late eighteenth-century narrators, it was necessary to address the fact that the murderer had dramatically deviated from a nature that was intrinsically comprehensible, reasonable, and endowed with an inborn moral sense. The image of the murderer as moral monster revealed the popular influence of eighteenth-century moral philosophy's understanding of evil as the twisting and distortion of original human nature. As Benjamin Whichcote wrote, "Nothing is more certainly true than that all Vice is unnatural and contrary to the nature of Man . . . . A depraved and vicious Mind is as really the Sickness and Deformity thereof, as any foul and loathsome disease is to the body."[56] The guilt of Captain Edward Tinker in murdering a young sailor to cover up a maritime insurance fraud was represented as a "shocking deformity"—his crime was said to "blur the face of Nature"—precisely because his conduct placed him outside *human* "nature" as it was comprehended within Enlightenment liberalism.[57]

53. *The Confession of John Battus, A Mulatto* . . . (n.p., [1804?]), p. 19.

54. Jonathan Plummer, *Murder!! Death of Miss Mack Coy, and the Young Teazer* (broadside) (Boston: [Coverly, 1813]); Welch, *Sketch of Caleb's life,* p. 27.

55. See *Trial of Edward Tinker,* p. 43; and *Report of the Trial of Dominic Daley and James Halligan* . . . (Northampton: S. and E. Butler, booksellers; T. M. Pomroy, printer, [1806]), pp. 33–34.

56. Quoted in Elizabeth MacAndrew, *The Gothic Tradition in Fiction* (New York: Columbia University Press, 1979), p. 23.

57. *Trial of Edward Tinker,* pp. 76, 84. As Elizabeth MacAndrew has argued, it is for this reason that the evil characters of sentimental and Gothic fiction—men such as Manfred in

For the image of the murderer as monster did not explain his great transgression so much as it captured its incomprehensibility within a liberal framework. In effect, this Gothic emphasis on the monstrosity of the evildoer served to protect Enlightened liberalism by suggesting that profound evil was an unnatural perversion of true human nature.

The moral monstrosity attributed to the new murderers effectively made them out to be something other than human, "a being cast in a different mould from those of mankind in general . . . ."[58] They were not exemplary sinners, publicly typifying the innate depravity of the entire race and inviting those present to acknowledge the corruption of their own hearts and turn to Christ; the new murderers were moral aliens, set apart from the run of humankind by their inexplicable moral otherness. This dramatically new stance towards the convicted criminal, which was replacing the earlier ritual of moral identification with an assertion of the impassable gulf dividing normal humanity from the condemned criminal, was enforced by the cult of horror that was emerging in popular murder literature during this same period. The vogue of horror that came to shape popular Anglo-American fiction in the last two decades of the eighteenth century was already at work in the American nonfictional literature of murder a few decades earlier, marking some important implications of the liberal worldview for the popular response to serious criminal transgression.

One of the earliest expressions of the new cult of horror was a growing tendency to regard murder as heinous less because it violated divine law than because it assaulted human feelings. As liberal clergyman Charles Chauncy wrote in 1754, "It is indeed a Crime that is *shocking* to the human mind . . . so associated with *Dread* and *Horror,* that we should tremble at

---

The Castle of Otranto or Ambrosio in *The Monk*—are represented as twisted distortions of their own good potential. Mary Shelley's monster is the best example of this convention: a creature in his original moral state harmless and childlike, brimming with sentiment and fellow-feeling, instinctively virtuous, who, when cast off by his creator and subjected to ill-treatment by others, becomes morally twisted and murderous. Significantly, Gothic villains are often endowed by authors with distorted bodies and ugly faces: Charles Brockden Brown's Carwin, George Lippard's Devil-Bug, Edgar Allan Poe's Hop-frog, Nathaniel Hawthorne's Roger Chillingworth, all demonstrate MacAndrew's argument that the Gothic novel made monstrosity "the outward show of the terrible inner distortion of man's innate good nature into evil" (p. 24). The Gothic novel, in MacAndrew's view, pointed toward the gradual emergence of a nineteenth-century view of evil as a form of psychological monstrosity, a warping of the natural mind.

58. *The Confession and Dying Words of Samuel Frost* . . . (broadside) (Worcester: Isaiah Thomas, [1793]).

the Thought of committing it."[59] Chauncy's words captured well the failure
of empathy, the absence of moral identification, at work in the liberal
response to criminal transgression. Other writers were soon dwelling on the
horrors of specific murders, such as "The bloody Murder of Miss Elizabeth
McKinstry" by the Negro youth Bristol, who struck her with a flatiron,
then knocked her into the fire where her face was burned, and finally
dragged her downstairs to finish her off with an axe: the author of an
appendix to the execution sermon for Bristol observed pointedly, "One
cannot call to mind the particular circumstances of this tragic scene without the deepest emotions of *horror*."[60] Most revealing was the new practice
of claiming that a given murder was the most horrifying murder ever
committed. The first American example I have found of such competitive
sensationalism appeared in 1778;[61] it quickly became a standard formula,
repeated every few years as one narrator after another attempted to upstage
all previous claims to horror.

This shift of cultural attention from the exemplary sinner, designedly
difficult to distinguish from the general run of the innately depraved, to
"the most shocking, inhuman and unnatural"[62] murderer ever, whose
violence was so heinous as to defy even the best-intentioned efforts to
empathize with him, was crucial to the new cult of horror. Domestic murders, in particular, began to draw a seemingly disproportionate share of
attention within the literature, in works such as *A Narrative of the Life of
John Lewis* (1762), in which the murderer himself identified the strangling
of his pregnant wife on their conjugal bed as a "horrid and devilish Jobb."[63]
One of the most infamous cases in the second half of the century was that
of Bathsheba Spooner, who in 1778 tired of her marriage and hired three
men to kill her husband Joshua. If domestic murder was unusually horrifying, the Spooner accounts made clear, then a wife's murder of her husband was particularly so: "What completes the *horridness* of the diabolical
act, and gives it the most of an infernal hue, is that these hard-hearted
ruffians should be instigated by the innocent victim's *wife*."[64] But the most

59. Charles Chauncy, *The horrid Nature, and enormous Guilt of Murder* . . . (Boston:
Thomas Fleet, 1754), pp. 12, 17.
60. Conant, *The Blood of Abel, and the Blood of Jesus*, p. 32.
61. Maccarty, *Guilt of Innocent Blood*, p. 24.
62. *The Confession of Mary Cole, who was executed on Friday, 26th June* . . . (New York:
n.p., [1812]) p. 3.
63. *Narrative of the Life of John Lewis*, p. 4.
64. Nathan Fiske, *A Sermon Preached at Brookfield March 6, 1778. On the Day of the
Interment of Mr. Joshua Spooner* . . . (Boston: Thomas and John Fleet, 1778), p. 7.

shocking murders were not all domestic in nature: the printed narratives of twelve-year-old Hannah Ocuish's murder of six-year-old Eunice Bolles, and John Joyce's apparently unmotivated killing of shopkeeper Sarah Cross, represented these murders as crimes so heinous as to defy any sympathetic identification by the reader with the convicted killer.[65]

One of the primary requirements of a truly horrifying murder was extensive gore and carnage. In the second half of the eighteenth century, the literature of murder became awash in blood, and filled with close descriptions of weapons, wounds and bruises, the scene of the crime, and the last words of the victim. *A Brief Narrative of the Life and Confession of Barnett Davenport* told the first-person story of a nineteen-year-old Continental Army deserter who slowly and savagely beat to death Caleb Mallory, his wife, and one of their three grandchildren, then set fire to the house and burned the remaining two children in their beds. Davenport offered abundant evidence to support his claim to have committed "the most horrid Murders ever perpetrated in this Country, or perhaps any other," detailing the sequence of murder weapons used, recording the shrieks and groans of the victims, describing their physical appearance when he was finished with them. The account is loaded with phrases that now sound like literary clichés, but which were relatively new to the American discourse of murder at the time: it was "a night big with uncommon horror"—"My heart trembles . . . at the relation of this bloody scene"—"the room [was] besmeared in blood, and filled with horrendous groans," etc.[66]

In other narratives, descriptions of the crime scene—the deck of the *American Eagle* after pirates murdered William Little in 1797, the inn room where Samuel Mayo and William Love killed lodger David Whittemore in 1807, the hat shop where James Anthony murdered Joseph Green in 1814—dwelt at length on the extent of the victim's blood.[67] Above all, the state of the corpse received growing attention. Whereas early American execution sermons had explicitly directed the attention of hearers and readers away from the "blood of Abel" to the "blood of sprinkling," the

---

65. Channing, *God Admonishing his People; Confession of John Joyce.*

66. *A Brief Narrative of the Life and Confession of Barnett Davenport Under Sentence of Death, for a series of the most horrid Murders, ever perpetrated in this Country, or perhaps any other* . . . ([Hartford?], 1780), title page and pp. 10, 12.

67. *The Interesting Trials of the Pirates, for the Murder of William Little* . . . (Newburyport: Herald Press, [1797]); *The Trials of Samuel M. Mayo and William Love, for the Murder of David Whittemore* (Augusta [Maine]: Chronicle Office, 1807); *Trial of James Anthony for the Murder of Joseph Green* . . . (Rutland [Vermont]: Fay and Davison, [1814]).

new horror accounts centered dramatic attention directly on the "mangled remains"[68] of the murder victim.

These new developments came together in 1783 in the first full-blown horror account in the literature of American murders. William Beadle was a retail merchant in Wethersfield, Connecticut, who fell on economic hard times during the American Revolution, became a Deist, and decided to kill his wife Lydia, their four children, and himself to send the family united into a happier state. The printed response to the Beadle murders was swift and extensive. Over the next fifteen years, more accounts and reprints were published than for any previous American murder, the most important of which was *A Narrative of the Life of William Beadle* (1783, 1794, 1795),[69] whose cover illustration immediately captured the full horror of Beadle's crimes. Headed "A HORRID MASSACRE," it consisted of three pictorial frames vertically stacked: at the top was a large coffin adorned with a black heart (Lydia), in the middle were four small coffins with black hearts (the children), and at the bottom was a supine body with a hatchet, knife, and two pistols floating above (Beadle himself). Earlier murder illustrations had been impersonally iconographic in their renderings of the skull-and-crossbones or the generic gallows motif; the cover of the Beadle *Narrative* was the first of its kind in American literature in its specific reference to the murders at hand.

"'Tis doubtful," wrote Stephen Mix Mitchell in the Beadle *Narrative,* "whether any history of modern times can afford an instance of similar barbarity, even in the extreme distress of war."[70] The *Narrative* of the Beadle murders exhibited all the identifying characteristics of horror narrative. The crime was shockingly aberrant, not just a domestic murder but a full-scale familicide: "What a monster of a man was this!," an affectionate husband and fond parent led by false theology to massacre his entire family.[71] It paid extensive attention to gory detail: Beadle's bloody footprints on the stairway, the position and condition of the bodies (e.g., the three daughters, "swimming in their blood," lying side-by-side on the floor "like

---

68. Fiske, *Sermon,* p. 5.

69. *A Narrative of the Life of William Beadle* . . . (Hartford: Bavil Webster, 1783); *A Narrative of the Life of William Beadle* (Bennington, Haswell, 1794); [Stephen Mix Mitchell], *A Narrative of the Life of William Beadle* . . . (Windsor: Alden Spooner, 1795).

70. *A Narrative of the Life of William Beadle* (1783), p. 17.

71. *A Narrative of the Life of William Beadle* (1783), "Extracts from the Rev. Mr. Marsh's Sermon at the Funeral of his Wife and Children," p. 19.

three lambs" with their throats cut), the discovery of brain fragments on the walls of the kitchen where Beadle shot himself, etc.[72]

Most important, the *Narrative* paid self-conscious attention to the power of these murders to horrify. In fact, it focused less on the sequence of actions taken by Beadle than on the step-by-step discovery of the murders by those who first entered the house, and on the nature of their horror-response. Indeed, what distinguished the second and third editions of the Beadle *Narrative* from the original was primarily their expanded attention to the discovery of the crime, which grew from four sentences to seven or eight pages treating the emotional response of those who first came upon the scene: detailing how the maid, "with trembling limbs," first entered the children's bedroom where "her horror was so great that she fainted and fell down stairs backward"; and how the doctor and two other men entered the same room, where "Surely a more distressing sight never agonized the human feelings than now presented itself to their view: the floor was swimming with blood," etc.[73] The reprintings of the Beadle murder narrative thus offer dramatic evidence of the rapid growth of the cult of horror in late eighteenth-century popular culture.

Frequently, as in the case of the Beadle murders, printed narratives focused attention specifically on the moment when the victim's body was first discovered: when Jacob Eshelman's brother located his corpse by tracking the stench of decay; or when Joseph Green's body was found under a pile of wood in the back room of James Anthony's shop; or when tenants found the body of Agnes Teaurs buried beneath the floor boards of the house rented to them by the victim's daughter and killer, Mary Cole.[74] As in the Beadle *Narrative,* the emphasis of such treatments was on the sense of horror evoked by that discovery: it was "with horror of soul" that searchers removed the murdered Marcus Lyon's body from the Chicopee River.[75] This close narrative attention to the moment when a murder was initially discovered was calculated to induce a horror-response in the reader that would replicate the horror-response of those who first came upon the scene of the crime. For the reader imaginatively to see "the

---

72. *A Narrative of the Life of William Beadle* (1783), p. 9; (1783), p. 9; (1794), p. 40.

73. *A Narrative of the Life of William Beadle* (1794), pp. 37, 37, 38.

74. *A Report of the Trial of James Jameson, and James M'Gowan* . . . (Harrisburgh: John Wyeth, 1806); *Facts relating to the murder of Joseph Green by James Anthony* . . . (broadside) (Rutland, Vt., Fay and Davison, 1814); *Confession of Mary Cole,* p. 4.

75. *Trial of Daley and Halligan,* p. 7.

mangled body of the deceased" was to experience "the horror which such a spectacle could not fail to inspire."[76] The corpse-discovery scene, which was growing increasingly central to American murder narratives in the late eighteenth century, illustrates the essentially spectatorial nature of horror, with its emphasis on what nonparticipants in the crime see. The ritual power of this narrative moment arose from its significance as a recognition scene: what was at stake was not merely the sight of blood but the recognition that murder had been committed. The element of surprise often present in such scenes of corpse-discovery was similar to the sudden revelation of a surprise-murderer: inexplicably, unaccountably—within the liberal worldview—a moral monster had once again been at work.

But the real locus of horror was not what was seen but the spectator's emotional response to what was seen. The nature of the horror-response was characterized with remarkable care and consistency throughout the new literature of murder. Horror involved, first, a numbing of the sensory faculties. The corpse of Sarah Cross was said to "petrify with horror" those who gazed upon it.[77] A violent murder "freezes the mind with horror"; one was said to be "struck with horror at the bloody deed."[78] When the soul is filled with horror, "its active and reasoning powers are for a moment suspended"; its "faculties" are "benumbed and petrified."[79] Such an understanding of horror was consistent with that set forth by one of the major theorists of Gothic fiction, English novelist Ann Radcliffe: she had distinguished between terror, which expands the soul and opens the faculties in a state of apprehension of an unknown threat, and horror, which contracts the soul and freezes the faculties in response to a direct confrontation with what is repellently evil.[80] Within Lockean psychology, horror thus involved a shutting down of those sensory faculties through which experience impinged upon the mind to become knowledge. In the face of what was overwhelmingly, repugnantly evil, the liberal mind simply refused to accept the evidence of the senses, in an act tantamount to moral denial.

A major part of this shutting down of the faculties in horror was speechlessness. In this, the response of the Beadles' maid to the revelation of

---

76. *Trial of Daley and Halligan*, p. 31.
77. *Confession of John Joyce*, p. 6.
78. Channing, *God Admonishing*, pp. 5, 8.
79. *Trial of William Hardy*, p. 23.
80. Ann Radcliffe, "On the Supernatural in Poetry," quoted in Malcom Ware, 'Sublimity in the Novels of Ann Radcliffe: A Study of the Influence upon Her Craft of Edmund Burke's *Enquiry into the Origin of our Ideas of the Sublime and Beautiful*," (Upsala: A. B. Lundequistska Bokhandeln, 1963), p. 16.

domestic massacre proved prototypical: "her horror and affright was [sic] so great that she fainted," and even when she regained consciousness, "horror stopped her utterance."[81] This failure of language in the face of horror quickly became one of the most pervasive conventions of the new murder literature. "No words can describe the horrors of my situation," reported one survivor of a murderous piracy in 1800.[82] When the first outsider arrived at the scene of the Purrinton murders, "a scene was presented which defies the powers of language, and beggars all description."[83] At the Fairbanks trial, the Attorney General referred to the scene of the murder as "an image from whence the eye turns with horror, and of which language refuses a description."[84] The narrator of the murder of Marcus Lyon in 1806 tried to convey his own speechlessness in the face of the crime with creative punctuation: "I—now—proceed—but—language fails me—terms cannot paint this doleful tragedy," he wrote, early in his account.[85]

To be petrified with horror was to experience a shutting down of the sensory faculties and of the mental powers that would ordinarily process the sensory impressions passing through those faculties; to be rendered speechless in the face of horror was to lose the capacity to articulate a coherent response based on such ordinary mental processing. The horror-response points again to the failure of the new Enlightenment etiology of murder to offer an intellectually satisfying explanation of the crime. For the convention of speechlessness indicated an inability to assign meaning to the act of murder. To be suddenly deprived of all language by the sight of a dead body was to be rendered incapable of rationally coming to terms with it, since language is the primary medium of cultural meaning. Horror was about the essential meaninglessness of evil within an Enlightenment intellectual worldview committed to the basic goodness of humankind.

But even as horror pointed to the intellectual failings of the liberal response to murder, it shaped a well-defined emotional response to the crime in the presence of those failings. The cult of horror was a major instrument in the gradual transformation of the murderer from an object

---

81. *A Narrative of the Life of William Beadle* (1783), p. 10; (1794), p. 37.

82. William Wheland, *A Narrative of the Horrid Murder & Piracy* . . . ([Philadelphia]: Folwell, [1800]), p. 6.

83. *Horrid Massacre!!*, p. 5.

84. *Report of the Trial of Jason Fairbanks on an indictment for the murder of Elizabeth Fales* . . . (Boston: Russell and Cutler, 1801), p. 73.

85. *Trial of Daley and Halligan*, p. 3.

of empathy and compassion into a monstrous moral alien, an inhuman fiend. "Human nature recoils with horror" in the face of murder;[86] "the bare mention" of the crime, admitted one defense attorney, "carries terror to the honest mind, and necessarily excites some degree of abhorrence and detestation, towards that being, who is suspected of imbruing his hands in the blood of a fellow-creature; this, it must be acknowledged is natural."[87] Even in the late eighteenth-century execution sermon, the earlier encouragement of empathy for the murderer on the grounds that every member of the congregation was equally vulnerable to such a criminal fall began quietly to disappear. In his execution sermon for William Shaw, the Rev. Moses Baldwin condemned the condemned murderer's sins of intemperance, swearing, quarreling, and domestic abuse, without then extending his lesson to other members of the congregation. Instead, he called upon the civil magistrates to suppress all forms of vice, and the masters of public houses not to serve vicious men, and delivered a specific warning to men of intemperance and passion, thus implying that such sins as had driven Shaw to murder were not shared by the entire community, but practiced by a vicious subgroup in need of social control by the morally upright.[88] Charles Chauncy explicitly reassured his congregation that he knew none of them was a murderer: in urging them to "detest" the "horrid" crime of murder "in our *Hearts,* and *keep at the utmost Distance from it* in our *Practice,*" he hastened to say that "I speak not thus from an Apprehension, as tho' there was any one here present, upon whom this *inhuman Crime* could be justly fastened, even by their *own Consciences,* or the *God who knoweth all Things:* I would rather hope, the Idea of this Sin, is, in all our Minds, so associated with *Dread* and *Horror,* that we shold tremble at the Thought of committing it."[89] In Chauncy's treatment, horror was a mechanism for reinforcing the moral distance between the murderous and the morally normal.

By the end of the century, the cult of horror had largely replaced an earlier view of the condemned criminal as sympathetic moral exemplum with a view of the murderer as moral alien. The cult of horror generated a new model sinner to replace the "exemplary" sinner of the earlier execution

---

86. *Biography of Fairbanks and Fales* (broadside).

87. *Trial of Jameson and M'Gowan,* p. 21. The attorney then called upon the jurors to try nonetheless to dispel all prejudice from their minds in considering the case.

88. Moses Baldwin, *The Ungodly Condemned in Judgment* . . . (Boston: Kneeland and Adams, 1771).

89. Chauncy, *The horrid Nature, and enormous Guilt of Murder,* p. 17.

sermon. The new model sinner did not claim to exemplify a sinful human-ity, but instead acknowledged his nature as moral alien, and even played up his monstrosity for the benefit of his reading audience. Such a sinner was John Battus, the indentured servant who in 1804 raped and then murdered thirteen-year-old Salome Talbott. *The Confession of John Battus, A Mulatto* offered a highly melodramatic account of Battus's crimes, the tone of which was calculated to maximize the reader's moral horror. Out of a "worse than brutal lust" which "would have disgraced and condemned even one of her own complexion," Battus had assaulted a "lovely and blooming damsel" and "disrobed her of that virgin purity, which is the flower and pride of her sex!" Then, "blind to the ruins of beauty!" and "deaf to the plaints of innocence and humanity!" he beat her with a stone, until "Her piteous cries and groans might now have melted to pity the surrounding flinty rocks, and caused the embowering trees to weep!" He then threw her into a pond and struck her with a rail until she sank. Even Battus's expression of regret that his account must "harrow up the very soul of humanity" and his warning to "Steel then your hearts, ye tender-hearted," were calculated to pile on the horror at his crimes, and convince readers that he was a moral alien. His was a "barbarity, unknown among savages or beasts," he claimed; he was "a monster" who had committed "the most horrid crimes ever done in this christian country"; he was "too disgusting and dangerous to intermix with civilized society!" Battus's editor had only to echo the murderer's own words: Battus's execution was lamen-table but necessary "to rid the world of a monster, too overgrown in iniq-uity, too pestilential to society, to live in it. He has cut asunder the cord of all the social affections."[90] Battus himself, not the society around him, was thus held responsible for the severing of the sentimental bonds uniting him to the rest of humankind. His criminal actions had placed him beyond the pale of human nature.

The larger purpose of the horror account of murder that emerged in the late eighteenth century was to induce the horror-response in the reader in order to arouse the proper feelings assigned to normalcy in the face of moral monstrosity. What was really being taught was a new relationship to the criminal, in which "nature recoils" from an evil that was defined as unnatural, alien, nonhuman. The emotional instructions conveyed by the early American execution sermon, to empathize with the murderer on the basis of the spectator's shared sinfulness, were thus giving way to new

90. *Confession of John Battus,* pp. 3, 8, 10–12, 18, 19, 22.

emotional instructions to shrink from him with revulsion, regarding him, in Dickensian terms, as "a horrible wonder apart." At bottom, the horror of these new murder accounts was a didactic concern: their blood-horror was in service to their new sense of moral horror. John Battus's close description of his murderous assault on Salome Talbott was not gratuitous; rather, it was intended to demonstrate his monstrosity, and to induce in the reader the proper response to such monstrosity. By inviting readers to gaze on the murderer and say, I am normal/moral, you are abnormal/evil, the cult of horror contributed to a more general hardening of social lines between "normality" and "abnormality" in late eighteenth-century Anglo-American culture, which was locking such social types as criminals, mad persons, and homosexuals into closed categories of deviancy.[91]

The early American cultural response to the crime of murder had been to acknowledge the existence of radical human evil and then invite the community's moral reconciliation with the heinous sinner on public display in an effort to put the crime to spiritual use in the interest of salvation; through the collective ritual of reconciliation, the community achieved spiritual transcendence of a highly disturbing crime. The eighteenth-century liberal response to the crime was to assert that human evil was not radical but extrinsic, alien, a monstrous distortion of normal human nature, and then invite individual readers to experience horror in its face. Through this private emotional experience of horror, isolated readers did not transcend the evil, but rather were mired down in it, immobilized and speechless in their alienation and disgust, without even the possibility of assigning meaning to it.

Why, then, did late eighteenth-century readers deliberately pursue this apparently painful experience? All horror literature poses the intellectual paradox that one critic has called the "dreadful pleasure,"[92] the enjoyment experienced by readers of the horror genre. One useful line of argument suggests that horror literature permits readers imaginatively to entertain images of the culturally forbidden within the safe confines of the printed

---

91. For an excellent discussion of this transformation of the criminal into moral alien, see Cynthia B. Herrup, "Law and Morality in Seventeenth-Century England," pp. 102–23. Also see Roy Porter, *Mind-Forg'd Manacles: A History of Madness in England from the Restoration to the Regency* (Cambridge: Harvard University Press, 1987); Keith Thomas, "Other Modes of Thought" (a review of Porter), *Times Literary Supplement* 4418 (4–10 December 1987): 1339–40; George L. Mosse, *Nationalism and Sexuality: Respectability and Abnormal Sexuality in Modern Europe* (New York: Howard Fertig, 1985).

92. See James B. Twitchell, *Dreadful Pleasures: An Anatomy of Modern Horror* (New York: Oxford University Press, 1985).

page, and then to put them away again at the end of the work—thus offering both the pleasure of vicariously performing forbidden acts and the pleasure of once again repudiating them through a reenactment of repression which reasserts the power of "normal" identity over that which is culturally forbidden.[93] Significantly, the horror genre emerged in the context of a dramatic expansion in the realm of the culturally forbidden in the late eighteenth century, as the liberal Enlightenment gave rise to new humanitarian views of pain, suffering, and physical coercion, views which were generating an intolerance for forms of violence that had gone unquestioned in premodern societies. The new tenderheartedness about suffering was at work in the growth of antislavery, the criticism of cruel and unusual judicial punishments, the growing disapproval of corporal punishment of children, sailors, and the insane, the rise of movements against blood sports, duelling, and prizefighting, and the beginnings of opposition to the cruel treatment of animals. Whereas earlier generations had tended to take pain for granted, the humanitarian revolution ushered in a new revulsion and dread of pain. The best indicater of this new attitude toward pain was the serious medical effort to stop it, which resulted in the isolation of morphine in 1806 and, a generation or two later, the invention of surgical anaesthesia. All these developments demonstrated the historical emergence of what James Turner has called "that dread of pain—that 'instinctive' revulsion from the physical suffering even of others—uniquely characteristic of the modern era."[94]

The new humanitarianism helps explain the pornographic quality of horror literature—pornographic in its implicit acknowledgment that it was willfully exploring forbidden matters. For the horror narrative appealed to precisely those human passions and appetites that were newly forbidden within the liberal humanitarian sensibility. That taste for suffering and

93. See Terry Heller, *The Delights of Terror: An Aesthetics of the Tale of Terror* (Urbana: University of Illinois Press, 1987).

94. James Turner, *Reckoning with the Beast: Animals, Pain, and Humanity in the Victorian Mind* (Baltimore: Johns Hopkins University Press, 1980), pp. xi–xii. Also see Myra C. Glenn, *Campaigns against Corporal Punishment: Prisoners, Sailors, Women, and Children in Antebellum America* (Albany: State University of New York Press, 1984); Elliott J. Gorn, *The Manly Art: Bare-Knuckle Prize Fighting in America* (Ithaca: Cornell University Press, 1986); Keith Thomas, *Man and the Natural World: A History of the Modern Sensibility* (New York: Pantheon, 1983); Michel Foucault, *Discipline and Punish*; Randall McGowen, "The Body and Punishment in Eighteenth-Century England," *Journal of Modern History* 59, no. 4 (December 1987): 651–79; Martin S. Pernick, *A Calculus of Suffering: Pain, Professionalism, and Anesthesia in Nineteenth-Century America* (New York: Columbia University Press, 1985).

violence that had once been openly and legitimately indulged at public executions, floggings, and brandings could now be satisfied privately and illicitly by reading horror accounts. (Here I am drawing on Walter Ong's argument that rising literacy helps create new emotional standards and experiences: the cult of horror must be understood as part of the social history of reading.)[95] The pornography of these accounts is thus primarily one of violence, with the sexual pornography of some accounts serving almost as a metaphor for the more deeply forbidden appetites for pain, suffering, and coercion. This consciously illicit quality to the horror narrative helps account for the "dreadful pleasure" readers might take in it: liberal humanitarianism was forcing pain, violence, and coercion into a kind of cultural underground, transforming them into obscenity within a pornography of pain.

The cult of horror thus provided a new idiom for addressing the problem of evil, which emerged historically side-by-side with the liberal humanitarian sensibility, and which was by no means limited to crime literature. Until now, scholarly attention to the cult of horror has focused on Gothic fiction, a new popular genre which immersed the Anglo-American mass reading market in horror during the last several decades of the eighteenth century, and proved a crucial influence on one of the best-known of early American novelists, Charles Brockden Brown. Gothic horror, it should be noted, does not necessarily involve an element of the supernatural, but simply a close attention to an evil expressed in heavily physiological terms calculated to arouse a powerful sense of revulsion and disgust.[96] At the same time, the distinctively American literary form of the captivity narrative, which had originated a century earlier as a symbolic religious work

95. Walter J. Ong, *The Presence of the Word: Some Prolegomena for Cultural and Religious History* (New Haven: Yale University Press, 1967), esp. pp. 133–35. Also see Ian Watt, *The Rise of the Novel: Studies in Defoe, Richardson and Fielding* (Berkeley: University of California Press, 1957), esp. chap. 6; Jack Goody and Ian Watt, "The Consequences of Literacy," in Jack Goody, ed., *Literacy in Traditional Societies* (Cambridge: Cambridge University Press, 1968).

96. A second explanation might suggest that the influence of Gothic fiction reoriented murder narratives toward horror. The problem here is that the shift toward horror was well underway before Gothic fiction became widely popular in America. Indeed, there is evidence that influence operated in the opposite direction: Charles Brockden Brown's *Wieland* (1798), the story of a man who kills his wife and children under the illusion that God has so commanded him, was based on contemporary accounts of the familicide committed by James Yates of Tomhanick, New York, in 1781. Both Gothic fiction and late eighteenth-century murder narratives were thus manifestations of a broader transformation of the American understanding of human evil in the late eighteenth century.

in the confessional mode, was in the late eighteenth century transformed into a visceral thriller, more concerned with blood and pain than with salvation.[97] By the early nineteenth century, the cult of horror was also at work transforming American journalism, replacing the staid sixpenny newspaper filled with news of commerce and politics with the sensationalistic penny press, which carried stories entitled "Double Suicide," "Awful Accident," "Bloody Murder," and covered alleged incidents of cannibalism and live burial. Significantly, the new literary form of pornography was heavily shaped by horror, with its peculiar combination of prurient sexuality and grisly gore: the pornographic novel *Mary Velnet* (1816), for example, included scenes of a nude woman tortured on a rack. And the literature of humanitarian reform itself internally revealed the close connection between the humanitarian sensibility and the cult of horror: opponents of such newly identified "evils" as slavery, public execution, intemperance, and the corporal punishment of sailors, criminals, children, and the mentally ill, generated a literature filled with graphic representations of the evils they opposed, calculated to convert new followers to the cause by arousing readers' sense of horror.[98]

The cultural pervasiveness of the conventions of horror points clearly to the inadequacy of dismissing the phenomenon, as a number of scholars have, as "cheap sensationalism," a crude exploitation of the lower side of human nature in an effort to broaden sales in a rapidly expanding commercial book market.[99] One problem with this interpretive approach lies in its elitism: its central assumption is that the emergence of a mass reading audience brings a vulgarization of taste. The "sensationalist" argument thus

97. Roy Harvey Pearce, "The Significance of the Captivity Narrative," *American Literature* 19 (March 1947): 1–20.

98. See David S. Reynolds, *Beneath the American Renaissance: The Subversive Imagination in the Age of Emerson and Melville* (New York: Alfred A. Knopf, 1988).

99. Roy Harvey Pearce, for example, has argued that the significance of the "captivity narrative as pulp thriller" was "mainly vulgar, fictional, and pathological," and attributed its "mass of crude, sensationally presented details" to a growing concern for the "salability of penny dreadfuls"; Pearce, "Significance of Captivity Narrative," p. 9. Similarly, Richard Slotkin explained that the rising tendency in eighteenth-century Negro crime narratives to depict crimes with sensationalistic detail reveals "the general tendency toward secularization and sensationalism of popular literary genres that accompanied the decline of Matherian Puritanism"; see "Narratives of Negro Crime in New England, 1675–1800," *American Quarterly* 25 (March 1973): 3–31. For both these scholars, horror is a matter of "sensationalism," a pursuit of sensation for its own sake, which emerged as a by-product of the eighteenth-century mass literary market.

replicates the contemporary critics' judgment of the novel's alleged promotion of shallow excitement for its own sake, and weighs in with those clergymen who could only regard the secularization of literature as a degradation. The treatment of horror literature as trash for the masses—"vulgar, fictional, and pathological"—rests on a dubious "high brow/low brow" distinction which was itself an historical creation, a distinction whose usefulness has recently come under serious attack. Another related problem with this argument is its implicit essentialism. It assumes a human nature that had always hungered for "sensation," that needed only the new opportunities provided by eighteenth-century commercialization to seize upon the literary pulp that would satisfy that hunger.[100] Such scholarly assessments of eighteenth-century sensationalism are, above all, ahistorical in their failure to explain why the cult of horror did not emerge earlier in the history of popular literature. Seventeenth-century New England execution sermons and captivity narratives were also popular forms of literature, produced for a largely literate population, yet these literary forms were not sensationalistic—that is, they did not appeal to sensation for sensation's sake.[101]

100. For example, James Twitchell's argument that "modern works of artificial horror originated in the late eighteenth-century discovery that by inducing extreme feelings of dreadful pleasures, both print and illustration could arouse and exploit powerful feelings deep within the human spirit," rests on the assumption that certain "powerful feelings deep within the human spirit" had been lying in wait to be "exploited" by a fully developed literary marketplace. See Twitchell, *Dreadful Pleasures*. Such a view treats readers as mere creatures of the marketplace, passively awaiting the moment when exploitation of their hunger might occur. The logical *ad absurdam* of this argument may be found in Joseph Grixti, *Terrors of Uncertainty: The Cultural Contexts of Horror Fiction* (London: Routledge, 1989), which argues that horror fiction, by cultivating fear within well-determined codes, propagates a sense of personal helplessness and political impotence which is central to the maintenance of consumer culture. By providing its own peculiar, passive, drug-like pleasure involving surrender, he argues, horror designs ideal consumers for the new commercial order.

101. In *Worlds of Wonder, Days of Judgment: Popular Religious Belief in Early New England* (New York: Alfred A. Knopf, 1989), David D. Hall identifies the execution sermon and the early captivity narrative as "sensational" without clarifying what he means by the term (despite his unexplained practice of occasionally using it in quotational form). Effectively, he has applied Pearce's argument linking sensationalism and the popular book to an earlier period, observing that the popular book and mass literacy had emerged by the seventeenth century. Such treatment gives short shrift to the professed purpose of the execution sermon, and tends to read the modern quest for "sensation" back into a premodern literary culture. Seventeenth-century English chapbook literature also generated nothing approaching the eighteenth-century horror account; see Margaret Spufford, *Small Books and Pleasant Histories: Popular Fiction and Its Readership in Seventeenth-Century England* (Athens, Ga.: University of Georgia Press, 1982).

Rather than dismissing the cult of horror as vulgar literature aimed at the newly literate masses buying books for the first time within a fully commercialized marketplace, it is important to look more closely at the precise nature of horror as it is set forth in the horror literature; to address, not the visceral response of the modern scholar to this emotionally charged literature, but the response that this literature explicitly and self-consciously intended to invoke in eighteenth-century readers—to take the horror account, that is, on its own terms. The problem with the term "sensationalism" as scholars have used it, is that it tends to trivialize what is best understood as a powerful new way of confronting human evil—whose power is evidenced, in fact, by these scholars' own strong revulsion from the new narratives, a disgust that testifies to their participation in the cult of horror. Only when that new way of confronting evil is taken on its own terms can its historicity be understood. For horror, like anger or romantic love, friendship or fear, has a cultural history, a point that most literary analysts of horror have overlooked. In some form or other, horror dates back to the earliest texts and artistic representations in human history. But the cult of horror at work in a range of American literary forms in the late eighteenth and early nineteenth centuries was a specific, highly defined experience that pointed to a major transformation in the understanding of human nature and moral evil.

The historical significance of the cult of horror lies in the Enlightenment noncomprehension of the problem of evil. Gothic horror—or, more broadly, modern horror—is the characteristic response to evil in an Enlightenment liberal culture that provides no systematic intellectual explanation for the problem. The Gothic view of evil at work in the cult of horror was not an irrationalist reaction against an excess of Enlightenment rationalism, as some literary historians have argued, but an indispensable corollary to Enlightenment liberalism which ultimately served to protect the liberal view of human nature. Within the cult of horror, the prevailing concept of human nature as basically good, free, and capable of self-government in the light of an innate moral sense was protected from the potential threat of major transgressions by the imaginative creation of a monstrous moral alien, divided from the rest of humankind by an impassable gulf. The modern cult of horror thus does not explain evil so much as it captures the raw experience of evil in a liberal humanitarian culture which offers no consistent and intellectually satisfying explanation of it.

This is why, in the modern cult of horror, evil tends first to hide and then to leap out at us: it is by nature the bogey under the bed, the dismembered corpse beneath the floorboards in Poe's "The Tell-Tale Heart," the mummy of Norman Bates's mother stowed in the fruit cellar in Alfred Hitchcock's *Psycho*—or the butchered bodies of the entire Beadle family, hidden behind the facade of their loving late eighteenth-century home, waiting for the arrival of unsuspecting neighbors. The eighteenth-century cult of horror worked something like an historical variant on Freud's theory of "the return of the repressed": every time a powerful affect is repressed because it is too "bad" to be confronted, that affect will return. "Horror has no end, no closure, no conclusion. . . . Extended horror can become a ritual, an endless loop. . . . [H]orror novels, horror movies, horror myths are never really satisfying intellectually, for we never get them under control."[102] Horror returns, it moves in an endless loop, it fails to satisfy intellectually, because liberal humanitarianism offers no way of articulating or transcending major acts of human transgression.

While the cult of horror does not explain the endurance of murder into the modern era, it has shaped the popular response to the crime down to the present. "Evil," posited the cover of *Time* magazine on 10 June 1991, "does it exist—or do bad things just happen?" The essay introduced by this ill-defined question is an exercise in liberal noncomprehension, well captured in the author's ventured definition of evil as "the Bad elevated to the status of the inexplicable."[103]

Two months later, on 5 August 1991, *Time* printed a story about accused serial sex murderer Jeffrey Dahmer, which demonstrated once again the relationship between the liberal "inexplicability" of evil and the modern cult of horror. Entitled "The Little Flat of Horrors," the story opens with a dramatic treatment of the discovery of the corpses by "shocked" policemen, listing the mutilated body parts that were found and offering a photograph of their removal, and describing the scene of the crime in lurid detail. Self-conscious of its own dominant literary conventions, the article refers indirectly to the camp horror film *The Little Shop of Horrors* and Hitchcock's *Psycho,* and explicitly compares Dahmer to Hannibal "the Cannibal" Lecter, a fictional serial killer in the recent horror hit, *The Silence of the Lambs.* And to emphasize its own protagonist's nature as monster, the story refers to Dahmer as "the *creature* who apparently turned Apartment 213 into a private slaughterhouse" (italics mine), and asserts that "throughout much of his life, there were warning signs that something was terribly

102. Twitchell, *Dreadful Pleasures,* p. 16.
103. Lance Morrow, "Evil," in *Time,* 10 June 1991, 50.

wrong with Jeffrey Dahmer." But what exactly went wrong with Jeffrey Dahmer is left unclear: readers are told that Dahmer's parents divorced when he was eighteen and his mother subsequently disappeared, but that he was engaging in bizarre behavior well before these difficult domestic experiences. Here, then, was a case study in "the Bad elevated to the status of the inexplicable." "The Little Flat of Horrors" concludes with a report of one person's inability to come to terms with what had happened. "How do you handle something like this?" Dahmer's stepmother is quoted as asking at the close of the piece.[104] For the readers of *Time* magazine, the answer to her question would seem to be, through the endless ritual of noncomprehension that is the modern horror experience.

104. Alex Prud-homme, "The Little Flat of Horrors," in *Time*, 5 August 1991, 26.

(*Top*): "The Modern Laocoon." *New York Daily Graphic,* 1 August 1874.
(*Bottom*): Portraits of Elizabeth Tilton, Henry Ward Beecher, and Theodore Tilton.
From *Frank Leslie's Illustrated Newspaper,* 8 August 1874.

4 Intimacy on Trial

Cultural Meanings of the Beecher-Tilton Affair

Richard Wightman Fox

"Elizabeth R. Tilton Dead"

The Beecher-Tilton file at the Brooklyn Historical Society is full of wordy Victorian commentaries on the "Scandal of the Age," Henry Ward Beecher's trial in 1875 for allegedly committing adultery with his parishioner Elizabeth Tilton. The file overflows with weighty contemporary treatments, pro and con, of Beecher's character and career, with satirical cartoons that pillory his apparent hypocrisy, and with ominous editorials about the sad state of an American culture that either produces such immorality or pollutes the public arena with sensationalist disclosures or concoctions about it.

A single stray clipping from the *Brooklyn Daily Eagle* centers on the other principal in the affair, and it is an obituary written a quarter-century later. The one-column story notes that although, because of the trial, Elizabeth Tilton's "personality has always been an interesting one to residents of Brooklyn," she strove to avoid all publicity after the trial. She refused all requests for interviews and was said to have allowed no newspaper to enter her house for the remainder of her life. While she did lead an active life among her small circle of friends and fellow believers in the "primitive" millenarian Christian sect called the Plymouth Brethren, she concealed herself from her contemporaries and, according to the story, sought to slip quietly off the historical stage. "To such an extent has Mrs. Tilton and her family avoided publicity that at the present time there is no crape [*sic*] on the door to tell passers by that death has visited the household. The blinds are not drawn down and there is an absence of the gloom which sometimes

For their counsel and criticism I want to thank the other contributors to this volume, as well as Elizabeth Beverly, Daniel Horowitz, Linda Kerber, Christopher Lowe, and a number of wise questioners in audiences at Harvard University, Indiana University, and the University of Oregon. Conversations with Laura Korobkin, herself hard at work on the Beecher-Tilton trial, have been indispensable, especially in thinking about the trial as narrative. For sharing materials gathered in their own research on related topics, I am grateful to Elizabeth Clark and Ellen DuBois.

surrounds the house in which one of the inmates has died. The fact of her death has been told only to a very few. Some of her intimate friends have called since her death to inquire how she was." Elizabeth Tilton's single clipping is buried under the browning, flaking pile of Beecher stories. "The internment will take place tomorrow," her obituary concludes, "and will be in the family plot at Greenwood. Mrs. Tilton will be laid to rest near the graves of her children who went before her."[1]

For some time I have been looking at late nineteenth-century liberal Protestantism and trying to grasp it as a "culture"—that is, as a set of practices, habits, and assumptions that inform a group's life. I am pursuing the elusive target of the liberal Protestants' "lived experience"—how they felt their lives as well as thought about them—and the perhaps still more elusive target of what such lived experience "meant," what it reveals to us, for example, about American historical development or about the drama of human life.

In this enterprise I am very conscious of embarking on a course that is novel for me, and relatively new to the American historical profession. Historians have typically defined their work as the quest to examine "change over time": to account for the development of society by tracing the key events, ideas, and institutions of this or that period and explaining what caused them. Cultural historians, whether (like me) attempting to probe the actual conscious or unconscious experience of people in the past or (like those of a more "antihumanist" poststructuralist bent) emphasizing the priority of discursive forms over individual experience, tend to be less interested in making cause-and-effect arguments and more interested in evoking and savoring the past and pondering its (experiential or linguistic-formal) resonances in contemporary life or thought. I am in fact eager to make some traditional cause-and-effect arguments about the role of liberal Protestantism in helping to transform modern industrial society in America, but I sense that those arguments will be fuller and more persuasive if they are grounded in a thicker than usual description of lived, felt, and thought experience.

It is a daunting task to look for and then, if it can be done, to look at the actual experience of those who came before us. After all, we have such

---

1. "Elizabeth R. Tilton Dead," *Brooklyn Daily Eagle,* n.d., n.p., Beecher-Tilton File, Brooklyn Historical Society. Elizabeth Tilton died on 13 April 1897. Short obituaries appeared in several New York newspapers, e.g., "Mrs. Elizabeth R. Tilton Dead," *New York Tribune,* 16 April 1897, p. 4, col. 2, which closely paraphrases the *Eagle* report.

trouble grasping what we mean by "experience" in our own lives—what do we really know about our inner feelings or about the personal habits or social rules that guide and shape our lives?—that we have to be skeptical about our capacity to know what earlier generations were experiencing. Looking for the liberal Protestant experience in late nineteenth-century America is doubly problematic, since looking for liberal Protestantism in that era is rather like looking for salt in the ocean. It is everywhere and it is so pervasive (not only a hundred years ago but today) that it is hard to see at all. And of course liberal Protestantism is not the only powerful cultural nexus in late nineteenth-century American life. It is difficult enough to separate liberal Protestantism even as a set of ideas from secular liberalism, from various scientific faiths, or from overlapping republican and democratic doctrines, without also having to distinguish it from other "cultures" or ways of life.

There is bound to be some slippage in our effort to know historical others, as there must be in our effort to know ourselves. But it is possible (and in today's Foucauldian academic climate very fashionable) to be too skeptical about the common ground we share even with those who inhabit what seem to be totally "other" cultures. Clifford Geertz, like Foucault an opponent (at least in the essays collected in *Local Knowledge*) of a "humanism" that celebrates too much the autonomous, self-driven integrity of the individual person, argues passionately against the view that we look at the "native" only from the "outside." We never know the other completely—as it were, from the "inside,"—and we never know "native" others the way their own people know them, but we do make real contact, even to the point that, because we are fellow human beings, we can encounter and "know" their experience.[2] Naturally this contact is a "construction," as the current academic formula puts it, but so is our experience of ourselves. The contemporary moral and intellectual task is not just, as Thomas Haskell has elegantly articulated it, to resist the epistemological extremes of a Nietzschean/Derridean relativism or a Straussian/Bloomian absolutist foundationalism—vital as that task is—but to offer a persuasive rebuttal to antihumanistic solipsism.[3]

I want this essay to contribute to that work by offering an encounter with the experience of Henry Ward Beecher and Elizabeth Tilton in the

2. Clifford Geertz, *Local Knowledge: Further Essays in Interpretive Anthropology* (New York: Basic Books, 1983), e.g., pp. 44, 58.

3. Thomas L. Haskell, "The Curious Persistence of Rights Talk in the 'Age of Interpretation,' " *Journal of American History* 74 (December 1987): 984–1012.

1870s. In describing and probing their experience I will also offer some ideas about what it means, how it illuminates the culture in which it took place and how it may also have helped shape the development of American culture. We will never know exactly what Henry and Elizabeth did or said together. We do know that, by their own account, they were deeply engaged, and felt their involvement as a richly emotional and spiritual Christian love. Their own *felt* experience was always *interpreted* experience, so that the interpretation they offered publicly to others (and thereby in the surviving historical record to us) gives us direct access to at least part of their own immediate experience. Justifying and explaining their tie as "Christian" was probably a wholly ingenuous mental strategy, one that allowed them to push with relative safety against established cultural norms. Under the Christian banner they could march into uncharted realms of feeling and behavior while claiming all the while to be drawing upon and extending a venerable moral tradition. What they could not manage, however, was their own complex of relations with and feelings about Elizabeth's husband and Henry's long-time friend and collaborator Theodore. A full account of the bond between Elizabeth and Henry would require pondering the intimate tie each of them had developed with Theodore since the 1850s, and examining Henry's long relationship with his wife Eunice, who stayed home while he consorted with the Tiltons. In this essay I will stress the Henry-Elizabeth side of a complex personal drama and a significant public event that disclosed and helped channel some central currents of post–Civil War American life.

The Story in Outline

In January, 1875, the foremost preacher in America, Henry Ward Beecher, surrounded by an entourage of his parishioners from Plymouth Church, entered Brooklyn City Court to defend himself against the charge of "criminal conversation." His old friend Theodore Tilton, himself, like Beecher, a famous writer and reformer in the abolitionist and suffragist movements, had accused Beecher, in the words of the civil complaint, of "wilfully intending to injure the plaintiff and deprive him of the comfort, society, aid and assistance of . . . Elizabeth, the wife of the plaintiff . . . . [W]rongfully and wickedly and without the privity or connivance of plaintiff, [Beecher] debauched and carnally knew the said Elizabeth . . . on or about the tenth day of October, 1868, and on divers other days and times after that day . . . at the house of the defendant . . . and at the house of the plaintiff, . . . by means whereof the affection of the said Elizabeth for the said plaintiff was wholly alienated and destroyed."[4]

Elizabeth Tilton, now estranged and separated from Theodore, was present in court throughout the trial, though she was not permitted to speak. She wanted to join Beecher in denying her husband's charge. But Beecher's defense lawyers refused to allow it on the stated grounds that the common law prevented a woman from testifying against, and therefore being unfaithful to, her husband. In fact they were worried she would buckle once she was face to face with Theodore, who had in 1870 extracted from her a written confession of guilt—a document which on a single harrowing winter evening, as she lay in bed recovering from a miscarriage, she first retracted (under pressure from Beecher, who composed a denial for her to sign), and then (under renewed pressure from Theodore) reaffirmed. At the trial, therefore, while lawyers and witnesses relentlessly scoured her life for the illumination of the jury and the edification of a national audience, she sat mute, ogled by the heavily male gallery just as she was by the mass newspaper readership. "She was very pale," commented the *Tribune* reporter who also served as official court stenographer, "and her manner was that of a timid, shy woman, who felt ill at ease under hundreds of staring eyes. The crowd instinctively instituted a comparison between her and Mrs. Beecher, and the result was not favorable to Mrs. Tilton . . . . Mrs. Beecher was cool and self-possessed throughout the proceedings, notwithstanding the bitter attacks upon her husband's honor. Mrs. Tilton was evidently nervous and embarrassed. Mrs. Beecher has a classical face, full of force and expression; Mrs. Tilton's face is of a commonplace type."[5] If she was nervous and embarrassed before such reports appeared, we may

---

4. *Theodore Tilton vs. Henry Ward Beecher, Action for Crim[inal] Con[versation]* (New York: McDivitt, Campbell and Co., 1875) [hereafter *TT v. HWB*], vol. 1, p. 1 [hereafter 1:1]. The three volumes of testimony, lawyers' summations, judge's instructions, and stenographer's commentary run to 2,700 double-column pages.

5. *TT v. HWB,* 1:34. At the start of the trial the judge selected the *Tribune* reporter as the "official" court stenographer. The official record of the testimony, assembled in the three volumes of *TT v. HWB,* also includes the reporter's daily "scene-setting" comments on the weather, the mood of the gallery, the moral standing of Beecher's and Tilton's wives, and other items. The identical comments and testimony are found in the daily columns of the *Tribune.* Since other newspapers had their own stenographers, their daily reports diverge from the *Tribune's.* Usually the difference is editoral: one paper is suspicious of Beecher, another of Tilton, and their commentary reflects their bias. Occasionally the difference is in their report of the testimony itself. "Verbatim" testimony as recorded by stenographers is not pristine: each of the texts that comes down to us must be taken ultimately as an approximation, not an exact recording, of what was said in court.

imagine how she felt afterwards, knowing she could look forward to a winter of such icy scrutiny.

Theodore Tilton had learned of Beecher's affair with his wife, he claimed, when she confessed it to him in 1870. For four years all the principals, including Beecher's and Tilton's "mutual friend" (as their designated intermediary came to be labeled, in a probable reference to Dickens' 1864 novel) Francis Moulton, had, in Tilton's version of the story, striven to avoid publicity. They all agreed that a cover-up of Tilton's charges was required not only by their personal interests—their good names and their children's—but by the interests of society. As Beecher explained to an investigating committee of his own church the summer before the public trial, "I cannot admit that I erred in desiring to keep these matters out of sight. In this respect I appeal to you and to all Christian men to judge whether almost any personal sacrifice ought not to have been made rather than to suffer the morals of an entire community, and especially of the young, to be corrupted by the filthy details of scandalous falsehoods, daily iterated and amplified, for the gratification of impure curiosity and the demoralization of every child that is old enough to read."[6]

Beecher and Theodore Tilton, both accomplished practitioners of the art of publicity, both dependent for their livelihood upon their carefully crafted public personas, might well have guessed that a successful cover-up was unlikely. Radical suffragist and spiritualist Victoria Woodhull was as devoted to publicity as they were, as committed as they had long been to a romantic self-image, that of the uncompromising crusader standing fearlessly against oppressive social institutions. In 1872 she published a report of the affair based on information she had heard from Susan B. Anthony, a friend of the Tiltons. That freed the newly emergent corps of news "reporters" around the country to investigate the scandal, and even turn up rumors of earlier Beecher escapades with female parishioners going back to his days in Indianapolis in the 1840s. And Theodore Tilton himself couldn't keep quiet. First he shared his secret with a few acquaintances, then, bitter over Beecher's apparent recommendation that he be fired as editor of the *Brooklyn Union,* with the press. His public accusation led to

6. Charles F. Marshall, *The True History of the Brooklyn Scandal* (Philadelphia: National Publishing Co., 1874), pp. 283–84. Marshall's compilation is a crucial source for the Beecher-Tilton affair because it contains the "verbatim" testimony of all of the principals—including Elizabeth Tilton—to Beecher's hand-picked church "investigating committee" in the summer of 1874, six months before the civil trial began. It also gathers a trove of letters exchanged by the principals—letters also found, though not in one place, in *TT v. HWB.*

the six-week Plymouth Church investigation in the summer of 1874. It was sensational, first-page news, day after day, in cities large and small across the country. When it was over, Beecher observed ruefully that "the nation has risen up and sat down upon scandal. Not a great war nor a revolution could more have filled the newspapers than this question of domestic trouble, magnified a thousand-fold, and, like a sore spot on the human body, drawing to itself every morbid humor in the blood."[7]

Not a great war or revolution, perhaps, but the public trial which began in January, 1875, did provoke even more publicity than the church investigation. For six months, until the jury announced in July that it could not reach a verdict (it was stalled with nine votes for acquittal, three for conviction), it was once again, as during the previous summer, the major story in newspapers all over the country. But now they also printed all the myriad documents of the case, sometimes, when they could get hold of the originals, in the newly developed "fac-simile" form for greater authenticity. Readers could ponder the actual hand-writing of Beecher and the Tiltons, no small treat at a time when handwriting was widely thought to be one indicator of inner character. In Troy, New York, a new newspaper, the *Thunderbolt,* named after Beecher's report of what the news of Tilton's charge felt like when he first heard it, consecrated itself solely to news of the trial. Major newspapers ran page after page of testimony even when they had to protest editorially, as the *Tribune* did in devoting three entire pages to a letter from one major witness, against its "insufferably prolix" character. Famous editorialists such as Charles Dana of the *New York Sun* argued the case alongside the nationally and internationally known lawyers. (Beecher's senior counsel, William Evarts, widely credited at the time with saving Beecher from conviction thanks to his scintillating summation, had been both U.S. Attorney General and Secretary of State.) Magazines also commented endlessly on the case—often, as in E. L. Godkin's frequent

---

7. Marshall, *True History,* p. 286. Perhaps the church investigation got more coverage nationwide during the slow news days of summer than it would have gotten in any other season of the year. In addition to New York and Brooklyn papers, I have checked the *San Francisco Chronicle,* the *St. Louis Dispatch,* the *Boston Globe,* and the *Chicago Tribune,* all of which provided detailed daily coverage. The *Tribune* devoted extraordinary resources to its reporting. It was the first paper to publish the collected love letters of Theodore and Elizabeth Tilton; its letter columns became a national forum for opinions on the case; during the civil trial in 1875 it hired renowned journalist George Albert Townsend (famous since his 1865 book on John Wilkes Booth) for on-the-spot reporting from Brooklyn. The *Tribune* seems to have attempted to establish its national credibility during the Beecher-Tilton affair by out-investigating the New York press.

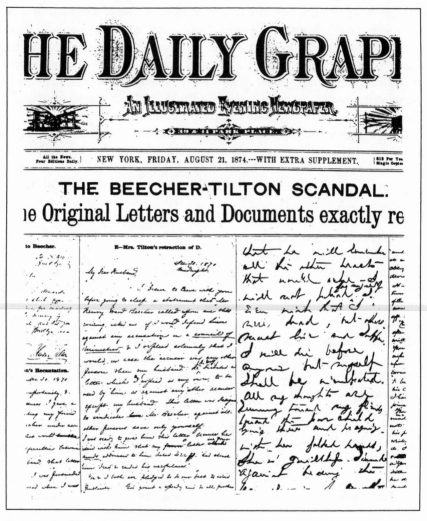

Daily Graphic, 21 August 1874

Nation editorials, chastising the newspapers for giving it so much attention. And the scandal entered popular culture at other levels: theatrical spin-offs (one of which, "Passion's Peril" in Boston, was shut down by the Board of Alderman because they viewed it as prejudicial to Beecher's case), satirical fiction and poetry (published in newspaper, pamphlet, and book form), children's humor ("Beecher, Beecher is my name—Beecher till I die! I never kissed Mis' Tilton—I never told a lie!"), and at least one circus spoof which Beecher sued successfully to stop on the grounds that it libeled him.[8]

The mass reading public could not get enough of the case, which read like a novel but had the alluring advantage of being "true." More: the key male players in the real-life drama were themselves well-known authors of sentimental fiction. Beecher's *Norwood,* the draft chapters of which Beecher had read to Elizabeth Tilton in her upstairs parlor—thus inaugurating their special friendship—had appeared in 1867. Theodore's *Tempest Tossed,* which featured a character patterned after Elizabeth and drew extensively on her actual love letters, came out in 1874, just before the trial began. Elizabeth Tilton, an accomplished reader of the genre—who by her husband's account had come to feel guilty about her infidelity to him only because of reading Charles Reade's novel *Griffith Gaunt,* in which Gaunt's wife Catherine suffers guilt over her relationship with a priest—was herself reported during the trial to be writing a novel. Newspapers supplied not only the "verbatim" text of the trial testimony, but the reactions of the audience in the courtroom, allowing those who "read" the trial at a distance to identify themselves with the spectators on the scene. Key letters or episodes were widely known by nicknames—the "Letter of Contrition," the "True Inwardness Letter," the "Day of Judgment Letter," "the Pistol Scene"—and even recognized by date. During the trial one of the lawyers announced he would soon begin analyzing a letter of 5 February 1872. The stenographer reported that the courtroom audience gasped: they knew it was Henry Ward Beecher's "Ragged Edge Letter," his confession that in his anxiety over the collapse of the cover-up, death itself seemed sweet. Readers around the country gasped in their turn.[9]

Historiography

Twentieth-century journalists and historians have been no more able to avoid the lure of the Beecher-Tilton Scandal than the Victorian public.

8. "Insufferably prolix": Marshall, *True History,* p. 505. Children's ditty quoted in Paxton Hibben, *Henry Ward Beecher: An American Portrait* (New York: George H. Doran, Co., 1927), p. 353. A *Chicago Tribune* editiorial reported that "three people in Washington have gone crazy over the great scandal, and have been sent to the insane asylum. Two of them were women who addled their weak brains with keeping track of the case, and the other, we regret to state, belonged to the masculine gender." 16 April 1875, p. 4, col. 1.

9. *TT v. HWB,* 2:825, reports the gasping audience. The Facts and Gossip column of the *Chicago Tribune* reported 19 May 1875 (p. 2, col. 7) that Elizabeth Tilton was writing a novel. I have found no evidence that she actually did.

Paxton Hibben's muckraking biography of Beecher in 1927, Robert Shaplen's *New Yorker* series published as *Free Love and Heavenly Sinners* in 1954, and Altina Waller's *Reverend Beecher and Mrs. Tilton* in 1982 are the most extensive treatments, but many other works have discussed the case. There are several remarkable things about this literature. First, there is an unspoken consensus on the proper goal of the historian in examining the affair: to determine the true facts and render a retrospective verdict. The assumption seems to be that although the jury couldn't do it, we, with our superior twentieth-century insight or critical methodology, can reconstruct the story and make a definitive judgment. Second, and more remarkably, there are many writers (such as Ann Douglas in *The Feminization of American Culture*) who go much further and believe, following Hibben's lead, that the true facts have long since been established and Beecher's guilt demonstrated. Finally, there is a nearly universal though unstated assumption that Henry Ward Beecher is the significant actor in the affair, Elizabeth Tilton a minor player interesting only because of her accidental proximity to the Great Man. In fact, even if Beecher the preacher does provide hefty clues to the character of mid-Victorian culture (as William McLoughlin argued in 1970 in the *The Meaning of Henry Ward Beecher,* the single best book about him), Elizabeth Tilton does too. Moreover, in the Beecher-Tilton affair she was an active presence, not a guileless bystander caught up in the heavy rush of Beecher's robes.[10]

It is easy to grasp why we should not ignore Elizabeth Tilton and why we should not assume her and Beecher's guilt without looking critically at the evidence. But we need to go even further and reject the historian-as-detective approach itself. No reexamination of the Beecher-Tilton case will ever yield a firm set of discrete facts that can ground a secure verdict. As the judge stressed to the jury when he gave them their charge: either you believe the story Beecher told or the conflicting one related by the three key prosecution witnesses—Theodore Tilton, "mutual friend" Frank Moulton, and his wife Emma (Beecher had confided in the Moultons and, they alleged, confessed to them). The only other evidence against Beecher was circumstantial. Beecher wrote letter after letter, for example, confessing

10. Hibben, *Henry Ward Beecher;* Robert Shaplen, *Free Love and Heavenly Sinners: The Story of the Great Henry Ward Beecher Scandal* (New York: Knopf, 1954); Altina L. Waller, *Reverend Beecher and Mrs. Tilton: Sex and Class in Victorian America* (Amherst: University of Massachusetts Press, 1982); Ann Douglas, *The Feminization of American Culture* (New York: Knopf, 1977); William G. McLoughlin, *The Meaning of Henry Ward Beecher: An Essay on the Shifting Values of Mid-Victorian America, 1840–1870* (New York: Knopf, 1970).

how guilty he felt about *something;* the prosecution argued that if he was *that* guilty he must have done something very naughty. As the judge explained, the jury would have to render delicate judgments about the credibility of witnesses. It is hardly possible for us, over a century after the events, to do better than the jury did at deciding who was lying and who was not.

But there is a second reason to give up the quest for a final verdict. Trying to decide whether Henry and Elizabeth committed adultery needlessly narrows our historical focus. Just because that was the key question the trial attempted to answer does not mean it needs to be the central question for us. It is much more important to think about the *acknowledged* relation of love and friendship that bound them together in the late 1860s. That relation—along with their separate, intimate ties to Theodore—offers us a unique entryway into the heart of Victorian northern middle-class culture. So does their effort at what in their private code they called "nest-hiding," the guarding of their relationship against public scrutiny. For it reveals the intricate, multilayered connection between private fidelity and public disclosure in the Beecher-Tilton affair, and between the "private" and "public" spheres in general in late nineteenth-century bourgeois culture.

At the simplest level of paradox, the private bond between Henry and Elizabeth, a bond that they believed required secrecy for is sustenance, led them inexorably to public displays of their attachment to one another. They were friends, not just (if they were at all, in the late twentieth-century sense) lovers, and as friends they sought a social expression of their bond. They did feel they had something to hide, and it may be that their public relationship was meant to cover up a sexual liaison. But it seems to me more likely that their private tie was a passionate spiritual romance, though one certainly enlivened with physical affection of the sort that was common in their circle among friends of both sexes. Beecher's whole ministry was devoted to breaking down the barrier between the public and private, to modeling for his Plymouth parishioners the public expression of intensely felt private emotions. And with Elizabeth as well as Theodore he had grown accustomed to the public cultivation of affection. Yet with Elizabeth he wanted more, and she responded willingly to his invitation to embark upon what in her view was a more fulfilling relationship than she had with Theodore. He felt the tug of an imagined secret nest where feelings of special urgency might lodge. It may even have been his eagerness to make his church a place of soulful and passionate feeling that made him crave another still deeper place of encounter that defied pious socialization and escaped (at least for a time) public notice.

When their publicly evident attachment prompted well publicized accusations first by Victoria Woodhull, then by Theodore Tilton, Henry and Elizabeth embarked on a path of accommodation to normal bourgeois expectations. They separated: each claimed innocence on the adultery charge, but each conceded a measure of moral error in having become such intimate friends. Ultimately each of them took refuge in culturally predictable resolutions: Beecher in detached, Olympian condescension toward Tilton's female irrationality, Tilton in silent isolation with her children. That withdrawal deepened in later years when she lost her sight. Her blindness was cured by an operation only a year before her death in 1897. For years passers-by had noticed her walking slowly, from memory, along the sidewalks of Brooklyn Heights. "All whom she had come to know by their voices alone she could [now] see," the obituary writer recorded, "and added to this was the greater pleasure of seeing again the friends she had known before she lost her sight."[11]

The Story in Sharper Focus

Henry Ward Beecher was in his late fifties, Elizabeth Tilton in her midthirties when they became intimate friends. He had known her and her husband since they were children; he baptized them at Plymouth Church and married them there in 1855. He came to be close to their family in the early 1860s. Elizabeth and Theodore were dazzled by Beecher's intense, conversational sermons, in which he strode up and down the platform, shared his innermost thoughts, wept freely about his fondest hopes and deepest longings. Elizabeth would come to him for consolation when babies died or her spirits were low, as they often were. Theodore, a skilled writer and ardent reformer, had assisted Beecher on the *Independent,* the foremost religious weekly of the 1860s, and had eventually replaced him as editor. During and after the war he urged Beecher to spend more time at his house, where suffragists like Susan B. Anthony and Elizabeth Cady Stanton often stayed while in New York. Beecher was happy to oblige since he shared with Theodore a self-conception as a latter-day Romantic who put feeling and bodily expression on a par with or ahead of reason and

11. "Elizabeth R. Tilton Dead," *Brooklyn Daily Eagle,* n.d., n.p.

middle-class conventions. They walked down the street with their arms around each other, kissed "Oriental style" when greeting or parting, sat on each other's laps. " You are my minister, teacher, father, brother, friend, companion," Theodore wrote him in 1865. "Whether you had been high or low, great or common, I believe that my heart, knowing its mate, would have loved you exactly the same."[12]

It was no surprise when Beecher followed everyone else's example and kissed Elizabeth Tilton the same way he kissed her husband. Beecher later unleashed a storm of laughter in the courtroom when he remembered that after one intense encounter between him and the Tiltons, "I kissed him and he kissed me, and I kissed his wife and she kissed me, and I believe they kissed each other." But all the warm contact in the Tilton household in fact concealed a harshness in Theodore that was his Romantic underside. Alive to passionate feelings and primed for dramatic encounters, he would often erupt in anger with Elizabeth. He would rage that she was too ortho-dox in religion, too conventionally domestic, too unappreciative of the new-thinking suffragists whom he invited over to converse into the night.[13]

By the late 1860s Theodore was frequently away on long lecture trips, and Beecher, with Theodore's knowledge, kept coming by. When he began writing his novel *Norwood,* a money-making sally into the realm of senti-mental fiction, he decided to read the manuscript to Elizabeth, because, he said, he needed a sympathetic critic. In fact, as an avid consumer of the genre Elizabeth probably rendered him very good advice. What he did for her, in turn, she expressed very eloquently to the Plymouth Investigating Committee several years later. She needs to be quoted at length. She has been so totally buried in the historical record that we must rely heavily on this testimony to get what little access we can to her own experience of the Beecher-Tilton affair.

"I do not know as I can make myself understood," she told the commit-tee. That initial self-deprecation—or self-doubt or nervousness or insight into the limited comprehension of her male listeners—was quickly refuted by an impassioned and utterly lucid statement. The lucidity of her testi-mony was widely noted at the time, and led to press speculation (unsub-stantiated as far as I can tell) that it had been written for her by a male friend. Her statement's force could not be disguised by the interrogative gesture that followed her hesitant opening.

12. *TT v. HWB,* 3:673.
13. *TT v. HWB,* 3:72.

But do you know what I mean when I say that [with Mr. Beecher] I was aroused in myself—that I had a self-assertion which I never knew before with Theodore; there was always a damper between me and Theodore, but there never was between me and Mr. Beecher; with Mr. Beecher I had a sort of consciousness of being more; he appreciated me as Theodore did not; I felt myself another woman; I felt that he respected me; I think Theodore never saw in me what Mr. Beecher did . . . . I never felt a bit of embarrassment with Mr. Beecher, but to this day I never could sit down with Theodore without being self-conscious and feeling his sense of my inequality with him.

After she had come to share this new intimacy with Beecher, her husband's "influence" was even more devastating to her spirit than it had been during his earlier periodic bursts of anger. She felt guilty now about not giving him "the all of my nature," about "giving to another what was due to my husband." But she also felt detached from Theodore and from the social norms to which she still expressed formal obedience. She realized she could not give to Theodore what he had never sought to "bring out" of her.

To the church committee she recounted a story that expressed the tangle of despair and resolve that marked her new life. It was an account of a real (and repeated) experience, but it reads like a parable carefully guarded, shaped, and polished, a parable about her search for peace and her quest to be heard. When she was living with Theodore, she wrote,

frequently I went out wandering in the streets; night after night I walked, with my waterproof cloak on, and would go back and creep into the basement and lie down anywhere, feeling utterly wretched; once I went away from home, thinking that I would not come back, but I found that I had left my purse at home, and had to return; Mr. Tilton owns a lot in Greenwood [Cemetery], and there I have two babies; I went there with my waterproof cloak on, and with the hood over my head, and lay down on the two graves, and felt peace; I had been there but a little while before the keeper of the grounds ordered me off; I paid no attention to him; I did not regard his order until he came again in a few moments and said, "I order you off these grounds; do you hear me?" I rose on my feet and said: "If there is one spot on earth that is mine, it is these two graves"; and he actually bowed down before me in apology; though he was a common workman, it was very hearty, and it was very grateful to me: he said, "I did not know that these were yours"; and he left me; I stayed there on the little graves the rest of the day.

The peace that she found on her babies' graves was a source of strength for speaking firmly to the male groundskeeper who had spoken harshly to her, just as the peace she found with Beecher was a source of strength for finally standing up to and leaving her husband. Repeating the story to the gentlemen of the investigating committee was also perhaps a means of gathering strength for the interrogation itself.[14]

If we look closely at her parable several interesting things emerge. The apparently gratuitous repetition of the detail that she had her "waterproof cloak on" conveys unintentionally her sense that when she was outside wandering she felt safer, more protected, than she did inside her house, where she would lie down in the basement "feeling wretched." She is frank about her experience of wretchedness, but does not grasp how bound she was to the place that made her wretched. Abused but used to the abuse, she could not quit her life even when she thought she was leaving once and for all: she "had to return" because of the forgotten purse.

In imagination, however, she dispossesses Theodore of his property even as she submits to his power to make her return home. She tells us that he owned the cemetery lot at Greenwood. She sneaks up to it "with the hood over her head" like a prowler, then lies on the graves to take possession. The groundskeeper, Theodore's stand-in, orders her off, but she summons the strength (no doubt partly because the actual groundskeeper is her social inferior) to stand up and inform him that this spot on earth "is mine," not Theodore's. It is her land because she has given her own, not Theodore's, babies to it. She is then free as the proprietor to lie down on the graves as long as she wishes. But the passage does not just signal a personal empowerment through ownership, indeed expropriation, of a piece of earth. It also expresses the dubious freedom of lying down, wrapped in a shroud-like cloak, on a cemetery plot. Feelings of liberation from Theodore mix with an older yearning for deliverance from her earthly travail.

Theodore Tilton's ideological commitment to intense, demonstrative friendships between friends of the same and opposite sexes gave Beecher and Elizabeth Tilton the social and psychic space they needed to attempt to create a friendship of their own. They conversed in her upstairs parlor (with the door sometimes closed, Beecher testified, to keep out her children's noise), took long walks holding hands, rode through the park (curtains sometimes closed) in Beecher's buggy, strolled through photograph galleries, talked about books and religion. Elizabeth, in Beecher's public judgment, was a "genius of religious sentiment" who in another era would have had "inspirations and ecstatic visions." As Theodore Tilton's ideas shifted during the 1860s toward skepticism about God, the church, and

14. Marshall, *True History,* pp. 196–97, 212–13.

(*Left*): Portrait of Elizabeth Tilton by William Page, N.A. Reprinted from Paxton Hibben, *Henry Ward Beecher*. (*Right*): Item from *New York Daily Graphic*, 22 July 1874.

MRS. THEODORE TILTON.

Mrs. Theodore Tilton, who is just at present an object of no little public curiosity, is the sister of Mr. Richards who was so long and favorably known in the business departments of the *Independent* and *Nation*, and subsequently the *Evening Post*. She is about forty years of age, a brunette, rather below medium height, inclined to stoutness, and although she cannot be said to be decidedly handsome is at least pretty, and so pleasing in her manner as to enhance largely her personal charms. Low-voiced, possessing a very sweet smile, and characterized by a constant and irrepressible yearning for sympathy and tenderness, she may be said to be an excellent type of the emotional woman, who, if she errs, does so through an excess of heart and not through vulgar passion. Mrs. Tilton has four children, the eldest now a young lady.

the institution of marriage, Elizabeth and Beecher were left behind to share the terrain of a romantic, sentimental, and revivalistic liberal Protestantism.[15]

The point for such liberal enthusiasts was to feel your faith as you felt the wind whistling through your hair. The religious was not the transcendent, but the natural infused with passion and vitality. Beecher's was a Gospel of Love, as he called it, in which God's wrathful judgment and the believer's scrutinizing conscience were replaced by God's universal acceptance and humankind's joyful response. It was in this ideological soil that radical utopian assaults on marriage had grown up in the early nineteenth century. Victoria Woodhull and the few other remaining postbellum advocates of "free love" justified sexual union outside marriage by invoking this standard split between love and law: the spirit had to be allowed to blow where it might; it could not be restricted by any legal convenant such

15. *TT v. HWB,* 2:893.

as marriage. Marriages without love should be ended; true love should not be suppressed simply because two lovers were not married, or married to other parties. This was not an endorsement of promiscuity; it was a call for the free experience of true love. In Beecher's religion as in Woodhull's, it was inappropriate to feel guilt about following one's feelings. In practice, of course, Beecher, like Elizabeth Tilton, felt enormous guilt, a "feeling" that led him to insist all the more on a liberal doctrine that subordinated conscience, judgment, and guilt to good, healthy feeling. Like many other first-generation immigrants to the world of liberal Protestant naturalism, he could never quite appropriate the freeing grace he frantically preached.

Meanings

Whether or not Beecher and Tilton consummated their love in sexual intercourse, they acted out an intimacy that forces us to rethink the simple connection we usually make between Christianity and bourgeois society. We typically assume that Christianity—especially the this-worldly, therapeutic faith of Henry Ward Beecher—operated as a firm support for bourgeois social norms, including the norm of the middle-class insular family. Certainly Christianity did function in a general way to buttress the family. But there was always an incipient cultural radicalism in the Gospel of Love, even in its neatly packaged Plymouth Church form. In his own living Henry Ward Beecher joined Elizabeth Tilton in stretching postbellum bourgeois boundaries to permit intimate friendships across gender and family lines. They did everything they could to persuade themselves that their love was religiously inspired and justified. They too subscribed to the mainstream assumption that Christianity could never undermine, but only defend, bourgeois social norms.

But in fact their Christianity was double-edged, as they may at times have suspected: it had a respectable, obedient side that celebrated middle-class family ideals, and it had a defiant, Romantic side that could slice right through them. We have to see Beecher, Tilton, and their therapeutic brand of Christianity not simply as a religious reflection of some seamless bourgeois culture, not simply as surrounded, tamed, and contained by culture, but as a potentially unpredictable force that could sometimes contradict culture. And we have to see bourgeois culture as deeply divided against itself, enforcing strict rules of "character" development while at the same time—and nowhere more extensively than in liberal Protestantism—sanctioning the much more open-ended flowering of "personality." Beecher's religion of intimacy was countercultural not in being antibourgeois, but in being an embourgeoisement of the Romantic assault on bourgeois convention.[16]

It was inevitable that Elizabeth and Henry would run afoul of convention for two reasons. First, in a culture increasingly committed to a commercialized publicity system for its sense of solidarity, agencies of information had emerged that privileged novel and, whenever possible, sensational revelations. Beecher and Theodore Tilton had themselves mastered this system of influence, supported themselves by keeping their names in the public light, so they must always have known that other publicists would seek influence by trying to discredit them. When Theodore decided the time had come to strike back at Henry, who he believed had been laboring behind the scenes to remove him from his editorship, the weapon of choice was publicity. And charges by Theodore against Henry were bound to stir profound interest because here were two famous writers and speakers who had public personas not just as celebrities in general, but as celebrity spokesmen for the private sphere, over which they were now at war. Two experts on the personal, each considering himself the proper protector of Elizabeth Tilton, who herself provoked extraordinary interest because she was not graspable simply as a woman in need of protection by a man. She was hard to "figure": which established category of female character could accommodate a selfless mother of four and Sunday School teacher who was a mystical "genius of religious sentiment," as Beecher put it, but also a woman who embraced intimate relations with a man not her husband?

Elizabeth Tilton stood at a point of particular tension in bourgeois culture. We have known for a long time that Christian reform impulses impelled nineteenth-century bourgeois women to cross the family threshold and enter the public realm. There they strove to develop their individual skills while uplifting, disciplining, and avoiding (what they often took to be) contamination by their frequently working-class charges. Some antebellum moralists had great difficulty accepting this new public vocation for women, but Henry Ward Beecher's older sister Catharine, among many others, eventually made it respectable: women had only to promise to keep affection and passion within the home, or else to suppress it altogether. Christianity posed a much more radical threat to bourgeois norms when

16. I have examined the development of "character" and "personality" in liberal Protestantism in "The Culture of Liberal Protestant Progressivism, 1875–1925," *Journal of Interdisciplinary History* 23 (Winter, 1993): 639–60.

it got women thinking not only about how they might save society, but about how they might save themselves by following love and friendship outside the marital compact. As long as a mother left home only to labor in the reform vineyard, she was not a major threat to the hegemony of bourgeois norms. If, however, she imagined herself to be an expressive being spiritually and emotionally tied to other men as well as women, as Christianity might always tempt her to do, bourgeois hegemony was truly in peril.

Even if Beecher and Tilton never did commit adultery, it was inevitable that someone would claim they did in order to clarify (not necessarily to bolster) social norms. Victoria Woodhull, who made the initial public charge, hoped to revolutionize social norms. She insisted on consistency: if Beecher was going to practice what she termed free love, he should follow her in preaching it. When confronted with that stark choice by Woodhull and the myriad accusers who followed in her train, Beecher (and Tilton) scampered back to respectability—Henry in a knowing, forgiving condescension toward her excessive attachment to him, Elizabeth in a silent, passive withdrawal from the web of publicity. Even Victoria Woodhull and Theodore Tilton lapsed into their own kind of cultural accommodation. In the wake of the trial a conservative wave inundated public discussions of family and sexuality; proponents of "free love" such as Woodhull and Tilton were now so far beyond the moral pale that they looked merely ridiculous. In their new incapacity to attract an audience for their own work they could occupy only the social role of deviant—each of them a convenient symbol of impropriety for the righteous middle class. Both Woodhull and Tilton soon chose exile over exclusion: Woodhull enacted a higher respectability by marrying a landed English nobleman, while Tilton moved to Paris where into the early twentieth century he wrote stories, played chess at sidewalk cafes, and entertained American tourists with tales of Whittier, Longfellow, and other writers he had known.

As a public event the Beecher-Tilton affair exhibited cultural meanings that lay beyond its meanings for individual actors. The Plymouth investigation of 1874, the civil trial of 1875, and all the printed discussions surrounding them operated as a vast catechetical enterprise. Newspapers tested and then taught one another new norms of exposure and sensation. For the mass public the press described a kaleidoscopic range of prescribed, proscribed, and as yet uncoded social practices and beliefs. In the act of informing people it formed them. It was a culture-shaping as well as a culture-reflecting event. Every disclosure was an implicit enactment: not always a prohibition or a permission, sometimes the seeding of a doubt, the planting of a hope, a hinting at confusion.

What did the trial disclose and teach about late Victorian culture? First of all, that it was a culture of celebrity, even though the participants in the trial did not all understand that it was, or grasp what that meant. The official court stenographer from the *Tribune* was forthright about his own confusion on the subject. He reported at the end of one wintery day of testimony that not even "slippery, sloppy sidewalks and a drizzling rainstorm" had prevented a large crowd from jamming the corridor leading to the courtroom. The crowd remained there all day even though "there was nothing to see but the closed doors of the court-room and two stalwart but shivering officers standing guard. There was nothing for them to hear but occasionally the faint murmur of lawyers' voices. Yet the crowd stood for hours upon the cold pavement, waiting Micawber-like for something to turn up. . . . Why they were there is one of those things past finding out." He could understand them scheming to get into the gallery, where they could participate by following the testimony. He could not get why they stayed in the hallway after all the scalped tickets (which went for $5) had been sold. It made no sense for them simply to *be* there in the penumbra. In fact they did not need "something to turn up" in the development of the case to feel that it was worthwhile freezing all day. All they needed was an end-of-the-day glimpse of one of the stars.[17]

The culture of celebrity was one manifestation of the culture of publicity that the trial both revealed and promoted. Dozens of reporters and artists covered it. The trial was about saving Beecher's national reputation, in which many men of means had substantial investments in the form of shares of his publishing concern and pews in his church; it was not just about persuading a jury to throw out the charges. But the key point is not the superficial observation that the trial was staged as a media event that could send him up or down the ladder of repute. The vital point is that publicity was becoming the culture's main medium of solidarity. Liberal individualism, a social theory and a daily practice of social relations, had

---

17. *TT v. HWB*, 1:231. Tickets were limited in number and distributed first come, first served, but they were not date-specific. Ticket holders therefore hoarded them in hopes of using (or selling) them on a day when the testimony was expected to be especially entertaining or memorable. This system produced a crush of visitors on certain days, a low turnout on others.

already devastated the community-based solidarity of the antebellum era. Beecher's nationally marketed sermons (not to mention his nationally marketed testimonials for such products as Chickering pianos, Pear's soap, Grover and Baker sewing machines, and Sapolio and Waltham watches) helped tie the culture together even as he preached, apparently, a merely laissez-faire gospel of individual feeling. Individual choice in one's feelings as in one's acts of consumption was compatible with social solidarity and stability. People could be united in their loyalty to a system of individual choice even if they did not all make the same choices. The system only required that designated (and, increasingly, celebrated) authorities such as Beecher define the outside boundaries of legitimate choosing. In the trial Beecher himself was chastised for choosing poorly, and he gladly accepted the mid-life correction.

Any national event of six-months' duration might have attracted broad attention and helped unite the country around its newspaper stands and reading rooms. The full cultural meaning of the trial emerges only when we look further into its distinctive shape. This event took place in a courtroom, a very particular kind of stage. The key actors were the lawyers. Witnesses such as Beecher might try to be expansive on the stand, but his attempts to interpret his role in his own way, complete with melodramatic body gestures and rhetorical digressions, were repeatedly undermined by his own attorneys as well as Tilton's. On the stage at Plymouth Church Beecher had the floor as long as he wished, and there he spun fine webs of feeling, sparking his three thousand worshippers to fits of laughter, applause, and weeping. His repeated plea was to go beyond logical analysis in the search for truth, beyond obedience to rules in the quest for fulfillment: dare to be vital, yearn to breathe the free air of nature, abandon the old-fashioned religious quest for rational demonstration. In the courtroom, by contrast, it was the lawyers who had the floor as long as they wished. And their favored theme was that logical analysis and rational demonstration (supported by often magnificent bursts of satiric oratory laced with classical and Shakespearean references) did lead to truth. The courtroom was a social space where virtually anything could be put on trial, including Plymouth Church. Beecher's own senior counsel, William Evarts, took the lead in passing negative judgment on the cult of feeling at Plymouth; Beecher had to sit quietly while Evarts expostulated on the "exaggeration not of fault, but of feeling" to which his client had given way in his conduct with Elizabeth Tilton as in his preaching at Plymouth. The court was a privileged sphere in which lawyers could speak endlessly and frankly on whatever subject they chose—the sole limitation being that they must not imperil their case.[18]

If the basic belief at Plymouth Church was that Christians attuned to their feelings could find God, the fundamental ideological tenet at the Brooklyn Court was that white male citizens could determine guilt or innocence by evaluating evidence and judging character. Beecher's trial was a massive sifting of evidence in the interest of proving or disproving his guilt, but also in the interest of reconfirming the legal process itself as the appropriate mechanism for resolving disputes about everyday life. Lawyers gathered the facts and presented them to twelve men of "character," who were thought able to assess the evidence and make nuanced judgments about the character of the witnesses. In a sense the trial promoted both an empiricist faith in truth-through-documentation and an essentialist, a priori faith in truth-through-authoritative-character. If the direct evidence did not add up to a decisive decision one way or the other, jurors could make up their minds on grounds of character. In the Beecher case, his lawyers appealed repeatedly to this standard: since the jurors knew Beecher's character to be pure in all of his other dealings, they could assume, in the absence of direct evidence, that he was also pure in this instance.[19]

Here the culture of publicity met a set of assumptions from an earlier era of imagined small-town community. The jurors did not actually know Beecher's character through personal acquaintance; they knew it from what they had heard about it or from watching his dramatizations of it on the Plymouth stage. Perhaps in a small-town environment, reputation did tend to correspond to real character. But in an urbanized society reputation floated free from actual social interactions; it could be marketed and rise and fall in value like a commodity. Of course the defense lawyers pretended that Brooklyn was still a small town in which everyone knew everything about everybody. The prosecution "would have you believe," Beecher's attorney intoned, "that the foremost man in the American pulpit, who lived in the blaze of noonday, who was known by every man and woman in Brooklyn, known to the school children, known to the serving girls, known to each poor negro that pursued his calling in the streets—that a man like this could be pursuing a secret amour in open day, that he should be debauched and live a year and a half in debauchery with a woman who

18. *TT v. HWB*, 3:791.
19. See, for example, *TT v. HWB*, 3:681.

worshiped God at his own altar, who took the bread of the covenant from his own hand. . . . Is it probable? Rational? Do you believe it?"[20]

Whether or not Beecher's lawyers believed their own rhetoric, they still preached a republican faith in a culture of character ruled by men of standing and patiently acquired wisdom. Beecher himself had long since abandoned that ideal, committing himself instead to a culture of personality in which authority resided in men of inspired feeling.[21] But the trial was not his forum, it was theirs, and the summations on both sides collaborated in disciplining him: each stressed the greatness of his character and agreed he was led astray by his passions and enthusiasms. The prosecution simply extended the point: in all likelihood he had succumbed to carnal tempta-tion, an expected lapse even for stalwart clergymen, as demonstrated by the long list of adulterous ministers through the centuries that the prosecu-tors put into the record.

The trial was a reprimand to Beecher and Elizabeth Tilton (as it was to Victoria Woodhull and Theodore Tilton, who were frequently vilified by lawyers and witnesses), even though Beecher's, and by extension Eliza-beth's, guilt was not proved. They had erred in loving too much, whatever the exact content of their lovemaking. Many observers then and since have argued that the trial therefore amounted to a ritual of cultural affirmation, a reassertion of central cultural norms. No doubt the trial did contribute its part to the moral belt-tightening of late 1870s America. But the cultural process is more paradoxical than that. The trial may have shored up tradi-tional practices while also unsettling their foundations. Beecher's lawyers may have argued for interpreting his career as the smooth growth of virtue and for seeing Brooklyn as governed by men immersed in a common pool of character. But several articulate witnesses, including one (Emma Moul-ton) whom the judge went out of his way to commend in his charge to the jury as a woman of high "moral character and worth," claimed he was a confessed adulterer. And at least three gentlemen of the jury were unable to discredit their testimony. What could a mass audience conclude but that Henry Ward Beecher might well have perjured himself, as the prosecution claimed? What else could they conclude but that he might well have been sleeping with Elizabeth Tilton, and that even if he had, the world would not end? The trial put liberal Protestant preaching of the Beecher-style "religion of love" on a kind of cultural probation, but a resurgence of

20. *TT v. HWB*, 3:561.
21. See my discussion of Beecher's formulation of "character" and "personality" in "The Culture of Liberal Protestant Progressivism, 1875–1925."

traditionalist themes in public discourse does not prove that cultural practice followed suit. The trial could, theoretically, have had equal and opposite effects: stirring up traditionalist defenders of a fixed moral order, while
also promoting liberal attitudes, such as the view that moral decision making was a matter of individual taste. The court, like commentators in the
broader culture, could put intimacy on trial, but not without giving intimacy a widely exposed trial run.[22]

The same holds true of the common belief that a legal proceeding was
a privileged pathway to the truth about personal relations. Anyone who
reads even a fraction of the Beecher-Tilton transcript will know that the
lawyers promoted a belief that the piling up of every possible shred of
circumstantial evidence would ultimately yield "the true story." But the
piling on of testimony may also have had the opposite result: the alerting
of many readers to the possibility that the truth was perspectival, that the
judge's final charge to the jury was ludicrous. He gave them fifty-four
separate things to think about, including a long list of "facts" for them to
"determine." But he was the first to acknowledge that in determining the
facts the jury would have to make assumptions about the credibility of
witnesses. A trial of six-months' duration ended by a hung jury, which
after a week's deliberation told the judge that "it is a question of fact, a
question of the veracity of witnesses on which we do not agree, your
Honor," may have helped prepare some Americans to give up the objectivist
faith that truth was "out there" waiting to be discovered. Neither the scandal nor even the trial was a single quake-like event with a set of outcomes
all moving in the same moral or epistemological direction. The trial and
scandal were not straightforward happenings but symbolic clearing houses
in which contending forces were galvanized. And they were a complex of
dramatic narratives in which readers could—like Elizabeth Tilton curling
up with *Griffith Gaunt*—experience a medley of desires, doubts, dangers.[23]

Some contemporary observers clamored for the court to hear the testimony of Elizabeth Tilton on the grounds that without it, the whole truth

22. *TT v. HWB*, 3:1032.
23. *TT v. HWB*, 3:1041. E. L. Godkin, writing in the *Nation* (6 August 1874, pp. 86–87)
before the public trial began, disputed what he considered the widespread view that trials
were effective forums for establishing truth claims. The "rules of evidence" prevented information relevant to a determination of truth from getting to the jury. The important point for
my purposes is not whether law courts were in fact good at ferreting out the truth, but
whether people believed they were, and were encouraged by lawyers, newspapers, magazines,
and other opinion-makers to believe they were. Godkin, writing in an effort to quash what
he felt was a widespread error, documents the pervasiveness of that viewpoint.

would never be known. But the exclusion of her testimony was quite compatible with the popular view that law courts were arenas for the full disclosure and patient establishment of truth. All it took was to categorize her as unreliable, as one whose speech was controlled by others. And since she had on that single night in 1870 changed her story twice, she was widely believed to be untrustworthy. At trial's end the defense and prosecution took turns avowing their readiness to have had her testify, but both sides had in fact been nervous about the risks and she never took the stand. Near the end of the testimony Elizabeth tried to be heard anyway, and her silencing by the court suggests another basic cultural meaning of the trial.

"One of the most dramatic scenes of the trial occurred at the opening of the day's session," the *Chicago Tribune* correspondent reported on 3 May 1875.

The court had no sooner been organized than [Mrs. Tilton], rising and facing the Judge, cried out in her low voice, a little tremulous from embarrassment: "Judge Neilson." The Judge heard without distinguishing her, and Mr. Tice, a spectator, repeated her call, at the same time pointing toward her. Mrs. Tilton again spoke up, saying: "Your Honor, I have a communication which I hope your Honor will read aloud." . . . As soon as Mrs. Tilton's voice had been heard, a hush had fallen upon the audience, and every eye had become fixed upon her slight figure, the only one standing in the centre of the room. Her face flushed a little when she perceived the general attention which she had attracted.[24]

The journalist told the story as a gendered drama of power and recognition: it required a male spectator to get Judge Neilson to notice her, even though everyone else in the nearly all-male gallery had already isolated her with silent stares. They awaited her further words, to be spoken not by her but by the judge. But after reading her message privately the judge refused to repeat it aloud or give it to the press. The next day Tilton released it herself, thereby testifying in the trial-by-newspaper that proceeded alongside the trial-by-lawyers. It was widely believed at the time that Beecher's defense attorneys had put her up to the drafting and releasing of the statement in order to make it appear that any testimony she might give in court would exculpate him. She would be spared, meanwhile, the drama (and risk to the defense) of cross-examination. Whatever the exact provenance of her statement, it very likely expresses some of her true feelings about her predicament.

"I ask the privilege from you for a few words in my own behalf," she said.

24. "Beecher," *Chicago Tribune,* 4 May 1875, p. 2, col. 1.

I feel very deeply the injustice of my position in the law and before the Court. . . . I have been so sensible of the power of my enemies that my soul cries out before you and the gentlemen of the jury that they beware how, by a divided verdict, they consign to my children a false and irrevocable stain upon their mother. For five years past I have been the victim of circumstances most cruel and unfortunate, struggling from time to time only for a place to live honorably and truthfully. Released for some months from the will by whose power, unconsciously, I crimi-nated myself again and again, I declare solemnly before you, without fear of man and with faith in God, that I am innocent of the crime charged against me. I would like to tell my whole sad story truthfully, to acknowledge the frequent falsehoods wrung from me through compulsion, though at the same time unwilling to reveal the secret of my married life, which only the vital importance of my position makes necessary.[25]

Victimized, cruelly treated, but determined to protect her children from "a stain upon their mother." Prone in the past, because of Theodore's influence, to speak falsely, but fully capable now of rising to speak the truth while shielding "the secret of my married life" from undue exposure. Whatever the validity of her refusing all responsibility for the multiple changes of mind, she composed a moving plea to be allowed to speak, instead of having merely to listen. It is plain that one of the profound messages of the trial was that under the law, not just in custom, a woman was not allowed to speak like a man. As the judge told her in his official response, it was one thing for a husband to testify about a wife, as Theodore had done at great length, quite another for a wife to testify about a husband. There were, to be sure, some legal questions even about the former, but the latter was barred by an actual statute of 1867 "expressly declar[ing] the wife to be incompetent as a witness for or against the husband."[26]

Yet the message of the trial transcript was still more complex. It was not only that the law barred Elizabeth Tilton from speaking, as the judge claimed. (Close readers of the testimony knew, as the judge did not point out, that upon consent of both counsels the law could be waived.) The point was that her voice, whether heard or unheard, was not considered credible. The men on both sides of the case—principals and lawyers alike —collaborated in discrediting her so that even if she did speak, she would not be believed. And the discrediting took the form not only of blame for her changeability but of praise for her saintly and mystical transcendence. She was too pure for mundane affairs, too high-pitched spiritually to render competent judgments about the affairs of the world (of men). Her voice in

25. "Beecher," *Chicago Tribune,* 5 May 1875, p. 2, col. 2.
26. "Beecher," *Chicago Tribune,* 5 May 1875, p. 2, col. 2.

"Mrs. Tilton Addressing the Court." *Frank Leslie's Illustrated Newspaper,* 22 May 1875.

such matters was literally not her own; it was a vocal channel for whichever man was at that moment speaking through her.

Of course it is possible that Elizabeth Tilton was an inveterate liar. It is more likely that she was incapable of telling a certain kind of truth. On the question whether she had committed adultery with Beecher, she may have found it difficult to answer one way or the other—or to always answer the same way—because she felt the question was too simplistic. She knew that her heart was divided. She knew, as she told the Plymouth Church investigators in 1874, that her relation to Beecher was pure and she also knew that she had dishonored her husband by withholding from him "the all of my nature." When forced to choose a yes or no on the adultery question she sometimes said yes, sometimes no, perhaps depending on whether she felt more keenly the promise of being "aroused in myself," the "consciousness of being more" with Henry, or the guilt of disloyalty to Theodore. Indeed, three years after the trial, in a last public statement before embracing her final silence on the case, she reversed herself again and claimed that she and Beecher had indeed committed adultery. By that time no one was listening, she was mocked in the press, and she marched resolutely off the historical stage.[27]

The important point is that the male principals in the trial taught a mass audience—or confirmed that audience in its prior belief—that a woman was less liable than a man to speak reasonably and truthfully. It was futile, they implied, to put a woman like Elizabeth Tilton on the stand, because her words were not rooted in the sort of controlled discourse that made possible the rational operations of the world of affairs. It may not be pressing the matter too far to suggest that by endorsing the figure of the irrational and irresponsible (however spiritual and vital) female, many bourgeois men reassured themselves that their own workaday web of legal and social conventions was firmly grounded in a natural, not merely a habitual, order of things. Of course here too the trial may have had more than one impact and meaning: some men and women nodded their consent at the official silencing of Elizabeth Tilton, others winced and bemoaned the injustice, even if not the malleability, of a starkly gendered cultural tradition.

Many commentators during and after the trial understood that the Beecher-Tilton affair was a culture-shaping and culture-disclosing event, and of course their commentary was part of the process of shaping and disclosing. In July 1875, after the conclusion of the trial, Frank Leslie published an editorial in his *Illustrated Newspaper* entitled "A Social Revival." It marked a sharp departure from his editorials of the previous summer, which had commented upon Theodore Tilton's initial accusation and the subsequent Plymouth Church investigation. In those early pieces Leslie could see only the individual dimension of the scandal: although the evidence was not all in, Beecher would probably be revealed to be another in the long line of pastor-hypocrites who couldn't distinguish comforting his female parishioners from seducing them. In "A Social Revival," however, he examined the cultural meaning of a major historical drama, and instructed his readers in how to interpret it. He began by noting that most business depressions in the past—he was probably referring to the panics of the 1830s and 1850s—had produced religious revivals, which allowed people at least to purify their souls if they could not make a living. But

27. "Mrs. Tilton Pleads Guilty," *New York Times,* 16 April 1878, p. 1, cols. 1–4; "Scandal," *Chicago Tribune,* 18 April 1878, p. 1, col. 3. The *Brooklyn Daily Eagle* obituary of 1897 inadvertently demonstrates that her 1878 confession of adultery with Beecher had little lasting impact. It claims that after the trial she made no further public statements.

the serious recession of 1873 had been prevented from having the usual moral effect because of "one wretched tale of huge dimensions, whose shadow extended to every corner of the land."

The Beecher scandal, Leslie asserted, had pushed history off its usual cyclical track of selfish excess followed by spiritual repentance. Instead it had provoked a new kind of revival, a culture-wide secular reformation to stop "the crusade of free love, or rather, unbridled license," which had penetrated "even to the church doors, and was knocking for admission to the sanctuary. It was feared that even those hallowed premises were invaded by the fanatics of the new gospel of lust, for a certain mawkish mode of expression had made itself manifest in the pulpit to the peril of pure doctrine." The very trial which had "threatened to scandalize Christendom" might ironically result in "an overthrow of the conspiracy against purity, and in establishing the supremacy of the family and the home. False ideas of society have been ventilated during the last six months as never before, and have been held up to the light to show that they are the merest drivel and insanity. No doubt this has been done at a terrible cost, but the price, great as it is, will be repaid in the increased sanctities which for the future will surround our social organization." The trial could be interpreted as a kind of inoculation: exposing the moral body to the microbe of impurity in order to provoke a retaliation by the cultural immune system.[28]

Leslie's editorial was utterly traditional in its plea for moral probity and family honor, but quite subtle in its recognition that revivals would now have to be "social," that is secular, rather than "religious," if they were to bolster the old moral order that the "gospel of lust" had mocked. Beecher's religion of feeling, which ungenerous contemporary commentators called, among other things, the "religion of gush," the "religion of lechery," and "cream-cheese religion," was ill equipped to provide a foundation for a strict, unchanging morality. It was too devoted to personal growth and to open-ended, intimate sentiment. Yet Leslie was agile enough to concede that whatever his hopes for a moral reformation, the trial had exacted a "great" and undetermined "price." That concession to the reality and depth of cultural instability sat awkwardly beside his strained prediction of "increased sanctities." The Beecher-Tilton affair brought drastic changes to many individual lives, but it also helped detach American culture from its familiar mooring and set it on a new course that no contemporary navigator could chart.

28. "A Social Revival," *Frank Leslie's Illustrated Newspaper,* 31 July 1875, pp. 358–59.

3 CONSTRUCTING AND CONTESTING "MASS CULTURE"

(*Top*): Milano Family Grocery Store, 9550 Avenue N, Chicago, ca. 1930. Courtesy of the Southeast Chicago Collection, Urban Culture and Documentary Program, Columbia College, Chicago. (*Bottom*): National Tea Company Store, 1300 block of 53d Street, Chicago, 1946. Photo by Elizabeth Felsenthal Kornblith. Courtesy of the Chicago Historical Society, ICHi 20831.

5 The Class Experience of Mass Consumption

Workers as Consumers in Interwar America

Lizabeth Cohen

The title of this essay, "The Class Experience of Mass Consumption," may sound like a contradiction in terms: mass consumption is usually meant to suggest that people are consuming as a mass, without class distinctions; that through the widespread accessibility of products Americans have become one mass market and hence one social community. This conceptualization surrounds us constantly—in the form, for example, of advertisements assuring all Americans that "This Bud's for you" or that Merit Ultra Light cigarettes will help you "Go from rags to enriches"—and has become the twentieth-century expression of America's commitment to its own exceptionalism. A classless society that in the nineteenth century was assured by republican rights and equal access to suffrage (at least for men), in the twentieth century is supposedly achieved by equal access to the fruits of our consumer society. Implicit in what, then, has become as much an ideological commitment as a sociological phenomenon is the assumption that through mass consumption people are effortlessly incorporated into a society where almost everyone can identify with the "middle class" by virtue of his or her access to a free market of goods.

Interestingly, the assumed benefits of a classless liberal society have changed little between the nineteenth century, when producers defined equality through political participation, and the twentieth, when consumers have expected to achieve equality through consumption. Although the twentieth-century version of American egalitarianism seems to imply an equality more economic than political, the broad accessibility of standardized material goods is intended to have significant political implications. The political ideal of the classless society—whether achieved through widespread electoral or economic participation—remains a harmonious

I presented an earlier version of this essay at the Social Science History Association Meetings, November 1988. I would like to thank the panel and audience members for their suggestions. I am also grateful to the Program in Technology and Society at Carnegie Mellon University for a grant to carry out research and to Jennifer Keene for research assistance. Editorial comments from Casey Blake, Herrick Chapman, Richard Fox, Jackson Lears, and Chris Wilson helped me immeasurably in writing this essay.

community of individuals, free of class-based social and political discord. Citizens within this society accordingly attribute their failures to personal rather than class inequities, their successes to individual achievement rather than class privileges. The manufacturers, merchandisers, advertisers, employers, and social critics who promoted this ideal of twentieth-century America as an egalitarian mass consumer society also counted among its benefits more pragmatic attributes, such as a larger market for mass-produced goods and a convenient strategy for motivating workers to perform. Mass consumption seemed to point the way toward fulfilling German sociologist Werner Sombart's 1906 portrayal of America as a place where Socialism would falter on "roast beef and apple pie," or, by the interwar era, automobiles and refrigerators.[1]

In the late twentieth century, Americans can congratulate themselves that they own more cars, telephones, and televisions than any other nationality in the world, but such comparative statistics mask some important questions about the reality of this consumer society. Before assuming that mass consumption has in fact led to the fulfillment of the ideal of classlessness, it is important to ask how well distributed in the society consumer goods actually are, and even more important, if the culture surrounding consumption is indeed a classless—rather than a class-specific—one. In other words, do people feel that through the process of consuming they are denying, or affirming, class identity? Does the purchase of a new car make a factory worker feel like a full-fledged participant in an egalitarian society or merely a working-class person who has managed to buy a new car, one marketed perhaps to his distinctive class tastes and financed in a characteristically working-class way, with longer and higher interest payments?

Relatedly, one needs to analyze the larger political implications of consumer behavior for the society as a whole, whether participation invests individuals in the status quo, fuels social discontent through raising unsatisfiable material desires, or provides people with a new way of expressing social and cultural differences. Analysts of consumerism argue, in fact, over the power relations involved in consumption: at the extremes, some insist that the expansion of mass consumption has contributed to the hegemonic authority of social elites who seek a depoliticized, homogeneous culture built around the consent of subordinate classes, while other critics empha-

---

1. Werner Sombart, *Why Is There No Socialism in the United States?* (White Plains, N.Y.: M. E. Sharpe, Inc., 1976).

size the free agency that people exercise as they consume and the variety of consumption patterns and meanings that occur in our society as a result. In between are analysts like myself who believe people make choices and provide their own meanings when consuming, but that those choices and meanings are carefully circumscribed by economic and political realities. In this last conception, consumers potentially can participate in private, class, and mass worlds at the same time. The consumer society can fuel, rather than suppress, class-based inequality, even though individuals have more autonomy within that culture than hegemonists often suggest.[2]

This essay cannot resolve all these questions definitively, and I should acknowledge at the outset that these are not questions that are easily answered at all. Understanding the experience of the masses with mass consumption is crucial to conceptualizing twentieth-century American culture and society, and yet it is much harder to identify and analyze than the ideas of elite ideologues of mass consumption. In this essay I will take an historical approach to the problem in the expectation that the passage of time has made cultural trends like these more visible, and in the conviction that the formative era of "the consumer society" during the 1920s and 1930s holds the key to understanding the larger significance of mass consumption in this century.

As a social historian, I bring some particular methodologies to this cultural investigation. My starting point is that ordinary people's experiences matter in interpreting a cultural activity such as consumption, even if the evidence they have left behind is more elusive than that left by elites. In place of more traditional cultural sources such as personal papers and literary texts, I peruse a wide array of evidence searching for insights into people's cultural activity, everything from contemporary sociological studies, oral histories, and newspapers to the records of organizations, businesses, and government agencies that impinged on individuals' lives. By moving back and forth between the personal, such as an oral history, and the public, such as the files of an employer or government department, I try to assess the interaction between individual choice and larger societal structure. In this study of mass consumption among Chicago workers, for example, such a strategy allows me to analyze how workers reshaped their cultural attitudes and actions during the 1930s, given the way economic depression and New Deal policies altered the institutional structure of their

2. For a useful discussion of the debate over the hegemony of mass consumption, see Richard Butsch, *For Fun and Profit* (Philadelphia: Temple University Press, 1989), Introduction.

lives. This kind of socially-based cultural analysis, moreover, can only be done by focusing on a particular population in a particular place. The historian has to be able to link sources—and the cultural activity they reveal—to actors who are well situated socially and economically. This does not mean, however, that the historian can only deal with homogeneous behavior. Wherever possible, I try to build comparisons into my analysis—between groups and across different times and settings—to sharpen my portrait of one popular experience by contrasting it with others. Rather than making the individual person or text exemplary, this kind of cultural history searches for patterns of cultural attitudes and behavior, and assesses their distinctiveness over time and in relation to other groups and the larger society.

In this essay I will argue that examining the way working-class people in an industrial city like Chicago reacted to mass consumption at a critical time in its expansion, during the interwar years, reveals that mass and class were not always at odds. For in that era at least, even as workers increasingly participated in mass consumption—particularly through chain stores and the standard brands they promoted—and mass culture like the radio, they did not deny their existing class and ethnic identities nor find themselves unconsciously incorporated into middle-class society. In fact, by the 1930s, workers even used common experiences resulting from their increased exposure to mass culture to forge the first permanent industrial unions in American history under the auspices of the Congress of Industrial Organizations (CIO). Moreover, as they watched the neighborhood and community institutions that had disseminated mass culture during the 1920s and early 1930s decline with changes in the economy and government policy, Chicago's working people fought to save them through class-based unions and electoral politics. This process suggests that workers were well aware that the political impact of mass culture depended on who controlled its distribution—locally-owned stores and theaters or corporate chains and studios. Motivated by their own ideal of political economy, which I call "moral capitalism"—the belief that capitalism was not corrupt in itself so long as it operated according to standards of morality and fairness—Chicago workers struggled to keep their own consumption within "working-class consumption communities." Their success or failure bears directly on whether postwar America became the classless ideal, or whether, as preliminary evidence suggests, the liberal consumer model persisted more as ideology than reality.

The first- and second-generation eastern and southern Europeans who worked in Chicago's mass production factories and lived in the city's ethnic, working-class neighborhoods were first exposed to many aspects of mass consumption during the 1920s. In that decade, manufacturers and advertisers aggressively promoted standard brand goods, while improved packaging methods, such as the wider use of cellulose wrappings, made mass-produced products more available, particularly through the chain stores which mushroomed during the twenties. Chains, which had been growing slowly since the mid–nineteenth century, suddenly underwent unprecedented expansion: in the seven years from 1920 to 1927, for example, the sales volume of chain stores tripled on the average, and in a case such as Walgreen's Drugs, grew to twenty times greater.[3] But although mass producers and distributors envisioned a "consumer revolution" that soon would have all Americans buying the same mass-produced goods from the same chain stores, workers like these ethnic Chicagoans developed their own distinctive pattern of consuming the new, standardized products designed for mass consumption.

Working-class people still felt comfortable buying in bulk out of barrels and sacks on the local grocer's floor, and to the extent that they did consume standard brand goods, they purchased them through these neighborhood shopkeepers, who often shared their ethnicity. Buying Del Monte canned goods from the familiar Italian grocer on the corner, along with other items in bulk, did not undermine workers' existing ethnic and class identity as it might have if they were purchased from an anonymous clerk at the A & P in the presence of strangers from all social spheres. Because their early consumption of mass-produced goods was mediated in this way, workers were not drawn into what has been labeled a "national consumption community" or "middle-class mass market" nearly as much as commonly assumed both then and now.[4]

Workers avoided chain stores and the standardized products they promoted because they both preferred and needed to preserve the social rela-

3. John P. Nichols, *The Chain Store Tells Its Story* (New York: Institute of Distribution, 1940), pp. 82–85.

4. For more in-depth discussion of workers' experience with mass consumption during the 1920s, see chapter 3 of my book, *Making a New Deal: Industrial Workers in Chicago, 1919–1939* (New York: Cambridge University Press, 1990) and my article, "Encountering Mass Culture at the Grassroots: The Experience of Chicago Workers in the 1920s," *American Quarterly* 41 (Spring 1989): 6–33.

tions they had established around consumption. For the many ethnic work-ing-class women who controlled family purchasing, the local store served as a social center and the means through which they perpetuated the food-ways that remained the core of ethnic culture. These working-class women and their families also had an economic dependence on the local grocer that the chain store, with its promise of "cash and carry" savings, could not compete with. Working-class people were dependent on credit from their local storekeepers during the seasonal and cyclical periods when they were laid off, and even between paychecks when they were employed. Ties of culture and credit, then, kept these workers loyal to the merchants of their ethnic communities.

Chain store management, moreover, recognized workers' reluctance to abandon their long-standing commercial relationships—even for a savings in price that experts estimated to be 10 percent in Chicago—and helped reinforce this preference by concentrating their stores in heavily trafficked locations in middle-class and upper-class neighborhoods where people were more favorable to chains. In Chicago, for example, two-thirds of the more than five hundred A & P and National Tea grocery stores of the late 1920s were located in neighborhoods of above average economic status. Similarly, in Atlanta, one chain store served 191 families in the "best" areas of town, while in the "third best" and "poorest" areas combined, the ratio was one store for every 740 families.[5] Chain store managers understood that just as the survival of working-class people depended on their provin-cial community connections, success for middle-class people required the opposite, with an openness to geographical mobility and national standards and fashions. Standardization in material life put the middle classes at ease as they climbed corporate ladders and improved their addresses.

5. Tabulations of A & P and National Tea grocery stores are based on *Chicago Telephone Directory,* Alphabetical and Classified, 1927, and *Polk's Directory of Chicago, 1928–29;* stores located in the census areas with the help of Charles S. Newcomb, *Street Address Guide by Census Area of Chicago, 1930* (Chicago: University of Chicago Press, 1933); identification of census tracts by economic level through "Economic Status of Families Based on Equivalent Monthly Rentals," Burgess Papers, Box 51, Folder 8, University of Chicago Special Collections (UCSC). For the distribution of chain stores in Atlanta, see Guy C. Smith, "Selective Selling Decreases Costs: Market Analysis Enables Seller to Choose His Customer, Saving Costly Distribution Wastes," *Chicago Commerce,* 14 April 1928, 24. Also see W. G. Marshall, "Know Your City! A Chain Store Executive Stresses the Importance of Constant Study of Local Developments," *Chain Store Age* 3 (March 1927): 61–64, 132; "The Science of Chain Store Locations," *Chain Store Progress* 1 (March 1929): 5; Charles Handelman, "We're Always Ready for More Stores," *Chain Store Age (General Merchandising Edition)* 6 (July 1930): 7–8, 96–98.

Furthermore, when workers purchased consumer items such as canned tomatoes or even a phonograph or a radio, they frequently used them to reinforce existing social identities: to continue to make a family recipe for spaghetti sauce when fresh tomatoes were not available during Chicago's winter, to play phonograph records of music from the old country on new American victrolas, or to listen to ethnic broadcasts such as Polish Hour on a local, noncommercial radio station like WCFL, the "Voice of Labor." The viability during the 1920s of small distributors like the independent merchant and the low-frequency, nonprofit radio station meant that workers' introduction to mass consumption and mass culture came on familiar ground.

By the early 1930s, however, the context in which workers experienced mass consumption began to change. To begin with, chain stores, confident of their hold over the middle-class market, became more aggressive about conquering the working-class market. They did so primarily by crowding out independent stores. On the supply end, they pressured manufacturers and wholesalers to engage in "selective selling," which meant increasing special privileges and pricing to large purchasers and shunning stores with poor credit ratings.[6] At the point of distribution, chains widened their own scope, leaving less of the market to small stores. Whereas originally little more than a standardized stock had distinguished the chain grocery or drug store from the independent one, that changed as soda fountains, cigars, and sundries joined drugs at Walgreen's, and baked goods, dairy products, vegetables, and finally meat found a place alongside groceries at the A & P, as managers developed the "combination grocery store" and later the self-service supermarket in the mid-1930s.[7] Chain stores also began to target the many small independent stores within working-class neighborhoods. As early as 1930, an A & P district supervisor told the manager of one of his Chicago stores which had just begun to sell fresh produce: "There is a Fruit store (independently owned) in our block of

6. Smith, "Selective Selling Decreases Costs," p. 13.

7. Kitty Joy Jamison, "The Drug Business," 1932, Burgess Papers, Box 157, Folder 2, UCSC; *Walgreen's Pepper Pod,* June 1951, p. 13; "A & P Study," *The Progressive Grocer,* February 1970, 12; National Tea Company, *Annual Report, 1929;* "Supreme Court of the District of Columbia in Equity No. 37623, United States of America Petitioner v. Swift & Company. Armour & Company, Morris & Company, Wilson & Company, Inc., and The Cudahy Packing Co., et al., Defendants, On Petitions of Swift and Company, and Its Associate Defendants, and Armour & Company, and Its Associate Defendants, for Modification of Decree of February 27, 1920 Petitioning Defendants Statement of the Case," 1930, pp. 18–29; on the development of self-service supermarkets, see note 21 below.

stores which must go broke at any cost. . . . The Great A & P will last longer than those people."[8]

Neighborhood storekeepers in working-class areas now faced aggressive chain competitors who were also working hard to overcome their poor public image as outsiders and "parasites," accused of depriving independent merchants of their lifeblood and draining money out of a community while giving little in return. Mr. J. C. Penney argued to other Chicago chain operators in 1930 that "the extent to which chain store units fulfill their obligations as citizens of the communities in which they operate is, to my mind, the measure by which their future success . . . will be determined." He particularly promoted "good citizenship" as the way to win "the wage earning family" who was unwilling to favor "a savings of from one to twenty per cent on its daily outlay against a friendly feeling toward the merchants with whom the wife or husband may be doing business." Knowing how integral local merchants were to the life of a neighborhood, he urged his peers to develop "community personality": get to know customers, involve yourself in local affairs, and support worthy charities. By the end of the thirties, the trade magazine *Chain Store Age* had developed Awards of Merit for Community Builders and in one issue singled out Harold F. May, manager of an F. W. Woolworth Store on Milwaukee Avenue in Chicago's oldest Polish neighborhood, for spearheading a community organization for "civic betterment."[9] Where the independent merchant had enjoyed an advantage—as community leader—chains mimicked him. Where he was limited—in size, stock, pricing and location—they strove to surpass him.

The challenge of chains to independent stores might not have succeeded very well, given the strength of workers' loyalty to their local merchants, had the Great Depression not altered circumstances so drastically. The reality, however, was that small stores proved far more vulnerable financially during the depression. Small retailers, particularly the ethnic neighborhood grocers who predominated in a city like Chicago, had always led a

8. Maurice Van Hollebeke to Mr. William Green, American Federation of Labor, 26 May 1930, Fitzpatrick Papers, Box 18, Folder 127, Chicago Historical Society (CHS), p. 2.

9. J. C. Penney, "Are Chain Stores Good Citizens? A Test of Human Relations," *Chicago Commerce,* 4 October 1930, 7–8; "What Some Community Builders Did," *Chain Store Age (Variety Store Managers Edition)* 15 (October 1939): 56; also see Francis G. Gibson, "Chain Personnel Pleases Women," *Chain Store Progress* 1 (October 1929); 5; "Come to Chicago," *Chain Store Progress* 1 (August 1929): 1. For a good summary of the attacks on chain stores and the defenses usually offered, see James L. Palmer, "Economic and Social Aspects of Chain Stores," *Journal of Business of the University of Chicago* 2 (1929): 272–90.

precarious existence. According to a 1923 study, only five out of a hundred grocers stayed in business more than seven years. Another study at the end of the decade determined that the rate of turnover of retail grocers in Buffalo, New York, between 1918 and 1926 exceeded 30 percent annually.[10] When the depression hit in the late 1920s, the fate of small shops became even more fragile. Many were caught in a bind: credit was one of the main reasons customers had patronized them over the cheaper chains, but now that many workers were unemployed and needed credit more than ever, giving too much credit could bankrupt a store. The daughter of one Chicago grocery owner remembered bitterly, "It got to the point where my Dad gave so much credit that he lost everything he had for giving the credit."[11]

Still, if a storekeeper refused credit to a family with a large bill, he risked losing the entire sum owed. Then, too, merchants had to beware of what was known as "grocery cheating"—getting all the credit you could from neighborhood grocers and then moving where people didn't know you. Worst of all, when customers had money, small shopkeepers often watched them beginning to patronize the cash-and-carry chain store—now more likely to be located nearby—where their money-in-hand bought more. In the midst of the depression, ethnic workers could less afford to indulge their preferences for the corner store, with its familiar food products and comfortable atmosphere. Even when people opposed the chain store in principle, economic realities were changing their buying habits. Ironically, by gradually introducing their customers to some standard brands over the decade of the twenties, thereby accustoming them to new products and tastes, ethnic grocers made it possible in the midst of the depression for consumers to switch to the chain store, where they could get the same products more cheaply.

State policy as well as economic imperatives contributed to the reorientation of workers' consumer behavior during the 1930s. Relief agencies run by the private United Charities, Cook County, and eventually, the state of Illinois and the federal government, preferred recipients to buy food at

10. David N. Walker, Jr., "The Great American Cupboard," *J. Walter Thompson News Bulletin* 103 (November 1923), p. 8, J. Walter Thompson Company Archives (JWT), New York City, now at Duke University, Durham, N.C.; Palmer, "Economic and Social Aspects of Chain Stores," pp. 287–88.

11. Interview with Theresa Giannetti, 16 April 1980, Chicago Heights, IL, "Italians in Chicago Project," University of Illinois, Chicago Circle, Manuscripts Division (UICC), pp. 5–6.

chain stores where prices were lower. At first, agencies tried to enforce this by writing grocery orders only for chain stores. When small shopkeepers, ethnic groups, and relief recipients protested, they relented and authorized purchases from "the retail grocer of the client's choice."[12] As one irate citizen had complained to officials in Washington, The National Tea Company, with its almost one thousand retail grocery units in Metropolitan Chicago, has

in the past three years . . . acquired the bulk of the business of furnishing 150,000 destitute families of the area as indicated with the necessities of life, through the medium of contracts awarded to them by the Illinois Emergency Relief Commission. The sum of approximately $100,000,000 was raised in the past three years for this purpose. The funds were derived from public subscription, sale of $18,750,000 of the State tax anticipation warrants and a $50,000,000 loan from the R.F.C. It is true that the National Tea Company did subscribe in the purchase of $50,000 of State tax warrants, for their act of benevolence they acquired untold millions of dollars in contracts furnishing the needy families with their merchandise.

The writer went on to argue that this special treatment of the National Tea Company hurt independent grocers in more ways than just depriving them of business. "Out of these profits in the past three years, they [National Tea Managers] installed 210 meat market units in connection with their grocery units in the Chicago area. Such meat market equipment cost them millions to install, and during this modern period of merchandising methods, which they boast about introducing[,] has wiped out hundreds of independent Grocers and meat dealers, forcing them into bankruptcy."[13] Not only had grocery chains like National Tea used the relief system to take dollars out of the small grocers' pockets, but they had then used this money to modernize chain operations in ways that hurt independents all the more.

Even after the policy of relief agencies was changed to allow all merchants to compete for the business of relief clients, the independent storekeeper still felt at a severe disadvantage. Many customers stayed with the chains. "We have lost about twenty-five customers through charity slips

12. "Minutes of Supervisors' Meeting," 31 March 1931, United Charities Papers (UnCh), Box 8, Folder 1, CHS, p. 3; "Minutes of Districts' Committee Meeting, April 15, 1932," 4 May 1932, UnCh, Box 8, Folder 2, CHS, p. 1; "People on Relief May Choose Their Own Grocers," *Osadne Hlasy,* 24 February 1933, Chicago Foreign Language Press Survey, Box 40, UCSC; Laura Friedman, "A Study of One Hundred Unemployed Families in Chicago, January 1927 to June 1932," M.A. thesis, University of Chicago, 1933, pp. 165–66.

13. Joseph Golcz to Hon. Frances Perkins, 4 August 1933, National Recovery Administration Papers (NRA), RG 9, "Meat Packing and Meat Stockyards," National Archives (NA).

on the chain stores. When a customer owes you money, he does not like to come in when he cannot pay you," complained one grocer who after twenty-nine years in business found himself suddenly $3,500 in debt.[14] Furthermore, although he could legally fill recipients' grocery orders, the small shopkeeper felt burdened by the relief bureaucracy in ways that the chains—with their professional bookkeeping—did not. Anna Blazewicz, who ran a grocery in a Polish neighborhood of Chicago, recalled that processing "charity tickets" was difficult. "They got food from the store like credit and every month we had to go and file and the city or county would pay back and it had to be just so because if you were a penny short or a penny over, then they would send the whole thing back to you."[15] And if that wasn't burdensome enough, the storekeeper had to cope with caseworkers who persisted in favoring chains, like the one who angered relief recipient Mrs. Carl Doyle so much by changing her grocery slip from the independent grocer she had selected to a Consumers' chain store, arguing "we'd get the most for our money" there, that Mrs. Doyle wrote to FERA head Harry Hopkins to complain. On the other hand, storekeepers felt squeezed by customers who threatened to have their grocery orders from the relief agency changed to another store if they did not receive additional credit.[16] It was no wonder that between competing with the chains, overextending credit, and coping with the relief system, many small stores were forced to close.[17]

Likewise, other New Deal strategies to cope with the crisis of the depression worked, intentionally or not, to the disadvantage of the independent neighborhood storekeeper. Despite the Roosevelt administration's rhetorical commitment to safeguarding the small businessman, the National Re-

---

14. "An Urban Famine: Suffering Communities of Chicago Speak for Themselves: Summary of Open Hearings Held by The Chicago Workers' Committee for Unemployment, January 5–12, 1932," Chicago Commons Papers, Box 24, CHS, pp. 16–17.

15. Interview with Anna Blazewicz, "Polonia Oral History Project," Box 1, CHS, pp. 92–93.

16. Mrs. Carl Doyle to Harry Hopkins, 10 June 1933, Federal Emergency Relief Administration Papers (FERA), RG 69, "Illinois Complaints, N–Q," NA.

17. John H. Cover, *Business and Personal Failure and Readjustment in Chicago* (Chicago: University of Chicago Press, 1933); Homer Hoyt, "One Hundred Years of Land Values in Chicago," Ph.D. dissertation, University of Chicago, 1936, p. 275; Interview with Ruth Katz in Sydelle Kramer and Jenny Masur, eds., *Jewish Grandmothers* (Boston: Beacon Press, 1976), p. 150; Interview with Lillian Cwik, "Polonia Oral History Project," Box 2, CHS, p. 20; from interviews, "Italians in Chicago Project," UICC: Joe Gentili, 2 June 1980, Chicago, Ill., p. 19; Margaret Sabella, 29 March 1980, Chicago, IL, p. 13; Rosalie Augustine, 5 August 1980, Melrose Park, Ill., p. 29.

covery Administration (NRA) of 1933–1935 established minimum prices for consumers and minimum wages and maximum hours for employees in ways that discriminated against the small retailer. Soon after the NRA was found unconstitutional in 1935, an investigation into the extent of compliance with the NRA code for the Retail Food and Grocery Industry in the Chicago Area found that the big chains were in almost full compliance. Instead, the most serious violators were independents and small chains who tried to compete with the big chains by lowering prices.

Smaller grocery stores complained that the large wholesalers were selling direct to chain organizations and the large independent units, thereby making it possible for the large units to sell an article at a price which was less than the small dealer could purchase the same article from the wholesaler. . . . If the small dealer met the sales price and sold below his cost price, he was often cited for violating the code and was hauled in the Code Authority's office by one of the chain or large stores.

The report also pointed to another common violation by small stores. In poor sections of the city, storekeepers usually worked alone in their shops and hired watchmen "to protect the merchandise while they are waiting on trade. Inasmuch as the merchants are unable to employ a relief watchman, the hours of those employees were far below the Code wage minimum."[18] In other words, small storekeepers who had to stay open long hours to survive, could not afford to pay the minimum wages set by the NRA.

Unfortunately, the end of the "First New Deal"—the era of the NRA and direct relief through the FERA—and its replacement by work relief under the Works Progress Administration (WPA) did not promise small independents in working-class neighborhoods much more help competing with the chains. In fact, store owners anticipated a whole new set of prob-

18. Illinois State NRA Office, "Compliance Status of the Retail Food and Grocery Industry in the Chicago Area with Particular Emphasis on the Large Chain Organizations," n.d. but c. 1935, NRA, RG 9, Region VI Papers. Also see numerous articles in the trade journal *Chain Store Age* for evidence that the chains monitored the NRA and its impact on them very carefully, for example, Godfrey M. Lebhar, "The Chains and the New Deal," *Chain Store Age (General Merchandise Edition)* 9 (July 1933): 87–88, 98; Frank E. Landau, "The Chains and the NRA," *Chain Store Age (General Merchandise Edition)* 9 (September 1933): 79–80, 115; "General Johnson Is Sorry," *Chain Store Age (General Merchandise Edition)* 9 (December 1933): 57–58; "Meeting Merchandising Problems Presented by the NRA, Based on Talks With Officials of G. C. Murphy Co.," *Chain Store Age (General Merchandise Edition)* 10 (June 1934): 24–25, 54–55; Paul H. Nystrom, "The Problem of the NRA Codes," *Chain Store Age (General Merchandise Edition)* 10 (August 1934): 24–25.

lems collecting from customers who were dependent on federal pay checks notoriously late in arriving. During the short life of the Civil Works Administration (CWA) from late 1933 to early 1934, independent merchants had suffered terribly from giving credit to customers awaiting government paychecks and then, when bills remained unpaid, discovering that "work relief wages were not attachable." In 1935, the Progressive Food Dealers Association of Chicago, "Organized for the Protection of the Independent Food Distributor," wrote New Deal administrator Harry Hopkins to warn how work relief might hurt them again.

A survey conducted among the members of this Association shows that practically every grocer has on his books from 20 to 35 accounts of the above mentioned character in amounts ranging from $15.00 to $30.00. When one considers there are over 5000 independent grocers in this city some idea of the loss incurred can be gained and this was for only the relatively short period the C.W.A. was in operation. With the principle of work relief to become the standard rather than the exception if gives a further idea of the loss which is going to confront the grocers.[19]

Government relief, whether in the form of direct payment or jobs, may have been a salvation for many citizens, but it rarely was for small independent storekeepers who were fighting for survival against the chains.

As a result of all these factors, by the mid-1930s working-class people were finding more chain stores near their homes and patronizing them more frequently. A survey of neighborhoods carried out in 1934 by the *Chicago Evening American,* probably to enhance the newspaper's advertising and marketing efforts, revealed that the percentage of stores that were chains in any particular community still increased with the average annual family income of its residents (in other words, they continued to be more common in better-off residential areas), but in neighborhoods of below average income—where workers were most likely to live—chains made up 7 to 21 percent of all grocery stores (see table 1). Jean Brichke, therefore, shouldn't have been very surprised in the early 1930s when she returned after a several-year absence to a working-class Jewish neighborhood in Chicago to find four chain groceries where there had been only one a few years earlier, a Walgreen's that had pushed out a privately-owned drugstore, two chain meat markets, a Grant's Dollar Store and a Woolworth's. The National Tea Store already present in the neighborhood had recently

19. E. M. Horton, Progressive Food Dealers Association to Harry L. Hopkins, 10 January 1935, FERA, RG 69, "Illinois Complaints, N–Q," NA.

Table 1   Chain Groceries as a Percentage of All Grocery Stores in Chicago Neighborhoods by Average Annual Family Income of Neighborhoods, 1934

Average Annual Family-Earned Income (City Average = $2,838)	Number and Percentage of Neighborhoods in This Income Category (n = 53)	Chains as Percentage of Total Groceries in Neighborhoods
Under $1,000	6 (11.3%)	6.8
$1,000–1,999	15 (28.3%)	9.6
$2,000–2,838	16 (30.2%)	20.6
$2,839–3,999	10 (18.9%)	24.1
Above $4,000	6 (11.3%)	25.1

Source: Data prepared by *Chicago Evening American,* 1934, and used by the Home Owners' Loan Corporation (HOLC) to evaluate Chicago neighborhoods. "File—Chicago, Illinois #13—Security Map and Area Descriptions Chicago Metropolitan Area and 32 Suburban Cities," HOLC City Survey File (RG 195), National Archives.

added fresh fruits and vegetables, further threatening independent stores nearby.[20]

It was not only a matter of the increasing number of chain stores in working-class neighborhoods. Even more significant, the market share of almost all kinds of chains grew during the Great Depression, as people changed their shopping habits to save a few dollars. As early as 1931, the major trade journal of chain store executives was predicting that "one of the most constructive features of the depression, so far as the chains are concerned, lies in the fact that it operated to make more people chain store conscious, a fact that will undoubtedly work to the advantage of the chains when better conditions return and consumer buying power increases. Thousands of people throughout the country have patronized chain stores this past year who never before felt it necessary to test the economies they claimed to offer." And as the depression persisted, chains continued to credit their survival to the new customers they were attracting.[21] By 1935, the 8 percent of retail stores that were chains in the nation were transacting

20. Jean Brichke, "Report on Term Paper under Miss Nesbitt's Direction," Paper for Sociology 264, c. 1931, Burgess Papers, Box 156, Folder 2, UCSC, pp. 15–18. The Lynds noted when they returned to Muncie, Indiana, in the mid-1930s that since doing their field work for *Middletown* in 1925, "Grocery chains have invaded the region 'South of the Tracks,'" the working-class part of town. Robert S. Lynd and Helen Merrell Lynd, *Middletown in Transition: A Study in Cultural Conflicts* (New York: Harcourt, Brace and World, 1937), p. 12, n. 17.

21. Godfrey M. Lebhar, "Chain Store Progress in 1930," *Chain Store Age* 7 (January 1931): 33; also see "To Bring Out Hoarded Dollars," *Chain Store Age* 8 (March 1932): 172 and Godfrey M. Lebhar, "Looking Ahead With the Chains," *Chain Store Age (General Merchandise Edition)* 9 (January 1933): 76.

23 percent of the business, up from 20 percent in 1929; chain grocery stores had an even larger percentage of sales, 39 percent, in 1935. By 1939 in a city like Chicago, that share had grown still larger, to 56 percent (see table 2).[22]

It was not that chains did not suffer at all in the depression. They, too, particularly in the early years, were beset by sharply decreasing profits. Chain strategy for meeting the economic crisis, however, took advantage of size in ways that were not possible for the small independent store. Chain stores, ranging from the A & P to Woolworth's, consolidated units, closing inefficient and unprofitable ones and modernizing others, since "the comparatively low cost of modernizing stores in times like these offers an advantage too great to be ignored," a group of chain executives agreed. Chain stores also developed new advertising and merchandising strategies, and lowered operating costs by introducing self-service and increasing the number of products they sold under their own label.[23]

By the end of the 1930s in Chicago, there was little doubt that the increased patronage of working-class customers had contributed significantly to this growth in chain stores' share of the consumer dollar. In the winter of 1936, when a DePaul University marketing professor conducted an extensive survey of the attitudes of Chicago housewives toward chain food stores, he found that indeed chain store popularity had increased greatly in recent years, particularly among factory workers. Another survey by the A. C. Neilsen Company revealed how much Chicago workers' shopping habits had changed by 1939. Ninety-three percent of those labeled "lower middle" and 91 percent of "lower" income buyers now paid by cash, not credit, an indication that they were patronizing chain stores. Although

22. Malcolm D. Taylor, "Progressive Retail Management," *The Annals of the American Academy of Political and Social Science* 209 (May 1940), special issue, "Marketing in Our American Economy," edited by Howard T. Hovde; Godfrey M. Lebhar, "Position and Outlook of Chain Stores," *Chain Store Age* 15 (August 1939): 69.

23. "Chain Store Expansion in 1930: A Survey of Chain Store Leasing Activities from Coast to Coast as Reported by Chain Store Specialists," *Chain Store Age* 7 (January 1931): 88; "Chain Store Modernization Active, Survey Reveals," *Chain Store Age (General Merchandise Edition)* 8 (November 1932): 635, 667; Hugh M. Foster, "The Chain Stores Come of Age: They Progress from Depths of Depression to New Heights in 1936," *Printers' Ink Monthly* 34 (April 1937): 79–94; Godfrey M. Lebhar, "Position and Outlook of Chain Stores," *Chain Store Age* 15 (August 1939): 69–70, 138; Nils Hansell, "American Food Counter," *Printers' Ink Monthly* 40 (February 1940): 5–8, 52; "A & P: Past, Present and Future," *Progressive Grocer Magazine*, New York, n.d., pp. 32–44; *Woolworth's First 75 Years: The Story of Everybody's Store*, pp. 29–30; *Walgreen Pepper Pod*, June 1951, pp. 15–19; "Seventy-Five Years of Walgreen Progress," special issue of *Walgreen World* 43 (September–October 1976): 7–10.

Table 2 Chain Stores in Chicago, 1923, 1929, 1939

Category of Store	1923			1929				1939			
	Total Units All Stores	No. Units Chain Stores	% Units Chain Stores	Total Units All Stores	No. Units Chain Stores	% Units Chain Stores	Chain % of Total Sales	Total Units All Stores	No. Units Chain Stores	% Units Chain Stores	Chain % of Total Sales
All Groceries	11,865	1,234	17.9	7,266	1,785	24.6	50.0	9,331	1,391	14.9	56.0
w/o Meat	x	x	x	5,151	1,700	33.0	68.5	5,757	989	17.2	54.7
Comb. w/Meat	x	x	x	2,115	85	4.0	8.7	3,574	402	11.2	56.9
Variety, 5 & 10	x	x	x	383	150	39.2	93.8	333	172	51.7	96.1
Dept. Stores	x	x	x	78	16	20.5	13.5	58	26*	44.8	67.2
Shoe Stores	1,206	92	7.6	1,016	292	28.7	59.6	764	275	36.0	66.6
Confectioners	2,440	102	4.8	x	x	x	x	2,286	195	8.5	35.5
Restaurants	x	166	x	3,436	256	7.5	23.7	4,193	302	7.2	30.0
Cigar Stores	1,204	216	17.9	1,380	249	18.0	44.1	751	177	23.6	60.7
Filling Sta.	x	307	x	1,255	476	37.9	36.4	2,161	190	8.8	19.0
Fuel Dealers	x	111	x	761	61	8.0	21.9	1,243	57	4.6	15.6
Drug Stores	1,283	90	7.0	1,969	231	11.7	35.2	1,903	237	12.5	41.2
Clothing	2,424	127	5.2	2,332	360	15.4	30.7	1,979	298	15.1	32.3
Furniture	x	x	x	501	73	14.6	27.3	420	40	9.5	29.3

Sources: Ernest Hugh Shideler, "The Chain Store: A Study of the Ecological Organization of a Modern City," Ph.D. dissertation, University of Chicago, 1927, chapter 4, pp. 18–20; U.S. Dept. of Commerce, Bureau of Census, *Fifteenth Census, 1930: Retail Distribution* (USGPO, 1933), p. 633; ibid., *Sixteenth Census, 1940: Retail Trade* (USGPO, 1943), pp. 218–219.

*includes mail order

x = data not available

figures on total sales are not available, the 7 to 21 percent of grocery stores in working-class neighborhoods that were chains likely handled a far higher percentage of the community's business than those figures might have led one otherwise to expect.[24]

The way that independent stores responded to the growing threat from chains only contributed further to the standardization of consumption during the 1930s. Increasing numbers of them joined what were called "voluntary chains," groups of independent retailers who banded together to gain the advantages of quantity buying and some assistance with merchandising while retaining separate ownership and management. As larger units, they were able to get better prices from wholesalers, to save in advertising, and to sell some products more cheaply under the voluntary chain's label. Nationally, between 1932 and 1935, the number of stores belonging to voluntary chains grew from 26 to 34 percent of total stores, and in sales volume from 28 to 35 percent.

Voluntary chains differed greatly in approach. In Chicago they ranged from the Independent Grocers' Association (IGA), which standardized its member stores so much that they differed little from chain units, to the Associated Grocers of Chicago (A-G), which only provided its six hundred local stores—predominantly owned by "foreign grocers"—with merchandise deivered C.O.D. and advertising material like handbills, window banners, and newspaper copy. Even in the case of the A-G grocer, however, participation in a voluntary chain encouraged small independent storekeepers to further standardize their operations, by, for example, favoring national brand goods and catering less to local and ethnic tastes. The end result was that the independents who survived the depression began more and more to resemble the chain stores with which they were trying to compete; the one sure way to beat chains seemed to be to join them. Workers, then, did not have to patronize chain stores to have more standardized shopping experiences by the late 1930s. Chances were that workers' neighborhood grocery stores resembled the ones their coworkers of different ethnicity shopped in across town much more than they had in the 1920s.[25]

24. L. M. McCermott, "Food Chains and the Housewife," *Chicago Commerce* 33 (June 1936): 22–24; Arthur C. Nielsen, "Solving Marketing Problems of Food Retailers and Manufacturers," based on an address to the National Association of Food Chains, Chicago, 11 October 1939, p. 24.

25. J. Walter Thompson Company, "Analysis of Retail Grocery Sales by Type of Outlet," February 1936, JWT, RG 5; "A & P Goes to the Wars," *Fortune,* vol. 17, April 1938, 94, 138;

This changing structure in the distribution of consumer goods and the resulting increase in workers' participation in "mass consumption" might suggest that by the 1930s "mass" had indeed overcome "class." But there is another side to the equation—the attitudes of consumers toward these structural changes—which is of crucial importance, albeit harder to substantiate than their behavior. What historical evidence exists, however, strongly indicates that the ideal—of a depoliticized working population who identified as middle class—which advertisers and mass marketers had anticipated in the 1920s, and many assume exists today, did not emerge. Rather, mass consumption, as part of workers' increased involvement with mass culture, contributed to the development of a more homogeneous working-class culture, which helped build bonds among workers of different ethnic and racial groups who long had found their efforts to organize into unions at the workplace thwarted by their cultural differences. Finally, by the late 1930s, factory workers in industrial centers like Chicago succeeded in creating unions under the auspices of the CIO to bargain with their bosses for better working conditions, pay, and rights as employees. Although many factors contributed to the CIO's achievement, including a more supportive federal government and a more effective national union leadership, the shared culture of rank-and-file workers should not be underestimated. More "Americanized" than an earlier generation who often could not even communicate in English, these workers were also consuming the same kinds of standardized products from the same chain stores instead of buying from local ethnic grocers; listening to the same national, commercial, network radio like the Jack Benny Program and Major Bowes' Original Amateur Hour in place of the local programming that they were used to in the twenties; and watching the same movies in theaters that were now owned by the Hollywood studio chains rather than frequenting the more intimate neighborhood theaters that they had previously preferred.[26]

The result was a more homogeneous working-class culture that was based on mass culture but yet distinguishable from the mass culture that the middle class participated in. One of the most important reasons that

and from *Printers' Ink Monthly* 18 and 19: Albert E. Haase and V. H. Pelz, "The Rapid Rise of National Voluntary Chains" (April 1929): 52–56, 98–103; Haase and Pelz, "The Significance of the Voluntary Chain" (May 1929): 52–56, 90–92; C. B. Larrabee, "Will the Independent Save Himself by Losing His Independence?" (September 1929): 38, 92–100.

26. See Cohen, *Making a New Deal*, chapters 7 and 8, for more discussion of the CIO drive and the new shared culture of working-class Americans.

these new cultural experiences remained working-class was that they were still encountered in working-class contexts such as chain stores and theaters in working-class neighborhoods and reinforced by working-class organizations like the CIO. CIO organizers, recognizing that workers were increasingly sharing these common cultural experiences—of which radio probably played the most important part—explicitly set out to build on this common culture. A South Chicago steelworker trying to rally fellow workers to challenge the company in 1935, for example, used the idiom of a popular radio program, "So if you are beginning to be a doubter too, pack your lunch and 'Come up'n see us' at the next meeting, and as Amos and Andy say, We'll talk the sichyation over."[27]

Several months later, workers at U.S. Steel's South Works held their first organizational meeting as a grassroots union the same night that Joe Louis established himself (unofficially) as world heavyweight champion against Max Baer. One thousand assembled steelworkers adjourned early to hear the 9:30 P.M. broadcast sponsored by the Buick Motor Company over network radio nationwide. It is not hard to imagine that this popular culture that they shared as working-class Americans contributed to the spirit of their own battle to start a union. That they were rooting for Louis, a black man, may have had a particular meaning for these workers whose success against U.S. Steel depended on building alliances across race. This is not to claim that white workers who supported Louis had overcome their racism, but sharing a black hero did have an impact on their attitudes.

A month earlier, Al Monroe of the black newspaper the *Chicago Defender* had written:

A few days ago your correspondent accepted an invitation to accompany Joe Louis to a festival that had never welcomed Race guests and the treatment accorded our party was almost unbelievable. Joe Louis was the hero of the assemblage. When we entered the place there was an air about it that did not seem free from discrimination. The little fellow who met us at the door appeared a bit bewildered. He had not seen Joe Louis in the background. A few moments later we had the best of everything about the place—they had discovered the presence of Joe Louis, the Bomber.

Furthermore, although it is difficult to know for sure if—and how—these working people understood the contest symbolically, Louis and Baer did have social-class images in the popular media that fans like these steelworkers likely were aware of. Joe Louis was a fighting symbol in the Great

27. *The Amalgamated Journal* 36 (23 May 1935): 20.

Depression, the man of simple roots who nonetheless was accomplishing great things. A long-time resident of industrial Detroit, he had until recently labored as a worker at the Ford Motor Company. Max Baer, in contrast, was the "rich guy"; in the words of sportswriter Jonathan Mitchell, "Baer . . . made wisecracks and went to parties and was a harbinger of the return of the old days. He was Broadway, he was California and Florida, he represented the possession of money once more and spending it." It didn't take much of a leap to see the Louis-Baer fight as a metaphor for industrial workers' own struggle against their bosses. In this case, then, mass culture, as broadcast over commercial network radio, was imparting not a depoliticizing message encouraging identification with middle-class America, but rather one that inspired class-wide political action.[28] Over the next several years, sit-down–strikers who charted baseball scores and danced to popular music together, CIO-sponsored programs over network radio, and labor newspapers which kept their readers informed about radio entertainment and inexpensive and healthful ways to cook with canned goods would testify to the important connections between culture and politics among America's workers.

A close look at workers' organizing activities in the CIO reveals another way that workers' experience with mass consumption in the 1930s differed from what one would have expected of people who had been successfully integrated into a middle-class consumption community: workers remained self-consciously ambivalent about this shift in their lives away from neighborhood-based exchange relations to the impersonality and corporateness of mass consumption in chain stores. This concern was part of a larger worldview which infused workers' political ideology in the 1930s, what I

---

28. Al Monroe quotation from *Chicago Defender* in Chris Mead, *Champion—Joe Louis, Black Hero in White America* (New York: Charles Scribner's Sons, 1985), p. 204; Jonathan Mitchell quotation from the *New Republic,* in Mead, *Champion,* p. 74. For more on the fight, see Mead, *Champion,* pp. 65–74 and Jeffrey T. Sammons, *Beyond the Ring: The Role of Boxing in American Society* (Urbana: University of Illinois Press, 1988), pp. 96–117. On the racial pride that Louis's victory engendered within Chicago's black community, see Richard Wright, "Joe Louis Uncovers Dynamite" in *New Masses: An Anthology of the Rebel Thirties,* ed. Joseph North (New York: International Publishers, 1969), pp. 175–79. For discussion of steelworkers' interest in the fight, see Interview with George Patterson, 2 February 1969, State College, Pa., United Steel Workers of America Papers (USWA), Penn State University Labor Archives, p. 12. Worker Clarence Stoecker remarked that the CIO at the McCormick Works of International Harvester Company often made initial contact with men by talking sports. Interview with Clarence Stoecker by Julia Reichert, 12 August 1978, Tape 1, Side 1, in possession of author.

have called their "moral capitalism." Workers' preference for small community merchants over what they viewed as national capitalist monopolies, grew out of their workers' conviction that capitalism itself was not bad, but that it must be—and could be—made fair. Nationally, when "poor" people were asked by *Fortune Magazine* if they favored taxing chain stores enough so that they would no longer have a price advantage over the independent store, about half of them responded "yes" even though they bought most of their groceries at chains because they were cheaper there. The editors were perplexed that the same people who regularly shopped at chain stores wanted to tax them, limiting their profitability and hence curbing the savings they could offer consumers.[29]

In Chicago, workers in locals of the Steelworkers' Organizing Committee (SWOC) and the Packinghouse Workers' Organizing Committee (PWOC), and their wives, daughters, sisters and other members of the Women's Auxiliaries that supported them, went out of their way to link the small independent storekeepers in their communities to the CIO union drive: they argued that higher wages for workers would profit local merchants as well; they organized joint labor-business organizations like the Calumet Merchants and Labor Association to work for common concerns; and they promoted local stores by awarding prizes donated by merchants and soliciting advertisements for union newspapers. The field minutes of the Chicago area SWOC record great satisfaction that "Businessmen have now been won over" in Chicago Heights, and that "Slovak saloon keepers in South Chicago are behind the steel drive." Despite all the changes that had occurred in consumer behavior during the depression, workers continued to value emotional as well as economic ties to their local merchants.[30]

29. "The Fortune Quarterly Survey: 7," *Fortune*, vol. 15, January 1937, 154, 156. On the controversy over taxing chain stores, see Maurice W. Lee, "Anti-Chain-Store Tax Legislation," Ph.D. diss. University of Chicago, 1939; Godfrey M. Lebhar, "The Robinson-Patman Act," *Chain Store Age (General Merchandise Managers Edition)* 12 (August 1936): 31; Otis R. Tyson, "California Votes 'No' On Chain Store Tax Issue," *Chain Store Age (General Merchandise Managers Edition)* 12 (December 1936): 27–30; "A & P Opens Fire against Patman's Proposed Tax," *Chain Store Age (Variety Store Managers Edition)* 14 (October 1938): 82–84.

30. Interview with Dorothy and George Patterson, 1 February 1969, State College, Pa., USWA, Penn State, p. 11; Interview with George Patterson by Ed Sadlowski, Chicago, Ill., Roosevelt University Oral History Project in Labor History, Book 21, pp. 89–90; "District Joyous over Steel Wage Increase: Merchants to Feel Effect in April," *Daily Calumet*, 3 March 1937; "Release to Daily Calumet on Establishment of Calumet Merchants and Labor Association," 6 January 1937, George Patterson Papers, Box 6, Folder 6, CHS; "From Our Minutes," in "We Women: Wives and Friends of Packing House Workers, Bulletin of the Women's

People's belief that a working-class victory was tied to the survival of a neighborhood economy was only reinforced by experiences that proved how easily chain stores could be drawn into the service of employers' interests. A particularly poignant instance for Chicago workers was Goldblatt's Department Stores' continued support of the repressive Hearst newspapers, through its placement of weekly advertising, during the bitter Newspaper Guild strike. In 1939, CIO members all over Chicago, including those in steel and packing, organized picket lines outside Goldblatt's stores, the centerpiece of most working-class shopping areas.[31]

Many workers also supported legislative efforts to tax chains on both the state and federal levels. This sentiment, for example, motivated the CIO's support of attorney Alfred Kamin for the Democratic nomination for state representative from the thirteenth district, which included South Chicago where the steel mills were located. One newspaper article from the spring of 1938 reported that Kamin's campaign headquarters "looks more like a union meeting hall than a political hangout. The men who roll steel over in South Chicago come into headquarters to report progress in their precincts much as if it were a campaign to unionize the boys in the plant." Kamin was a liberal who had the previous year been secretary of the Citizens' Joint Commission of Inquiry, which investigated the infamous "Memorial Day Massacre" where ten workers were killed and over a hundred wounded when Chicago police, protecting Republic Steel from striking workers, shot at picketing workers and their supporters without provocation. Obviously, Kamin had good credentials to win labor's support, but of particular relevance here, he built his campaign around consumer issues. Kamin had helped to organize the Consumer's League of Chicago, and the first two items on his nine-point platform spoke directly to workers' concerns about consumption: one called for "high taxes on chain stores as an

Auxiliary of the Packing House Workers Industrial Union," vol. 1, no. 1 (October 1937), CHS, p. 5; "A Happier Life," in "We Women," vol. 1, no. 2 (December 1937), p. 2; Arthur Kampfert, manuscript, United Packinghouse Workers of America Papers, State Historical Society of Wisconsin, part 2, p. 14; SWOC Field Workers' Staff Meeting Minutes, 5 November 1936 and 28 December 1936, USWA District 31 Papers, CHS.

31. "Council Aids News Guild, Hits Goldblatt Stores on Hearst Advertising," *CIO News–Packinghouse Workers' Organizing Committee Edition (PWOC)*, 16 January 1939; "Chicago Locals to Picket Goldblatt Store April 8," *CIO News–PWOC Ed.*, 3 April 1939; "PWOC Pickets Unfair Store, Rap Ads in Hearst Papers," *CIO News—PWOC Ed.*, 17 April 1939; Edward Andrew Zivich, "Fighting Union: The CIO at Inland Steel, 1936–1942," M.A. thesis, University of Wisconsin-Milwaukee, 1972, pp. 34–35.

aid to the small businessman, whose profits remain in the community, and who gives credit to workmen who are his neighbors in the event they are out on strike" and item two demanded "repeal of the sales tax, which hits workingmen and small retailers."[32]

Kamin understood that workers were still concerned about ensuring credit in hard times, now as likely to be caused by a strike as by a downturn in the business cycle, and that they still felt most comfortable entrusting those needs to the small, independent merchant of their own communities, even when they did much of their regular shopping at chain stores. Only when established CIO unions began to sponsor credit unions and other kinds of credit arrangements during the next decade would workers be able to imagine forsaking their allegiance to small storeowners. But even at that point, they were vesting their credit needs as consumers in the working-class institution of the union, not in the mainstream institutions of "mass consumerism" like the chains. While participation in national consumption trends may have helped facilitate workers' collective action through the CIO, to say nothing of their economic survival during the depression, workers nonetheless seemed to have lamented the social, political, and cultural costs precipitated by the nationalization and standardization of consumption. In supporting Kamin's candidacy and platform, they were acknowledging the importance of reforming state policy for improving their own ability to put political and cultural preferences before economic necessity.[33]

Despite the sentiments of workers, chain stores had a momentum by the late 1930s that could not be stopped. After Congress's passage of the Robinson-Patman Act in 1936, which had little effect on chain operation

32. "Kamin's Support Increasing in Steel District," *People's Press,* 2 April 1938; articles entitled "Kamin's Slate for Labor and Small Business," "Kamin Supports Small Merchant," "Kamin Active in Consumers League Here," "Progressives Urge Support for Al Kamin," "They're All for Kamin," "These Men Back Kamin," "Paul Douglas Backs Kamin," "Meyer Levin for Al Kamin in Primary," *People's Press,* 9 April 1938.

33. Chain stores, meanwhile, were defending themselves against the agitation for chain store taxation by arguing that efforts to penalize them would only hurt the low-income customers who had begun to patronize chains during the depression. Godfrey M. Lebhar, "As We See It," *Chain Store Age (General Merchandise Edition)* 10 (April 1934): 91–92, 98; Newton Maxwell, "Intelligent Advice Boosts Sales of Summer Cosmetics," *Chain Store Age (Variety Store Managers Edition)* 14 (July 1938): 50, 56; "Are Chain Stores in the Public Interest? A Broadcast by Congressman Patman and Godfrey M. Lebhar over Station WGN, Chicago, October 19, 1938," *Chain Store Age (Variety Store Managers Edition)* 14 (November 1938): 27–28.

despite its supporters' intentions, agitation for chain taxing died, small stores continued to struggle, and candidates like Kamin tended to lose their bids for office. But the attitudes of workers uncovered here at least suggest that working people did not enthusiastically, nor unconsciously, embrace these changes. They continued to harbor a sense of being different, of being outside the maelstrom of "mass consumption," and an awareness of the political significance of keeping consumption within working-class communities.

This examination of workers' consumption patterns suggests the importance of the context in which people consumed; purchasing a canned good or mass-produced item like a phonograph did not in itself produce an inevitable result. When workers encountered mass-produced goods mediated by their ethnic communities in the 1920s, they were not uprooted culturally. When they purchased them without that mediation in the 1930s, these goods did help to bring them out of their former ethnic isolation, but given the political context of a national drive towards unionization, consumption patterns remained working-class. While the goods purchased by working-class and middle-class consumers became more similar in the thirties, important differences in the contexts surrounding people's consumption continued to distinguish them.

The emergence of a class-differentiated mass market was reinforced by the late 1930s as mass producers and marketers recognized that social classes had distinctive tastes, and that they, therefore, must think more in terms of segmented markets. Advertising agencies, for example, lost no time—once the CIO unionization campaign began to succeed—in recognizing that profits would result when factory workers were making a decent living. In the October 1937 issue of the J. Walter Thompson Advertising Company's monthly bulletin, entitled *People,* the lead story, "Your Customer, the Worker: With New Wants and a Fattening Purse, He Enlarges Many Markets," probed the distinctive tastes of American workers with the aim of satisfying them. The trade journal *Chain Store Age* began in this period to speak of serving three markets, with "the price customer" and "the quality customer" at either end of the class spectrum. And A & P made the unique shopping needs and cooking habits of a working-class family, the Steinmillers, the subject of an early issue of *Woman's Day* magazine, which the store began to publish in 1937 as a way of showcasing its own Ann Page label and other standard brands, to convince working-class customers that the chain grocery was adapting to suit their lives. Nobody put it more bluntly than the research manager for NBC, who was convinced by 1940 that "radio offers a 'class' as well as a 'mass' market."[34]

By the 1950s, social class considerations informed every aspect of marketing. Landmark marketing studies such as *Workingman's Wife,* carried out by the sociologists Lee Rainwater, Richard P. Coleman, and Gerald Handel for Macfadden Publications, Inc., told manufacturers and advertisers that social class identity carried with it a whole constellation of values that shaped the way particular groups of Americans consumed. "These class differences have important implications for the manufacturer or merchant. Here is a vast group of consumers who have their own special dreams and desires, their own value systems, their own way of reacting to products, to advertising, or to sales messages. The advertiser who wants to talk meaningfully to these people must understand the symbols and messages which will have the most meaning to them. He must, in short, understand *how* to talk to them," the authors wrote. Measuring consumption capacities by income alone would not do. Likewise, by 1969 blacks had prospered enough to focus capitalists' attention on defining a distinctive "black" market. A study such as D. Parke Gibson's *The $30 Billion Negro* identified the special preferences of black consumers. Although the perceptions of advertisers cannot be equated with the realities of consumer behavior, there was greater likelihood, as marketing research became more sophisticated in the postwar era, that what marketing experts discovered did approach reality. How successfully producers and advertisers geared products to identifiable class-, ethnic-, and race-based "constellations of values" is another issue, but business historian Richard Tedlow has argued in a recent book that during the postwar era mass marketers have increasingly prospered through successful market segmentation.[35]

34. J. Walter Thompson Company, *People,* October 1937; see also the issues of July 1937 and November 1937, JWT; *Chain Store Age,* 1935–1940, passim, particularly Leo Warren, "First Showings of National Toilet Brands Win Quality Patronage for Store," *Chain Store Age (Variety Store Managers Edition)* 13 (May 1937): 58–62; "Oven Meals Win Prize for Toledo, Ohio, Woman," *A & P Menu, a Weekly Food Supplement to Woman's Day,* 16 November 1937; H. M. Beville, Jr., "The ABCD's of Radio Audiences," *Public Opinion Quarterly* (June 1940): 196.

35. Lee Rainwater, Richard P. Coleman, and George Handel, *Workingman's Wife: Her Personality, World, and Life Style* (New York: Oceana Publications, 1959), p. xii; Pierre Martineau, "Social Classes and Spending Behavior," *Journal of Marketing* 23 (October 1958): 121–130; D. Parke Gibson, *The Thirty Billion Dollar Negro* (London: Macmillan, 1969). Richard S. Tedlow, *New and Improved: The Story of Mass Marketing in America* (New York: Basic Books, 1990).

Thus, beginning in the 1930s, at the same time that workers were haltingly becoming more integrated into mainstream "mass culture," mass culture was altering to accommodate their distinctive tastes. A working-class version of mass culture was taking shape in both the experience of working people and the consciousness of promoters. Workers' conviction that they had unique needs and tastes was being underscored by marketers increasingly committed to identifying them. Although workers' desire to protect their long-standing community-based consumption relationships is not the same thing as Madison Avenue and Detroit gearing products to a working-class market, both contributed in their own ways to the survival of class along with mass culture.

During the pivotal era of the 1930s, workers' behavior and attitudes toward mass consumption were increasingly at odds; economic imperatives were forcing them to patronize chain stores in preference to their familiar, local merchants, while their moral sympathies and fears about credit kept them loyal to the small, noncorporate—and endangered—shopkeeper. As a result, workers like these in Chicago seemed at times intensely ambivalent, if not inconsistent, in their attitudes and behavior, as is so often the case with human beings despite the best efforts of historians to make everything fit. What is clear, however, is that rather than being unconscious victims of large cultural processes like "mass consumption," workers were trying to grapple with the contradictions of the consumer society in which they saw themselves steadily becoming entrenched. Even as they were joining a growing "mass" market, they were using those common experiences to build a class-based institution like the CIO. Once workers achieved political recognition through this struggle, moreover, producers, advertisers, and merchandisers came to identify them as a distinctive group within the larger mass market, worthy of unique products. Over time, stores, goods and other items of mass consumption would become coded for social class. Although much has transpired since the late 1930s that needs careful investigation, we should at least be wary of ideological assertions that class integration and cultural homogenization have accompanied the ascendancy of mass consumption.

Advertisement printed by permission of Henry Holt and Company, Inc.

6 Between Culture and Consumption

The Mediations of the Middlebrow

Joan Shelley Rubin

In the three decades following the First World War, American authors, publishers, entrepreneurs, and broadcasters collaborated to make literature and humanistic discourse available to a wide reading public on an unprecedented scale. The Book-of-the-Month Club, founded in 1926 by the advertising man Harry Scherman, mailed subscribers newly published volumes endorsed by expert judges like the writer Dorothy Canfield Fisher. The biggest nonfiction sellers of the 1920s were "outlines," such as Will Durant's *The Story of Philosophy,* which attempted to simplify and organize specialized knowledge for a generalist audience. During the same period, Columbia University English professor John Erskine implemented his pioneering "great books" curriculum for undergraduates and then, in novels and periodical articles, carried his approach to the classics outside the classroom. In 1924, Stuart Pratt Sherman, another refugee from the academy, attached himself to the *New York Herald Tribune's* innovative book review section, *Books;* from that base, he extended his brand of literary criticism beyond the pages of rarefied journals. Throughout the 1930s and 1940s, such commentators as Alexander Woollcott and Clifton Fadiman talked about books on the new, far-reaching medium of radio. To those developments, one might add the popularization of the humanities through correspondence courses, university extension programs, public lectures, library services, women's study clubs, anthologies, and reprint series.

The proponents of book clubs, "outlines," and similar efforts liked to describe them as contributions to "adult education" or "the humanization of knowledge." Yet, at least since the 1940s, commentators on American culture have more often characterized the sensibility such activities represented by calling it "middlebrow." The categorization by brow height—"high," "middle," and "low"—derived from the pseudoscience phrenology, which linked behavior to the shape of a person's skull. "Highbrow" and "lowbrow" came, by 1900, to denote the presence or absence of refinement. Van Wyck Brooks thereafter appropriated the terms to depict a rift in American life between pallid art and crude materialism. Later, Virginia Woolf, Clement Greenberg, Russell Lynes, Dwight Macdonald, and others

163

added their own definitions of the area between "high" and "low," revaluing the ends of the spectrum in the process. "Highbrows" now became laudably serious intellectuals; "lowbrows" exhibited honest, uncomplicated pleasure in jazz and comic books; but "middlebrows" (except in Lynes's view) were dangerous enemies of good taste. "Midcult," as Macdonald derisively called it in 1960, "pretends to respect the standards of High Culture while in fact it waters them down and vulgarizes them." By way of example, Macdonald singled out the Book-of-the-Month Club, the *Saturday Review of Literature* (first edited by Club judge Henry Seidel Canby) and the "great books" publishing project.[1]

The delineators of that supposedly treacherous middle ground were especially concerned about the connection between middlebrow enterprises and the marketplace. Greenberg, for instance, warned in 1948 that the avant-garde's "growing acceptance by official and commercial culture" threatened genuine creativity. Corroborating the surge of popularization in the early twentieth century, he added, "It must be obvious to anyone that the volume and social weight of middlebrow culture, borne along as it has been by the great recent increase of the American middle class, have multiplied at least tenfold in the past three decades. This culture . . . insinuates itself everywhere, devaluating the precious, infecting the healthy, corrupting the honest, and stultifying the wise." The solution, Macdonald argued, was to fortify the barrier protecting "high" art from debased, commodified imitations. "So let the masses have their Masscult," Macdonald concluded in admittedly elitist terms, "let the few who care about good writing, painting, music, architecture, philosophy, etc., have their High Culture, and don't fuzz up the distinction with Midcult."[2]

That dismissive posture in turn licensed both literary scholars and historians to omit middlebrow activities from their accounts of the twenties, thirties, and forties. As a result, today students of American literature are

---

1. Lawrence W. Levine, *Highbrow/Lowbrow: The Emergence of Cultural Hierarchy in America* (Cambridge: Harvard University Press, 1988), pp. 221–22; Van Wyck Brooks, "America's Coming of Age," in *Three Essays on America* (New York: E. P. Dutton, 1934), pp. 15–35; Virginia Woolf, "Middlebrow," in *The Death of the Moth* (New York: Harcourt, Brace, 1942), pp. 180–84; Clement Greenberg, "The State of American Writing," *Partisan Review*, no. 8 (1948), 879; Russell Lynes, "Highbrow, Lowbrow, Middlebrow," *Harper's*, February 1949, 19–28; Dwight Macdonald, "Masscult and Midcult: 2," *Partisan Review*, Fall 1960, 592. Macdonald used the term "middlebrow" as early as 1953, in "A Theory of Mass Culture," reprinted in *Mass Culture: The Popular Arts in America*, ed. Bernard Rosenberg and David Manning White (Glencoe, Ill.: Free Press, 1957), pp. 63–64.

2. Greenberg, "American Writing," p. 879; Macdonald, "Masscult," p. 628.

more likely to become acquainted with Hemingway and Fitzgerald or the writers for "little magazines" than with Woollcott or Fisher. Moreover, recent efforts to offset the biases implicit in the received hierarchy of "great books"—or "great men"—have continued to slight middlebrow artifacts while constructing an alternative pantheon out of the materials of popular culture. Similarly, American history survey texts, influenced by the well-intentioned precepts of the "new social history," have tended to counteract the prior focus on politicians and diplomats by stressing the development of movies and amusement parks, not book clubs and educational broadcasts.[3]

My own intention here, by contrast, is to restore attention and nuance to the study of American middlebrow culture by looking closely at what its promulgators actually thought and felt. The questions I have posed belong to the cultural historian's stock in trade: What values did middlebrow critics espouse? What biographical factors shaped those values? From what intellectual traditions did they derive? How did middlebrow actors themselves understand their roles? What tensions and contradictions did their outlooks conceal? How did the form, as well as the content, of their projects reflect those strains? To what broader social transformations were middlebrow anxieties connected? In answering these questions, I have also tried to test and rethink two generalizations that have become part of the standard portrait of American life in the early twentieth century. The first is the view that, by 1917, the nineteenth-century critical establishment, or "genteel tradition," embodied in its most rigorous form by figures like Charles Eliot Norton, E. L. Godkin, and Frederick Law Olmsted, had lost all of its control over American standards of taste.[4] The second is the

3. An important exception to the neglect of "middlebrow" forms is the compelling work of Janice Radway on the Book-of-the-Month Club, which seeks to rescue the Club from the scorn of intellectuals by arguing that its criteria for book selection are no less valuable to its readers than those governing academic criticism. See Radway, "The Book-of-the-Month Club and the General Reader," in Cathy N. Davidson, ed., *Reading in America: Literature and Social History* (Baltimore: Johns Hopkins University Press, 1989), pp. 259–61. For a full-length study of the issues I raise in this essay, see my book *The Making of Middlebrow Culture* (Chapel Hill: University of North Carolina Press, 1992).

4. The phrase "genteel tradition" now conveys so many pejorative associations that it may be impossible to use it positively or to restore any complexity to the term. I have retained the phrase (using it interchangeably with "Arnoldian"), and undertaken these efforts, however, because it is the phrase in common usage among historians. Here I limit its reference to the Boston wing of the group, omitting the less intellectually serious New York poets and critics (e.g., E. C. Stedman, Richard Stoddard) who are sometimes also described as exemplars of gentility. For the assumption that the genteel tradition was dead by 1917, see, for example,

related idea that a vision of the self predicated on "character" entirely gave way, in this period, to an emphasis on selfhood as "personality." By delineating the presence, instead, of mingled, competing ideals, I hope to enrich our understanding of the complexities involved in the United States's shift from a producer to a consumer society.[5]

While I have thus sought to take the making of middlebrow culture on its own terms, and to locate it historically, I do not mean to imply, however, that I have adopted a neutrality that eluded earlier explorers of the topic. On the contrary, I have operated (like the other contributors to this volume) from a sense of responsibility not merely to report (if that were even possible) but also to evaluate the developments I have investigated. In so doing, I have continually bumped up against my own ambivalence toward my subject. On the one hand, I have conceived of my task as, in part, the reinforcement of the premise that critical theorists have so convincingly established in the last few years: the idea that the literary canon—in the shape of a list of "classics" or a "book-of-the-month"—has always derived from the experiences and presuppositions of the canonizers.[6] Yet, on the other hand, along the way I have noticed the degree to which the challenge to the canon has often depicted its instigators monolithically: that is, merely as dictatorial members "of a privileged class and of the male sex." Almost conspiratorial in some formulations, that approach presumes that the men engaged in "distorting and misreading the few recognized female writers and excluding the others" did so arrogantly and unhesitatingly; that they harbored no reservations, conscious or otherwise, about their warrant to act as literary experts; that (except for a desire to subordinate those threatening

---

John F. Kasson, *Amusing the Million: Coney Island at the Turn of the Century* (New York: Hill and Wang, 1978), p. 6; Malcolm Cowley, *After the Genteel Tradition: American Writers, 1910–1930* (Carbondale, Ill.: Southern Illinois University Press, 1964); Henry F. May, *The End of American Innocence: A Study of the First Years of Our Own Time, 1912–1917* (New York: Knopf, 1959); Dee Garrison, *Apostles of Culture: The Public Librarian and American Society, 1876–1920* (New York: Free Press, 1979), p. 14.

5. The now-classic discussion of selfhood construed as "character" and "personality" is Warren I. Susman. "'Personality' and the Making of Twentieth-Century Culture," in *Culture as History* (New York: Pantheon, 1984), pp. 271–85.

6. On the canon, see, in addition to the article by Janice Radway cited above, Sharon O'Brien, "Becoming Noncanonical: The Case against Willa Cather," in Davidson, *Reading in America,* pp. 240–58; Jane Tompkins, *Sensational Designs: The Cultural Work of American Fiction, 1790–1860* (New York: Oxford University Press, 1985), pp. xi–39 and passim; Gerald Graff, *Professing Literature* (Chicago: University of Chicago Press, 1987) and the essays in Elaine Showalter, ed., *The New Feminist Criticism* (New York: Pantheon, 1985).

them) their own variable psychological needs had no effect on their judgments. One of my purposes is to suggest otherwise.[7]

In particular, I have been struck by the democratic loyalties animating middlebrow critics. While scholars like Lawrence Levine have depicted a process of "sacralization" that, beginning in the mid-nineteenth century, increasingly imposed a pernicious "hierarchy" on what had been a more egalitarian culture, I see my protagonists as engaged in an effort at "desacralization" by disseminating literature to a wide audience. That is, as Macdonald and his colleagues knew all too well, the middlebrow agenda entailed not the creation of an aristocratic preserve but the mediation between realms of "high" art and popular sensibility.[8]

To complicate the matter further, my insistence on recognizing my subjects' democratic orientation nonetheless coexists with my reservations about the phenomenon that enabled them to carry out their disseminating mission: the broadening, in the interwar period, of an American consumer culture. Granted that the growth of a mass market permitted more readers to obtain more books, and that such readers benefitted from those books in ways Macdonald never acknowledged, I share the opinion that consumer priorities made inroads on laudable values associated with the genteel tradition. These values include an affirmation of inward selfhood that minimized the judgment of others and a conviction that critics owe readers an opportunity for disciplined training. My endorsement of these values does not mean that I also condone the lifelessness and conformity some genteel arbiters of taste fostered; in fact, my awareness of gentility's repressive potential is another component of my ambivalent stance. Yet, if, as I believe, the genuine democratization of literature requires the creation of a cultural heritage that is both widely possessed and life-enriching, the cases of two middlebrow critics—Stuart Sherman and John Erskine—remind us that, in the context of American society between 1917 and 1950, the attenuation of genteel commitments did not necessarily serve that end.

Stuart Pratt Sherman's appointment as editor of *Books* in 1924 was a signpost on a circuitous intellectual journey that had begun in his youth.[9] Born

---

7. Lillian S. Robinson, "Treason Our Text: Feminist Challenges to the Literary Canon," in Showalter, *The New Feminist Criticism,* pp. 106, 111–12.

8. Levine, *Highbrow/Lowbrow,* passim. See also Fredric Paul Smoler, "The Bard of Red Dog," *Nation,* 30 January 1989, 132.

9. The basic source for Sherman's life is Jacob Zeitlin and Homer Woodbridge, *Life and Letters of Stuart P. Sherman,* 2 vols., (New York: Farrar and Rinehart, 1929). Hereafter cited as ZW.

in 1881, Sherman grew up on the frontier, but moved East following the death of his father in 1892. As an undergraduate at Williams College between 1900 and 1903, he hoped for a career as a poet. Melancholy by nature—his verse celebrated "black bread" as his portion while others had "cake and wine"—he nonetheless drew sustenance from a vision of self-reliance. In particular, the moral philosopher John Bascom, who personified resolute idealism, taught Sherman that the "austerest beauty of character" derived from lonely adherence to "truth."[10]

Imbued with that conviction, Sherman embarked after graduation on doctoral study in English literature at Harvard. There he came immediately under the influence of one of the university's famous mavericks: Irving Babbitt. Babbitt opposed the critical approach known as philology, a technical method of language analysis that, in the early twentieth century, captivated powerful Harvard scholars such as George Lyman Kittredge. Barred from the Classics Department for his refusal to obtain a Ph.D., Babbitt symbolized the resistance of the generalist to the pressures of specialization and the prestige of science. From that perspective, Babbitt (together with Paul Elmer More) enunciated the doctrine known as the New Humanism. Starting from the premise that every person possessed both a passion-ridden "lower self" and a "higher self" that nourished the life of the spirit, New Humanists argued that human advancement depended on the exercise of restraint, or the "inner check." As a corollary, Babbitt and More rejected the siren call of a consumer culture that offered only the temporary fulfillment of material needs; instead, they dedicated themselves to a search for what they considered less transient, more universal values.[11]

As a program for literary criticism, this quest translated into an insistence on what Babbitt and More called "standards": measures of whether or not a work expressed mankind's "higher" capabilities. The critic's function, according to the New Humanists, was to gauge the degree to which a writer approximated the "best" literature of the past—for example, the Greek classics. Here Babbitt and More revealed a heavy debt to Matthew Arnold, whose definition of culture as "the best that has been thought and said in the world" made him virtually the patron saint of the New Humanist

10. ZW, pp. 75–76, 98.

11. Thomas Nevin, *Irving Babbitt: An Intellectual Study* (Chapel Hill: University of North Carolina Press, 1984), p. 14; Graff, *Professing Literature*, pp. 67–72, 81–97; J. David Hoeveler, *The New Humanism: A Critique of Modern America, 1900–1940* (Charlottesville: University Press of Virginia, 1977), p. 32; Richard Ruland, *The Rediscovery of American Literature: Premises of Critical Taste, 1900–1940* (Cambridge: Harvard University Press, 1967), pp. 14–20.

movement. In determining the "best," Babbitt announced, critics were to exhibit "judgment and selection and only secondarily comprehension and sympathy." Moreover, they were obligated to convey the bases for such judgment to society at large. That is, although deeply skeptical of democracy, New Humanists (again following Arnold) assigned themselves the responsibility of inculcating "standards" in a wide audience. Only with such outreach, they concluded, could human advancement occur. To that end, Babbitt and More embraced the practice of journalism: not the lax, effusive prose of the mass-market periodicals but the discriminating, impersonal style denominated by the phrase the "higher journalism."[12]

Receptive to New Humanism by temperament and education, Sherman became one of Babbitt's chief disciples. As such, he positioned himself (along with his mentor) as a latter-day exemplar of genteel criticism. Ever since George Santayana dubbed the New Humanism the "genteel tradition at bay," scholars have striven to disentangle the two viewpoints—arguing, for example, that Babbitt's position was more reactionary and less romantic than Charles Eliot Norton's. Yet, because historians have assumed that, in the early 1900s, the genteel tradition collapsed under the weight of avantgarde protest and the rise of mass entertainment, it is essential to reiterate the continuities between the genteel ideology and Sherman's developing sensibility.[13]

For Norton, E. L. Godkin, Frederick Law Olmsted, and like-minded reformers, culture was inextricably bound to ethical and aesthetic strictures. Drawing on both Unitarian and Transcendentalist legacies, they defined the cultured person as someone imbued with inward integrity and self-control. The aim of education, Norton explained, was "the development of the breadth, serenity, and solidity of mind, and . . . the attainment of that complete self-possession which finds expression in character." That conception of the self, Warren Susman persuasively argued, reflected the "producer" mentality animating nineteenth-century Americans; it bespoke an entire "culture of character" predicated on the importance of duty, work, and moral order. At the same time, genteel critics counterposed culture to

12. Hoeveler, *New Humanism,* pp. 40, 61–62, 67; Ruland, *Rediscovery of American Literature,* pp. 23–56, 61; Christopher Kent, "Higher Journalism and the Mid-Victorian Clerisy," *Victorian Studies* 13 (1969–70): 181–98. For a discussion of the "higher journalism" in the American context, see David D. Hall, "The 'Higher Journalism' and the Politics of Culture in Mid–Nineteenth-Century America," manuscript, 1988, in my possession.

13. George Santayana, "The Genteel Tradition at Bay," in Douglas L. Wilson, ed., *The Genteel Tradition: Nine Essays by George Santayana* (Cambridge: Harvard University Press, 1967), pp. 153–96.

the pursuit of "tangible profit" and "cheap personal distinction." In terms of literary values, they also demanded that cultured individuals acquire the "fine" perception that would enable them to discern "freshness" of language, "simplicity" of structure, and "beauty" of style. Dedicated, in Daniel Aaron's phrase, to "the craft of writing," they shouldered the obligation to undergo the "training" required to uphold their commitments to art as well as virtue. Finally, genteel leaders founded such institutions as the *Nation* magazine to transmit their views to the public. From those positions of authority, they prescribed attaining autonomy by submitting to the expert guidance of an educated minority: themselves. Yet they were simultaneously motivated by the democratic belief that all citizens deserved a better fate than life in what Norton dubbed a "paradise of mediocrities."[14]

Connected by personal acquaintance and sympathy to a network of British thinkers, the American exponents of the genteel tradition incorporated into their philosophy their friend Matthew Arnold's proposal for diffusing the "best." For that reason alone, the New Humanists can be counted as intellectual descendants of Norton and his colleagues. As Sherman's Emersonian portrait of Bascom underscores, however, the two groups were linked as well by their common emphasis on autonomy, their alienation from the marketplace, and their shared confidence in the "higher journalism." The affinities between Norton's and Babbitt's circles argue that genteel values were redirected, rather than eradicated, in the early twentieth century. In particular, the emergence of New Humanism challenges the chronological boundaries Susman erected around the "culture of character" and the supposedly subsequent "culture of personality." If, as Richard Fox has maintained, Susman's confinement of a concern with personality development to the period after 1900 overlooked earlier manifestations

14. Charles Eliot Norton, "Harvard University in 1890," *Harper's New Monthly Magazine,* September 1890, 590; Kermit Vanderbilt, *Charles Eliot Norton: Apostle of Culture in a Democracy* (Cambridge: Harvard University Press, 1959), pp. 73, 182; Susman, "'Personality,'" pp. 271–85; Charles Eliot Norton, review of "Le Prime Quattro Edizione Della Divina Commedia," by G. G. Warren Lord Vernon, *Atlantic Monthly,* May 1860, 628; Charles Eliot Norton to Edward Lee-Childe, 18 August 1874, and Charles Eliot Norton to W. D. Howells, 28 July 1895 in *Letters of Charles Eliot Norton,* vol. 2, ed. Sara Norton and Mark A. DeWolfe Howe (Boston: Houghton Mifflin, 1913), pp. 47, 230; Charles Eliot Norton, "Notices of Gillett's Huss," *North American Review,* July 1864, 270–71; Thomas Wentworth Higginson, "Literature as an Art," *Atlantic Monthly,* December 1867, 745–54; Thomas Wentworth Higginson, "A Plea for Culture," *Atlantic Monthly,* January 1867, 33; Daniel Aaron, "An Informal Letter to the Editor," *Daedalus* (Winter, 1983): 29; Charles Eliot Norton, "The Paradise of Mediocrities," *Nation,* 13 July 1865, 43–44. See also David D. Hall, "The Victorian Connection," *American Quarterly* (December 1975): 571–74.

of that mentality, the history of Sherman and his teachers supports the complementary point: that (as Susman himself briefly acknowledged) the character ideal flourished, in some quarters, well into the twentieth century.[15]

In 1906, Sherman left the precincts of the genteel tradition to carry its message westward: after a year on the faculty of Northwestern University, he took up an appointment in the English Department of the University of Illinois. There he was free to turn his back on philology and to perpetuate, in his classroom, Babbitt's generalist orientation. He also found time to voice his New Humanist convictions in frequent essays for the *Nation,* which More began editing in 1909. Condemning "decadence" and sentimentality in literature, Sherman set himself against the stance Joel Spingarn and others were then defining as "impressionism": the idea that a book's success lay in the extent to which it re-created in its readers the emotions of the author. Some "impressionists" even went so far as to argue that the function of criticism was not "pedagogical" but "to provide a means of self-expression for the critic." Sherman's countervailing effort, as he explained in a collection of his *Nation* articles, was to foster "the instructed and disciplined heart." His directive to the readers of his *Matthew Arnold: How To Know Him* (1917)—a study that was at once disguised autobiography and critical manifesto—perhaps best summarizes his view of his role at this time: "[I]f you make an earnest effort to perceive the stylistic distinctions which Arnold tells you are there," Sherman urged, "you will find the process highly exciting to your esthetic sensibility; you will undergo an esthetic discipline which you will never forget, and which will leave you with a sense of augmented power in these matters." Both the authoritative tone of that statement and the connections it presumed among culture, training, and self-reliance represent the highwater mark of Sherman's genteel critical practice.[16]

In particular, Sherman vigorously opposed literary naturalism. As is well known, he focused his animosity on the work of Theodore Dreiser, calling it "barbaric" because it depicted the animalistic side of human beings rather than their "higher selves." This position, which Sherman larded with a good bit of anti-German prejudice after the outbreak of World War I, drew

15. Richard Wightman Fox, "The Culture of Liberal Protestant Progressivism, 1875–1925," *Journal of Interdisciplinary History* 23 (Winter, 1993); Susman, "'Personality'," p. 274.

16. J. Middleton Murry, "A Critical Credo," *New Republic,* 26 October 1921, 251; Stuart P. Sherman, *On Contemporary Literature* (New York: Henry Holt, 1917), p. 17; Stuart P. Sherman, *Matthew Arnold: How to Know Him* (Indianapolis, Bobbs-Merrill, 1917), p. 174.

the opprobrium of H. L. Mencken, who saw him as boorish and provincial. It also alienated Randolph Bourne, Van Wyck Brooks, and other so-called Young Intellectuals just then championing modernism and artistic freedom. To them, Sherman typified the benighted older generation: Sherman himself imagined the "radicals" derisively howling at him, "Go up, bald head!"[17]

But more was involved than questions of censorship, taste, or generational conflict. At the core of the controversy was Sherman's conception of the canon of American literature. Since the early 'teens, when his former student Carl Van Doren had invited him to contribute to the *Cambridge History of American Literature,* Sherman had been exploring the nation's literary traditions. ("How interesting American literature is after all," he wrote Van Doren, "when you really get down to it!") Exemplifying the argument of Jane Tompkins and others that critics have repeatedly reconstituted the "same" ostensibly "classic" texts in light of their own presuppositions, Sherman began refashioning that tradition in terms of the New Humanist program. As Richard Ruland has demonstrated, his construction of the canon included an interpretation of the Puritans that (influenced by More) construed them as homegrown models of the "inner check." Similarly, his *Cambridge History* article on Franklin portrayed him as a premature Arnoldian. When Mencken unleashed his attack, Sherman accused him and the young "cosmopolitans" of cutting themselves off from the "builders of American civilization." Condemning his adversaries' celebration of naturalism as a liberation from the past, he insisted that great literature would only arise when writers drew upon a national heritage of moral idealism. In support of his case, Sherman depicted Emerson and Thoreau as appropriately concerned with the "higher self."[18]

While Sherman's rereading of American literature upheld Babbitt and More's conviction that culture depended on familiarity with the "best," his version of the national legacy nevertheless contained one element that made his mentors distinctly uncomfortable: a more positive view of democracy than they could stomach. In place of Babbitt and More's grudging

17. Sherman, *On Contemporary Literature,* pp. 85–101; Ruland, *Rediscovery,* p. 154; ZW, p. 345.

18. ZW, p. 259; Tompkins, *Sensational Designs,* pp. 196–99; Ruland, *Rediscovery,* pp. 61, 78–90; Stuart P. Sherman, "Benjamin Franklin," *Cambridge History of American Literature,* vol. 1, ed. William Peterfield Trent, John Erskine, Stuart P. Sherman, and Carl Van Doren (New York: Cambridge University Press, 1917), pp. 90–110; Stuart P. Sherman, *Americans* (New York: Charles Scribner's Sons, 1922), pp. 14, 98; Stuart P. Sherman, *The Genius of America* (New York: Charles Scribner's Sons, 1923), p. 28.

concession of the need for the dissemination of taste, Sherman accepted democratic government and even affirmed its benefits. In an essay begun for the *Cambridge History,* he faulted Henry James for advocating "aesthetic aristocracy"; by the same token, he applauded Whitman as a figure who sought "distinction" for the "average man." No less the Arnoldian, Sherman distinguished between pandering to a "new public now swarming up the avenues of democratic opportunity" and raising the populace by preserving an "aristocracy of talent." Yet his stance as canonizer involved not so much the self-serving entrenchment of elite interests as the recognition of a dilemma: How, in a democratic society, should the critic mediate between art and politics, "standards" and accessibility? To W. C. Brownell, he outlined a preliminary (if vague) solution:

The line I have taken and intend to follow is the encouragement of the native tradition, with all its imperfections on its head, . . . the adventurous, daring, exploring, spirit, democracy. . . . I got a couple of volumes of [Santayana], and these with the works of Arnold and your books and whatever appeared in the older *Nation* style—the Charles Eliot Norton tradition, and Babbitt's and More's books— whatever, in short, was most hostile, on the surface, to the earthy, rough Jacksonian element in our life and literature seemed the things to cultivate. They seem so still. . . . [But] I want to get the Emersons and the Jacksons together, and their offspring to intermarry. I believe the American breed will profit by the misalliance.[19]

Sherman's political position thus drew him somewhat closer to figures such as Brooks and Bourne than they recognized. Moreover, both factions' sense of the generation gap dividing them overlooked striking similarities between Sherman's state of mind and the quest for "experience" and free expression that animated many Young Intellectuals. As one of his colleagues remembered, there were "two Stuart Shermans": the scholar increasingly ensconced in academia and the romantic who perpetuated another facet of the Emersonian tradition by clinging to his early poetic ambitions. In a letter to a friend in 1907, for example, Sherman contradicted the genteel vision of integrated, interior selfhood by observing that man was "a hungry living case enclosing the cadaver of a soul." Seeking emotional release but weighed down by academic strictures, he reported that his own spirit was "nearly dead." Two years later, envying some construction workers outside his window, he recorded in his journal, "Brain sensation as of nausea at 'intellectual life.'" This undercurrent of discontent flowed into his study of Arnold, who, in Sherman's view, subordinated his "instinctive and spontaneous feelings" to the demands of "duty" and

19. Ruland, *Rediscovery,* pp. 78–81, 85–86; Sherman, *Americans,* p. 2; ZW, pp. 521–22.

self-mastery. In 1918, the same tensions surfaced in a letter to Carl Van Doren: "I waver between the delight of losing touch with the world in the pages of Giraldus Cambrensis and the Grettir Saga, and on the other hand wishing I were a muddy journalist cuffing and taking cuffs in the thick of the struggle."[20]

Interestingly, Sherman's restlessness included resistance to the form as well as the content of genteel ideology. As early as 1912, he articulated to More the beginnings of a dissent from the requirements of the "*Nation*-essay" that would eventually lead him out of the New Humanist camp altogether: "In the space at our disposal it is necessary to be very curt. . . . We break [writers'] necks in a *Nation*-essay and wash our hands of them. We ought to have space to show that we, too, understand all the seductions of their hyacinthine locks before we break their necks. . . . [W]e should oppose enthusiasm to enthusiam." Such reservations constituted, at bottom, a demurrer about the legitimacy of the critic's authority. More was predictably alarmed. "[A]n excess of judgment," he told Sherman, "is no bad thing these days, and 'enthusiasm' makes me afraid."[21]

Sherman's fight against naturalism served to abate his desire for "real life" somewhat. Yet, in place of the inward serenity he officially admired, his Arnoldian and romantic aspects remained in conflict. Around 1921, when he turned forty, Sherman's longings for experience finally erupted in a "definite crisis." Although literary scholars have portrayed the episode as idiosyncratic, the terms in which Sherman conceptualized his malaise were clearly indicative of a larger cultural transformation: the shift, to invoke Susman again, from the culture of "character" to the preoccupation with "personality." Those attitudes most widely identified with the latter phenomenon—a concern with growth, therapeutic renewal, and self-expression for its own sake—now broke through the dam of Sherman's New Humanism.[22] Protesting against the capacity of the genteel outlook to value decorum over spontaneous feeling, he announced his plans hence-

20. Christopher Lasch, *The New Radicalism in America, 1889–1963: The Intellectual as a Social Type* (New York: Vintage, 1965), pp. 99–103 and passim; ZW, pp. 142, 160–61, 297, 299, 367; Sherman, *Matthew Arnold,* pp. 4, 10, 18.

21. ZW, pp. 233–36.

22. See, for example, T. J. Jackson Lears, "From Salvation to Self-Realization," in Richard Wightman Fox and T. J. Jackson Lears, eds., *The Culture of Consumption: Critical Essays in American History, 1880–1980* (New York: Pantheon, 1983), pp. 3–38; T. J. Jackson Lears, *No Place of Grace: Antimodernism and the Transformation of American Culture, 1880–1920* (New York: Pantheon, 1981); Christopher Lasch, *The Culture of Narcissism* (New York: W. W. Norton, 1978).

forth to stop "hammering out his 'solid character.'" In lieu of adherence to restraint and moral obligation, he substituted a new creed: "Unfold leaf by leaf. . . . Push on into untrodden forests, up unexplored valleys, seeking new springs of refreshment, crying at the foot of every mountain ridge, 'Let us see what is on the other side.'"[23]

It is crucial to recognize that, despite his resolve to "gather up and concentrate and intensify," Sherman did not entirely abandon his earlier perspective; in fact, he periodically reiterated his commitment to the construction of character while pursuing his therapeutic quest. In an essay entitled "The Shifting Centre of Morality" (1923), which at once beautifully documents the changes cultural historians have delineated and points out that dedication to both visions of the self could coexist, Sherman even denounced the tendency of young Americans to turn away from an "inner monitor" toward an "external, socially-centered" ethic. "In the violence of their reaction against the idealism and inwardness of their fathers," he lamented, "they rejoice in their intention of living on the surface of things."[24] Nevertheless, to the extent that Sherman himself joined that youthful rebellion, he became an apostle of the culture of "personality" in its most solipsistic form. Unlike Randolph Bourne, for example, who urged the liberation of an individual's creative capacities in the context of a socialist community, Sherman failed to link his concern with personal development to radical politics. Instead, his reorientation facilitated surrender of the most laudable features of the genteel tradition to the ethos of self-realization through consumption. To borrow Sherman's image, those unintended consequences of Sherman's new position with respect to his stance as critic "unfolded" gradually in the mid-1920s.[25]

His first move was to step up his protest against the formal constraints the "higher journalism" imposed. In language that, again, nicely captures the paradigms of selfhood involved, he wrote Henry Seidel Canby the year before the onset of the "crisis": "For some time, I have 'sort-of' hankered

---

23. Stuart P. Sherman, "Forty and Upwards"; reprinted in *Points of View* (New York: Charles Scribner's Sons, 1924), pp. 29–46.

24. Stuart P. Sherman, "Flappers and Philosophers," *McCall's*, May 1923, 14ff.; reprinted as "The Shifting Centre of Morality," in *The Genius of America* (cited in note 18), pp. 95–124.

25. Casey Nelson Blake, "The Young Intellectuals and the Culture of Personality," *American Literary History* (Fall 1989): 510–31; Casey Nelson Blake, *Beloved Community: The Cultural Criticism of Randolph Bourne, Van Wyck Brooks, Waldo Frank, and Lewis Mumford* (Chapel Hill: University of North Carolina Press, 1989); Richard W. Fox, review of *Walter Rauschenbusch: American Reformer*, by Paul M. Minus, *Journal of American History* (December 1989): 953.

to pull out an essay stop which is somewhere in my melodeon. . . . I hanker for the freedom of the 'informal essay' and particularly for the 'personality' of it, as allowing an expression of 'suppressed desires'; and flatter myself that once the outlet is found, I might produce like a flowing well." Acting on the same impulse, he contributed a series of articles for the *Atlantic Monthly* later published as *My Dear Cornelia* (1924). In the guise of fiction, Sherman assayed the conflict between the genteel tradition (represented by Cornelia, a well-bred middle-aged *Atlantic* reader) and "modern" morality (symbolized by Cornelia's husband and daughter). Sherman himself appeared as a "professor of literature" who understands Cornelia but wants her to reassess her antiquated views. By arguing that contemporary American fiction actually fostered standards because it illuminated the misery degeneracy created, Sherman effected a rapprochement with naturalism. (In the same period, he admitted Sinclair Lewis to his canon on similar grounds.) The *Cornelia* project as a whole, Sherman explained to one correspondent, was an "experimental" attempt to "see how much of a case can be made out for the 'externalized life.'" It outstripped all of Sherman's other books in terms of sales and popular acclaim.[26]

The most dramatic embodiment of Sherman's reorientation, however, occurred in the fall of 1924, when he moved his experiment to a different laboratory: the offices of *Books* in New York. Earlier that year, after buying the *Herald* and merging it with the *Tribune,* Ogden and Helen Rogers Reid had decided to add to the new paper an ambitious literary weekly. Interested in hiring an editor who was "both competent and readable," they approached Sherman. By this time, Sherman's ongoing discontent had strained his relationships at Illinois: even the university president's Christmas greeting praising him for figuratively constructing his "house" of "marble" triggered a hostile response in which Sherman equated character-building with embalming. In addition, he was tired of teaching and wished only to write. Once the Reids promised to hire Irita Bradford Van Doren (then Carl Van Doren's wife) for the day-to-day management of the supplement, he accepted their offer.[27]

26. ZW, p. 477; Stuart P. Sherman, *My Dear Cornelia* (Boston: Atlantic Monthly Press, 1924); ZW, p. 620.

27. Royal Cortissoz to Geoffrey Parsons, 6 January 1923, Helen Rogers Reid Papers, Library of Congress, Washington, DC; Maynard Britchford, "Notes from the Archives," *The Laputa Gazette and Faculty News* (University of Illinois at Urbana-Champaign), 20 March 1969; ZW, pp. 643–48. On the *New York Herald Tribune,* see Richard Kluger, *The Paper: The Life and Death of the New York Herald Tribune* (New York: Knopf, 1986).

As he prepared to leave academia behind, Sherman confided to his journal an especially illuminating set of observations about the task that awaited him. On the one hand, his Arnoldian background survived in a persistent sense of educational mission. He was, he noted, merely substituting "one classroom for another." In several entries, he displayed vestiges of New Humanism, reiterating the theory of the "inner check" on base impulses and the partnership of literature and ethics. On the other hand, he declared his determination to "write, so far as possible, about happiness, and where it is, and how it got there; and every paragraph that I write shall have the word, or the record of happiness in it." Accompanying that Whitmanesque hymn to gratification was a redefinition of his purpose in terms that made the critic not the enemy of the marketplace but, rather, its agent. "As you widen your audience," he told himself, "you omit your parentheses; you eliminate dependent clauses; you reduce subordination. . . ; you reduce allusion; you erase shades; you don't soften lines; you remember you are advertising—a 'Poster' not an etching." Moreover, he explicitly rejected the model of selfhood Bascom and Babbitt had provided in favor of an explicit rendering of the critic as social performer: "We don't want soliloquy. Personality. Megaphone at Stamford Bridge— jollying the American crowds—Mark Twain did it. . . . Now comes my chance to try it." More concretely, repudiating the tenets of the "higher journalism," he conceded that part of a literary supplement's function was to help publishers sell their wares. In that spirit, he imagined himself in a role diametrically opposed to that of guardian of a sacred canon; he would be, instead, a "cheer leader" promoting "fair play" and "enthusiasm"—the word that had made More shudder—even if the contestants failed to "break a world record."[28]

Sherman's ambivalence about the "cheer leader" conceit was so strong that, shortly after he actually assumed the *Books* editorship, he disparaged Canby as a "sportsman" who merely encouraged all sorts of literary "games" without committing himself to any. Similarly, in the lead reviews he wrote for each issue, he announced that Dreiser had "the imagination of a chemist," affirmed the virtue of "self-denial," and insisted on Robert Louis Stevenson's greatness. His allegiance to the genteel aesthetic shone through in his praise for accurate character portrayal and "luminous" language. Nonetheless, Sherman implemented his decision to explore personality and mimic advertising by ladening his prose with intimate biographical or

28. ZW, pp. 654, 679, 682–83, 685–86, 691.

autobiographical detail, evocative imagery, and captivating sentence rhythm. A few months into his new job, he noted to his son the assumption behind his style: "Your vulgar reader can dispense almost with thinking if you prod his senses sharply enough." That statement, worthy of a copy-writer's manual, was not exactly what Arnold had in mind when he called for "carrying" the "best knowledge" from "one end of society to the other."[29]

At the same time, Sherman's pursuit of self-expression paradoxically inclined him increasingly to muffle his authoritative voice. By the end of 1925, when he issued his first collection of *Books* articles, his uncertainty about his right to pass judgment had overwhelmed his image of himself as moral arbiter. "No man," he remarked, "should state very emphatically what the 'good life' is until he has found it." Instead, he pledged himself simply to supply "a fairly full and veracious report of what is going on." The critic, Sherman added, would have "his own convictions regarding the permanent value of various parts of the contemporary spectacle. . . . But his first duty is not to exploit his own predilections; it is rather to under-stand the entire 'conspiracy' of forces involved in the taste of his day." Thus he would from then on try "on all possible occasions to keep his theoretical and didactic mouth shut."[30]

This reconception of himself as a reporter rather than an educator was the ultimate result of Sherman's assent to the values modern American consumer culture enshrined. Moreover, his stance operated, in turn, to strengthen those values. The idea that book reviews (especially those in the daily press) should be primarily a form of news stretched back to the early nineteenth century. Yet it acquired more power after the Civil War, when specialized knowledge, instead of broad cultivation, was increasingly essential for success. It was not only that the fivefold expansion of the book market between 1880 and 1930 enhanced the appeal of bulletins sorting out the latest titles; it was also that, in the context of a bureaucratic, mass society, ready information about books could appear a more useful weapon against anonymity than the slow, disciplined preparation genteel

29. Stuart P. Sherman, "Recognizing One of Our Contemporaries," *Books,* 12 October 1924, 1; Sherman, "Vanity Fair in 1924," *Books,* 16 November 1924, 1; Sherman, "Style or the Quest of Perfection, *Books,* 19 October 1924, 1; Sherman, "R. L. S. Encounters the 'Modern' Writers on Their Own Ground," *Books,* 25 October 1926, 3; Sherman, "Anatole France," *Books,* 26 October 1924, 3; Sherman, "Lawrence Cultivates His Beard," *Books,* 14 June 1925, 3; ZW, pp. 718–19; Matthew Arnold, *Culture and Anarchy,* ed. J. Dover Wilson (Cambridge: Harvard University Press, 1969), p. 70.

30. Stuart P. Sherman, *Critical Woodcuts* (New York: Charles Scribner's Sons, 1926), pp. xii–xiii, xviii.

critics recommended. Sherman's reportorial posture enhanced that perception, narrowing the definition of culture to an item that, like other trappings of "personality," could enable its procurer to stand out from the crowd. What is more, Sherman's equation of culture with news reinforced the modern premium on efficiency; implicitly, it helped readers conserve resources for more important pursuits such as business. As one advertisement explained, "The less time you have for reading, the more important it is for you to consult *Books* in order that none of your reading time may be wasted."[31]

It is true that Sherman's realignment of the "higher journalism" with reportage well served his egalitarian commitments: instead of flaunting his superior expertise, he now swung over to the Jacksonian side of the "marriage" he had arranged earlier. That stance, moreover, could function as a kind of strategic adaptation to the challenges the rise of mass culture posed to genteel authority. As pluralism became a fact of American political life, Sherman's identification of himself as "an inveterate and incorrigible average man" could accommodate and deflect resistance to the power of experts in a democratic society. To one reader, for example, Sherman insisted that "you have in your own mind some of the material needful for a judgment, with standards." That abdication of the critic's responsibility superficially restored the audience's autonomy. Yet as Sherman abandoned adjudicating "the best," the exploration of "personality" rushed in to fill the resulting vacuum. The same reader, aware that something was lost in the bargain, thus complained that Sherman had reduced criticism to "personal likes and dislikes"; to his dismay, he found in Sherman's reviews only "that subjective flavor" that made him conclude "Oh, well, that's the way it affects him." In that respect, Sherman's espousal of a less elitist outlook actually heightened the tendency to think of culture as a commodity useful for distinguishing oneself from others and deprived readers of the aesthetic training to which, in a democracy, they were arguably entitled.[32]

By 1926, the affinity for the marketplace permeating Sherman's criticism and politics had so unraveled his role as genteel canonizer that Edmund Wilson cast him as the ringmaster in what Wilson disparaged as the "all-

---

31. For the book market, see Hellmut Lehmann-Haupt, Lawrence C. Wroth, and Rollo G. Silver, *The Book in America: A History of the Making and Selling of Books in the United States* (New York: R. R. Bowker, 1951), p. 321; *Books*, 8 July 1928, 16.

32. Stuart P. Sherman, "Philosophy and the Average Man's Adult Education," *Books*, 20 June 1926, 1; Stuart P. Sherman, "The Man in the Street Protests," *Books*, 22 February 1925, 12.

star literary vaudeville." Highlighting Sherman's appropriation of copywriting techniques, Wilson declared that Sherman and his colleagues tended to "forget critical standards"; as "salesmen" for "contemporary literary goods," they made it impossible to "tell the reviews from the advertising." During his years at *Books,* Sherman's compliance with consumer culture also solidified into a thoroughgoing acceptance of American capitalism. "I am a strong believer in the American bourgeoisie," he wrote in one review, "and feel great pride in its virtues and achievements." To the members of New York's Rotary Club, he took to the extreme his conflation of criticism and news, counseling executives to treat literature as an "information department" that would increase profits.[33]

Still, it would be a mistake to follow Wilson in depicting Sherman's reorientation as a process of selling out. The tensions governing his sensibility remained—his poetic longings counteracting his boosterism, his painful awareness of human loneliness offsetting his preoccupation with "happiness," his respect for inner selfhood surviving his attempt to live "on the surface of things." Speaking to a colleague of his determination to pursue pleasure, he once conceded, "I would, you know, approach amusement in that way, as a duty." If he had lived longer, Sherman might ultimately have achieved more serenity. In the summer of 1926, however, he died of a heart attack while swimming in Lake Michigan. By an odd coincidence, even the placement of his death notice in American newspapers epitomized the conflicts with which he struggled in life. His obituary shared space with those for two other figures, one representing the genteel tradition, the other the "culture of personality": Charles W. Eliot, the former president of Harvard, and the actor Rudolph Valentino.[34]

The strains marking Sherman's career comprise what one might call the "middleness" of middlebrow culture: not only its location between the "high" and the "popular," but also its capacity to preserve aspects of gentility while reinforcing the priorities of a modern "business civilization." To apprehend the psychological and cultural sources of that doubleness and

33. Edmund Wilson, "The All-Star Literary Vaudeville," reprinted in *The Plastic Age, 1917–1930,* ed. Robert Sklar (New York, 1970), pp. 152–53; Stuart P. Sherman, "Middle Class Strategy or a Call to the Converted," *Books,* 22 February 1925, 3; Sherman, "Speaking to Successful Executives and Business Men Only on the Literary Profession," in Stuart P. Sherman, *The Emotional Discovery of America* (New York: Farrar and Rinehart, 1932), p. 128.

34. ZW, pp. 699, 800; Stuart P. Sherman, "Miss Sinclair Presents Magnanimous Love," *Books,* 5 October 1924, 1.

to see, in Sherman, its poignant result, is to move beyond Macdonald's portrait of middlebrows as dissembling vulgarizers.

At the same time, to recognize that, as *Books* continued on the course Sherman charted, it drifted further toward an emphasis on news and personality is to wish for more, not less, exercise of middlebrow authority. Succeeding him as editor, Irita Van Doren conceived of herself as office manager rather than critic. Her guiding principle, she explained in a rare interview, was "fairness"—reviewing books "from the point of view from which they were written, so that they will ultimately find the audience for whom they are intended." That version of journalistic "objectivity" had a number of consequences: it eradicated the presumption that some books should not find an audience at all; it rejected Arnoldian commitments to discerning, aesthetically and morally, the "best"; it made neutrality itself a virtue (thus quelling Marxist demands, in the 1930s, for "proletarian literature"); it weakened critical authority to the point that, as observers on both the political right and left complained, the book supplement became a hodgepodge of competing viewpoints. Coupled with Van Doren's straightforward determination to combine literary gossip with an emphasis on the "news value" of current books, and with the *Herald Tribune*'s crusade to garner as much advertising linage as possible, *Books* by the late forties exhibited even greater congruence with consumer priorities than in Sherman's day. Ironically, Sherman himself eventually came to symbolize for Geoffrey Parsons, the editor who most influenced the *Herald Tribune*'s cultural coverage, an evanescent harmony of format and intention—even as Parsons called for fewer reviews and greater emphasis on information about books and personalities. Only the demise of the paper after the New York newspaper strike of 1962–63 laid those lingering tensions to rest.[35]

The explicitness with which Sherman registered his apostasy from gentility—notably his dichotomous use of the terms "character" and "personality"—make him an especially strong example of the middlebrow configuration I have been sketching. By way of indicating that Sherman was not unique, however, it is worth a briefer look at another figure at the center

---

35. "*Books* Covers the World of Books," *Publishers' Weekly*, 30 September 1939, pp. 1339, 1346; Ishbel Ross, *Ladies of the Press: The Story of Women in Journalism by an Insider* (New York: Harper and Brothers, 1936), p. 404; Geoffrey Parsons Memos, 1 September 1952, quoted in notes, Richard Kluger Papers, Yale University Library, New Haven, Conn.; Kluger, *The Paper*, pp. 201, 346, 465.

of American middlebrow culture in the first half of the twentieth century: John Erskine. Sharing Sherman's restiveness and desire for self-expression, Erskine nonetheless remained more closely tethered to gentility than Sherman did. Hence, in a different but equally powerful way, his career throws into high relief the dualities at the heart of the middlebrow perspective.

Born in 1879, Erskine grew up in Weehawken, New Jersey, in surroundings he labeled "aristocratic." As a child, he learned a set of rituals—dressing for dinner, afternoon piano recitals, formal etiquette—that instilled in him a respect for genteel definitions of refinement and decorum. Along with manners, he also acquired a commitment to the Episcopal church and to white Anglo-Saxon Protestant leadership in matters of civic concern and taste. Within the aura of stability his home represented, the character ideal flourished. His father, James Erskine, strove for Emersonian self-reliance; he was "affectionate but slightly reserved, always balanced and self-controlled." Another fixture in the household, Erksine's maternal uncle William Hollingsworth, similarly exhibited "iron" restraint. Thus sheltered, the young Erskine regarded Weehawken as permanent and preeminent.[36]

Yet the genteel milieu of Erskine's youth—and its concomitant vision of the self—were already disappearing under the influence of the new industrial order. As Erskine later recognized, Union Hill—the immigrant community where his father's ribbon factory was located—symbolized the "real life" of the future, while Weehawken was receding into the past. More palpably, James Erskine suffered severe financial reverses in the early nineties and gradually lost all of his assets. To his son, he seemed a victim of the pressure for practicality at the expense of art. Like the creative misfits Van Wyck Brooks described as wounded by the "catchpenny realities" of American capitalism, James Erskine became, in these years, a figure whose outward stoicism concealed thwarted energies and dreams. Furthermore, while his father's unhappiness arose from the assault on genteel ideals, Erskine's uncle's history suggested another source of the same discontinuity: the demand for conformity that gentility itself could generate. Hollingsworth, in his nephew's view, was courtly, superficially conventional, and miserable; beneath his distant manner there was "a furnace or boiler, which might blow up at any minute." Faced with those two examples of fragmented selfhood, the adolescent Erskine came to understand that both

---

36. John Erskine, *The Memory of Certain Persons* (Philadelphia: J. B. Lippincott, 1947), pp. 14, 18, 21, 23, 43–46, 51.

Union Hill and Weehawken exacted a price—at least from sensitive men. The conflicts he witnessed in his father and uncle were portents of the tensions he would soon evince himself.[37]

Still, Erksine continued, much like Sherman, to endorse and pursue genteel notions of self and culture. As an undergraduate at Columbia University between 1896 and 1900, he gravitated toward the generalists and traditionalists on the faculty who were defending liberal study against the advocates of specialization. In particular, Erskine became devoted to the poet George Edward Woodberry. A student of Charles Eliot Norton and a disciple of Emerson, Woodberry represented an unbroken link to the genteel tradition in its literary manifestation. While aspects of his idealist outlook emphasized growth and self-development, his fundamental commitments were to aesthetic sensitivity rather than social performance. Woodberry himself embodied to Erskine the unity that had eluded his male relatives: he imparted the idea, Erskine recalled, "that poetry is the flower of life but still an integral part of it" and that "all human activities are related, and—unless one is stupid or a hypocrite—must be harmonious." Although William James, for one, implied that Woodberry's autonomy came at the expense of action, the young Erskine found his mentor's outlook "a thrilling vision," adding that "in its power many who sat in Woodberry's classes have tried to live."[38]

Upon graduation, Erskine remained at Columbia for doctoral work in English under Woodberry's direction. Like Sherman, he also wrote poetry. His literary pursuits, conducted in the confines of the university, enabled him, for a time, to stave off the threats to gentility outside its gates. The inauguration of Nicholas Murray Butler as the institution's president in 1902, however, signalled the triumph at Columbia of practicality over idealism. When Woodberry became embroiled in a feud with his worldly colleague Brander Matthews, Erskine took his teacher's side, but acknowledged the doubts that had begun to invade his sense of his role: "Our university would grow, its graduates would be legion," he mused, but "would there be a place on its staff for original minds? On the other hand. . . , why should not a poet like Woodberry be a man of action,

37. Erskine, *Memory,* pp. 14, 21, 23, 47–48; Brooks, "America's Coming-of-Age," p. 17.
38. Joel Spingarn, "George Edward Woodberry," *Dictionary of American Biography* 20 (New York: Charles Scribner's Sons, 1936), pp. 478–81; George Edward Woodberry, *The Appreciation of Literature* (New York: Baker and Taylor, 1907), pp. 53, 107, 175; *Letters of William James* 2 (Boston: Atlantic Monthly Press, 1920), p. 89; Erskine, *Memory,* p. 94.

competent in daily affairs? These questions, posed by swift changes at Columbia, filled my head almost as much as my studies."[39]

Appointed assistant professor of English at Amherst College in 1903, Erskine continued to operate from Woodberry's pedagogical premises. Nonetheless a crisis about his potential as a poet triggered anew the misgivings he had managed to suppress earlier. Dismayed by the Amherst community's preoccupation with parlor rituals, he hungered as well for a less contemplative existence. Although his writings from the period permit only speculation and inference, he appears to have formulated the same question that troubled many twentieth-century intellectuals: How to embrace life beyond the printed page while sustaining an integrated self? Less willing than Sherman simply to throw "character" aside, Erskine also differed from the "antimodernists" Jackson Lears has identified by dissenting from their conviction that self-realization required breaking away from outworn prescriptions for restraint and control. Rather, for the rest of his career Erskine struggled to reconcile the expectations of the genteel tradition with a yearning for unbridled experience.[40]

Two circumstances enabled Erskine to attain a measure of the engagement he desired. The first was his return to Columbia as a member of the English Department in 1909. (In that role, he collaborated with Sherman, Van Doren, and Trent on the *Cambridge History,* contributing the chapter on Hawthorne.) The second—perhaps the most significant moment in Erskine's career—resulted from the entry of the United States into World War I. Early in 1918, Erskine went to France to take charge of an educational program for American soldiers waiting to be demobilized. The work was exhausting, but also more exhilarating than the "petty world" and "small things" that had occupied him at Amherst and Columbia. Randolph Bourne, who, as Erskine's former student, sarcastically assailed him as aloof and superficial in "The Professor" (1915), actually could not have had Erskine in mind when, two years later, he published his famous analysis

---

39. Erskine, *Memory,* pp. 110–11; Lloyd Morris, *A Threshold in the Sun* (New York: Harper and Brothers, 1943, pp. 81–84; Lionel Trilling, "The Van Amringe and Keppel Eras," in *A History of Columbia College on Morningside* (New York: Columbia University Press, 1954), p. 24; Laurence Veysey, *The Emergence of the American University* (Chicago: University of Chicago Press, 1965), pp. 426–27.

40. Henry Morton Robinson, "John Erskine as I Knew Him," *Columbia Alumni News,* March 1957, 9; Erskine, *Memory,* p. 182; John Erskine to Melville Cane, 3 October 1906, John Erskine Papers, Columbia University Library, New York; John Erskine, *My Life as a Teacher* (Philadelphia: J. B. Lippincott, 1948), pp. 32–49; Lears, "From Salvation to Self-Realization," pp. 10–17.

of "The War and the Intellectuals," because Bourne's piece appeared prior to Erskine's enlistment in the war effort. Yet Erskine's response precisely matched Bourne's argument that the conflict satisfied a "craving for action" among "practitioners of literature." As Erskine's second wife recalled, "He often said that his first trip to France . . . was a subconscious liberation. . . . How often he said, 'Remember to live! Be the active participant, not the onlooker!' . . . He preferred the Front. He said he found there the peace of decision, the calm that comes when you've made up your mind, when there is no turning back, when the die is cast." In addition, however, the discipline and sacrifice the war exacted overlaid Erskine's liberation with familiar genteel ideals. It was the knowledge that he was both doing his duty and forgoing restraint that, one suspects, fully accounts for Erskine's comment that he had "a feeling of peace all the time."[41]

That serenity receded upon Erskine's resumption of his position at Columbia. But he strove to reconstitute it, as best he could, by waging a different fight: a battle for curricular reform. As early as 1908, Erskine, influenced by Woodberry and others, had begun formulating a remedy for his contemporaries' perception that American college students were ignorant of the "best" literature. Because "great" books were, by his definition, capable of speaking to diverse audiences, Erskine urged instructors merely to let students relate them to their own lives. When first published, Erskine reasoned, the "classics" addressed readers who were unfamiliar with the historical background, philology, and bibliography his colleagues insisted undergraduates master. Why not permit the same sort of encounter with the text in the modern American classroom? In 1916, Erskine presented to the Columbia faculty a formal plan along those lines for the study of "great books." In addition to a list of required titles, it prescribed a structure and approach: classes were to consist of small discussion groups guided by two teachers who were "not to lecture nor in any way behave like professors." Too controversial to win immediate approval, Erskine's proposal hung in abeyance until he returned from Europe. By then, however, a war-inspired interdisciplinary course on "Contemporary Civilization" had

41. Morris, *Threshold in the Sun,* p. 80; John Erskine to Eliza Hollingsworth Erskine, 18 March 1918 and 23 February 1919, Box 1, 1975 addition, John Erskine Papers; Randolph Bourne, "The Professor," in *History of a Literary Radical and Other Essays,* ed. Van Wyck Brooks (New York: B. W. Huebsch, 1920), pp. 91–97; Randolph Bourne, "The War and the Intellectuals," in *The War and the Intellectuals: Collected Essays, 1915–1919,* ed. Carl Resek (New York: Harper Torchbooks, 1964), pp. 3, 11; "The Reminiscences of Helen Worden Erskine" (1957), p. 113, Columbia Oral History Collection, Columbia University, New York.

paved the way for the format Erskine had in mind. In 1920, under the rubric "General Honors," Columbia offered its first "great books" seminar. Exported to the University of Chicago by Erskine's student Mortimer Adler and carried into the lay community by such figures as Adler, Mark Van Doren, Clifton Fadiman, and Erskine himself, the course inspired both General Education curricula and "great books" discussion groups throughout the country.[42]

Today, the controversy about the latter-day versions of Erskine's innovation—particularly Adler's and Allen Bloom's assumption that the canon of "great books" includes almost exclusively works by white men in the Western tradition—has sensitized us to the biases in Erskine's design. He can be faulted not only for omitting women and non-Western writers but also for slighting modernists and Americans. Erskine's prejudices, moreover, were not confined to literary matters: in his letters of the period, he expressed dismay at the influx of immigrants at Columbia.[43] Yet, even so, far from merely attempting to preserve the hegemony of a cultural elite, Erskine actually aimed to open up, rather than restrict access to, his admittedly skewed canon. By discarding historical and philological exegesis, and by licensing the use of works in translation, he sustained a place for the generalist in an increasingly specialized society. Similarly, although Richard Brodhead has observed that, at least in the case of American literature, the promulgators of the canon in the early twentieth century worked to "underwrite their own new cultural authority" by selecting texts so difficult as to require "expert assistance," the original "great books" ideology was predicated on precisely the opposite idea. In much the same way that

42. *Columbia College Gazette,* December 1916, 3–6 and May 1917, 1; John Erskine, "The Teaching of Literature in College," *Nation,* 3 September 1908, 202–4; John Erskine, *The Delight of Great Books* (Indianapolis: Bobbs-Merrill, 1927), pp. 21, 23. Erskine, *My Life as a Teacher,* pp. 168, 170; John Erskine, "General Honors at Columbia," *New Republic,* 25 October 1922, Supplement, 13; Trilling, "Van Amringe and Keppel Eras," pp. 44–47; Justus Buchler, "Reconstruction in the Liberal Arts," *Columbia College on Morningside,* pp. 48–54; James Sloan Allen, *The Romance of Commerce and Culture* (Chicago: University of Chicago Press, 1983), pp. 81–99; Jacques Barzun, *Teacher in America* (Boston: Little, Brown, 1945), pp. 154–59; Mortimer J. Adler, *Philosopher at Large: An Intellectual Autobiography* (New York: Macmillan, 1977), p. 55; Graff, *Professing Literature,* pp. 133–36.

43. Allan Bloom, *The Closing of the American Mind* (New York: Simon and Schuster, 1987); John Erskine to Eliza Hollingsworth Erskine, 5 May 1918, Box 1, 1975 addition, Erskine Papers; John Erskine, *Democracy and Ideals: A Definition* (New York: George H. Doran, 1920), pp. 129–30; Daniel Bell, *The Reforming of General Education: The Columbia College Experience in Its National Setting* (New York: Columbia University Press, 1966), pp. 14–15.

Sherman's reportorial stance reassigned power from critic to audience, Erskine advised the "great books" reader to "get yourself a comfortable chair and a good light—and have confidence in your own mind." In fact, like the interpreters of the Bible whose works permeated early New England, Erskine enacted his role as mediator between "high" culture and the reading public by constructing the fiction that his scheme permitted readers to encounter entirely unmediated texts.[44]

Erskine's belief in returning to ordinary people the "powers that, for a while, we delegated to the expert" thus prevents an easy categorization of his politics. Like Sherman, he amalgamated both elitism and democracy. If Erskine's "great books" plan derived from more than narrow political self-interest, however, it is equally important to see that it reflected other compelling personal needs. In Erskine's hands, reading the classics became an instrument for creating a self—predominantly not the consumer culture's other-directed performer but the genteel tradition's autonomous individual. To read "great books," Erskine explained (here with particular reference to Sir Walter Scott), "to be on familiar terms with the noble men and women who dwell in them, to share their courage, their zest in life, their self-reliance, their intellectual sincerity, until their outlook on life becomes our own—this would be good protection against . . . those social cure-alls which still offer to make us good and happy at low cost, with just a little rearranging of the environment." That conception kept alive the heritage of Arnold, Emerson, Norton, and Woodberry long after its reputed demise. At the same time, Erskine's idea that readers relate to "great books" simply on the basis of their own lives offered the prospect of participating in a human drama stretching from ancient to modern times. The spectacle of submergence in community—what Erskine called a liberation from the "prison of egotism"—paralleled his hope that the reading group itself would supply fellowship and "human understanding." Coupled with his language about immersion in the text, those images suggest Erskine's countervailing impulse to eradicate autonomy by surrendering to experience. His expectation that the unmediated encounter would release readers'

---

44. Richard H. Brodhead, *The School of Hawthorne* (New York: Oxford University Press, 1986), p. 5; John Erskine, "Outline of Great Books," p. 4, Uncatalogued Manuscripts, Helen Worden Erskine Papers, Columbia University Library, New York, N.Y.; Erskine, "Teaching of Literature," p. 203; John Erskine, "My Life in Literature," p. 260, Uncatalogued Manuscripts, Helen Worden Erskine Papers; David D. Hall, *Worlds of Wonder, Days of Judgment: Popular Religious Belief in Early New England* (New York: Knopf, 1989), p. 27.

"zest" and "energy" even endowed it with the promise of self-realization integral to the culture of personality.[45]

Hence, instead of resting on immutable, self-evident principles, as later "great books" training manuals were to imply ("It is absolutely essential that all the participants face each other"), the shape of Erskine's ideology of reading was in part a projection of the psychic tensions his historical circumstances generated. Erskine's program, moreover, was not merely an effort, as historians have often characterized it, to defend the classical tradition against the incursions of mass consumption and "the fact-finding ethos of science." Rather, in ways that he did not anticipate, his perspective, like Sherman's, was capable as well of fortifying both those tendencies.[46]

First, as Brooks, Bourne, and Macdonald understood, the emphasis on mastery of a list of the "best" books prepackaged aesthetic tradition in a way that left Americans free, as Brooks put it, to live "for practical purposes." In the late 1940s, Erskine's ideology of reading was literally transformed into a commodity—the Encyclopedia Britannica's *Great Books of the Western World,* or what Macdonald called "a hundred pounds of Great Books." Similarly, Erskine's stress on "greatness," although hardly unique to his approach, melded all too well with two features of American consumer culture between the wars: the rise of the star system, which thrust celebrities into the spotlight on the basis of image more than substance, and the widespread use of testimonial advertising, which linked products to famous personalities. Finally, along with democratizing access to literature, his insistence that feelings supplied the right basis for comprehending the classics and his notion of conversational exchange eradicated the genteel supposition that becoming cultured required work. The headline accompanying a group of articles on "great books" Erskine wrote for the *Delineator* in 1926 makes clear just how vulnerable his stance was to self-sabotage: The banner declared, "There's fun in famous books!" It was a short distance from that point to the plot summaries Erskine provided in *The Delight of Great Books* (1927); it was only another step to Adler's promotion of the Britannica set's "Great Ideas" feature as a "device" which would save pur-

45. John Erskine, "The Twilight of the Specialist: A Program for Mastering Our Own Lives," *Journal of Adult Education* (June 1932): 231; Erskine, *Delight of Great Books,* p. 200; John Erskine, *Prohibition and Christianity and Other Paradoxes of the American Spirit* (Indianapolis: Bobbs-Merrill, 1927), p. 250; Erskine, "Teaching of Literature," p. 203.

46. "A Manual for Discussion Leaders," p. 131, Box 17, Folder 5, Robert M. Hutchins Papers, Joseph Regenstein Library, University of Chicago, Chicago, Ill.; Allen, *Romance of Commerce and Culture,* p. 87.

chasers from having to "read a whole book through"; and, from there, an easy stride to William Benton's pitch that consumers buy the set to "become popular and successful."[47]

The most significant aspect of the initial "great books" movement was thus its pliability—or, again, its "middleness": its ambivalent politics, its accommodation of both genteel and therapeutic visions of the self, its vacillation between alienation from and assent to the ethos of the market-place. Its appeal, one might hypothesize, derived from its capacity to keep alive familiar constructs ("self-reliance," "liberal education") in a world grown impersonal and specialized, while meeting newer demands for information, social performance, and personal growth.

If Erskine's program executed that balancing act, however, he himself never quite regained the "feeling of peace" he had enjoyed during the war. By the time he turned forty-five, in 1924, his desire for an escape from genteel inhibitions (and, in particular, from a repressive marriage) was stronger than his ideology of reading, by itself, could satisfy. Gradually, he turned to other pursuits. Combining, in a different way, classic texts and modern values, he wrote the best-selling American novel of 1926: an ur-bane, racy satire entitled *The Private Life of Helen of Troy*. (In the next several years, he wrote several more stories based on the same formula.) Simultaneously, a series for the *Century*—on such topics as "Culture," "Self-Reliance," and "Integrity"—pulled him back toward genteel ideals. Restless and controversial at Columbia, he resigned from the university to become president of the Juilliard School of Music. Beginning in 1931, a relationship with the journalist Helen Worden (whom he married in 1946) provided some of the liberation he sought. His mood in this period, how-ever, was often one of self-reproach. In the late 1930s, a year after a serious automobile accident, he suffered a stroke and a nervous breakdown.[48]

Cut adrift thereafter from any institutional base, he published more novels (incurring less and less critical acclaim) and continued to lecture

---

47. Van Wyck Brooks, "Letters and Leadership," *Three Essays on America*, p. 135; *History of a Literary Radical*, p. 33; Dwight Macdonald, "The Book-of-the-Millennium Club," *New Yorker*, 29 November 1952, 171; John Erskine, "There's Fun in Famous Books," *Delineator*, December 1926, 14; Adler, *Philosopher at Large*, p. 237; "The University of Chicago Round-table: The Great Ideas," p. 1, Box 35, Folder 2, Presidents' Papers 1925–45, University of Chicago Library, Chicago, IL; William Benton to Robert Maynard Hutchins, 18 October 1949, Box 35, Folder 1, Presidents' Papers.

48. John Erskine, *The Private Life of Helen of Troy* (Indianapolis: Bobbs-Merrill, 1925); "The Reminiscences of Helen Worden Erskine," p. 121; John Erskine to Helen Worden, 12 May 1933 and 16 May 1933, Uncatalogued correspondence, Helen Worden Erskine Papers.

on "great books." In what seems a forced attempt to adjust to new realities, he spent some time in Hollywood, but he was a fish out of water: the magazine articles he wrote about the film industry explicitly indicted the star system's premium on personality. In the same vein, he issued *The Complete Life* (1943), a volume which resurrected the autonomous individual as model self. Yet his decision to write four autobiographies, each on a different aspect of his career, suggests the extent to which his own life was fragmented rather than "complete." By the late forties, Adler and his associates had eclipsed Erskine's role in the great books movement. In those years, he was—very much like Sherman—a touching and ulti- mately sad figure: clutching photographs of his World War I activities, returning to France for a last look at where he spent his happiest days. When he died in 1951, Erskine most resembled what he called the defeated romantic hero: "Failing ever to live completely, he carried with him to his grave the memory of much experience which he had yearned for, but which had escaped him."[49]

Today the works of Sherman and Erskine, categorized—and abandoned— as middlebrow, turn up mainly on the shelves of summer cottages and used book stores. Yet perhaps it is time to dust such volumes off. At the very least, understanding Sherman's and Erskine's ambivalent perception of self and role amplifies our sense of the past, helping us to resist drawing too sharp a distinction between nineteenth- and twentieth-century values. But the dilemmas middlebrow critics mediated also remain relevant and instructive for the future. Since 1950, certain features of American society have sharpened and made more urgent many of the issues the popularizers of the interwar period faced. The accelerating proliferation of knowledge has heightened the demand for information as a prerequisite to success; the quest for personality development has hardened into a virtual science of "impression management"; the American's apparently shorter attention span and more frenetic busyness has further elevated ease of learning into a virtue; the idea that consumption—of culture and anything else—will enhance self-realization is taken for granted.

49. Trilling, *Van Amringe and Keppel Eras,* p. 28; e.g., John Erskine, "Can Hollywood Stars Afford to Be Good Actors?," *Liberty,* 2 December 1939, 14–15; John Erskine, *The Complete Life* (New York: Julian Messner, 1943); Erskine, "The Delight of Great Books," p. 220. In addition to *The Memory of Certain Persons* and *My Life as a Teacher,* Erskine published *My Life in Music* (New York: William Morrow, 1950). A fourth memoir, "My Life in Literature," remained unpublished at his death.

For all their respective merits, both the determination, in the name of democracy, to temper the authority of the critic, and the insistence, in the name of "cultural literarcy," on acquiring knowledge about "great books," still risk exacerbating the very tendencies they seek to curb. Consequently, while recognizing its biases and drawbacks, we might ask whether and how we might recover and sustain (as Sherman and Erskine could not) the genteel tradition's best hopes: its commitment to a widely shared aesthetic sensitivity; its emphasis on autonomy and integrity; its view of moral and social obligation. Exploring the merits—and the limitations—of that outlook would seem a prerequisite to creating what Arnold called an "adequate" culture in the future.

4 CULTURAL POWER AND
THE PUBLIC LIFE

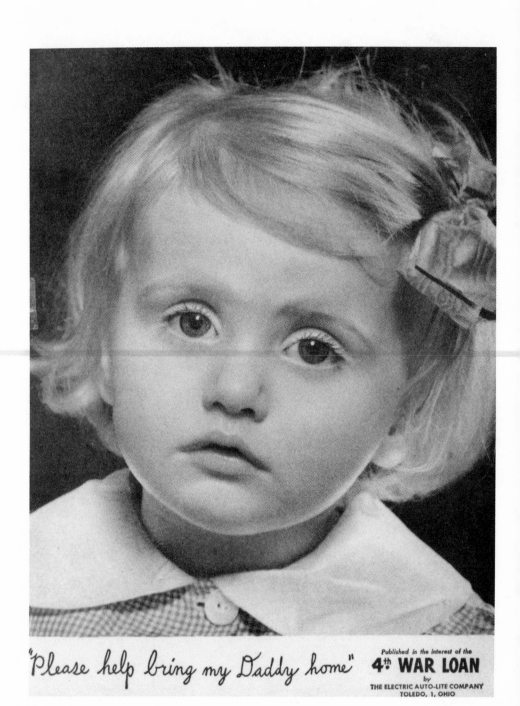

Electric Auto-Lite advertisement, *Time,* 7 February 1944. Courtesy of Allied Signal, Inc.

7 Fighting for the American Family

Private Interests and Political Obligation in World War II

Robert B. Westbrook

Prologue: A Note on Method

Cultural history is an ill-defined field of inquiry, and I suspect this is one reason why it is so attractive to so many scholars these days. It is the sort of undisciplined discipline where one can easily break with convention because there are so few conventions. One consequence of this latitudinarianism is that cultural history is a rubric under which a variety of interdisciplinary marriages have been arranged. The most well-publicized of these engagements have seen historians in search of past *mentalités* courting anthropology and literary academics in quest of a "new historicism" romancing history, or at least Michel Foucault.[1]

I have in my own work been interested in the possibilities of an interdisciplinary cultural history somewhat outside the mainstream of contemporary "cultural studies," one that would bring together history and ethics (broadly conceived to include much social and political theory) in order to better understand what anthropologist Clifford Geertz has called the "social history of the moral imagination." With Martha Nussbaum, I share a puzzlement and concern about the manner in which contemporary literary studies have readily turned to philosophers (mostly French) for epistemological guidance but have neglected the work of others (mostly Anglo-American) who have had much of great value to say about the central ethical question of human life: "How should one live?" I worry as well that cultural historians, who seem these days especially eager to emulate their literary colleagues, will follow suit. As Nussbaum says, "this is a rich and

This essay is for Jean-Christophe Agnew, for without his example, I doubt I would ever have done the sort of cultural history I do here.

1. I will not attempt to cite the considerable literature of methodological dispute produced by these two interdisciplinary efforts, but for starters see Lynn Hunt, ed., *The New Cultural History* (Berkeley: University of California Press, 1989); and H. Aram Vesser, ed., *The New Historicism* (New York: Routledge, 1989); and a pair of essays by Jean-Christophe Agnew worrying over the consequences of each of these enterprises: "History and Anthropology: Scenes from a Marriage," *Yale Journal of Criticism* 3 (1990): 29–50 and "History and Literature: The Family Romance," manuscript.

wonderful time in moral philosophy," and it would be a shame if historians did not share in these riches.[2]

I am at the moment particularly interested in the light that contemporary moral philosophy can shed on the history of what might best be called popular political theory, a history of American political thought that centers on "ordinary" people or at least on people who are not intellectuals by conventional definition. Such history argues that just because most citizens are not political philosophers does not mean that they do not on occasion advance significant theoretical arguments or that we should not subject these arguments to the same scrutiny that we give to those of intellectual elites. The rationale for this conviction has been nicely stated by philosopher Michael Sandel:

> Our practices and institutions are embodiments of theory. We could hardly describe our political life, much less engage in it, without recourse to a language laden with theory. Political institutions are not simply instruments that implement ideas independently conceived; they are themselves embodiments of ideas. . . . [W]e live some *theory*—all the time. . . . If theory never keeps its distance, but inhabits the world from the start, we may find a clue to our condition in the theory that we live. Attending to the theory implicit in our public life may help diagnose our political condition. It may also reveal that the predicament of American democracy resides not only in the gap between our ideals and institutions, but also within the ideals themselves, and within the self-image our public life reflects.

This view points toward a critical cultural history of American politics that aims, as Sandel says, "to identify the public philosophy implicit in our practices and institutions, and to show how tensions in the philosophy show up in the practice." Historians who pursue this task must be prepared to find political theory not only among political theorists and politicians, but in some unusual places—even, I have suggested elsewhere, in pin-ups of Betty Grable.[3]

2. Clifford Geertz, "Found in Translation: On the Social History of the Moral Imagination," in Geertz, *Local Knowledge* (New York: Basic Books, 1983), pp. 36–54; Martha C. Nussbaum, *Love's Knowledge: Essays on Philosophy and Literature* (New York: Oxford, 1990), pp. 169–70. To my mind, the exemplary practitioner of the social history of the moral imagination among contemporary American historians is Thomas Haskell, an acute and imaginative student of modern moral philosophy. See his "Capitalism and the Origins of the Humanitarian Sensibility," *American Historical Review* 90 (1985): 339–61, and "The Curious Persistence of Rights Talk in the 'Age of Interpretation,'" *Journal of American History* 74 (1987): 984–1012.

3. Michael Sandel, "The Political Philosophy of Contemporary Liberalism," manuscript, p. 2; Robert Westbrook, "'I Want a Girl, Just like the Girl That Married Harry James': American Women and the Problem of Political Obligation in World War II," *American Quarterly* 42 (1990): 587–614.

There need not be a sharp divide between the historical study of the ethical imagination of those to whom we are willing to grant the title of philosopher and those to whom we are not. Just as one can better understand the work of the former by understanding the life they share with the latter, so clues to the assumptions and tensions in the thinking of the latter can be found in the work of the former, where they are often more elaborated. Just as the study of preeminent intellectuals can benefit from an understanding of the larger culture in which they are embedded, so too can the investigation of the reflective life of less articulate men and women profit from an awareness of the concerns of those who have made it their business to engage more explicitly with the conundrums of the moral life. If the history of popular political theory finds its documents in strange places, so too it finds many of the best questions it poses to these documents in the work of philosophers, as I hope the essay that follows will suggest.

Why We Fight

One of these occasions on which we realize that we are living political theory in the way Sandel describes is when our nation goes to war. In this event, we reflect especially on the problems of political obligation. We ask ourselves why we are obliged not only to obey the laws of our state but why we (or our loved ones) are obliged to risk our lives to defend that state. That is, with Frank Capra, we ask "why we fight." In the research in which I am currently engaged, I am exploring the ways Americans thought about this question during World War II. But I am also interested in what such a study might help us understand more generally about political obligation in modern American political culture. My aim, that is, is to identify the philosophy of political obligation at work in American practices and institutions, and to highlight its distinctive features by means of a case study of a moment when Americans had reason to be more explicit than usual about such matters. In particular, I want to ask whether the peculiarities of the conception of political obligation that a number of theorists have identified in the liberal tradition of political philosophy are manifested in the political culture of a polity like that of the modern United States in which liberalism is the dominant public discourse.

World War II is a particularly good choice for a case study of this sort. For one thing, as a "total war," it mobilized most of the society, and, as a consequence, the number of people who worried over issues of obligation was broad and diverse. World War II was also the first American war to follow the consolidation of mass culture and social science, and there is a wealth of material to draw on: advertisements, movies, radio programs, photographs, mass circulation newspapers and magazines, and the reports of researchers who ran around asking people what they thought about the war. Also, because of widespread criticism of the operations of the Creel Committee in World War I and public identification of centralized propaganda agencies with the totalitarian enemy, the production of propaganda in World War II was more decentralized and much was left to private initiative. Thus one can more reasonably posit that the common themes evident in this prescriptive material reflect more widely-shared attitudes than one could if it had been the product of a single bureaucracy. Matters are also simplified somewhat in World War II because it was regarded by the vast majority of Americans as a just war, and hence people's thinking about why they should fight for their country—the issue that interests me most—was not complicated and overwhelmed by the need to consider why they should fight for their country in this particular war.[4]

In the research I have done so far I have arrived at the working hypothesis (consistent with the expectations derived from political theory) that, with some exceptions, Americans during World War II were not called upon to conceive of their obligation to participate in the war effort as an obligation to work, fight, or die for their country as a political community. The contention of some critical philosophers that liberalism lacks a coherent conception of *political* obligation seems to be reflected in wartime discourse. By and large, the American state and other propagandists relied on arguments—such as those in the Atlantic Charter or Franklin Roosevelt's "Four Freedoms" speech—positing moral obligations that transcended those to a particular political community. Or more interestingly, they appealed to Americans both as individuals and as families to join the war effort in order to defend *private* interests and discharge *private* moral obligations. Moreover, the more elusive evidence I have examined thus far of the felt obligations of Americans suggests that it was the latter sort of appeals that were most compelling and coincided most often with their own notions of "what we are fighting for."

4. On the production of propaganda in World War II see Alan M. Winkler, *The Politics of Propaganda: The Office of War Information, 1942–1945* (New Haven: Yale University Press, 1978); John M. Blum, *V Was for Victory: Politics and American Culture during World War II* (New York: Harcourt, Brace, Jovanovich, 1976), pp. 15–52; and Clayton Koppes and Gregory Black, *Hollywood Goes to War* (New York: Free Press, 1987).

In the discourse of obligation during World War II, no private interest outranked that of the family, and it is the place of the family in the prescriptions Americans were offered for "why we fight" that I would like to address here. But before I do so, I should say a bit more about the difficulties that liberalism and the liberal state have with political obligation in order to better indicate the questions and hypotheses I have taken from my reading in contemporary political philosophy.

The Limits of Liberalism

It is fair to say that the liberal theory of political obligation is in deep trouble these days. Arguing from a variety of perspectives, a number of philosophers have offered a powerful critique of the efforts of the philosophical giants of the liberal tradition from Hobbes to Rawls to provide an adequate basis for political obligation and have concluded that, as Carole Pateman puts it, "political obligation in the liberal democratic state constitutes an insoluble problem; insoluble because political obligation cannot be given expression within the context of liberal democratic institutions."[5]

This critique of the liberal theory of political obligation has advanced on at least two fronts. On the one hand, such philosophers as John Simmons have used the tools of analytic philosophy to demonstrate that such traditional foundations for the liberal theory of political obligation as the tacit consent of citizens to the authority of the state or the reciprocal exchange of benefits between citizens and the state cannot provide an adequate account of or justification for obligation. On the other hand, such communitarian critics of liberalism as Michael Walzer have slighted these difficulties in favor of raising doubts about whether the liberal theory can be said to be an account of *political* obligation, that is, of obligations that men and women have as citizens. It is this latter critique that is most pertinent to my discussion here of the centrality of familial obligations and interests in the thinking of Americans about their commitment to the war effort in World War II.[6]

In an essay on "The Obligation to Die for the State," Walzer addresses

5. Carole Pateman, *The Problem of Political Obligation: A Critique of Liberal Theory* (Berkeley: University of California Press, 1985), p. 1.

6. See A. John Simmons, *Moral Principles and Political Obligations* (Princeton: Princeton University Press, 1979); Michael Walzer, *Obligations* (Cambridge: Harvard University Press, 1970). Pateman's *Problem of Political Obligation* might be said to give it to liberalism with both barrels.

the problem of obligation in the context of war and raises the question of whether the obligation citizens have to the state can be made the motive for risking their lives. The answer to this question, he suggests, depends in critical respects on the nature of the state, and, in the case of the liberal state, the answer is no. The reason for this, he argues, is that the end of the liberal state, as conceived in the social contract tradition of Hobbes, Locke, and their successors, is the security of the life of the individuals who form it, and, consequently, "a man who dies for the state defeats his only purpose in forming the state: death is the contradiction of politics. A man who risks his life for the state accepts the insecurity which it was the only end of his political obedience to avoid: war is the failure of politics. Hence there can be no political obligation either to die or to fight."[7]

When a war begins, political authorities in a liberal society may, as Hobbes put it, invite their subjects to "protect their protection," but this is an admission on the part of these authorities to a failure to hold up their end of the bargain on which the state rests. Peculiar in any case as a call to men and women to risk their lives for their instrument, the invitation is doubly peculiar as one to defend an instrument that has failed its function. As Walzer says, when individuals "protect their protection they are doing nothing more than defending themselves, and so they cannot protect their protection after their protection ceases to protect them. At that point, it ceases to be their protection. The state has no value over and above the value of the lives of the concrete individuals whose safety it provides. No man has a common life to defend, but only an individual life." The liberal state at war is like a bodyguard hired to protect the lives and property of a family who then gets into a fight with a gang threatening that family and turns to his clients and asks them to protect him. They have no obligation to do so since they hired the bodyguard precisely to avoid this kind of situation. If they fight the gang, they do so because of obligations they have to protect themselves and one another and not out of any political obligation to the bodyguard-state.[8]

Walzer links this difficulty liberalism has with political obligation to its atomistic individualism and largely negative view of liberty, which make for a conception of the citizen as an individual who is protected by the state from interference by other individuals or by the state itself. The liberal position suggests "an indefinite number of distinct and singular relations

7. Walzer, "The Obligation to Die for the State" in *Obligations*, p. 82.
8. Ibid.

between the individual citizens and the authorities as a body—a pattern that might best be symbolized by a series of vertical lines. There are no horizontal connections among citizens as citizens." The state is thought of "as an instrument which serves individual men (or families) but not or not necessarily as an instrument wielded by these men themselves" as constituents of a political community. Walzer concludes that any theory like liberalism which "begins with the absolute independence of freely willing individuals and goes on to treat politics and the state as instrumental to the achievement of individual purposes would seem by its very nature incapable of describing ultimate obligation."[9]

It is important to add, as Walzer does, that this difficulty in liberal theory does not mean that citizens will not go to war and fight and die on behalf of ethical, if not political, obligations. As he says:

Moved by love, sympathy, or friendship, men in liberal society can and obviously do incur ultimate obligations. They may even find themselves in situations where they are or think they are obliged to defend the state which defends in turn the property and enjoyment of their friends and families. But if they then actually risk their lives or die, they do so because they have incurred private obligations which have nothing to do with politics. The state may shape the environment within which these obligations are freely incurred, and it may provide the occasions and the means for their fulfillment. But this is only to say that, when states make war and men fight, the reasons of the two often are and ought to be profoundly different.[10]

The fact that an argument is a bad one does not mean that it will not be made, and during World War II the American state did occasionally call upon its citizens to protect their protection, as if this amounted to something more than a plea to protect themselves. Less often, it "poached" on other nonliberal traditions in search of more persuasive grounds for political obligation. More frequently, it invoked commitments to such abstract, universal values as "freedom" that Americans shared with others not as citizens but as fellow human beings. Yet what is most striking about propaganda for the "Good War" is the degree to which, as if acknowledging that these were not compelling arguments for political obligation in a liberal society chastened by the failure of an earlier war to make the world safe for democracy, proponents of the war openly attempted—as Walzer's arguments suggest they might—to exploit private obligations in order to con-

9. Walzer, "The Problem of Citizenship" in *Obligations*, pp. 205–207; Walzer, "The Obligation to Die for the State," p. 89.

10. Walzer, "Obligation to Die for the State," p. 89.

vince Americans to serve the cause of national defense. As I can only begin to suggest here, such obligations—to families, to children, to parents, to friends, and generally, to an "American Way of Life" defined as a rich (and richly commodified) private realm of experience—were tirelessly invoked in the campaign to mobilize Americans for World War II and formed the centerpiece of the propaganda produced by the state and its allies in Hollywood, the War Advertising Council, and elsewhere.

Norman Rockwell's War

The study of popular political theory will often find it in some unusual places, and I would like to begin my discussion of the mobilization of familial obligations in World War II with a story about the work of an American not usually numbered among the nation's great political philosophers: Norman Rockwell.

Sometime in 1942 Rockwell and his friend, neighbor, and fellow illustrator, Mead Schaeffer, decided to contribute to the war effort by offering their services as painters to the American government, but they were delayed initially by Rockwell's inability to come up with any ideas for posters that he really liked. "I wanted to do something bigger than a war poster," he wrote in his autobiography, "make some statement about why the country was fighting the war."[11]

Rockwell thought the idea he was looking for might be found in Franklin Roosevelt's proclamation of the "four essential human freedoms"— freedom of speech, freedom of worship, freedom from want, and freedom from fear—that Americans hoped to secure abroad, but he was deterred by Roosevelt's language which he found "so noble, platitudinous really, that it stuck in my throat": "No, I said to myself, it doesn't go, how am I to illustrate that? I'm not noble enough. Besides, nobody I know is reading the proclamation either, in spite of the fanfare and hullabaloo about it in the press and on the radio." One night, while tossing and turning in bed with this problem, the solution struck him:

I suddenly remembered how Jim Edgerton had stood up in town meeting and said something that everybody else disagreed with. But they had let him have his say. No one shouted him down. My gosh, I thought, that's it. There it is. Freedom of Speech. I'll illustrate the Four Freedoms using my Vermont neighbors as models. I'll express the ideas in simple, everyday scenes. Freedom of Speech—a New En-

11. Norman Rockwell, *Norman Rockwell: My Adventures as an Illustrator* (Garden City, N.Y.: Doubleday, 1960), p. 338.

gland town meeting. Freedom from Want—a Thanksgiving dinner. Take them out of the noble language of the proclamation and put them in terms everybody can understand.[12]

Rockwell and Schaeffer then set out for Washington armed with rough sketches of their ideas. Here they met with little success. The Office of War Information, one administrator told them, intended to use only the work of "real artists."

On the way back to Vermont, a discouraged Rockwell stopped off in Philadelphia to meet with Ben Hibbs, the editor of *The Saturday Evening Post,* and happened to show him his sketches for *The Four Freedoms.* Hibbs found the sketches very exciting, pledged to publish them in the *Post,* and urged Rockwell to drop everything else he was doing. Early in 1943 the illustrations were published in four consecutive issues of the magazine.

The illustrations elicited an enormous response. Requests to reprint them poured into the *Post* offices, including many from government agencies that now found a use for them. Millions of reprints were made, and they were distributed all over the world. Subsequently, the Treasury Department used the original paintings as part of a war-bond tour that garnered nearly $133 million in bonds. "Those four pictures," Hibbs wrote, "quickly became the best known and most appreciated paintings of that era. They appeared right at a time when the war was going against us on the battle fronts, and the American people needed the inspirational message which they conveyed so forcefully and so beautifully."[13]

What was the message that these pictures conveyed so forcefully and beautifully? It was, with one notable exception (to which I shall return), that Americans were fighting World War II to protect essentially private interests and discharge essentially private obligations. And, in two of the four paintings, the message was that the people of the United States were fighting for the family.

Freedom from Fear (fig. 1) was the only one of the four paintings that made a direct reference to the war. In this painting a concerned mother and father look in on their sleeping children. Their concerns on this occasion are, however, extraordinary (perhaps, this is indicated by the fact that both are in the children's room simultaneously), for they have been reading of the bombing of London in the newspaper that the father holds in his hand. As Rockwell said, the painting is supposed to say: "Thank God we

12. Rockwell, *My Adventures,* pp. 338–39.
13. Rockwell, *My Adventures,* p. 343.

can put our children to bed with a feeling of security, knowing they will not be killed in the night." The threat of bombing conveyed in the illustration, as Stephen Vincent Benét said in the essay accompanying it in the *Post,* is a threat that the geographical isolation of the United States cannot withstand, and hence children must rely on the courage of their parents to protect them from death and the fear of death. Freedom from fear, Benét intoned, "goes to the roots of life—to a man and a woman and their children and the home they can make and keep."[14]

Familial interests and obligations were also central to Rockwell's vision of *Freedom from Want* (fig. 2). This painting portrayed a Thanksgiving dinner for which an extended family has gathered (and to which the viewer is invited). This was intended to convey the message that Americans are fighting to protect the opportunities they had, as Americans, to provide for the material needs of themselves and their families. Here Roosevelt's most controversial "freedom" was rendered not, as Henry Wallace would have had it, as the foundation of a Global New Deal in which every child was guaranteed a quart of milk a day, but rather as the defense of the familial surfeit of a peculiarly American holiday.[15]

14. Stephen Vincent Benét, "Freedom from Fear," *Saturday Evening Post,* 13 March 1943.

15. Norman Rockwell, "Freedom from Want," *Saturday Evening Post,* 6 March 1943; Rockwell, *My Adventures,* p. 343. (Rockwell reported that many Europeans resented this painting "because it wasn't freedom from want, it was overabundance, the table was so loaded down with food.") "Freedom from want" was the most controversial of the war aims proclaimed by Roosevelt because it introduced into the reciprocal relationship between the liberal state and its citizens the obligation of the state to provide and protect a minimal level of subsistence for the individuals who compromise it. This obviously is not conveyed in Rockwell's painting, but it is something that Benét appears to have worried over on behalf of more traditional liberals in his essay on fear, in which he went out of his way to make it clear that "freedom from fear" did not mean "freedom from struggle and toil, from hardship and danger. We do not intend to breed a race wrapped in cotton wool, too delicate to stand rough weather." On the other hand, the *Post* essay on "Freedom from Want" by Carlos Bulosan, a Philippine immigrant who had suffered a good deal of rough weather in the thirties as a labor organizer, articulated the position of the welfare-state liberal and stood in curious contrast with Rockwell's illustration on the facing page as well as, it should be said, with Roosevelt's implicit contention that freedom from want was something that the New Deal had secured for Americans who now wished to extend it to the rest of the world.

Speaking on behalf of those in America who are "not really free" because they have not been granted freedom from want and who wonder "if we are really a part of America," Bulosan advanced what might be termed the "immanent" critique of a liberal theory of political obligation grounded in the receipt of benefits from the state. This critique was most forcefully argued during the war by some black Americans, who contended that, if citizens were obligated to defend the state because of the benefits they received from it, then they were less obliged than others to defend the American state because it provided them with fewer benefits than it did other citizens.

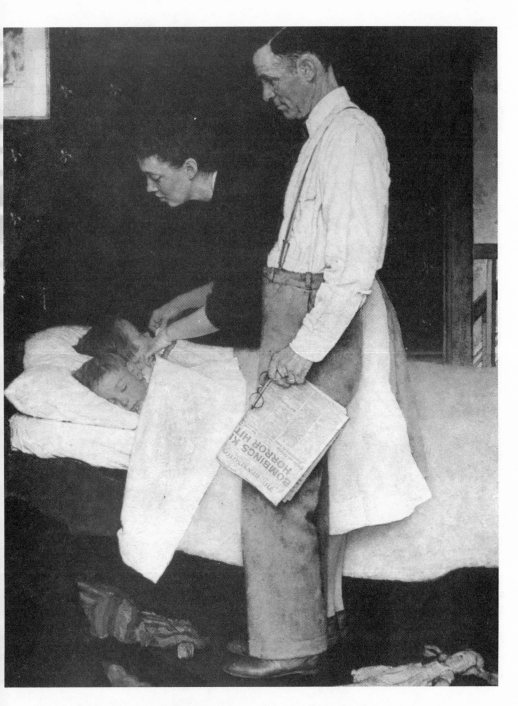

Figure 1. Norman Rockwell, *Freedom from Fear*. Printed by permission of the Norman Rockwell Family Trust. Copyright © 1943, the Norman Rockwell Family Trust.

Figure 2. Norman Rockwell, *Freedom from Want.* Printed by permission of the Norman Rockwell Family Trust. Copyright © 1943, the Norman Rockwell Family Trust.

The Homefront

Rockwell's translation of Roosevelt's noble, platitudinous, abstract, and universalist moral language into a more concrete, particular moral language centering on private obligations and interests was far from idiosyncratic. Indeed, I would maintain that this sort of translation is one of the most significant features of American propaganda during World War II. Again and again, propagandists explicitly or implicitly contended, as an advertisement for U.S. Rubber put it, that "words like *freedom* or *liberty* draw close to us only when we break them down into the *homely fragments of daily life*." And, more often than not, those fragments were literally "homely," that is, familial.[16]

Like Norman Rockwell, the American state and private corporations interpreted the obligations of Americans to support the war effort as a duty owed to the family in which they were raised, the family they were themselves raising, the family they would someday raise, and/or, somewhat more abstractly, to the family as a social institution (fig. 3). The war, one ad said, was "this fight to keep our country a safe place for the wives we love, a place where our children can grow up free and unafraid," and no obligation ranked higher in American war propaganda than the obligation to protect the family.[17]

The enemy was repeatedly portrayed in posters and ads as a threat to the family, particularly its weaker members (fig. 4). The state, in turn, was seen in good liberal fashion as the protector of the family (fig. 5). In one very illuminating example of this argument (fig. 6), we find the Axis powers portrayed as Halloween vandals on a rampage. They have burned a family farm, an essentially private icon tied to "Our Democratic Institutions." Behind a tree Uncle Same (literally "Uncle" Sam)—the American state— waits to foil their further mischief, armed with the rifle of American industrial might. In ads such as this, private corporations like Philco announced their eagerness to be a part of the family's arsenal, emphasizing that the sacrifices made in converting to war production would, as another ad put it, "help Daddy lick" the enemy.[18]

The Philco ad is interesting not only because it clearly indicates that it was home and family that Americans were fighting for when they came to

16. United States Rubber Company, "What Are We Fighting For?" *Life,* 12 October 1942.

17. Union Central Life Insurance Company, "War . . . and the Family Man," *Life,* 23 February 1942.

18. Western Electric, "More aluminum up there, less in new telephones—for victory!," *Life,* 23 February 1942.

Figure 3. Community Silverplate advertisement, *Life*, 19 October 1942. Courtesy of Oneida Ltd.

"Are they coming over here to fight, daddy?"

NO, Sister, they're not coming over here — not if all the power of American ships and planes, and all the sacrifice of American men can stop them.

But they may try.

If they try, some may get through, for it is a wide sky, and bombs may crash here as they crashed on far-away Hawaii and in the distant Philippines.

Or even if they don't try, the work of enemies within our own gates may bring fires, explosions, damage to our busy defense plants.

So we must be ready—just in case.

Ready with quick help for the hurt and the suffering. Ready with merciful aid that is still great in America's heart, even in a world where such things as mercy and decency seem no longer to exist.

That's the job of the Red Cross — to dispense that merciful care and help wherever and whenever pain and suffering exist.

It's a big job, that will call for every effort the hundreds of thousands of Red Cross workers — nurses, disaster fighters and volunteer helpers — can put forth.

It will call for vast stores of medicines and supplies, food and clothing, bandages and equipment.

It will demand every penny of the fifty million dollars the Red Cross is now asking for, and more.

So every bit helps, Sister.

Every dollar your Daddy can bring up from the bottom of his pocket, every penny any man or woman can add to the check he or she writes now for the Red Cross.

The brave men awing, afloat and afield who take care of us sometimes need care too, and we must give it.

We give it when we give to the Red Cross, whether it be a little or a lot.

Send contributions to your local chapter

American Red Cross War Fund Campaign

Give and give generously — to your local chapter — to volunteer solicitors. Give when you can, where you can, as much as you can.

This page contributed to the American Red Cross by the publishers

Figure 5. Dixie Cup advertisement, *Life*, 16 March 1942

"He won't let them hurt us ...will he, mommy?"

YOUNG flying officer...civilian air-raid warden...both enlisted to make America safe. He fights...she serves ...and both must be kept well and strong.

Illness, contagion must not be permitted to slacken our speed — or weaken the staggering blow our nation has set itself to deliver. Common colds, influenza, trench mouth and the like must not black out the work of thousands of willing hands. And health officials everywhere tell us that these illnesses are most commonly spread by indirect mouth-to-mouth contact at the common drinking place.

It is not surprising then that you meet Dixie Cups so frequently at soda fountains these days, at milk bars, at Army canteens, aboard our Naval ships...wherever thirst is quenched in public. Used but once and thrown away, these fresh clean paper cups break the chain of contagion.

DIXIE CUPS

DIXIE-VORTEX COMPANY, EASTON, PA., CHICAGO, ILL., TORONTO, CAN.

DIXIE CUPS are safeguards of health at all times ...everywhere. In the office, in the shop, in public places, at soda fountains, on trains and airplanes, the common drinking vessel is a thing of the past. The expanding uses of Dixie Cups are but an indication of the trend of the times.

Our Way to Handle Vandals!

THE Army-Navy "E" flags that fly above the Philco plants at Philadelphia, Trenton and Sandusky are citations of *Excellence* in the production of war equipment from our fighting forces to the men and women of Philco. They are symbols of the vital partnership between our soldiers of the front and our soldiers of production.

More than that, they are *battle flags* for America at home, symbols of the devotion and sacrifice beyond the line of duty which are the price of Victory. For that is the spirit in which industrial America, as the War Department citation reads, is "accomplishing today what yesterday seemed impossible."

The Philco laboratories, machines and assembly lines are producing communications equipment, radios for tanks and airplanes, artillery fuzes and shells, electric storage batteries for the Army, Navy and War Production plants. They are doing their share to the end that America's might may strike the decisive blow for Victory. And that mankind may enjoy in freedom the more abundant life which will arise from the scientific miracles born of war.

This cartoon by Herbert Johnson is another in the series being drawn for Philco by America's leading editorial cartoonists to interpret the spirit of Philco's soldiers of production. It is being posted on bulletin boards of the Philco factories as a symbol to the men and women of Philco of the purpose and significance of their work in the united effort for Victory.

Free Limited Offer . . . While available, a full size reproduction of the original drawing by Herbert Johnson will be furnished gladly upon request. Simply address Philco Corporation, Philadelphia, Penna., and ask for Cartoon Number 27D.

PHILCO CORPORATION

FOR VICTORY
BUY
UNITED
STATES
WAR
BONDS
AND
STAMPS

America is conserving its resources for Victory. As you save on sugar, rubber, gasoline and all products of peace-time consumption, remember too to preserve the use of the things you own. Through its national service organizations, Philco offers, at reasonable and uniform charges, the means of prolonging the life of Philco products.

RADIOS, PHONOGRAPHS, REFRIGERATORS, AIR CONDITIONERS, RADIO TUBES ★ ★ INDUSTRIAL STORAGE BATTERIES FOR MOTIVE POWER, SIGNAL SYSTEMS, CONTROL AND AUXILIARY POWER

The Army-Navy "E" Flag flies above the Philco plants in Philadelphia, Trenton, N. J. and Sandusky, Ohio.

Figure 6. Philco Corporation advertisement, *Life,* 2 November 1942. Reprinted with permission of White Consolidated Industries, Inc.

the defense of democratic institutions. It is also a nice example of the way the liberal state could use the representation of itself as a family relative, "Uncle Sam," to obscure the fact that a declaration of war marked its failure to hold up its end of the bargain struck with its citizens to protect them from death in exchange for their obedience. It was not "Uncle Sam" that was protecting the family during the war but fathers, mothers, and other relatives who went to war to keep Hitler, Mussolini, and Tojo from the door, and it was their private obligation to do so that the American state mobilized. Thus, to be true to the character of obligation in World War II, one would have to say that "Uncle Sam," as depicted in this ad, represents not the American state but the host of real Uncle Sams organized by the state to fight for their families. The gun he wields is a representation of the others, "our soldiers of production," who went to work in war plants in order to protect their homes.

Americans were instructed that they might discharge their obligation to protect home and family in a number of ways. Soldiers, of course, were called upon to risk their lives in combat for their loved ones, and their mothers—who, according to *Life,* stood for "home, love, faith, all the things they are fighting for"—were presented with blue stars to signify this commitment and gold stars to signify that their sons had made the ultimate sacrifice. Hollywood portrayed soldiers fighting for mothers, children, brides, and brides-to-be back home. For example, in the most poignant scene in one of the best combat films, *Guadalcanal Diary* (1943), a marine captain lying fatally wounded on the beach reaches in death for his helmet and the photograph of his family tucked in its webbing. For those who had no personal pin-ups of wives or girl friends to plaster to the machines of war, the studios in cooperation with the state provided surrogates like Betty Grable. Grable, far and away the most popular pin-up of the war, was offered to soldiers less as an exotic sex goddess than as a symbol of the kind of woman for whom American men were fighting. Grable, as Jane Gaines has said, was "model girlfriend, wife, and finally mother," and her popularity increased after she married bandleader Harry James in 1943 and had a child later that year.[19]

---

19. "Mother: She Keeps Home Warm for Her Sons When They Go Off to War," *Life,* 28 December 1942, 59–62; Westbrook, "'I Want a Girl Just like the Girl That Married Harry James,'" 592–606; Jane Gaines, "The Popular Icon as Commodity and Sign: The Circulation of Betty Grable, 1941–1945," Ph.D. dissertation, Northwestern University, 1982, p. 502.

On the home front, civilians were urged to aid their soldier-protectors in the war for the family by working in defense plants, supporting the Red Cross, conserving vital materials, and buying war bonds. One life insurance company warned that men deferred in 1942 because they were fathers should be aware that "upon victory rests everything that means most to you as a father . . . the security of your home . . . the safety and freedom of your children . . . the very *way of life* that America stands for" and recommended that these men supplement the protection victory afforded with the added fortification of a new insurance policy. Women who worked in factories to provide their protectors with the weapons they needed to protect them were assured that in so doing they were "fighting for freedom and all that means to women everywhere. You're fighting for a little house of your own, and a husband to meet every night at the door. You're fighting for the right to bring up your children without the shadow of fear."[20]

Some corporations argued that the war was not only being waged to protect the family, but that it was a blessing in disguise that would actually enhance family welfare. Restraints on consumer spending coupled with high wages and savings invested in war bonds had provided consumers with the opportunity to engage in "installment buying in reverse" that would enable them to have the home of their dreams. "After the war," Revere Copper declared, "youth has a new world to look forward to. For today's young men and women can plan instead of dream, can be sure that the homes their parents merely wished for can become a reality for them. . . . In this war, we are fighting not only against our enemies, but *for* a better way of life for many more of us." The homes pictured in its ad (fig. 7) were an example of what American families could have "by fighting, and sacrificing, and winning."

A few companies like furniture manufacturers W. & J. Sloane urged consumers not to wait for war's end to begin living this dream but to invest immediately in at least one major purchase that "can mean home . . . the root, the core, the propulsion of our lives." The better way of life, the "American Way of Life" that these ads and other propaganda described had little to do with citizenship. It was above all a rewarding domestic life for which Americans were fighting, a private sphere filled with goods and

20. Union Central Life Insurance Company, "The person named herein has been classified 3A," *Life*, 23 March 1942; Eureka Vacuum Cleaners, "My Heart's Overseas but My Hands Are on the Job," *Saturday Evening Post*, 21 August 1943.

Beyond the war waits happiness

After the war youth has a new world to look forward to. For today's young men and women can plan instead of dream, can be sure that the homes their parents merely wished for can become a reality for them.

Here is such a home where every window can frame a garden view, where there is space for all the pleasures and purposes of living, where doors can move aside to enlarge favorite rooms or to include garden and terrace as part of the living area.

Here is more than shelter from the weather, and more than simple provision for physical comfort. This house is designed to surround you with the things that lift your heart and make you glad.

It is a house to be lived in for a lifetime. If your family grows so that more rooms are needed, you can add them. They have already been provided for in the original plan. Even the closet and storage space have been carefully worked out to hold the many possessions which all families accumulate through the years.

Complete with the new inventions and conveniences which copper has brought to modern living, such a house can be made available, through mass production, for not more than $2,000. And the 36 parts of which it is built can be assembled in diversified arrangements, so it never need look or be just like your neighbor's. For you and those you cherish, it can always be—Home.

A. LAWRENCE KOCHER

In this war, we are fighting not only against our enemies, but *for* a better way of life for many more of us. Homes such as those Mr. Kocher has designed are an example of what we can have by fighting and sacrificing, and *winning*.

Great architects and engineers have developed brilliant plans for homes after the war. New techniques will be available for building them at lower cost. Enduring, rust-proof copper will be waiting to give them protection against weather and termites, to help heat them more economically, to insure rust-free water, to afford new comforts and conveniences — to make your home of tomorrow better to own, or rent, or sell.

All of us today are working for Uncle Sam. There is no copper for building, or for any other purpose except winning the war. But in Revere's laboratories, research is continually pressing forward in preparation for the better, happier living that victory can bring us all.

Floor plan showing one of the many attractive arrangements possible with this house.

Naturally, in this limited space, Mr. Kocher could give you only a bare outline of his conception. Revere has prepared an illustrated booklet with complete details. We will gladly send it to you, free. Write us.

Figure 7. Revere Copper advertisement, *Life,* 20 July 1942. Courtesy of Revere Copper and Brass Inc.

services provided by those who had for the duration halted production in order that their customers might effectively defend homes that would in the wake of victory be even more densely cluttered with commodities.[21]

I could easily multiply these examples of "why we fight" documents that argue that "we fight for the family." All this is evidence, it should be said, of *prescriptions* about obligation and provides little direct evidence about the *felt* obligations of Americans during the war. But one can at least say that American propagandists—especially those working for private corporations—appealed to attitudes and convictions they believed (or their research told them) were widespread in their audiences. Moreover, the widespread popularity of Rockwell's paintings suggests that he struck a nerve as well. Nonetheless, I can for now merely assert that what little research I have done on the felt obligations of Americans (principally soldiers) suggests that the claim that Americans were fighting for the family was not an adman's fabrication. But substantiating this hypothesis will have to await another occasion.[22]

Nonliberal Obligations

If the only theory Americans lived in World War II was liberalism and if they only thought about their obligations to the war effort in liberal, nonpolitical terms, the story would be neat and probably wrong. Historians no longer contend that liberalism is the only American political tradition, even if few doubt its hegemony, and though I am less disposed than some to stress the persistence in the United States of an adversarial republican ideology, one can now and again hear its faint echoes in World War II. Moreover, theory—especially lived theory—is rarely consistent. We shore up the weak flanks of our thinking with arguments to which our most cherished premises may not entitle us, preferring a jerry-built structure of thought that covers all the bases to a logical masterpiece that leaves us without benefits that logic would deny. I would like to conclude then with

21. W. & J. Sloane, "I'm Too Old to Dream," *New Yorker,* 14 October 1944. See Charles F. McGovern, "Selling the American Way: Democracy, Advertisers and Consumers in World War II," paper delivered at the National Museum of American History, Smithsonian Institution, 1987.

22. My arguments are also borne out by research on contemporary American attitudes about citizenship. See Pamela J. Conover, Ivor M. Crewe, and Donald P. Searing, "The Nature of Citizenship in the United States and Great Britain: Empirical Comments on Theoretical Themes," *Journal of Politics* 53 (1991): 800–32.

a look at two documents that reflect nonliberal perspectives that occasionally crept into the discourse about obligation during the war.

In a 1942 Birds Eye Foods advertisement (fig. 8) one can see an attempt at a nonliberal argument that imparts a quite different meaning to "fighting for the family" than what I have discussed. Occasionally, to borrow some terms from political philosopher Amy Gutmann, Americans tried to think of themselves during the war not as a "state of families" but as a "family state" or, as a General Electric ad put it, "just one fighting family . . . 130,000,000 of us!" In the Birds Eye ad, which offers a nice contrast to Rockwell's later use of the Thanksgiving theme, the nation is portrayed as a family sitting down to Thanksgiving dinner at a table headed by Uncle Sam. Expressions such as this, it seems to me, grew out of anxieties about the capacity of a nation of "individualists" or even individual families to achieve the level of cooperation and solidarity necessary to win a total war. If the nation was to win the war, the ad suggests, its citizens must think of themselves as members of a single family, bound together by affective ties akin to those they shared with their closest relatives.[23]

Yet arguments such as this were rare, for they presented a grave difficulty: they came perilously close to the theories of political obligation advanced by the enemy, particularly the Japanese, who justified dying for the state (the emperor) on the grounds that its state was (quite literally) a family state. This theory was widely attacked by Americans and perceived by many as evidence that the Japanese were a subhuman race. Americans were urged, in effect, to see themselves as defending liberalism and its thin conception of citizenship from the evil of a nation wedded to a much thicker and thereby oppressive conception of citizenship and political obligation. Yet a note of grudging admiration for the family state sometimes snuck into these denunciations, and it is evident as well in this ad.[24]

But what the ad perhaps suggests best is the difficulty of coherently reconciling stronger theories of political obligation with liberal premises. The representation of the American state as an uncle and not a father (or mother) made it difficult to effectively depict the family state because it

23. Amy Gutmann, *Democratic Education* (Princeton: Princeton University Press, 1987), pp. 22–33; General Electric, "This Fight Is a Family Affair!" *Life,* 24 August 1942.

24. On Japanese prescriptions for political obligation see *Kokutai no Hongi: Cardinal Principles of the National Entity of Japan,* ed. Robert K. Hall (Cambridge: Harvard University Press, 1949). For a superb discussion of these presciptions and the American response to them see John Dower, *War without Mercy: Race and Power in the Pacific War* (New York: Pantheon, 1986), pp. 28–32, 279–85.

Your Government *urges* you, please, to eat WELL and HEARTILY!

AMERICA, THERE'S A WAR ON!

A war for our survival as a free country. A war whose winning will take *greater* efforts than we ever dreamed possible. Heroic efforts and sacrifices from our fighting men. Grim, endless toil from the men and women who back them up on production lines.

To supply the energy for this daily battle, you need more than *will* and *heart*. You need FOOD. *Lots of it.* And your Government, through the National Nutrition Advisory Committee, urges you—in these hurried days —*not* to get in the habit of the "gulp-and-run" meal.

Get food that *looks* good . . . *tastes* good. Nourishing food that gives your body the *vital elements* it must have for sustained drive!

On the list of such foods are Birds Eye Frosted Foods. They are *appetizing . . . delicious . . . nutritious*. Appetizing, because they are painstakingly selected for quality. Deli-

cious, because they are *ocean-fresh* or *farm-fresh*—quick-frozen at their *peak of goodness!* For this same reason, Birds Eye Foods are *naturally rich* in healthful vitamins and food values.

With Birds Eye Foods, there is little, if any, loss of important food values through exposure to air, or en route to markets. Instead —and we must repeat this—they are *quick frozen* and *held for you* at zero temperature. This captures not only flavor and freshness, but vital vitamins and minerals which your body needs!

EAT—and *eat well!* There are over 60 varieties of Birds Eye Frosted Foods—Meats, Seafood, Poultry, Fruits, and Vegetables.

BIRDS EYE
BRAND
FROSTED FOODS
REG. U.S. PAT. OFF.

U.S. NEEDS US **STRONG**

EAT NUTRITIONAL FOOD

Every day, eat this way

MILK and MILK PRODUCTS . . . at least a pint for everyone—more for children—or cheese or evaporated or dried milk.

BREAD and CEREAL . . . whole grain products or enriched white bread and flour.

ORANGES, TOMATOES, GRAPEFRUIT . . . or raw cabbage or salad greens—at least one of these.

MEAT, POULTRY or FISH . . . dried beans, peas or nuts occasionally.

GREEN or YELLOW VEGETABLES . . . one big helping or more —some raw, some cooked.

EGGS . . . at least 3 or 4 a week, cooked any way you choose —or in "made" dishes.

OTHER VEGETABLES, FRUIT . . . potatoes, other vegetables or fruits in season.

BUTTER and OTHER SPREADS . . . vitamin-rich fats, peanut butter, and similar spreads.

Then eat other foods you also like

OFFICE OF DEFENSE HEALTH AND WELFARE SERVICES
PAUL V. McNUTT, DIRECTOR, WASHINGTON, D. C.
Property of Federal Security Agency, may be reproduced by permission only

Figure 8. Birds Eye Frosted Foods advertisement, *Life,* 29 June 1942

was not at all clear what avuncular authority amounted to. On the other hand, placing Uncle Sam at the head of the table rather than portraying a father-surrogate deflected too close an approximation of the ideology of the enemy. Had the artist put the carving knife in the hands of, say, FDR, howls of protest against creeping dictatorship would have gone up from the precincts of the Republican party if not elsewhere. Hence this ad stands less as a statement of collective than of aggregate purpose and, at most, a description of wished-for social rather than political bonds.

Nonliberal theories of political obligation need not be undemocratic, and sometimes during the war Americans were offered a glimpse of this alternative. Perhaps the best example of such a democratic theory was *Freedom of Speech* (fig. 9), the exceptional painting in Rockwell's series to which I alluded above.[25] It is the only picture of the four to portray a public scene, and it envisions a political community and a democratic, participatory politics. It would not be stretching too far, I think, to say the painting provides a celebration of public life and speech akin to that later eulogized by Hannah Arendt: "a way of life in which speech and only speech made sense and where the central concern of all citizens was to talk with each other." Yet, unlike Arendt, Rockwell imagined the *polis* as a socially egalitarian community in which a working-class man (modeled on a filling station attendant) speaks as an equal among men with white collars and in which even women are allowed to participate. He thus painted a moment in the politics of the sort of state that some democratic philosophers have contrasted to the liberal state as one in which the state is not a bodyguard or insurance company for the private interests of citizens but a political community providing a common life for citizens as citizens.[26]

Rockwell's portrait of this sort of political community was, I think, unwitting. As the anecdote about the origins of *The Four Freedoms* indicates, what impressed him about this meeting was the fact that Jim Edgerton was allowed to voice his objections on a proposed policy without being shouted down by his neighbors. It was not political community that Rockwell saw himself celebrating here, but tolerance of individual dissent, the use of free speech to protect private conscience from the state. This is also the meaning Booth Tarkington gave to free speech in his accompanying essay, a fable about a meeting of Hitler with Mussolini in the Alps

25. I will say nothing here about *Freedom of Worship* because it portrays a set of nonfamilial (albeit private) and nonpolitical obligations and interests.

26. Hannah Arendt, *The Human Condition* (Chicago: University of Chicago Press, 1958), p. 27.

Figure 9. Norman Rockwell, *Freedom of Speech*. Printed by permission of the Norman Rockwell Family Trust. Copyright © 1943, the Norman Rockwell Family Trust.

in 1912 in which each plots to become dictator of his respective country by means of the destruction of free speech. However, the painting eluded Rockwell's intentions, principally because he happened to live in a part of the country where a remnant of participatory democracy survived, and he placed his dissenter (who it is difficult to recognize as such) in the midst of this remnant.[27]

Such a participatory democracy would be one for which citizens would be obliged to die in order to protect the common life they share; such a state could lay claim to *political* obligations. Walzer finds this conception of the state in Rousseau's republican version of the social contract in which individuals undergo a qualitative transformation in moving from nature into civil society, a move that makes all the difference. Here the citizen receives from his active participation in a political community "a second life, a moral life, which is not his sole possession, but whose reality depends upon the continued existence of his fellow-citizens and of their association." From this perspective:

A good society is one in which the new man, a moral member of a moral body, achieves his fullest development. The very instincts of pre-social man are overwhelmed and above all the instinct for self-preservation. When the state is in danger, its citizens rush to its defense, forgetful of all personal danger. They die willingly for the sake of the state . . . because the state is their common life. So long as the state survives, something of the citizen lives on, even after the natural man is dead. The state, or rather the common life of the citizens, generates those "moral goods" for which, according to Rousseau, men can in fact be obligated to die.[28]

This is obviously a quite different conception of the state and of citizenship, one in which the citizen has "the lively sense of oneself as a participant in a free state, concerned for the common good" rather than "a lively longing for private pleasure." Walzer is obviously attracted to this nonliberal alternative, though he admits that it makes for a "hard politics" and is an ideal that "fails to describe any reality we know or can project for the future." Moreover, one cannot completely discount the worries liberal critics have expressed about the harmonies one finds between Rousseau's descriptions of this hard democratic politics and the organic ideologies legitimating the even harder politics of authoritarian states. For my purposes, what is most important is Walzer's contention that this democratic ideal does inhere in the feeling that some Americans have that citizenship

27. Booth Tarkington, "Freedom of Speech," *Saturday Evening Post,* 20 February 1943.
28. Walzer, "Obligation to Die for the State," pp. 91–92.

must amount to more than liberalism allows and in the sense that these citizens (now a bare majority of registered voters) have that they should continue to participate in the minimal public life that the liberal state has conceded to democracy. Important as well is his suggestion that this participatory ideal plays a very important role in the liberal state as an *ideology* designed to counteract the absence in the liberal theory of obligation to a "horizontal" political community. "This imposing and difficult ideal," he notes, "becomes an ideology whenever we are told that we are already citizens, men at or near our very best, and that our country is a nation of citizens." This is "mystification of the worst sort," yet it serves a useful purpose in that it keeps the ideal alive: "ideology is the social element within which ideals surive."[29]

Freedom of Speech was Rockwell's favorite painting in the series and the favorite of much of his audience as well, and I suspect this may be because it argued for a communitarian and thoroughly political conception of obligation that many found an attractive alternative to the liberal conception of fighting for the family and other private obligations and interests, though these obligations and interests were no less moral than those represented in the portrait of the town meeting. This was also the most thoroughly ideological of the illustrations, for it portrayed the hard politics of a nonliberal, democratic state unavailable to most yet appealing to many Americans; contended that it was their politics; and asked that they risk their lives for it. Yet *Freedom of Speech* also served to keep alive the ideal it represented. And those who remain wedded to this difficult and distant ideal may take some comfort in its appearance in a painting by Normal Rockwell, for this, one would think, would guarantee that it cannot be dismissed as un-American simply because it is not liberal.

29. Walzer, "The Problem of Citizenship," pp. 211–13.

U.S. Royal Giant Tire, 1964–65 New York World's Fair. Collection of The Queens Museum of Art, New York; gift of Bob Golby.

8 Making Time

Representations of Technology at the 1964 World's Fair

Michael L. Smith

The year is 1961. A commercial jetliner en route from London to New York encounters a problem when it attempts to land at Idlewild International Airport: there is no Idlewild. When the pilots contact La Guardia, they are denied permission to land; the air traffic controllers have never heard of their flight, or of jets or radar. As the aircraft passes over Flushing Meadow, the pilots stare in disbelief at two geometrically distinct objects: the Trylon and Perisphere, emblems of the 1939 New York World's Fair, which were dismantled in 1940, their steel girders melted down for wartime production.

"The Journey of Flight 33," as this *Twilight Zone* episode was called, left the aircraft circling, suspended in time and space. But at about the time this program aired, committees were meeting to plan a second New York World's Fair on the site of the old one. Robert Moses, New York City's planning representative for the 1939 Fair and president of the 1964 Fair Corporation, declared that the upcoming Fair would be "an Olympics of Progress," "an endless parade of the wonders of mankind." He personally solicited Walt Disney to apply his state-of-the-art audio-animatronic display techniques to four of the Fair's exhibits. Thomas J. Deegan, Jr., chair of the Corporation's executive committee, predicted that the Fair would be "the greatest single event in history."[1]

Despite its futuristic claims, the 1964 Fair bore a remarkable resemblance to its 1939 predecessor. The Trylon and Perisphere were replaced by the Unisphere, a 140-foot, hollow steel grid of the earth encircled by satellites. The Fair's vision of the future, however, appeared not to have changed much in those twenty-five years. Moses, Disney, and the other exhibit designers were apparently on board Flight 33: circling over the

---

1. "Your Day at the New York World's Fair, 1964–1965" (brochure, Organization Day Office, World's Fair Headquarters, 26 July 1963), Hagley Library, Wilmington, DE; John Brooks, "Onward and Upward with the Arts: Diplomacy at Flushing Meadow," *New Yorker*, 1 June 1963, 41. Moses saw the 1964 Fair primarily as a vehicle for developing Flushing Meadow into an elaborate state park bearing his name. Robert A. Caro, *The Power Broker: Robert Moses and the Fall of New York* (New York: Alfred A. Knopf, 1974), pp. 1084–1114.

Trylon and Perisphere, unable to touch down in 1939, and unsure how to navigate their way to 1964.

A number of social critics and historians (including this one) have challenged the versions of the past and the future presented at twentieth-century America's triad of distinctly "futurist" fairs: the 1939 and 1964 New York World's Fairs, and EPCOT Center, the Disney Corporation's permanent world's fair in Orlando. Generally we have expressed disdain at the failure of these depictions to approximate our own sense of the past, our own hopes for the future.[2] In so doing, many of us have overlooked not only the particular dynamics by which these fairs (and corporations, and governments) codify and represent cultural values, but also the tactics with which the "audience" receives or reappropriates what they see. Elsewhere in this volume, Lizabeth Cohen and Casey Blake focus on the reception and redefinition of consumer culture, or of public art by those who receive it. My current examination of visitors' reactions to depictions of technology at EPCOT suggests to me that consumer response, however elusive, is essential to our understanding of the everyday life of ideas and beliefs in mass culture.

It remains important, however, to include the first half of the equation. Like Robert Westbrook's examination of depictions of the national "family" during World War II, this essay will focus on the images themselves, exploring the underlying themes with which the designers of the 1964 Fair sought to encapsulate the relation between public and private, power and community at the height of postwar U.S. affluence. What assumptions reside within the pavilions' corporate and national depictions of change over time? What are the cultural implications of these assumptions? What

2. Michael L. Smith, "EPCOT, Camelot, and the History of Technology," in Bruce Sinclair, ed., *New Perspectives on Technology and American Culture* (Philadelphia: American Philosophical Society, 1986), pp. 69–79; John F. Kasson, "The Invention of the Past: Technology, History, and Nostalgia," in Steven E. Goldberg and Charles R. Strain, eds., *Technological Change and the Transformation of America* (Carbondale: Southern Illinois University, 1987), pp. 37–52; Wade Roush,"The Futures Market: Myths of Technological Progress in Consumer America," B.A. thesis, Harvard, 1989; Mike Wallace, "Mickey Mouse History: Portraying the Past at Disney World," *Radical History Review* 32: 33–57. See also Louis Marin, "Utopic Degeneration: Disneyland," chapter 12 of *Utopics: Spatial Play,* trans. Robert A. Vollrath (Atlantic Highlands, N.J.: Humanities Press, 1984). Because my emphasis is on representations of advanced industrial technology, I have not addressed expressions of cultural and racial differences contained in the pavilions sponsored by various national governments. A full comprehension of the fair, I believe, would require such an inquiry. For an example of the codification of racial attitudes in earlier fairs and expositions, see Robert W. Rydell, *All the World's a Fair* (Chicago: University of Chicago Press, 1984).

(and who) has been omitted from the story as told? How closely do the fair's representations of technology, culture, and progress mirror the patterns of change within U.S. society?

Time Capsules

Following in the tradition of world's fairs and expositions, the 1964 Fair's corporate exhibits tended to fixate on the products of technology, rather than on the social processes that created them. To the pantheon of wonders at previous fairs—steam engines, electric lights, telephones, streamlined locomotives, "cars of the future," television—this one added space stations, nuclear generators, picture-phones, computers and a variety of new plastics and synthetics. Repeating a gesture from the previous New York World's Fair, Westinghouse filled and buried a time capsule containing artifacts of life in 1965. Its contents leaned heavily, though not entirely, on recent technological innovations. Items chosen for immortality included a section of the heat shield from a Mercury space capsule, graphite from the first nuclear reactor, a computer memory board, contact lenses, credit cards, polyester, birth control pills, filter cigarettes, tranquilizers, an electric toothbrush, and a bikini.

Some of the exhibits were playful, like the U.S. Royal Tires ferris wheel in the shape of a huge tire, or the Chrysler pavilion's "zoo" of whimsical sculptures fashioned from auto parts. But for the most part, the brightly lit machines signified more than the sum of their precision-crafted parts. Designers of the 1964 pavilions were even more reluctant than their 1939 counterparts to portray workers, or the process of production embedded in each displayed artifact; they were eager, however, to offer scenarios of consumption for each product. No longer just halls of machinery, corporate pavilions had become their own realms of simulation: three-dimensional advertisements that sold not just products but consumer environments, ways of life receptive to the necessity of those products.[3]

3. On simulation, see Jean Baudrillard; I am more persuaded by his earlier arguments in *For a Critique of the Political Economy of the Sign* (1972), trans. Charles Levin (St. Louis: Telos, 1981), than by the all-devouring "third-order simulacra" of his *Simulations* (New York: Semiotext(e), 1983). Visitors to the major exhibits generally found themselves mildly dislocated in one of two varieties of simulation: time-travel, through corporate-sponsored visions of technology past and future; and space-travel, with glimpses of the cultures of other nations, sponsored by their governments. The corporate exhibits were primarily for U.S.-based sponsors, and it was America's past and future, not just those of General Motors or General Electric, that their pavilions claimed to represent. These corporate pavilions provided the Fair's most sustained composite image of American culture.

By and large, the fair's technological exhibits claimed to situate exhibited objects within a consumer-based narrative of progress, stepping off from the present into stylized pasts and futures. In this way, time itself becomes commodified, insinuating the sponsor's products into leading roles in the pageant of progress. Within the image-worlds of the pavilions, the "future," like the "past," created for the fairgoer a sensation of well-being about the present, and about the exhibit's sponsor. (Speaking to a conference of corporate exhibitors for the 1964 Fair, J. E. "Jiggs" Weldy, an advertising and sales manager for General Electric, explained "the show, flow, glow and dough elements" of Fair exhibits: "we want people to leave us with a glow. We want them to feel well about General Electric. We want them to make big decisions about our product.")[4] In this setting, visions of the future strive to be comforting, to evoke a sense of change only in the most cosmetic and unthreatening forms. Indications of social struggle therefore disappear.

Seen in this light, the 1964 Fair's resemblance to its earlier namesake was a measure of its success; the future it depicted, like its versions of the past, was an exercise in nostalgia. Its corporate exhibits applied images of technology as a way of dressing belief systems of the past in the trappings of future wonders.

At the core of this enterprise was the notion of progress conveyed by the Fair's corporate sponsors. The rhetoric of democratic participation appeared in some of the exhibits' narratives; but the variety of progress dominating the major corporate pavilions (General Motors, General Electric, Du Pont, Ford) was an automatic succession of new mass-produced products visited upon grateful consumers. In 1939, when the nation was still struggling to emerge from a decade of Depression, few faulted the Fair's vision of a progress typified by passive consumer abundance. But by 1964, when the culture of plenty was at its height, many of the social problems of 1939 had only grown worse. By adhering to the familiar "future" of 1939, the 1964 Fair's exhibitors obscured the social changes that had occurred—or failed to occur—in the intervening quarter-century.

It is in the nature of representations to omit more than they portray; yet the patterns of their omissions sometimes reveal more than the most vivid image. To understand what the 1964 Fair reveals about postwar

4. J. E. ("Jiggs") Weldy, "Using Fairs Effectively: The Show, Flow, Glow, and Dough Elements of World's Fair Participation," in *Key Facts for Advertisers on the New York World's Fair 1964–1965: Third Report* (New York: Association of National Advertisers, 1 December 1962), p. 19.

American culture, we have to invoke what it did *not* depict, and reintroduce people and relationships into a vision of technology and culture inhabited primarily by gleaming machines and disembodied voices.[5]

In recent years, sociologists of science, anthropologists, and historians of technology have sought to look behind discoveries and inventions, to uncover the process of contention through which competing explanations and designs move toward closure. While they are "doing" science or engineering, participants cannot separate the content of their work from its context. But when one explanation or design has succeeded in overtaking all the others, it tries to banish context, to hide all traces of struggle from view. As Bruno Latour characterizes it, the once-disputed open terrain becomes enclosed in a "black box," passing itself off as an inevitable product of scientific inquiry or technical application.[6]

This process of moving toward closure is not so elegant or complete as Latour and others have described it. Even the finished artifact can be recontextualized or redefined.[7] By focusing on cultures of reception for the products of science and technology, we can argue that closure is a designer's desire, never fully realized. Always the resistance by "users" pressures and reshapes the artifact.

Gravitation toward closure, however, is an important aspect of design—one that begins again when a new product is poised for marketing. In *portraying* dimensions of science and technology, sponsors and designers of world's fair exhibits, like advertisers, must devise strategies of representation that lean toward one of two contrasting approaches: they can focus on the products of research and development as black boxes, portraying

5. Alan Trachtenberg, *The Incorporation of America: Culture and Society in the Gilded Age* (New York: Hill and Wang, 1982), p. 209, passim; James Gilbert, *Perfect Cities: Chicago's Utopia of 1893* (Chicago: University of Chicago Press, 1991); Rydell, *All the World's a Fair*. One commentator described the 1964 Fair as "a city engineered for machines but not designed for people" (Peter Lyon, "A Glorious Nightmare," *Holiday,* July 1964, 54).

6. Bruno Latour, *Science in Action: How to Follow Scientists and Engineers through Society* (Cambridge: Harvard University Press, 1987); Wiebe Bijker, Thomas P. Hughes, and Trevor Pinch, eds., *The Social Construction of Technological Systems: New Directions in the Sociology and History of Technology* (Cambridge: MIT Press, 1987); Bryan Pfaffenberger, "Humanized Nature," manuscript (author thanks author), see especially part 1, "Semiological Materialism"; Robert Frost, "Semiotics, Narrative, and the Technological Artifact: Hardware Meets the Software Script (and They Contend Endlessly Thereafter)," paper presented to the 1988 Annual Meeting of the Society for the History of Technology, Hagley Museum and Library, Wilmington, Delaware (author thanks author).

7. See, for example, David F. Noble's account of the struggle between workers and managers over the use of NC (numerical counter) technology in *Forces of Production: A Social History of Industrial Automation* (New York: Knopf, 1984).

them as markers on the unwavering path of progress; or they can endeavor to open the black box, and usher the observer into the rich mix of voices, the cacophony of social process that is embedded in each artifact like the sound of the ocean inside the seashell.[8]

Consider, for example, the automobile—one of America's most cherished black boxes. At the 1939 Fair, the Ford pavilion featured a "Road of Tomorrow," in which visitors got to ride in new Ford automobiles, and an animated "Cycle of Production" exhibit, created by industrial designer Walter Dorwin Teague. Mounted on a hundred-foot-wide revolving turntable, the Cycle of Production employed a legion of elaborately animated objects illustrating the automobile manufacturing process, from the mining of ores to the end of the assembly line. Teague's exhibit attempted to open the black box of automobile production, although not quite wide enough to reveal the people behind the machines; pistons, gears, and metal frames all came together through magical self-animation. The absence of workers from the Cycle of Production helped to disassociate the exhibit from the violent struggles between Henry Ford and his workers in the years immediately preceding the Fair.[9]

For the 1964 Fair, representations of Ford's manufacturing process disappeared altogether. The company hired Walt Disney to update the "Road of Tomorrow" into a "Magic Skyway" ride that served as an animated advertisement, creating a succession of exotic backdrops for Ford's new product line. Visitors were ushered through select moments in the earth's past and future—dinosaurs in battle, cavemen inventing the wheel, a distant City of Tomorrow—all while riding in brand-new Ford convertibles. For time-travelers from the twenty-first century, the Magic Skyway might have appeared to be a prescient comment on the automobile as the dinosaur of its era. But the Disney team's design implied that those shiny new Mustangs were helping to carry, not just their passengers, but humanity itself, out of the sulfurous mists of prehistory and toward a luminous, high-rise future.[10]

8. "Success in building black boxes has the strange consequence of generating these UFOs: the 'irreversible progress of science,' the 'irresistible power of technology,' more mysterious than flying saucers floating without energy through space and lasting forever without aging or decaying!" Latour, *Science in Action,* p. 132.

9. Stanley Appelbaum, *The New York World's Fair 1939/40 in 155 Photographs by Richard Wurts and Others* (New York: Dover, 1977), p. 24.

10. William L. Laurence, *Science at the Fair* (New York: New York World's Fair 1964–65 Corp., 1964). See also Daniel Cohen, "Preview of Disney's World's Fair Shows," *Science Digest,* December 1963, 9–15; and "*Look's* Guide to the N.Y. World's Fair" (pamphlet), *Look,* 11

The black-box approach to technological display lends itself to techno-logical determinism, hiding the people behind the machines, polishing the metal surfaces clean of fingerprints, obscuring the social relations and so-cial choices that are the very substance of technological development. It is a determinism visited upon the present by imagined pasts and futures. At the risk of oversimplification, we might call the black-box approach *closed,* and its opposite *open.* Has the depiction of technology in twentieth-century American culture become more closed with each decade, and if so, why? How can we break open the black box that was the 1964 World's Fair? What hidden cultural assumptions does it harbor?[11]

Elsewhere, Roland Marchand and I have examined the ways in which corporate displays of science and technology at the 1964 Fair and EPCOT recapitulate the Fairs of 1933 and 1939.[12] In this essay I would like to explore the persistence of corporate futurism from a different perspective, by examining the 1964 Fair's depiction of space travel and nuclear power— two technologies that emerged between the first New York World's Fair and the second. Since no clear models existed for displaying them, were they depicted as "open" and emerging technologies, or were they forced into black boxes by the same forces that shaped the other exhibits sur-rounding them? I will devote particular attention to "Futurama II," the featured ride-exhibit in the General Motors pavilion. After considering the ride's display strategies, I will offer some possible roads of inquiry into its significance.

Domesticating the Atoms and the Stars

"Space" and "the atom" were by no means the only new arenas of techno-logical change to emerge between 1939 and 1964; but they were certainly two of the most dramatically and pervasively portrayed applications of

February 1964. The Magic Skyway was "the first known association of American cars and dinosaurs," according to one Disney employee and celebrant. Randy Bright, *Disneyland: Inside Story* (New York: Harry N. Abrams, 1987), p. 173.

11. A "closed" future is as inflexible as the past, for it serves to anesthetize the viewer's awareness of present alternatives. Disney's EPCOT Center is a model of closed future depic-tion. An "open" future is flexible and vibrant, but very difficult to display, for it points toward multiple possibilities that emerge from each choice confronting us. A model of open future depiction is the Exploratorium, a participatory museum of science and technology in San Francisco, founded by Frank Oppenheimer.

12. Roland Marchand and Michael L. Smith, "Corporate Science on Display," forthcoming, in Ronald Walters, ed., *Science and Social Reform in Industrial America* (Baltimore: Johns Hopkins Press).

technology in postwar America. The federal government sponsored major projects in both areas; soon, postwar mass culture was saturated with celestial and nuclear images, and with links between the two. Science editors and comic book characters alike assigned special significance to the striking similarity between the "orbital" model of the atom and diagrams of the solar system. Between the vastness of space and the tiniest particles of matter all around us, there appeared to be correspondences as compelling as any in religious belief systems. At least one of the '64 Fair exhibits directly exploited this association. In the Transportation and Travel pavilion, the Cinerama film "To the Moon and Beyond" propelled the viewer "through billions of miles of space" and "into the center of the minutest atom," using for both the same model of a nucleus orbited by particles.[13]

Public events in the years preceding the Fair kept the interplay of nuclear and space issues on the front pages. The Soviet launch of Sputnik I in October 1957 had inaugurated "the space age," and an accompanying space race between the superpowers. Two months later, the nation's first civilian nuclear power plant came on-line, and political leaders declared that the age of "the peaceful atom" had begun. In April 1961, Yuri Gagarin became the first human to orbit the earth; less than a month later, Alan Shepard was the first American in space. The Cuban missile crisis of October 1962 kept the possibility of nuclear exchange in the headlines. In July 1963, the United States, the Soviet Union, and Britain signed the first Partial Test Ban Treaty, banning atmospheric testing of nuclear weapons.

For corporate and government elites, however, space and the atom suggested a different sort of correspondence. The atom promised unlimited power (political as well as physical); and outer space offered an unlimited scope for that power. Taken together, rockets and atoms constituted the hardware (payload and delivery system) for the arms race. They also provided Cold War surrogates for military competition, with each superpower measuring its superiority in peaceful atoms and space launches. Nuclear technology and the space program played an expressive role far beyond their technical functions: they provided a vocabulary of terms and images by which much of American culture and ideology were articulated in the 1950s and 1960s.[14]

13. Sheldon J. Reaven, "New Frontiers: Science and Technology at the Fair," in *Remembering the Future: The New York World's Fair from 1939 to 1964* (New York: Queens Museum, 1989), p. 80.

14. Michael L. Smith, "Selling the Moon: The U.S. Manned Space Program and the Triumph of Commodity Scientism," in Richard W. Fox and T. J. Jackson Lears, eds., *The Culture*

Government and corporate publicists alike continually faced one of the inherent contradictions of impression management in the nuclear age: to potential adversaries, they needed to maximize the impression of America's destructive capacity and will; but to citizens and consumers, they sought to *domesticate* space and the atom, emphasizing "pioneer" analogies, images of childlike wonder and discovery, and characterizations of nuclear and space technology as artifacts of everyday life.[15]

Like every other international setting, world's fairs in the Cold War era tended to become arenas of image warfare between East and West. U.S. exhibits at the 1964 Fair, however, did not have to compete with their Soviet counterparts for attention. The Fair was not granted international recognition as a world's fair, because of a provision that no country would host two such fairs within ten years of each other. (The Seattle Fair in 1962 enjoyed official status). Accordingly, the Soviet Union, the East Bloc countries, and most of Western Europe declined to sponsor exhibits in New York. American exhibit designers were thus freer to concentrate on images of technological domesticity.

The Fair's unofficial status also translated into less federal involvement in science-based exhibits. If this meant less propaganda, it could also mean less science. The early planning sessions for the 1962 Seattle Fair coincided with the furor created among U.S. policymakers by the Soviet Union's October 1957 launch of the world's first orbiting artificial satellite. In the wake of Sputnik, the federal government created the National Aeronautics and Space Administration, poured money into programs to enhance science education in the nation's schools—and devoted nearly ten million dollars to the design of a sophisticated U.S. science pavilion at the Seattle World's Fair. In the absence of such funding, the 1964 New York Fair relied primarily on the efforts of corporate exhibitors, which focused more on attaching meaning to their own products than on "science for science's sake."[16]

---

of Consumption: Critical Essays in American History, 1880–1980 (New York: Pantheon, 1983); Michael L. Smith, "Advertising the Atom," in Michael J. Lacey, ed., *Government and Environmental Politics: Essays on Historical Developments since World War Two* (Washington, D.C.: Wilson Center Press, 1989); Pfaffenberger, "Humanized Nature," p. 21 ("technology is by no means essentially instrumental, but rather essentially *expressive*" [emphasis mine]).

15. Michael L. Smith, "If Atoms Could Talk: Ventriloquism, Gender, and Domesticity in Nuclear America," forthcoming, in Robert L. Frost and Bryan Pfaffenberger, eds., *Material Discourse* (Johns Hopkins University Press).

16. John Walsh, "Science Exhibits: At Seattle Fair, Federal Funds, Scientists Helped, New Yorkers Try a Different Tack," *Science* (31 May 1963): 960–62 ("science for science's sake," p. 960). See Walsh's discussion of the controversy surrounding the 1964 Fair's New York

Visitors to the 1964 Fair encountered images of space and the atom at every turn. The Unisphere itself, with its three orbiting satellites, was a self-proclaimed talisman of the space age. Two of the rejected theme center proposals for the Fair had been even more space-minded. Industrial designer Walter Dorwin Teague, one of the principal designers of the 1939 Fair, submitted a proposal called "Journey to the Stars," a 170-foot, aluminum inverted spiral with wands of star-shaped balloons at the top. (Robert Moses thought it looked too much like a bedspring.) Also rejected was Yale architect Paul Rudolph's "Galaxon," a 160-foot-high, 340-foot-long, saucer-shaped concrete structure with "star viewing stations."[17]

Far from evoking the bizarre or daring scenes of 1950s science fiction films, most of the fair's depictions of space travel made a special effort to domesticate outer space. In the U.S. Space Park, cosponsored by NASA and the Defense Department, visitors could walk among, touch, and pose beside full-scale models of an Apollo capsule, a Telstar satellite, the "business end of [a] Saturn C-5" rocket, and "Scott Carpenter's actual Mercury capsule." The normally unapproachable, massive hardware of space and missile technology thus seemed tamed by its very proximity.[18]

Other exhibits lent a sense of familiarity to space travel by linking it to more earthbound activities of the past. The Missouri Pavilion featured the St. Louis-based McDonnell Corporation's full-sized models of Mercury and Gemini capsules; by exhibiting them alongside a replica of Lindbergh's "Spirit of St. Louis," McDonnell placed space exploration in the familiar context of aviation history, while associating both air and space technology with the site of its corporate headquarters. And just as Lindbergh's trans-

---

City–sponsored Hall of Science. On the tension between science and the Cold War at the 1958 Fair, see Howard Simons, "Brussels Fair and Science," *Science News Letter,* 11 January 1958, 26–27.

17. Marc H. Miller, "Something for Everyone: Robert Moses and the Fair," in *Remembering the Future,* pp. 62–65. Teague was a member of the design committee for the 1939 Fair; he contributed designs for the Ford, U.S. Steel, Du Pont, Kodak, and Con Ed pavilions, among others.

18. "P[opular] S[cience] Reader's Guide to the Fair," *Popular Science,* June 1964, pp. 56, 182. The guide was designed to "pinpoint things a PS-type man won't want to miss." NASA and the Defense Department later expanded the Fair's "space park" approach when the Kennedy Space Center in Florida was transformed into a major tourist attraction. Surrounding the visitors' center, several generations of missiles, boosters, and rockets are displayed on an expansive lawn—many on their sides, with children permitted to climb them and families allowed to photograph themselves gathered around them. By transforming the hardware of the arms race into a playground, the Space Center neatly domesticates both space and the atom.

Atlantic flight had been widely hailed in 1927 as a marriage of the frontier spirit of the past with the technology of the future, so the 1964 U.S. pavilion's 135-screen presentation, "Past as Prologue," portrayed outer space as a natural extension of the nation's pioneer ethic, ushering viewers from the scenes of Conestoga wagons to glimpses of lunar and galactic frontiers.[19]

Most depictions of space, however, anticipated the future. The roof of the Kodak pavilion offered a stylized "moonscape" for "family snapshots in outer space." In Martin-Marietta's "Rendezvous in Space" exhibit at the Hall of Science, scale-model prototypes of Skylab and the Shuttle performed docking maneuvers overhead, like amiable puppets. The Pavilion of American Interiors included a "Moon Room," where spare, minimalist surfaces and transparent furniture anticipated "gracious dining, even in outer space."[20]

The Fair's representations of nuclear technology pursued even more emphatically the domestication of a new technology. The Swiss pavilion included an "atomic clock." At General Electric's "Progressland" pavilion, visitors could witness a "Fusion Demonstration"; GE scientists appeared with instruments to provide the audience with "bonafide evidence that true nuclear fusion was accomplished as they watched." The Atomic Energy Commission sponsored "Atomsville, USA" at the Hall of Science, described by Fair publicists as "a pint-sized atomic city, in which youngsters can activate two dozen simulated nuclear experiments." A "Children Only" sign forbade parents beyond a low-slung entrance. "Everything in the universe is made of atoms," the exhibit's first panel reassuringly announced. Inside, children found playful, interactive exhibits such as the "pedal driven generators"—stationary bicycles on which young visitors could compare their own energy-generating capacity with that of a nuclear power plant.[21]

The Fair's sunny assertions of the wonders of the peaceful atom were not enough to dispel all of the shadows cast by the Cold War and the arms

19. John William Ward, "The Meaning of Lindbergh's Flight," *American Quarterly* (Spring 1958): 3–16. The U.S. pavilion's "Lindbergh strategy" later became the organizing principle for the Smithsonian's Air and Space Museum, where in a single overview, the visitor can see the Wright brothers' first plane, Lindbergh's "Spirit of St. Louis," John Glenn's Mercury 7 capsule, a moonrock, and a cosmic wall mural depicting the space-bound trajectory of human evolution.

20. Patricia Leigh Brown, "Fifty Years after the Fair," *New York Times,* 2 March 1989, p. C6.

21. Laurence, *Science at the Fair;* 1964/65 New York World's Fair Papers, New York Public Library (cited hereafter as NYPL), Box 663.

race. The Office of Civil Defense sponsored a Fair exhibit on the causes and nature of radiation; but by downplaying the dangers, the exhibit provided reassurance more than information. Perhaps the clearest example of the Fair's approach to the dark side of nuclear technology was the Underground House. Based on a prototype built by Jay Swayze, a former instructor in chemical warfare, the Underground House was essentially a luxury fallout shelter. The Fair's newsletter and publicity releases, however, cast the planned exhibit in the most favorable light possible, describing it as a "modern home and garden" designed to demonstrate the "advantages of underground living." Visitors were invited to "dial proper blends of electrical sunshine, twilight, moonlight and starlight," and to adjust geography and the seasons with "dial-a-view" simulated picture windows. Swayze himself characterized his shelter as "the ultimate in privacy," and publicity brochures praised the house for providing protection from "the hazards of modern living, including pollution, pollen, noise and radioactive fallout."[22] The Underground House domesticated the Bomb itself by assigning comparable "annoyance status" to smog, rowdy neighbors, and thermonuclear war.

Futurama

By far the most intricate vision of a future world shaped by nuclear and space technologies was Futurama II, the ride featured in the General Motors pavilion. The highlight of GM's original Futurama ride in 1939 had been its depiction of the "highway world of 1960." Designed by Norman Bel Geddes, it simulated an aerial view of the near future, with teardrop-shaped vehicles gliding along broad superhighways en route to the streamlined skyscrapers and elevated streets of the City of Tomorrow. The most popular attraction at the 1939 Fair, Futurama was more of an innovation in display technique than in substance. Most of the ingredients of the City of Tomor-

22. *Fair News,* 22 November 1963, NYPL, Box 669; Brown, "Fifty Years after the Fair," p. C6. Contrasting a recent press conference on the need for fallout shelters with the boundless optimism of the Fair's advance publicity, radio commentator Dorothy Kilgallen complained of the "inconsistency of men in high places": "The Governor [Nelson Rockefeller] and the President [Kennedy] think we are going to be devastated by bombs, but if we have [fallout] shelters maybe a certain number will be saved. On the other hand, Robert Moses thinks everything is coming up roses, or everything's coming up Moses, and we're going to have a World's Fair" to celebrate the inevitable sweep of progress. "Breakfast with Dorothy [Kilgallen] and Dick [Kollmer]," transcript, Radio-TV Reports, 6 June 1962, WOR Radio, NYPL, Box 406.

row—symmetrically arranged mega-skyscrapers, elevated multilevel super-highways, and aerial moving sidewalks, all sporting sleek, curved edges in a world liberated from friction and sharp corners—were borrowed from sources that had already influenced mass culture: the Italian Futurists, Le Corbusier, Hugh Ferriss, Fritz Lang's *Metropolis,* and the "streamlining" industrial designers among whom Bel Geddes himself was one of the most prominent.[23]

Its sweeping, utopian narration notwithstanding, Futurama served primarily as a lobbying device for a national superhighway system; its elaborate futurescape was predicated on the triumph of the private automobile over mass transit. And while visitors were marveling at the City of Tomorrow's multilevel highways, General Motors was in the midst of a "motorization" campaign, aimed at eliminating electric streetcars from the nation's cities. In 1947, a federal jury convicted GM, Firestone Tire, Standard Oil, and a number of smaller companies for conspiring to replace the nation's electric rail lines with buses. Between 1936 and 1946, their umbrella company, National City Lines, bought and destroyed the streetcar lines in forty-five American cities; in many cases, they also excavated the tracks to ensure a permanent conversion. By 1955, when Congress passed the Interstate Highway Act, almost 90 percent of the nation's electric streetcars were gone.[24]

In 1964, the new superhighway system which Futurama had envisioned was well under construction, although the 1939 exhibit's predicted conges-

---

23. Reaven, "New Frontiers," p. 96; Caroline Tisdall and Angelo Bozzola, "The Futurist City," in *Futurism* (London: Thames and Hudson, 1977), pp. 121–35; Manfredo Tafuri, "The Disenchanted Mountain: The Skyscraper and the City," in Giorgio Ciucci et al., *The American City: From the Civil War to the New Deal,* trans. Barbara Luigia La Penta (Cambridge: MIT Press, 1979), pp. 389–503; Philip Strick, "The Metropolis Wars: The City as Character in Science Fiction Films," in Danny Peary, ed., *Omni's Screen Flights/Screen Fantasies: The Future According to Science Fiction Cinema* (Garden City, N.Y.: Doubleday, 1984); Andreas Huyssen, *After the Great Divide: Modernism, Mass Culture, Postmodernism* (Bloomington: Indiana University Press, 1986), pp. 65–81; Rem Koolhaas, *Delirious New York: A Retroactive Manifesto for Manhattan* (New York: Oxford University Press, 1978), pp. 226–41, passim.

Le Corbusier's "Radiant City" was more directly mirrored by "Democracity," the model city of tomorrow exhibited inside the Perisphere. Hugh Ferriss, whose *Metropolis of Tomorrow* (1929) envisioned a city of dramatic setback skyscrapers cloaked in romanticized urban chiaroscuro, served as an official renderer for the 1939 Fair's Board of Design.

24. The jury's findings, which were upheld on appeal, were that GM and the other corporations had conspired with intent. The federal prosecutors recommended that individual corporate officers be imprisoned. The judge, however, treated the case as a traffic violation, and fined the offenders $1 apiece; the corporations received the maximum penalty of $5,000. (GM alone sold $25 million worth of buses to National City Lines over the years.)

tion-free, seven-lane motorways with hundred-mile-per-hour speed limits still seemed out of reach.[25] General Motors decided to try to repeat its success at the previous New York World's Fair by featuring a "Futurama II" in 1964—designed, this time, by GM's own team of stylists. But the future could no longer be invoked with superhighways. In a world of space travel and nuclear power, surely a new Futurama would require a new vision of the future.

Like its namesake, Futurama II promised "a look at developments that await man in the very near future—predictions," the public was assured, "solely based on fact." Once again, superhighways linked the countryside to a "Metropolis of Tomorrow." This time, however, the highways of the future ventured to "the far reaches of our planet" and beyond.[26] For a third of a mile, visitors rode past a succession of dramatic animated dioramas, while voices emanating from individual speakers inside their seats provided a narrative to accompany what they saw.

This fifteen-minute "multi-sensory experience" began by carrying visitors to the moon, where an all-terrain lunar vehicle crossed the face of a crater on rows of huge spherical "wheels" resembling soccer balls. In the distance, a permanent lunar colony provided a base for "man and machines exploring the surface of the moon." Returning to earth, Futurama explorers found themselves in Antartica, a "bleak, stark, uninhabited" realm transformed into a new site for colonization. Scientists could be seen at work at "a weather station cut deep into the Antarctic shelf," where they monitored global climate. A climate-controlled harbor had been excavated from the ice for settlers. Goods were shipped in via "atom-powered submarine trains" to avoid the fierce Antarctic winter.[27]

Visitors then journeyed to the floor of the ocean, where guests at "the beautiful Hotel Atlantis, an undersea resort," could watch an "underwater well pump[ing] oil into a train of [nuclear powered] submarine tankers." Nearby, underwater miners operated aquacopters, "probing the ocean's

25. In his report on the opening of the Fair, WCBS-TV reporter Douglas Edwards spoke of the "GM soothsayers" who "trust that progress will solve the problems of city traffic just as the superhighways they predicted made road travel easier in our own time." "Late News," typescript, 8 April 1964, Radio-TV Reports, NYPL, Box 406.

26. General Motors, "Let's Go to the Fair and Futurama: NYWF 1964–1965" (guidebook, undated).

27. Ibid.; "Will This Be the No. 1 Show?" *Science Digest,* April 1964, 14–15. "The headquarters is located here," *Science Digest* explained, because according to GM press releases, "it is here that most of the Southern Hemisphere weather originates. It in turn affects, to a marked degree, much of the weather of the Northern Hemisphere."

caverns" for "riches of the deep." Next came a "jungle deep in the tropics" where "we observe a vibrant new quality in tomorrow's jungle—the sound and look of progress. Revolutionary new earth-moving and jungle equipment are helping to construct modern highways, towns and industrial plants." GM's vision of taming the jungle focused on replacing its natural transportation medium, an "aimlessly wandering river," with modern superhighways. First, a jungle harvester felled great swaths of trees with laser beams. Then the area was sprayed with chemical defoliants, and "a road-building vehicle as high as a five-story building and as long as three football fields" leveled the cleared ground, set steel pilings, and extruded a multilane highway "in one continuous operation!" GM press releases predicted that this massive "road-builder," powered by its own mobile nuclear reactor, would be "capable of producing from within itself one mile of four-lane, elevated superhighway every hour."[28]

The jungle gave way to "desert lands—a vast, arid sea of sand which, until the future, had been another no-man's land. Here, too, a miracle has taken place." Massive nuclear-powered irrigation projects fed large-scale, remote-control "electronic farms," which produced bumper crops from "land too long sterile."[29]

Finally, "the graceful beauty of modern multi-lane highways" carried visitors to the "Metropolis of Tomorrow," with streamlined skyscrapers, elevated highways and moving sidewalks very much like the 1939 City of Tomorrow. But the Metropolis of Futurama II also introduced new kinds of vehicles and roadways custom-designed to match specific functions, whereas the original Futurama had pictured universal ownership of private vehicles—a virtual automobilization of America—which in turn would lead to maximum, effortless mobility on the highways of the future.

By 1964, advertising still associated the private automobile with total mobility; but with over sixty million cars on the road (not the thirty-eight million predicted by Futurama I), fairgoers were all too familiar with the realities of traffic jams and congestion. Futurama II's solution was to introduce an "autoline," where drivers entering the city would relinquish control of their vehicles to electronic traffic control centers. This suspension of GM's doctrine of automobility arose from Futurama II's struggle to achieve

28. "Let's Go to the Fair and Futurama"; "Will This Be the No. 1 Show?" 16–17; GM press releases, quoted in Rosemarie Haag Bletter, "The 'Laissez-Fair,' Good Taste, and Money Trees: Architecture at the Fair," in *Remembering the Future*, p. 119.

29. "Let's Go to the Fair"; Joyce Martin, "Transportation Area Exhibits" (press release), 21 April 1965, NYPL, Box 393; Laurence, *Science at the Fair*.

the benefits of mass transit without diminishing reliance on private auto-mobiles. The exhibit's publicity, however, assured visitors that an abundance of on-board recreational appliances (television, refrigerator, hi-fi) would compensate drivers for their temporary loss of the wheel. (Similarly, to streamline trucking and shipping, containerized goods—and, presumably, longshoremen—would be relegated to automated underground corridors reminiscent of Fritz Lang's *Metropolis*.)

Futurama II's specialized vehicularization reflected its designers' conception of gender roles as well. For shopping districts, GM engineers had designed "easily maneuverable, three-wheeled 'Runabouts' " with built-in, detachable shopping carts. The Runabout, according to GM press releases, was an experimental car "especially designed for housewives," who were widely recognized to be "avid shoppers" but "poor drivers."[30]

Technocolonialism

Even more than its 1939 namesake, Futurama II ventured far beyond promoting GM products. To be sure, the ride's dioramas featured an exotic variety of futuristic vehicles, many of them nuclear-powered (lunar crawlers, aquacopters, the jungle road builder, the Runabout). But Futurama's settings were not simply backdrops for transportation fantasies. The moon, Antarctica, the sea floor, the jungle, and the desert materialized before fairgoers as a succession of "techno-colonies." Collectively, they conveyed an unacknowledged but powerful cluster of related messages concerning the social meanings of technology.

These messages were not limited to Futurama. Images of the techno-colonies were scattered throughout the corporate pavilions at the 1964 Fair; and this same vision dominates the Future World pavilions at EPCOT Center.[31] How did this particular vision of the future come to displace all of the other possibilities? And what did it convey?

30. Bletter, "The 'Laissez-Fair,' " p. 121.

31. Michael L. Smith,"EPCOT's America: Disney, Technology and Amnesia in the Nuclear Age," paper presented at the 1989 Annual Meeting of the Organization of American Historians, St. Louis. Five of EPCOT's eight Future World pavilions—Kraft's "The Land," United Technologies' "Living Seas," AT&T's "Spaceship Earth," Exxon's "Universe of Energy," and General Motors' "World of Motion"—reenact some portion of the Futurama II array of colonies; a sixth, General Electric's "Horizons" pavilion, is virtually a remake of the Futurama II concept.

During my most recent visit to EPCOT Center in August 1990, I asked visitors, in interviews and questionnaires, to share their thoughts about the colonies. Most people responded that they believed such colonies would exist in their lifetime, but did not feel inclined to live in one of them.

Futurama's depictions of the colonies portrayed rather unremarkable activities; they owed most of their futuristic allure to their settings. In this future, then, people would live in places presently considered uninhabitable. The exhibits offered no reasons why people should want to live on the moon or the ocean floor; nor did they have to. The techno-colonies were at the heart of the 1964 Fair's black box of futurism; approached properly, they might also provide the key to open it.

To understand the messages of the colonies, we should begin by recognizing the *visual imperative* that pressured all exhibit designers. World's Fairs and theme parks are ads disguised as museums. To make its presentation strategies succeed, Futurama required a series of instantly recognizable *tableaux,* identifiable by viewers as "the future."[32] To accomplish this task, exhibit designers chose images that expressed values and themes their audiences would recognize; the techno-colonies were visual elaborations of a *global engineering* ethos that flourished in the United States from the 1930s until the 1960s. The 1964 Fair may be considered one of the last unselfconscious expressions of global engineering—and one of the most baroque.

A principal attribute of this vision was a rhetoric of conquest. Above all, it characterized the human mission as the conquest of nature. ("Everywhere you go," the Futurama guidebook promised, "you will see man conquering new worlds.") Natural environments were depicted as challenges, or as backdrops for large-scale projects.[33] Global engineering thrived on giantism; from dams to thousand-megawatt nuclear plants to space stations, scale denoted human triumph over nature. (The Unisphere handsomely expressed this quality. The world's largest model of the earth, it really depicted almost nothing of the planet; metal silhouettes of the

---

32. Exhibit designer James Gardner explained to Fair exhibitors that "If your aim is to interest an exhibition crowd, you are in show business." When fairgoers enter exhibits, he observed, "they are tuned in to a much higher pitch of critical appreciation than they normally are. In fact, let's face it, most people are tuned in to no pitch of critical appreciation." In such a state, they "are psychologically ready for you to influence them." James Gardner, "Exhibit Designs and Techniques That Attract the General Public," in *Key Facts for Advertisers on the NYWF 1964–1965: Third Report* (New York: Association of National Advertisers, 1 December 1962), 25–26.

33. Between the 1930s and the 1960s, GM produced innumerable "ephemeral films"—short subjects to be screened between features in movie theatres. These films celebrated every aspect of American production and consumption. "American Engineer," produced in 1956, is the consummate expression of global engineering at its cultural peak. (I am grateful to Richard Prelinger of Petrified Films for making this and many other ephemeral films available to me.)

continents were superimposed onto an empty sphere of gridwork, with lines of latitude and longitude substituting for the earth's substance.)

For New Yorkers, Fair Corporation President Robert Moses personified global engineering. As New York City Park Commissioner, Moses was responsible for most of the parkways, bridges, parks, and zoos constructed in the area from the twenties through the fifties. By the sixties, however, Moses had outlived the public's unquestioning acceptance of each new large-scale project. The 1964 Fair occurred at just the moment when giant-ism and the growth imperative, two mainstays of global engineering, were encountering serious public challenges. One of Moses's final projects, a new freeway cutting through Greenwich Village, was canceled because of the severity of public protests.[34]

For American viewers, the colonies evoked a familiar frontier metaphor for technological change. Historically, they had thought of the westering of the geographical frontier as a salient feature of their culture. In the twentieth century, advocates for diverse causes spoke of the nation's tech-nological frontier as a kind of conceptual West. In this context, the Fair's techno-colonies appeared to extend the parameters of national conquest. Their visually arresting settings may have described questionable expendi-tures of human effort; but as futurist updates of frontier settlement, they served as vivid signifiers for science, technology, and national progress.

By 1964, this association of remote settlement with technological and national frontiers had acquired explicit political overtones as well. Presi-dent Kennedy presented the space program as a "new frontier" in the literal as well as the metaphorical sense. Futurama's colonies simply extended this interchangeability of geographic and intellectual frontiers.

At the Fair, as in the nation, political and corporate frontiers corre-sponded nicely. For General Motors and the other private sponsors, the colonies reflected the mandate for continuous growth and expansion within corporate culture. GM may not have anticipated an impending need for aquacopters; but the techno-colonies provided dramatic visual expression of corporate management's need for ever-expanding markets.

In these corporate and political adaptations, the colonies' implied tri-umph over nature served as a surrogate for the conquest of adversaries in the marketplace or the world of nations. Futurama II's gargantuan, jungle-devouring, nuclear-powered road-builder perfectly articulated this conquest-of-nature stance and its many levels of cultural meaning. In retro-

34. Caro, *The Power Broker.*

spect, the road-builder might have served as a more appropriate theme center for the Fair than the Unisphere. The reign of the road-builder, however, was about to undergo a powerful challenge. The publication of Rachel Carson's *Silent Spring* in 1962, and the passage of the Wilderness Act in 1964 were only small indications of the full-scale environmentalist temperament that was destined to emerge in the years immediately after the Fair closed. By the late 1980s, children in suburban shopping malls would wear "Save the Rainforest" T-shirts; but in 1964, few thought to question the need for highways in the Amazon.

Environmentalism also contributed to a shift in public attitudes toward nuclear power, global engineering's technology of choice. The 1964 Fair embraced the unchallenged nuclear optimism of the fifties and sixties. But between 1969, when the mass media discovered an unprecedented array of critics warning of nuclear-related health and environmental hazards, and the accident at Three Mile Island a decade later, the atom became contested terrain. The nuclear industry and its government supporters characterized the "anti-nukes" as "hysterical," an "idiot fringe" using nuclear fear to attack "the American philosophy of life." The most effective critics of nuclear technology, however, were scientists and technicians from within the Atomic Energy Commission and the nuclear industry itself.[35]

Even the revered automobile, after a half-century as a cultural icon, found itself targeted for safety and environmental hazards; and its critics, in turn, found themselves targeted by automakers. While fairgoers marveled at the road-builder, detectives hired by General Motors were tailing Ralph Nader, hoping to find ways to silence him after the publication of his *Unsafe at Any Speed* in 1962. In the 1970s, the new Environmental Protection Agency threatened to tighten and enforce air quality standards; and two energy crises created federal pressure for more fuel-efficient automobiles. While foreign models won an increasing share of the market, America's automakers spent many millions of dollars on these new challenges—if not to solve them, then at least to lobby against them.

If an environmental challenge was emerging from within global engi-

35. Chet Holifield, "Let Us Get the Facts Straight," *Congressional Record,* 30 June 1970, Washington, DC; "Remarks of Harry G. Slater," Atomic Industrial Forum, Workshop on Reactor Licensing, Glen Cove, NY, 2 July 1969; Theos J. Thompson, "Improving the Quality of Life—Can Plowshare Help?" *Symposium on Engineering with Nuclear Explosives,* 14–15 January 1970, vol. 1 (Washington, DC: Atomic Energy Commission), p. 104. See also Smith, "Advertising the Atom," pp. 253–57; and Daniel Ford, *The Cult of the Atom: The Secret Papers of the Atomic Energy Commission* (New York: Simon and Schuster, 1982).

neering's images of the conquest of nature, a form of *cultural* conquest was also implicit in the "new frontiers" represented by the techno-colonies. Futurama II promised to demonstrate "how the frontier lands of today— desert, jungle, polar regions and ocean floor—can be made livable and productive." In spite of GM's extensive operations in Brazil and other Third World countries, Futurama gave no indication that for indigenous populations, many of those jungles and deserts were already "livable and productive." What depths of national and corporate imperialism were implied by the road-builder's intolerance of unpaved surfaces? A clear cultural judgment was implicit in the Futurama II guidebook's assertion that "[n]uclear power is being used to transform this land of impenetrable vegetation into civilization—to give motion to people and usefulness to resources too long dormant." During the Fair's second season, the Gulf of Tonkin Resolution granted President Johnson the power to dramatically escalate U.S. involvement in Vietnam. America's percepton of the jungle was about to undergo a considerable change.[36]

Gender messages, another arena of contention implicit in Futurama II's global vision, were encoded into the road-builder's alter ego, the Runabout. Designed to reflect GM designers' "Stepford Wives" notions of the role of women, the Runabout unwittingly revealed the culturally enforced "masculine" code of values that shaped the global engineering perspective. Enthusiastic response to the publication of Betty Friedan's *The Feminine Mystique* in 1963 only hinted at the eagerness with which the emerging women's movement would identify and challenge the gender politics of the global engineers in the years that followed.

The Fair's blind spots regarding race and class provided additional targets for challenges to Futurama II's worldview. Picket lines at the Fair reminded visitors that they lived in the most volatile period of Civil Rights activism since Reconstruction; during the Fair's two-year run alone, Americans witnessed passage of the two most sweeping Civil Rights acts in the

---

36. LBJ, a firm believer in global engineering, said that he expected to win the hearts and minds of the South Vietnamese by promising to "turn the Mekong Delta into a goddamn T.V.A."; he was shocked when they showed little interest in such projects. He was also unwilling to believe that North Vietnam, a "fourth-rate little pissant of a country," could resist the military might of the most technologically advanced nation on earth. Yet in spite of a protracted defoliation effort, and the most extensive bombing campaign in history, the United States failed even to halt the flow of troops and supplies along the Ho Chi Minh Trail. This "land of impenetrable vegetation," it turned out, had a "civilization" of its own: one that gained the military advantage by viewing technology as interaction with—rather than conquest of—nature.

nation's history, the Watts Riots, and the assassination of Malcolm X. Publication of Michael Harrington's *The Other America* in 1962 revealed that poverty was not confined to the ghettos; the legislation that launched the "War on Poverty" was also initiated during the Fair's tenure. Yet Futurama II, like most of the Fair, "solved" these problems by simply omitting any reference to them. Everyone in the future was white and middle-class.

Again, aspects of Robert Moses's career demonstrated how other social and political issues (in this case, race and class) become embedded in the artifacts of engineering design. By opting for extremely low overpasses above his Long Island parkways, Moses was able to block buses, with their minority and low-income patrons, from ready access to his prized public park, Jones Beach. "Many of his monumental structures of concrete and steel embody a systematic societal inequality," observes Langdon Winner, "a way of engineering relationships among people that, after a time, become just another part of the landscape."[37]

All visions of conquest in postwar America, however, were profoundly altered by the ever-present shadow of the Bomb. Cold War political leaders found the rhetoric of conquest strangely up-ended by the nuclear threat. For the first time in history, the superpowers couldn't openly pursue total military victory over their adversaries. Instead, each side spoke of its arsenals and strategies as "defense" and "deterrence." Weapons, like Fair exhibits, became useful primarily for their display value. Both the United States and the Soviet Union, however, depicted the other side as suicidally unrestrained in its lust for conquest. Each nation's desire for victory was thus projected onto its adversary, and ricocheted back in the form of fallout shelters and "mutually assured destruction."

The contradictions implicit in nuclear age militarism reveal a deeper inversion: in the nuclear age, the rhetoric of *conquest* describes a strategy of *escape*. In the inverted world of the nuclear age, the rulers desert the palace for a cave beneath the mountains, and the techno-colonies become the Underground House.

Futurama II's designers, no doubt, would not agree. How can a glorified hole in the ground compare with the colonies' vistas of limitless expansion? Yet on closer examination, we can see that the colonies, like the Underground House, are the ultimate fallout shelters. The colonies were described as frontiers of unfettered freedom; their inhabitants, however,

37. Langdon Winner, *The Whale and the Reactor: A Search for Limits in an Age of High Technology* (Chicago: University of Chicago Press, 1986), p. 23.

would have to live in conditions of severe confinement. Postwar culture's unwillingness to confront the realities of the nuclear threat fueled a technology of escapism. Perhaps the Fair's most expressive symbol of the age was not the Unisphere, or even the road-builder, but the Underground House.

We began our inquiry by flying over the site of the 1964 Fair on the eve of its inception. We close at a site *under* the fairgrounds after its demolition. Unfortunately, as is often the case with time-travelers, we have taken too long; space and the atom have already been trapped inside the black box of techno-colonies; and Flight 33, having run out of fuel, has crashed into Flushing Meadow. To understand the culture we now inhabit, we must emerge from our Underground House and sift through the wreckage for survivors. As is customary after a plane crash, we will also search for the black box. And learn how to open it.

Federal Plaza immediately after the removal of *Tilted Arc*. Photo by Addison Thomson Architectural Photographs.

9 An Atmosphere of Effrontery

Richard Serra, *Tilted Arc,* and the Crisis of Public Art

Casey Nelson Blake

At stake in every struggle over art there is also the imposition of an art of living, that is, the transmutation of an arbitrary way of living into the legitimate way of life which casts every other way of living into arbitrariness.
—Pierre Bourdieu

I

On the night of 15 March 1989 the federal government removed *Tilted Arc* from Federal Plaza in Manhattan. Ten years after it had commissioned the work for the space in front of the Jacob K. Javits Federal Building and the United States Court of International Trade, the General Services Administration (GSA) ordered a crew to dismantle the enormous steel sculpture and store it in a Brooklyn warehouse. The debate about *Tilted Arc* conducted throughout the 1980s in the media, public hearings, and the courts made it one of the best-known pieces of contemporary public art in the United States. Opponents of *Tilted Arc* had condemned the modernist sculpture since its installation in July 1981 as an ugly, aggressive intrusion that obstructed the use of the plaza overlooking Foley Square by office workers in the area. William Diamond, the GSA regional administrator

I wish to thank the following people for providing me with materials relevant to the *Tilted Arc* case: Trina McKeever, an associate of Richard Serra; Leslie Cornfeld-Urfirer of Paul Weiss Rifkind Wharton and Garrison, Serra's legal counsel; Dale Lanzone and Susan Harrison of the Arts and Historic Preservation Program, General Services Administration (Washington, D.C.); Peter Sneed of the New York GSA Regional Office; Paul Goldstein and the staff of Community Board No. 1, New York City; and the staff at the Museum of Modern Art Library. I am also very grateful for the comments I received on early versions of this essay from Thomas Bender, Richard Fox, Shelley Gurstein, Arlene Shaner, Michael Smith, Rosalind Williams, and Richard Wolin. In addition, I am indebted to the participants in the multidisciplinary faculty seminar in Cultural Studies at Indiana University, for their comments on a paper based on this material, and to Miriam Levin and David Samson for bibliographical suggestions.

Figures on pages 246, 263, and 289 are reproduced by permission of the publisher from Clara Weyergraf-Serra and Martha Buskirk, eds., *The Destruction of Tilted Arc: Documents,* ©1991 by MIT Press.

responsible for dismantling the work, argued that "the atmosphere of the plaza turned into affrontery [sic]" with the appearance of the piece. For Richard Serra, the creator of *Tilted Arc,* and his supporters, removal of this "site-specific" sculpture meant its destruction. The team that worked until 4:30 in the morning uprooting *Tilted Arc* from the pavement of the plaza, cutting it into movable pieces, and hauling it away for storage was engaged in government censorship of the arts. For Diamond, the sculpture's removal was a democratic triumph over "a group of elitists in Washington." "This is a day for the people to rejoice," he announced, "because now the plaza returns rightfully to the people."[1]

Less than four months later, on 6 July, "the people" reclaimed Federal Plaza in an official ceremony celebrating the fortieth anniversary of the GSA and the victory of government workers over the offensive artwork. Some two hundred GSA employees attended the lunchtime event, in many cases under order from their supervisors, and listened as Diamond "rededicated" the plaza "to the public." The sculpture's removal was a "victory for New York," he explained, and "a victory for the concept that the federal government will correct a mistake." Effrontery gave way to the familiar anonymity of an undistinguished urban space. Park benches, trees, and flags took the place of "elitist" art, making the plaza safe again for outdoor lunches and ceremonial occasions.[2]

Many commentators noted at the time that the *Tilted Arc* controversy involved two quite different publics—a public of government employees located geographically at Federal Plaza and a cosmopolitan art public that visited the site from elsewhere specifically to see Serra's work. Such a view confirms a liberal-pluralist theory of cultural differences, best represented by Herbert Gans's sociological writings, that divides cultural audiences into distinct "taste publics" choosing from a menu of "taste cultures." The problem with *Tilted Arc,* in this analysis, is that it forced two different

1. Quotations are from Letter from William Diamond to Dwight Ink (p. 143), Interview with William J. Diamond (p. 271), and Richard Serra's introduction (p. 3), in Clara Weyergraf-Serra and Martha Buskirk, eds., *The Destruction of Tilted Arc: Documents* (Cambridge: MIT Press, 1991). For more on the *Tilted Arc* debate see *Public Art, Public Controversy: The Tilted Arc on Trial* (New York: Council for the Arts Books, 1987), and the 1985 video documentary by Shu Leang Cheange, *The Trial of Tilted Arc.* The controversy was extensively covered in hundreds of articles in newspapers, magazines, and art journals, many of which are cited below.

2. Herb Lash, "Sculpture's removal puts Fed. Plaza on Square 1," *Daily News,* 7 July 1989; Harriet Senie, "Richard Serra's *Tilted Arc:* Art and Non-Art Issues," *Art Journal* 48 (Winter 1989): 301.

"taste publics" to occupy the same public space: upper-middle-class aesthetes were rubbing elbows with civil servants from the outer boroughs. This simple dichotomy hardly does justice, however, to the range of responses to *Tilted Arc*. Nor are the issues of power at stake in the debate over Serra's sculpture illuminated by a view of a public rent only by tastes in cultural consumption.[3]

Recent revisionist accounts of American artistic Modernism are equally unhelpful in making sense of the *Tilted Arc* affair, despite their greater attentiveness to the political context of artistic practice. The destruction of *Tilted Arc* is not simply another chapter in the struggle between culture and commerce that has preoccupied radical historians of American art over the last two decades—and which, as we shall see, shaped Serra's response to the conservative attack on his sculpture. A single-minded focus on capitalism's ability to co-opt a once-pure avant-garde ("how New York stole the idea of modern art") obscures the extent to which modern art itself enjoys a significant degree of power as a result of its institutionalization over many decades and its claim to an autonomous aesthetic divorced from the practical considerations of the majority of people. At the end of the twentieth century, ritual denunciations of corporate control of the avant-garde are less helpful to a democratic project in the arts than a sustained examination of how and why the assumptions of avant-gardism now fit so easily with forms of professional and governmental authority that are hostile to popular scrutiny and public deliberation.[4]

Close examination of controversies over public art can recast the discussion about art and power by revealing the profound cultural fissures with respect to appropriate public activity and authority that lie at the heart of the most seemingly arbitrary assertions of artistic taste. Discussions of the function and aesthetic of public art inevitably turn to questions about the very possibility of a common public life in a heterogeneous industrial soci-

3. See Herbert J. Gans, *Popular Culture and High Culture: An Analysis and Evaluation of Taste* (New York: Basic Books, 1974), esp. pp. 10–13, 69–70; and Herbert J. Gans, "American Popular Culture and High Culture in a Changing Class Structure," in Judith H. Balfe and Margaret Jane Wyszomirski, eds., *Art, Ideology, and Politics* (New York: Praeger, 1985), pp. 40–57.

4. For examples of the revisionist accounts of American Modernism, see Serge Guilbaut, *How New York Stole the Idea of Modern Art: Abstract Expressionism, Freedom, and the Cold War*, trans. Arthur Goldhammer (Chicago: University of Chicago Press, 1983), and the essays collected in two recent anthologies: Francis Frascina, ed., *Pollock and After: The Critical Debate* (New York: Harper and Row, 1985); and Serge Guilbaut, ed., *Reconstructing Modernism* (Cambridge: MIT Press, 1990). For a critique of the revisionist literature on the American avant-garde, see my review of Guilbaut's earlier book in *Telos* 62 (Winter 1984–85): 211–17.

ety. In the case of *Tilted Arc,* debate fractured along the lines of three fairly coherent discourses rooted in different forms of power: one articulated by artists and art administrators that upheld the exclusive competence of cultural professionals; another put forth by conservative judges, officials, and commentators who sought to reassert their power against the "New Class"; and a third discourse that, however hostile to *Tilted Arc,* broke out of the confines of the conservative polemic against the adversary culture in its insistence that the public be given more control over public affairs. This essay examines those positions and seeks especially to reconstruct the aesthetic and political implications of the third position—the arguments about *Tilted Arc* and Federal Plaza made by hundreds of anonymous petitioners—that both the avant-garde and conservative officials ignored.

Employees in the area seized the political space opened up by the controversy to voice anger at the arrogance of powerful elites in art circles and the federal bureaucracy and expressed a desire for participation in decisions affecting their everyday lives that went far beyond the cultural issues conservative officials exploited to mobilize popular opinion. Their interventions may have displayed ignorance about artistic traditions and prejudices against innovative art, but they also revealed a longing for the democratic debate indispensable to a vigorous public culture.

As these petitioners keenly recognized, much more than aesthetic preference was at stake in the long and emotional debate surrounding *Tilted Arc.* Fundamental issues of power inhere in the very terms of the debate about the artistic merits of Serra's piece, its impact on the plaza and its occupants, the function of public art, and the role of the government in sponsoring cultural production. By raising the question of who should decide about the placement and aesthetics of art in public places, the *Tilted Arc* affair exposed the often obscure but never absent connections between cultural and political representation. Public art is in crisis for many reasons, notably the collapse of consensus about a symbolic public language and about the values and ideals to be embodied in that language. But the *Tilted Arc* controversy also demonstrates that the most important source of the aesthetic crisis of public art is the ongoing political crisis of the public sphere. Bitter disputes over the aesthetic and social functions of public spaces both reflect and contribute to a waning belief in the very possibility of a democratic public sphere constituted by collective deliberation.[5]

5. Barbara Hoffman examines the implications of *Tilted Arc* for free speech in the public realm in her "Law for Art's Sake in the Public Realm," *Critical Inquiry* 17 (Spring 1991): 540–73.

II

Those familiar with Richard Serra's career were probably not surprised to find him at the center of one of the most contentious controversies in American art in the 1980s. By the time he received the commission for Federal Plaza in 1979, Serra—then forty years old—had already established himself as one of the most daring and challenging contemporary artists in the United States. The ambition of his sculptural innovations during the late 1960s and 1970s, the scale and energy of his public works, his repeatedly stated intention to elaborate on and explode the conventions of twentieth-century Western sculpture, and his passionate pronouncements on artistic process suggested that in an age of cool postmodernist professionals, Serra alone had inherited the first New York School's romantic vision of artistic heroism. Beginning in the late 1960s, Serra had taken advantage of the fluid situation of the New York art scene to launch an artistic project that, however loyal to Modernist conventions of artistic autonomy, would expose and heighten the contradictions within contemporary artistic production. From the outset, he created works that deliberately sharpened the tensions inherent in the practices associated with high art in order to redefine the viewer's experience of sculpture.[6]

Serra initially made his mark as a sculptor with two important works in lead, *Splashing* (1968) and *One Ton Prop (House of Cards)* (1969), that set the stage for his later explorations of sculptural materials and the politics of the New York art world. In these paradigmatic examples of sixties "process art," the apparent solidity of the sculptural object was betrayed by its

---

6. For information about Richard Serra's work and career, see Deborah Solomon, "Our Most Notorious Sculptor," *New York Times Magazine*, vol. 138, 8 October 1989, 38–40, 74–77; Ernst-Gerhard Guse, ed., *Richard Serra* (New York: Rizzoli, 1988); Laura Rosenstock, ed., *Richard Serra/Sculpture* (New York: Museum of Modern Art, 1986); Rosalind E. Krauss's influential essay, "Richard Serra, a Translation," reprinted, among other places, in *The Originality of the Avant-Garde and Other Modernist Myths* (Cambridge: MIT Press, 1985), pp. 260–74; "Richard Serra," *Current Biography Yearbook* 46 (January 1985): 380–84; Harriet Senie, "The Right Stuff," *Art News*, vol. 83, March 1984, 50–59; and Richard Serra and Clara Weyergraf, *Richard Serra: Interviews, Etc., 1970–1980* (Yonkers, N.Y.: The Hudson River Museum, 1980). I have also found the following interpretations of Serra's work helpful in understanding his career: Arthur C. Danto, "Richard Serra," in *The State of the Art* (New York: Prentice Hall, 1987), pp. 177–82; Kenneth Baker, "Vectors of Viewer Response," *Artforum*, vol. 25, September 1986, 103–108; Hilton Kramer, "Richard Serra at MOMA," *The New Criterion* 4 (May 1986): 1–5; David Craven, "Richard Serra and the Phenomenology of Perception," *Arts Magazine*, vol. 60, March 1986, 49–51; Yve-Alain Bois, "A Picturesque Stroll around *Clara-Clara*," *October* 29 (Summer 1984): 32–62; Donald B. Kuspit, "Richard Serra, Utopian Constructivist," *Arts Magazine*, vol. 55, November 1980, 124–29.

material construction and the local conditions of its placement. To create *Splashing,* Serra occupied the warehouse for the Leo Castelli Gallery for several days in December 1968, flinging molten lead at the intersection of the floor and wall. The result was not so much a finished product as a temporally and spatially situated act of guerilla theater, with Serra (his face covered by a gas mask) assuming the roles of both Jackson Pollock at work "inside" his paintings and antiwar protesters tossing tear gas cannisters back at police. *One Ton Prop (House of Cards)* consisted of four square plates of soft lead, each four feet by four feet and weighing about 480 pounds, which Serra and his friends carefully propped up against one another to form an open-ended pyramid. Without structural support of any kind, the piece combined a minimalist aesthetic with a not-so-concealed threat that its precarious balance might collapse. The warring tendencies at play in these two sculptures came to define what was distinctive about Serra's work: aesthetic purism, manifested in geometric design and a concern for the innate properties of materials, resulting in a sense of danger that disrupted any formalist reading of the sculpture; the redefinition of the gallery, a place of privileged leisure-time artistic consumption, as the site for industrial production techniques; and a challenge to the fetishism and commodification of art objects carried out in the heart of the most prestigious American spaces for exhibiting and marketing art. *Tilted Arc* was not the first act of effrontery in his career.[7]

Serra's early sculpture drew on the language of sixties Minimalism and his personal experience of industrial labor to challenge the autonomous aesthetic of High Modernism. A child of working-class parents in San Francisco, Serra had worked in steel mills to support himself as an undergraduate and art student. He retains a lifelong interest in the relationship between industrial processes and the creation of fine art that fit perfectly with the sixties generation's rediscovery of the early twentieth-century avant-garde and its assault on the separation of art and everyday life. The work of such kindred spirits as Donald Judd, Carl Andre, Dan Flavin, Sol LeWitt, Robert Morris, Eva Hesse, Frank Stella, and Philip Glass provided a supportive context for his initial experiments in sculpture. These Minimalist artists and their critical enthusiasts appropriated the theoretical language of phenomenology to make the now-familiar, post-structuralist case that art enables a multiplicity of readings resulting from the interactions

7. See the discussion of these early works in Rosalind E. Krauss, "Richard Serra/Sculpture," and Douglas Crimp, "Serra's Public Sculpture: Redefining Site Specificity," in Rosenstock, *Serra/Sculpture,* pp. 14–39, 40–56.

between objects and viewers located in specific contexts. Along with their contemporaries in the Pop Art movement, the Minimalists eschewed the psychological interiority of Abstract Expressionism for an art of surfaces and exterior spaces. But in contrast to Pop, Minimalists employed an austere, geometric aesthetic to reach beyond the art object to its surroundings, erasing boundaries between the art work and the world. A heightened awareness of the passage of time, of inhabiting spaces with art objects and other viewers, and of changes in perception dictated by one's motion through a specific terrain became the "content" of Minimalist art.[8]

By the early 1970s, however, Serra's sculpture had moved significantly beyond Minimalism in its scale, its use of materials, and its relation to its site. Serra felt that the Minimalists' work was insufficiently attentive to purely sculptural properties; it remained trapped within the confines of the traditional fine art market. Rejecting the shiny polished surfaces of much Minimalist sculpture, Serra turned to unfinished steel as the primary material for his sculpture—hot-rolled steel for indoor works and self-oxidizing Corten steel for outdoor pieces. He also started to create large-scale "site-specific" objects, installed permanently or for long periods of time, that functioned outside gallery and museum spaces and escaped the market for art commodities. In one work after another throughout the 1970s—from his gallery pieces *Circuit* (1972) and *Delineator* (1974–76), to such outdoor works as *Pulitzer Piece* (1971), *Sight Point* (1971–75), and *Terminal* (1977)—Serra expanded on the implications of his early "process" pieces to create "anti-environments" that dramatically altered public and private spaces: "I think that sculpture, if it has any potential at all, has the potential to create its own place and space, and to work in contradiction to the spaces and places where it is created in this sense. I am interested in work where the artist is a maker of 'anti-environment' which takes its own place or makes its own situation, or divides or declares its own area."[9]

Whereas his early sculpture had deconstructed the art work into process, these new pieces were huge and unavoidable objects. They asserted their command over space by providing visual markers for motion across landscapes and by imposing their mass—often in threatening ways—in closed exhibition spaces. Serra's original desire to make the reception and experience of art works as much a matter of sculptural space as the works

8. On Serra and Minimalism, see (in addition to the critical literature by Krauss, Crimp, Baker, Bois, and Craven cited above) Gregory Battcock, ed., *Minimal Art: A Critical Anthology* (New York: Dutton, 1968).

9. Serra and Weyergraf, *Serra: Interviews*, p. 128.

themselves led him to sculptures (especially for outdoor sites) that recalled the monumentalism of pre-Modernist civic and religious statues even as they renounced the metaphysical and political scaffolding of traditional monumental sculpture. "They do not relate to the history of monuments," Serra has insisted. "They do not memorialize anything. They relate to sculpture and nothing more." Yet Serra has also denied that his work is self-referential or formalist; its "site specificity" requires a recognition that "there is no neutral site," that "art is always ideological" insofar as it "manifests a value judgment about the larger sociological context of which it is a part."[10]

Therein lies the great paradox—or the great challenge—that has been at the heart of all Serra's work since 1970. With the absence of a consensually-derived iconography for large-scale sculpture, only an aesthetic rooted in purely sculptural concerns can avoid being manipulative agitprop, sentimental decoration, or artistic affirmation for powerful institutions. But in order to function as "anti-environments," rather than as "corporate baubles" embellishing skyscrapers, Serra's site-specific sculptures must deny their status as autonomous high-art commodities and achieve mastery over their given spaces. Sites are "redefined not re-presented" as their original spatial organization comes into confrontation with the language of sculpture. The result is not a stylistic reconciliation of architectural and sculptural motifs, but a conflicted space that lays bare its internal divisions to inhabitants. "Every language has a structure about which one can say nothing critical in that language," Serra has written. "There must be another language dealing with the structure of the first and possessing a new structure to criticise the first." In works as precariously balanced as *One Ton Prop,* Serra has monumentalized the nonmonumental idiom he derived from Minimalism and set the "anti-environment" of sculpture against the logic of public and private spaces.[11]

III

The difficulty with this project is that Serra has conceived of his move into public spaces almost entirely in negative terms. He does not view public spaces as sites with an appealing social or symbolic logic of their own. Going public with sculpture has value primarily because it frees art from

10. Ibid., p. 178; Richard Serra, "Extended Notes from Sight Point Road," in *Richard Serra: Recent Sculpture in Europe, 1977–1985* (Bochum, Germany: Galerie m, 1985), p. 13.

11. Serra and Weyergraf, *Serra: Interviews,* p. 166; Serra, "Extended Notes," p. 15.

traditional exhibition spaces. "If you show work in the confines of a private gallery or cultural institution," he has said, "it is evaluated and protected. Urban and landscape work built in place by-passes commerce and cultural institutions by not being available for secondary sales in the ahistorical space of the museum." His goal remains the subversion of a private market for art commodities. "What I'm trying to do is get sculpture off the pedestal and into the street." But for Serra, such a move demands no dialogue with those already occupying the street and no effort to respond aesthetically to the culture they have created. "Placing pieces in an urban context is not synonymous with an interest in a large audience even though the work will be seen by many people who wouldn't otherwise look at art," he explains. "The work I make does not allow for experience outside the conventions of sculpture as sculpture. My audience is necessarily very limited." In "Extended Notes from Sight Point Road," a 1984 statement on public sculpture, Serra writes: "When I conceive a structure for a public space, a space that people walk through, I consider the traffic flow, but I do not necessarily worry about the indigenous community. I am not going to concern myself with what 'they' consider to be adequate, appropriate solutions." This is a prescription for public art without a public.[12]

It is easy to understand how Serra has arrived at such a position at the end of the twentieth century. If one means by "public" a large self-conscious, informed audience participating in the creation and criticism of aesthetically demanding works in public spaces, then no such public exists for public art. Nor is there a vital tradition of public sculpture to orient and give meaning to discussions about the aims and aesthetics of organized civic life. As Lawrence Alloway observed in 1972, "The nineteenth century closed the tradition of public sculpture and the twentieth century has not established one." Western fine art sculpture from Rodin's *Thinker* to the present has repudiated any unifying civic, moral, or metaphysical intention. By taking sculpture off its pedestal, Modernists simultaneously demystified such art—negating its cultic, authoritarian status—and personalized it, making sculpture a vehicle for the artist's own vision and a commodity for private collections. Civic sculpture has, for its part, gone into a similar decline during this century, as a viable iconography for its commemorative and reformist aspirations has become increasingly elusive.[13]

12. Serra and Weyergraf, *Serra: Interviews,* p. 149; Solomon, "Our Most Notorious Sculptor," p. 74; Serra, "Extended Notes," p. 14.

13. Lawrence Alloway, "The Public Sculpture Problem" (1972), in *Topics in American Art Since 1945* (New York: Norton, 1975), p. 245. On the predicament of American public sculp-

The collapse of a public art tradition that inspires and embodies the ideals of a democratic public sphere provides the context for Serra's thinking about the political implications of his own work. In spite of his leftist politics, Serra rejects social realism and agitprop strategies because they entail unacceptable aesthetic compromises and condescend to the public they claim to champion. Public sculpture, in his view, can be radical only by embracing and exposing its own historical predicament. His pieces are political insofar as their unsettling juxtaposition of site and sculpture make available to viewers an alternative understanding of the organization and display of power in public places. Their very refusal to offer consolation, or to reconcile the disparate components of a given space, opens the viewer's imagination to possibilities unavailable in the current organization of modern cities.

Serra's radicalism is thus closer to the left pessimism of the early Frankfurt School, with its grim vision of a "totally administered" or "one-dimensional" society, than to a Deweyan faith in participatory democracy. Given the affirmative premises of consumer culture, Serra argues, art re-

---

ture since the late nineteenth century, see Michelle H. Bogart, *Public Sculpture and the Civic Ideal in New York City, 1890–1930* (Chicago: University of Chicago Press, 1989), esp. chap. 12; Marianne Doezma and June Hargrove, *The Public Monument and Its Audience* (Cleveland: The Cleveland Museum of Art, 1977); Daniel Robbins, "Statues to Sculptures: From the Nineties to the Thirties," in Tom Armstrong, et al., *Two Hundred Years of American Sculpture* (New York: David R. Godine and the Whitney Museum of American Art, 1976). See also Miriam R. Levin, *Republican Art and Ideology in Late Nineteenth-Century France* (Ann Arbor: UMI Research Press, 1986); and Albert E. Elsen, *Rodin's "Thinker" and the Dilemmas of Modern Public Sculpture* (New Haven: Yale University Press, 1985) for discussions of European public sculpture.

Michelle H. Bogart describes how the case of *Civic Virtue*—a sculpture commissioned in 1909 for Manhattan's City Hall, but erected in 1922—demonstrated the predicament of civic monuments in the twentieth century. This sculpture of a semiclad male embodiment of "Civic Virtue" trampling two female symbols of "Vice" invited almost immediate ridicule and protest from feminists who objected to its subordination of women. The work was eventually moved to the backwater of Queens Borough Hall in 1941 by Robert Moses, who had learned the lesson that twentieth-century public art could aspire to entertainment or to innocuous decoration, but not to lessons in civic virtue.

In recent years, it is almost impossible to think of American civic monuments that represent significant artistic achievements. Two notable exceptions—Eero Saarinen's *St. Louis Arch* (the *Jefferson National Expansion Monument*) and Maya Lin's *Vietnam Veterans Memorial* in Washington, D.C.—prove the rule. Both disavow any pictorial or allegorical content, and both elaborate on Modernist, even Minimalist aesthetic principles. (Lin's enormously successful Vietnam memorial is, in fact, deeply influenced by Serra's 1970s landscape pieces; Serra was a visiting faculty member at Yale's architecture and art schools while Lin was an architecture student there.)

tains a critical perspective only if it remains resolutely dysfunctional. Echoing Theodor Adorno's aesthetics, Serra defends a "non-utilitarian, non-functional" art as a means of asserting a dissonant perspective in an administered world. "As soon as art is forced or persuaded to serve alien values it ceases to serve its own needs," he insists. "To deprive art of its uselessness is to make other than art." Serra's use of industrial materials and construction techniques in his urban sculptures appears a deliberate attempt to invert the usual expectation of both production and consumption in modern capitalism. By creating these steel works, industrial processes serve a decidedly "useless" purpose, while the resulting art product confounds expectations of what a finished aesthetic work should look like by retaining the rough, rusting exterior associated with steel bridges and factories. In contemporary urban spaces, such sculptures appear almost as ruins from the age of Andrew Carnegie and Eugene Debs that haunt downtowns given over to neon and chrome. Huge steel structures that serve no apparent function evoke repressed memories of the past and posit alternative uses for such materials, inviting the viewer to imagine a more expansive conception of what counts as useful.[14]

What cannot be tolerated in this aesthetic politics is any concession to popular taste, which Serra views as pandering to a consumerist public. Serra reminded an interviewer in 1984 that in the sixties "it was your job as an artist to redefine society by the values you were introducing, rather than the other way around." "Trying to attract a bigger audience has nothing to do with the making of art," he argued. "It has nothing to do with making yourself into a product, only to be consumed by people. Working this way allows society to determine the terms and the concept of art; the artist must fulfill those terms. I find the idea of populism art-defeating."

14. Serra, "Extended Notes," p. 13; Kuspit, "Richard Serra, Utopian Constructivist." Two films that Serra made in the 1970s—*Television Delivers People* (1973) and *Steelmill/Stahlwerk* (1979)—are revealing in their crude restatement of the Frankfurt School indictment of mass culture and alienated labor. In *Television Delivers People,* a manifesto against television appears on the screen accompanied by muzak. "POPULAR ENTERTAINMENT IS BASICALLY PROPAGANDA FOR THE STATUS QUO," the credits read. "You are the product of TV. You are delivered to the advertiser, who is the customer. He consumes you. . . . You are the end product delivered en masse to the advertiser. You are the product of TV." In *Steelmill/Stahlwerk,* a documentary about German workers in a mill in the Ruhr Valley where one of Serra's pieces was cast, individuals appear entirely enslaved to their machines, incapable of communication with one another and devoid of private hope or class solidarity. Outward conformity and inner despair appear as the common state of affairs in advanced capitalist societies. (The text of *Television Delivers People* is quoted in Serra and Weyergraf, *Serra: Interviews,* p. 104; see pp. 110–17 for a discussion of *Steelmill/Stahlwerk.*)

Despite his keen sensitivity to the precarious position of art in a culture of consumption, Serra remains indifferent not only to the popular reception of avant-garde art works in public spaces but to the potential social activity that might take place there.[15]

In Serra's case, fear of art's co-optation by the marketplace obscures the more problematic political issues at stake in public art. His stance takes no account of the authority that public art enjoys in its own right, an authority that is recognized, and often resented, by inhabitants of public spaces. When installed, public sculptures can function as totemic emblems of power that, however antagonistic to corporate or government authority, assert a claim on the attention and physical space of viewers. Above all else, such works advertise the privileged position of a new cultural elite of administrators, bureaucrats, and critics, whose authority was ironically enhanced by the avant-garde innovations of the 1960s. The struggle to disentangle artistic production from the art market that inspired Serra's generation appears, in retrospect, to have been a campaign against an archaic patronage system that was already in decline at the time. The proliferation of works incapable of commodity exchange since the sixties has accelerated the growth of a bureaucratic art market, which now relies on the mobilization of large sums of money to fund installations for universities, foundations, corporations, and government agencies. The avant-garde protest against the separation of art from everyday experience has had unintended consequences. Artistic production and consumption have indeed become more like "real life," with artists more dependent than ever on the support of large-scale bureaucratic institutions.[16]

Serra's urban sculpture may escape the pitfalls of commodity exchange or museum display, but it assumes a knowledge of Modernist traditions that is generally available only to those at home in the gallery and the museum. For the rest of the population, such art may seem less an invita-

15. Serra quoted in Senie, "The Right Stuff," p. 55.

16. The neoconservative critic Hilton Kramer is wrong to argue that the sixties process art and site-specific sculpture movements were "easily assimilated into the patronage system they were ostensibly designed to challenge," since they did conflict with traditional patterns of patronage and exchange, but his suspicion that such efforts were less disruptive of the social relations of artistic production than anyone believed at the time is certainly on target. Hilton Kramer, "Richard Serra at MOMA," p. 3. On the transformation of the art market since the mid-1960s, see Diana Crane, *The Transformation of the Avant-Garde: The New York Art World, 1940–1985* (Chicago: University of Chicago Press, 1987), esp. chap. 6.

tion to critical thinking than a brazen assertion of privilege by groups whose education and social position permit what Pierre Bourdieu calls "an ethos of elective distance from the necessities of the natural and social world." Public sculptures that challenge conventions specific to artistic Modernism or exhibition spaces rely on those conventions and spaces to define who has sufficient "cultural capital" to assess and appreciate them. The installation of such pieces reminds viewers that they are divided by their ability to influence the design of public space and by their competence to consume art objects in a professionally prescribed manner. Cultural outsiders may very well feel that such works are not really "public" at all—that they convey, in Bourdieu's words, "a refusal to communicate concealed at the heart of the communication itself."[17]

Together, the deliberate neglect of the local culture of public places and the association of public sculpture with elite cultural bureaucracies set the stage for the hostile reception of *Tilted Arc*. As the debates over the sculpture would make abundantly clear, Serra's decision to join an autonomous aesthetic to a program of site-specific sculpture entailed political risks that were made even worse by his explicit antipopulism, which conservatives happily exploited for their own purposes. The prospects for a radical public art, already hindered by the waning of radical politics after the 1960s, grew even dimmer as its supporters invoked bureaucratic proceduralism and aesthetic formalism—and not popular participation—to legitimate their work in public.

---

17. Pierre Bourdieu, *Distinction: A Social Critique of the Judgment of Taste,* trans. Richard Nice (Cambridge: Harvard University Press, 1984), pp. 5, 12, 34.

The austere neo-Minimalism of Serra's steel sculptures may in fact heighten viewers' sense that they are confronting an aggressive work that orders their experience according to a hierarchy of social distinction. As Anna C. Chave has argued, "what disturbs viewers most about Minimalist art may be what disturbs them about their own lives and times, as the face it projects is the society's blankest, steeliest face; the impersonal face of technology, industry, and commerce; the unyielding face of the father: a face that is usually far more attractively masked." Neoconservatives have seized upon these features of Serra's work to protest its supposed contempt for humanistic values. After the 1977 installation of *Terminal* in the steel-producing town of Bochum, Germany, by a Social Democratic municipality, Christian Democrats drew up a campaign poster with a drawing of the sculpture, juxtaposed against steel mills, and the slogan: "This will never happen again—CDU for Bochum." Christian Democrats invoked a populist mythology of working-class heroism and denounced the work for its failure to "provide the possibility of positive identification for . . . the steelworkers." Anna C. Chave, "Minimalism and the Rhetoric of Power," *Arts Magazine,* vol. 64, January 1990, 55; Crimp, "Serra's Public Sculpture," in Rosenstock, *Serra/Sculpture,* p. 50.

IV

The process that led to the installation of *Tilted Arc* in Federal Plaza in July 1981 was almost guaranteed to bring out the political ambiguities of Serra's understanding of public sculpture. Two years earlier, the Art-in-Architecture Program of the General Services Administration had called upon a National Endowment for the Arts (NEA) panel to nominate a sculptor for a public work in the plaza. Such a work would normally have been commissioned with the construction of the Federal Building and the Court of International Trade in 1968, but the Kennedy-era Art-in-Architecture Program had gone into decline after the 1966 installation of a controversial Robert Motherwell mural at the John F. Kennedy Federal Building in Boston. Architects of the two buildings in Federal Plaza has imagined an unobtrusive sculpture located near or in the plaza's fountain, but funding cuts brought the program to a halt, until it was revived under the Nixon Administration. Eleven years after the buildings were completed, the commission for Federal Plaza went to an artist renowned for his conception of site-specific "anti-environments."

Federal Plaza was an especially challenging site for Serra. Its two buildings, joined at the corner by a breezeway, are undistinguished slabs of steel and glass that give the plaza a cold, impersonal quality. Before the installation of *Tilted Arc*, the semicircular plaza was organized around a large turquoise fountain that had to be turned off almost immediately after its construction because winds that swept through the area sprayed water on pedestrians. In its original form, Federal Plaza had the characteristics of many other "empty" spaces in front of corporate or government buildings. Too big to allow for intimacy, too formless to suggest organized social functions, the plaza was primarily a place employees walked through on their way to or from work. Employees ate lunch there in good weather, but the absence of benches or other amenities, the nonfunctioning fountain, and the high winds made this a less than hospitable site. The sole virtues of the plaza were the circular design of its pavement (already in disrepair by the early 1980s), which echoed the fountain's shape and gave the plaza some coherent visual structure, and the elevation of the entire area above street level. The latter was especially important, since it afforded an unusual degree of open space by Manhattan standards and a view looking out over Foley Square and beyond, to nearby neoclassical courthouses built at the turn of the century.

The site also presented Serra with a political challenge. By the late 1970s, he had come to believe that "one way of avoiding ideological co-optation is to choose leftover sites which cannot be the object of ideological misinterpretation." One such "leftover" space was a plot of ground in Manhattan surrounded by an exit ramp from the Holland Tunnel, where Serra located his *St. John's Rotary Arc* in 1980, one of his most successful works. *St. John's Rotary Arc* occupied a semiabandoned area almost entirely inaccessible to pedestrians; viewers experienced the work as they drove around it. Federal Plaza was an entirely different space. Dominated by large, anonymous office buildings, the plaza was a showcase for bureaucratic power.[18]

Serra spent two years designing a work that would respond to the scale and style of the surrounding buildings and counter the ideological definition of the plaza. In the meantime, he reacted to GSA's concerns about the sculpture's impact on pedestrian traffic, wind currents, sunlight, and access to Foley Square. The result was *Tilted Arc,* a work of Corten steel, 120 feet long, 12 feet high, and 2½ inches in width, covered with a surface coating of brown rust. Tilting vertically one foot off its axis, *Tilted Arc* also slowly curved off its horizontal axis as it bisected the space between the Court of International Trade and the plaza's fountain. When viewed from different angles, *Tilted Arc* was alternately graceful and threatening, lyrical and overbearing. It was a work simultaneously capable of unifying the plaza around its gestural energy and closing off the space with all the subtlety of a massive steel wall. At various points in the plaza, the sculpture mediated between the human scale of pedestrians and the enormous size of the buildings; at others, especially when viewed head-on, it towered over employees in an aggressive, even menacing manner. What could not be denied, however it was viewed, was that the sculpture completely transformed Federal Plaza. The curve of the work cut directly against the pattern of the pavement in defiance of the area's original design. *Tilted Arc* divided the plaza itself into two distinct spaces, so that those who sat on the rim of the fountain and looked at the sculpture's convex side confronted an imposing steel plane. The concave side of the work created an amphitheater space facing the steps leading into the two federal buildings, but it also obstructed the view of Foley Square for those exiting the same buildings. As Serra explained in 1980, his intention was "to dislocate or alter the decorative function of the plaza and actively bring people into the

18. Serra and Weyergraf, *Serra: Interviews,* p. 154.

Tilted Arc (1981–89). Steel, 12′ × 120′ × 2½″. Federal Plaza, New York.
Photo by Allen Freeman.

Tilted Arc. Photo by David Aschkenas.

Tilted Arc. Photo by Glenn Steigelman, Inc.

sculpture's context." "After the piece is created, the space will be under-stood primarily as a function of the sculpture."[19]

In retrospect, the *Tilted Arc* commissioning and installation process was a disaster of public arts policy that misled the artist and mystified his audience. As he worked on *Tilted Arc* in 1979 and 1980, Serra was repeat-edly reassured by Donald Thalacker, director of the Art-in-Architecture program, and other GSA officials that the commission was for a permanent installation. Yet Serra's contract did not reflect these verbal guarantees, a crucial mistake that critics later exploited to press for the sculpture's re-moval. Serra was commissioned under the Carter Administration and was thanked personally by Carter at a White House ceremony. His sculpture was installed in 1981, however, after the Reagan Administration had come into power with the intention of overhauling the GSA and reorienting the federal government's arts policies. As a result, New York GSA officials who might have been expected to defend the sculpture sought instead to dis-tance themselves from a controversial relic of a previous administration.[20]

To make matters worse, GSA policies in effect at the time did not require any significant consultation with the local community during the selection process, nor did the installation include any serious effort to educate the public as to the artist's intentions, the sculpture's relationship to the area, or its context in modern art history. The resulting vacuum in public discus-sion of the sculpture was instantly filled by its opponents. *Tilted Arc*'s appearance in Federal Plaza in the summer of 1981 provoked immediate criticism from Judge Edward D. Re of the Court of International Trade, who wrote to the GSA Administrator in Washington protesting the work's "stark ugliness," and from some 1,300 employees (of a total of 10,000 in the plaza) who signed petitions calling for the sculpture's removal. Grace Glueck, an art critic for the *New York Times,* denounced *Tilted Arc* in a highly influential article as "an awkward, bullying piece that may conceiv-ably be the ugliest outdoor work in the city." She was seconded by Peter Schjeldahl of the *Village Voice,* who congratulated the petitioners for pro-testing a work espousing the "absolutely hateful" and "puritanical" ideology

19. Ibid., p. 168.
20. Testimony of Richard Serra, in Weyergraf-Serra and Buskirk, *Destruction,* p. 67. See also the material presented regarding Article Six by the plaintiff in *Richard Serra v. United States General Services Administration.* The commissioning process for *Tilted Arc* is analyzed in Judith H. Balfe and Margaret J. Wyszomirski, "Public Art and Public Policy," in Pam Korsza, ed., *Going Public: A Field Guide to Developments in Art in Public Places* (Amherst, Mass.: Arts Extension Service, 1988), pp. 268–79.

of Minimalism. "They can complain," he wrote of the protesters, "that everything that is right about *Tilted Arc*, on its own terms, is wrong in terms of what they humanly want and need."[21]

Criticism died down until November 1984, when Judge Re again condemned the "ugly, rusted, steel wall," this time in a letter to Ray Kline, a new Acting Administrator for the GSA who agreed to hold a public hearing on the sculpture early the following year. Re's letter reopened the *Tilted Arc* controversy and set in motion the process leading to its destruction. William J. Diamond, the new Regional Administrator for GSA in New York appointed by the Reagan Administration, made it clear from the start that he favored relocation of the work on the grounds that "it has made it impossible for the public and the Federal community to use the plaza." Diamond played the critical role in directing the campaign that culminated in the hearing in March 1985 and a subsequent recommendation to the federal GSA office in Washington that *Tilted Arc* be relocated. The absence of any forum for public discussion and education about *Tilted Arc* allowed Re, Diamond, and other powerful opponents of the work to seize the initiative and claim that they spoke for widespread popular revulsion against the sculpture.[22]

In the months surrounding the 1985 hearing, the *Tilted Arc* case became a *cause célèbre* in New York's art world and a focus of national media attention. Confronted with a renewed petition drive against the sculpture and largely hostile press coverage, Serra and his supporters mobilized artists, critics, gallery and museum directors, and art administrators from around the world in defense of *Tilted Arc*. Their efforts resulted in a petition drive to retain the sculpture in Federal Plaza, a letter-writing campaign to GSA offices in New York and Washington and to President Reagan, and a remarkable turnout at the raucous three-day hearing. By a margin of 122

21. Edward R. Re to Gerald P. Carmen, 18 August 1981, in Weyergraf-Serra and Buskirk, *Destruction*, p. 26; Grace Glueck, "An Outdoor-Sculpture Safari around New York," *New York Times*, 7 August 1981; Peter Schjeldahl, "Artistic Control," *Village Voice*, 14–20 October 1981.

22. Edward R. Re to Ray Kline, 5 November 1984, in Weyergraf-Serra and Buskirk, *Destruction*, p. 27; Douglas C. McGill, "Art People: Hearing Near on Sculpture," *New York Times*, 22 February 1985. It is fair to say that Diamond went out of his way to mobilize opinion against *Tilted Arc* through a series of misstatements and administrative sleights of hand. Regardless of one's opinion of *Tilted Arc*, one must agree that Serra is absolutely right to argue that "Diamond acted as both prosecutor and judge in this case" and that the ad hoc procedure that led to the sculpture's removal "was a mockery of due process." Weyergraf-Serra and Buskirk, *Destruction*, p. 7.

to 58, Serra's partisans dominated the hearing and offered a variety of arguments against relocation. The work was site-specific, they explained, and could not be moved without destroying it. Serra had scrupulously followed the selection and installation procedure mandated by the GSA; to remove his sculpture now would break a contract and destroy the trust necessary to any future working relationship between artists and the government. The hearing itself was illegitimate, as was the entire reassessment of the sculpture. Diamond was simply trying to provide cover for a decision he had already made to censor the work.

Serra himself gave a vigorous and eloquent presentation at the hearing in which he summarized his artistic aspirations and described *Tilted Arc* as a work intended for a mobile audience of pedestrians. He was joined in his defense of the work's placement in Federal Plaza by Rosalind Krauss, Douglas Crimp, and other prominent art critics, who argued that *Tilted Arc* embodied a phenomenological aesthetic and made viewers newly conscious of their own movement through space and time. Several speakers explicated Serra's politics, including the social theorist Joel Kovel, who praised *Tilted Arc* as a deliberately dissonant work that challenged the "homogenization of contemporary bureaucracy" by its bisection of Federal Plaza. "The *Tilted Arc* is, I must admit, subversive," Kovel testified, "and this very hearing proves its subversiveness and hence its value." Sculptor Claes Oldenburg agreed: "the problem with the *Tilted Arc* is that it's *too* honest."[23]

In the face of mounting criticism of the work, and of administrative maneuvers by the local GSA officers to remove it, Serra and his allies moved beyond the aesthetic and political implications of *Tilted Arc* to a series of propositions about the public reception of abstract art, and the relationship of the avant-garde to society, that amounted to a fierce antidemocratic polemic. During the first years of the controversy, Serra repeatedly questioned the "weird notion that sculpture should somehow serve what are being called 'human needs.'" "So much of so-called affirming human needs is just reaffirming the values of our culture," he explained, "and most human needs in our culture are created by advertising and corporations." Serra's defenders made similar arguments at the 1985 hearing, insisting that *Tilted Arc* was unpopular because it did not pander to the consumerist mentality of the general public. Sculptor George Sug-

---

23. Testimony of Joel Kovel and Claes Oldenburg, in Weyergraf-Serra and Buskirk, *Destruction*, pp. 94, 78.

arman, who had himself experienced a similar controversy over one of his public works, lectured the audience, "We are not appealing to a TV taste. We are not appealing to . . . McDonald's hamburger, you know, quick taste." Given the transformation of a critical public into a mass audience, the argument went, concern for "human needs" only legitimated a culture of oppression.[24]

As the debate continued into the late 1980s, Serra became less openly hostile to the idea of serving "human needs." Instead, he and many of his supporters resurrected the left's age-old hope of addressing a working class uncontaminated by capitalist ideology. Several speakers at the hearing referred to the ways Serra drew on his own experiences in steel mills to create an unsentimental art that resonated with the practice of industrial labor. Film professor Annette Michaelson testified to Serra's concern "that the working man and the office worker be presented with that same kind of challenge that the middle and upper classes have found so interesting." In a 1986 interview, Serra found it "condescending to say that the art of the museums is not for the people." The campaign against *Tilted Arc* divided a natural coalition. "The government pitted the artist against the workers in an unrealistic manner," Serra complained in 1987. "It established a condition that ought not to be present—basically, artists are part of the working class." Conservative politicians, Serra and his partisans pointed out, offered office workers a chance to vote on the art in Federal Plaza, but denied them any say about other important matters. "The people in the government buildings are not asked about their working conditions," Serra noted. "They are not asked about the quality of the food in the cafeteria. They don't vote on whether their offices have windows. But a petition was circulated that invited them to comment on the 'artistic merit' of my work."

24. Gerald Marzorati, "Artful Dodger," *Soho News*, 17 November 1981; Don Hawthorne, "Does the Public Want Public Sculpture?," *Art News*, May 1982, 56; testimony of George Sugarman in transcript of "A Public Hearing on the *Tilted Arc* Outdoor Sculpture Located in Front Plaza of Jacob Javits Federal Office Building," 6–8 March 1985, p. 91. (Wherever possible, I quote from transcriptions of the hearing testimony based on audio tapes, such as the Weyergraf-Serra and Buskirk collection, as opposed to the less reliable typed transcript. In some cases, when quoting from the transcript, I have made corrections of obvious typographical or other errors.)

After the hearing, critic Martha Rosler joined those who attributed hostility to *Tilted Arc* to the hegemony of a consumer culture: "the current perceived crisis of art stems from the apparent swamping of the relative social prestige and significance of elite culture by mass culture, with the consequent evaporation of any dimension of *remove*—whether critical consciousness, aesthetic transcedence or some more spiritualized aim." Martha Rosler, "The Birth and Death of the Viewer: On the Public Function of Art," in Hal Foster, ed., *Discussions in Contemporary Culture*, No. 1 (Seattle: Bay Press, 1987), p. 11.

Serra's wife, Clara Weyergraf-Serra asked at the hearing, "Where is 'direct democracy' used other than to get rid of art?"[25]

Weyergraf-Serra's question was exactly the point where the political battle against Diamond and the official opponents of GSA might have begun. A truly radical approach to public art, one could argue, would start by viewing the challenge of "direct democracy" in the arts as an opening to other political and aesthetic issues—including the anonymous space at Federal Plaza—rather than dismissing talk of "human needs" as so much vigilantism or consumerism. Despite their rhetorical nods to the working class, Serra and his allies failed to pursue this option. Instead, Serra claimed that the commissioning of the work by the GSA, "a public entity," proved that "the selection of the sculpture . . . was made by, and on behalf of, the public." If it is true, as Michael Brenson argued in the *New York Times,* that "almost no one opposed to the work even *tried* to understand it," it is equally the case that virtually none of *Tilted Arc*'s defenders tried to understand the complaints against the work. Their statements led to the inescapable conclusion that the employees at Federal Plaza deserved the powerlessness they experienced in every sphere of social activity, including the arts. Direct democracy was apparently inappropriate for them in any form.[26]

Serra's defenders repeatedly distinguished between those who were competent and incompetent to judge *Tilted Arc.* Donald Thalacker told a reporter, "You go to a medical expert for medical advice; you go to a legal expert for advice about the law. We go to experts for real estate and gardening. Yet when it comes to art, it seems they want the local gas station attendant in on things." "Since the piece was commissioned by the General Services Administration by proper professional channels," architect Philip Johnson wrote Diamond, "it strikes us professionals that only a similar process can authorize its removal." "Public feelings," he added, "have no validity in this matter." Robert Buck, Director of the Brooklyn Museum, told the hearing that "all one can strive for in this affair is the largest consensus of informed opinion," adding that "other opinion actually doesn't matter very much." Many at the hearing noted that Diamond and

25. Testimony of Annette Michaelson in "Public Hearing," p. 70; Carter Ratcliff, "Whose Art Is This Anyway?," *Elle,* March 1986, 226; Karin Lipson, "When the Public Turns against Public Art," *Newsday,* 27 September 1987; Margaret Moorman, "Arc Enemies," *Art News,* vol. 84, May 1985, 156; testimony of Clara Weyergraf-Serra in Weyergraf-Serra and Buskirk, *Destruction,* p. 89.

26. Testimony of Richard Serra in Weyergraf-Serra and Buskirk, *Destruction,* p. 68; Michael Brenson, "The Case in Favor of a Controversial Sculpture," *New York Times,* 19 May 1985.

the other panelists presiding over the hearing lacked the expertise to judge modern art. "I haven't heard one person with credentials," said one speaker, "with good credentials as an expert witness in aesthetics or art testify here in favor of removal of the piece."[27]

The case for retaining Serra's sculpture degenerated, on several occasions, into outright contempt for those outside established art circles. Defenders of *Tilted Arc* described a war between "right-thinking experts," on the one hand, and "barbarians," on the other. There were "VFW guys in their eighties and their blue caps from the First World War" testifying against "intellect of unquestioned credibility, unquestioned credentials." "If we begin destroying art for any reason," one speaker said, "we become as philistines, vandals, animals"—epithets that opponents of the work in the audience believed were directed against them. Mary Kilroy, a leading Philadelphia art administrator, warned, "The Philistines are in the wings sharpening their long knives. Don't let them draw blood." "Is Archie Bunkerism going to win the field," asked sculptor Robert Murray, "and drive our artists underground again?"[28]

Throughout the hearing, artists, art administrators, and critics openly ridiculed the idea of a public art rooted in democratic processes. The testimony of Jonas Mekas, Director of the Anthology Film Archives in New York, captures the tone and content of this line of argument.

I have a proposal to avoid any other misunderstandings in the future. It's simple. Ask the workers. Mr. Smith works in the cubicle there, he says he likes a poem, that is fine. Margie says she would prefer a cupid. Now, Peter who works in the cubicle next to her, he says he likes Michelangelo, but Margie says she likes Michael Jackson, so why don't we get all these into the computer and the computer will spit out a perfect composite sculpture that will make everybody happy. A perfect expression of the people's will. George Lucas, Disney or Spielberg could do this for us for nothing.

In Mekas's imaginary scenario, collective reasoning about artistic matters was out of the question. Ordinary people were capable only of venting diffuse, irreconcilable prejudices that resisted rational mediation. Their tastes were fodder for a homogenizing culture-industry, not the starting-point for a discussion of art for public places. Starting from such premises,

27. Hawthorne, "Does the Public Want Public Sculpture," p. 62; Philip Johnson to William J. Diamond, 1 March 1985, in *Tilted Arc* file, Arts and Historic Preservation Program, GSA, Washington, D.C.; testimony of Robert Buck and Gerry Rosen in "Public Hearings," pp. 373, 630.

28. Testimony of Barbara Jacobson, Donald Judd, Gerry Rosen, Terry Wilcox, Mary Kilroy, and Robert Murray, in "Public Hearing," pp. 252, 450, 629, 609, 92, 325.

it was a short step to the argument tht fine art was meant only for a learned elite. Thus gallery owner John Weber let the audience into "one of the most closely guarded secrets of the art world," namely "that art is not democratic. It is not for the people." Jessie McNab, Curator for the Metropolitan Museum of Art, likened *Tilted Arc* to the great cultic art of the ages. Stonehenge and the Gothic cathedrals "were not for the general public," she explained. "They were only for the esoteric few in each tribe, in each people or in each culture that could tolerate the stress of embodying what was happening to their consciousness at that moment and forcing it through and mediating it for the people as a whole."[29]

With remarks like these, the American avant-garde traveled full circle back to the position it had rejected twenty years earlier, when it railed against the art establishment, the fetishism of the autonomous art work, and the cultic aura that separated fine art from everyday experience. In fact, such arguments resurrected rigid conceptions of cultural hierarchy that Modernists and avant-gardists had hoped to demolish in the early twentieth century. It's not altogether surprising, then, to find the sculptor George Segal resorting to a version of Matthew Arnold's dictum that culture is the best that has been thought and said in the world. Art, Segal told the hearing, "has this value of trapping or encapsulating the best thinking of a generation." When pushed hard by their conservative opponents, defenders of *Tilted Arc* fell back on the argument that ordinary people were incapable of aesthetic judgment and that art should only address "the esoteric few in each tribe"—the best thinking for the best people.[30]

The artists who resurrected the ideal of an autonomous art for a knowledgeable elite found their strongest supporters in the very art establishment whose control of cultural production had driven Serra and his generation into the streets in the first place. The artists' defense of aesthetic autonomy went hand-in-hand with a defense of professional standards of art administration. "My understanding was that I was involved in a national program," Serra testified. "I thought the idea was to strive toward excellence. I understood this to mean that this program would not be subject to political currents, prejudices, ephemeral tastes, or bureaucratic pressures." Several comments by Serra's defenders revealed the symbiotic relationship between avant-garde art and its official apparatus of interpreters and administrators. "Art is often misunderstood by people who see it for the first time," Joan

29. Testimony of Jonas Mekas, John Weber, and Jessie McNab in "Public Hearing," pp. 532–33, 401–2, 284.

30. Testimony of George Segal in "Public Hearing," p. 98.

Mondale explained. "Initial public opinion," Donald Thalacker wrote in a letter to the *New York Times,* was "against the work of the French Impressionists, Picasso and even Michelangelo." Fortunately, informed professionals were on hand to certify the greatness of art and interpret difficult works to the public. " 'Tilted Arc,'" he wrote, "has been hailed as a bold and masterful work by the curators of the Museum of Modern Art, the Guggenheim Museum and the Whitney Museum of American Art and by New York City's Commissioner of Cultural Affairs." In a reversal of 1960s avant-garde polemics, the case for *Tilted Arc* became a vindication of New York's powerful cultural institutions.[31]

The specialization of knowledge and the fragmentation of culture have proceeded too far to admit any easy resolution of the tensions between artistic innovation and participatory democracy. It is undeniably true that many of the critics of *Tilted Arc* were ignorant of its art-historical context and hostile to the idea of public support for any kind of art. Yet Serra's aspirations to a radical art in public places and the sculpture's public location demanded more from the sculpture's advocates than they proved willing to concede. Specifically, it demanded from them a public imagination—the capacity to imagine a public for public art—that they never demonstrated. For the artists and their allies, public space was empty space until art entered the scene; its inhabitants were either ignorant Archie Bunkers or informed viewers whose appreciation of public art met the standards of professional interpreters. Serra and his allies never fully envisioned the possibility the office workers—as opposed to some heroic image of an earlier industrial proletariat—could constitute such a public. Even when they endorsed public education about abstract art, the avant-garde and the art establishment imagined a missionary project in which art would uplift the benighted masses to their standards. "I guess I believe in the trickle-down theory," Serra explained; "I choose to work in public spaces to get beyond the gallery and engage people who don't go there." But such "engagement" had to be a one-way process, given the assumption that public spaces were filled with people drunk on the promises of a consumer culture. Despite the claims that Serra's aesthetic offered up a multitude of interpretations, the message from the hearing was that public art flourished in an atmosphere of unanimity premised on professional standards. One correspondent let on to more than he realized when he proposed a facetious

31. Testimony of Richard Serra in Weyergraf-Serra and Buskirk, *Destruction,* pp. 68–69; testimony of Joan Mondale in "Public Hearing," p. 317; Donald W. Thalacker, letter to the editor, *New York Times,* 3 October 1981.

solution to the controversy in his letter to Diamond. "Take all the individuals working at the Javits Federal Building who do not like the Sculpture and move *them* somewhere else. They are not as heavy, not as expensive and most important not site specific."[32]

V

For their part, the judges, politicians, and pundits who attacked Serra's sculpture gave voice to the wide-ranging cultural lament of neoconservatives, free-market libertarians, and cultural traditionalists that preoccupied the media and policy-making elites in the 1980s. These three conservative factions differed in important respects when they addressed public art. Neoconservatives supported federal support for the arts, albeit at reduced levels of financing, but argued that the radical movements of the sixties and seventies had politicized art commissions and devalued cultural standards. The neoconservatives' goal was to discipline federal arts programs by reminding art bureaucrats of the need to promote "excellence," instead of entertainment or social engineering. Advocates of a free-market approach to the arts disagreed with the entire notion of government sponsorship of the arts. These libertarian conservatives saw such funding as an unconstitutional arrogation of powers by the federal government and a dangerous mixing of public and private spheres. By contrast, public financing of the arts was not in itself objectionable to cultural traditionalists allied with the New Right; what they wanted was government sponsorship of art that reaffirmed "traditional values" in morality, resurrected classical standards of aesthetic beauty, and celebrated the nation-state through commemorative and civic monuments. Whereas neoconservatives sought to resurrect a High Modernism untainted by mass culture or politics, and free-market conservatives wanted to keep avant-garde art in private homes or galleries where it belonged, cultural traditionalists expressed a long-standing conservative animosity toward Modernism for its subversion of aesthetic and moral conventions.

Despite these differences, conservatives united on a number of issues of central importance to the *Tilted Arc* case. First and foremost, they all held to the neoconservatives' theory that a "New Class" of professionals, intellectuals, and administrators had seized control of cultural institutions and put

32. Marzorati, "Artful Dodger"; Mikel Frank to William J. Diamond, 1 March 1985, *Tilted Arc* file, Arts and Historic Preservation Program, GSA, Washington, D.C.

them in the service of an "adversary culture" hostile to civic obligation, artistic integrity, and self-discipline. Despite the right's use of populist rhetoric in its argument against the "New Class," such a program in practice often boiled down to a clash between two elites. A cultural New Class employed in museums, universities, foundations, and government cultural agencies, which ranged politically from liberal to radical, found itself under attack in the 1980s by a more conservative economic and political elite represented in the *Tilted Arc* case by judges, local GSA officials, and the media.[33]

"The neoconservatives," according to Jurgen Habermas, "see their role as, on the one hand, mobilizing pasts that can be accepted approvingly and, on the other hand, morally neutralizing other pasts" that invite critical thinking about the present. The same could be said of the other two wings of the cultural right, which responded to the perceived crisis in public cultural symbols with a selective revision of the past. Conservatives referred vaguely to an edenic moment in the past when the symbolic language of public art reflected strong public consensus on values and iconography, a time when signifiers and signified were one and the same and easily accessible to all citizens. And although they disagreed on the appropriate nature of the relationship, conservatives all gestured to a time when Americans properly understood the balance between public and private spheres. "In reality," wrote one critic of *Tilted Arc*, "the greatest public art comes when there is the greatest unanimity of cultural, political, and religious aims." "A hundred years ago," James F. Cooper agreed, "everyone understood the purpose of public art. In stone, marble, and bronze were glorified the ideals and triumphs of the nation and the community." Such unanimity had given way to Babel, thanks to the radical chic of New Class liberals foisted upon an unsuspecting public. "With the ascension of Modernist art," Cooper

33. On neoconservatism and the critique of the New Class, see Peter Steinfels, *The Neoconservatives: The Men Who Are Changing America's Politics* (New York: Simon and Schuster, 1979); Barbara Ehrenreich, *Fear of Falling: The Inner Life of the Middle Class* (New York: HarperCollins, 1989), pp. 146–60; and Christopher Lasch, *The True and Only Heaven: Progress and Its Critics* (New York: Norton, 1991), pp. 512–22. It's worth noting that the neoconservative argument requires not just the preservation of distinctions between high and low culture, or between art and politics, but the introduction of new distinctions into the corpus of twentieth-century modern art itself. In the neoconservative version of the history of Modernism, formalist innovation is shorn of any association with political radicalism, bohemianism, sexual liberationism, or the avant-garde effort to eliminate the boundaries between art and life. The neoconservative campaign against the "adversary culture" of the "New Class" is thus partly aimed at the legacy of modern art itself.

argued, "it became increasingly difficult to create appropriate designs or to decide what in fact there was to memorialize. The result was to leave the decision to art 'experts' who usually opted for abstract forms."[34]

In the *Tilted Arc* debate, the lament about cultural decline took the form of a nostalgic narrative in which outsiders from Washington and New York's art world invaded a once tranquil Federal Plaza and transformed it from an oasis in the urban desert to an arena for avant-garde effrontery. Judge Edward Re complained that "a once beautiful plaza" was "rendered useless by an ugly, rusted, steel wall." Before Serra's intrusion, "the plaza served as a pleasant and humane open space for federal employees and the citizens of New York." Those testifying at the March 1985 hearing in favor of relocation of *Tilted Arc* made equally expansive claims for what had been lost in Federal Plaza. Donald Nawi, an attorney who spent much of his work life in the Foley Square area, composed a poem for the hearing:

> There was a plaza once.
> Now there is a steel wall.
> There was light there, air once.
> Now there is a steel wall.
> There were people once, mingling, looking, talking, sitting.
> Now there is a steel wall. . . .
> There was something once.
> Now there is nothing.

Joseph L. Liebman, another attorney, rhapsodized about the pastoral pastimes disrupted by Serra's sculpture.

I remember the cool spray of the fountain misting the hot air. I remember the band concerts. I remember the musical sound of neighborhood children playing on the plaza, while their mothers, sheltered under the courthouse, rocked baby carriages, still minding their children at play. I remember walking freely in the plaza, contemplating the examination of a witness, undisturbed by the presence of other people engaged in conversation or young lovers holding hands.

The old Federal Plaza allowed individuals to engage in solitary, anonymous pursuits together—"undisturbed by the presence of other people," in Liebman's revealing phrase. But all this was just a memory now. "The *Arc* has

---

34. Jurgen Habermas, "Neoconservative Cultural Criticism in the United States and West Germany," in Shierry Weber Nicholsen, ed. and trans., *The New Conservatism: Cultural Criticism and the Historian's Debate* (Cambridge: MIT Press, 1989), p. 43; Claire Stein, "Challenge: Sculpture in Public Places," *Sculpture Review* 32 (Spring 1983): 22–23; James F. Cooper, "Our Age Has Abandoned Beauty and Truth for the 'Gospel of Ugliness,'" *New York Tribune*, 9 February 1988.

condemned us to lead emptier lives," he testified; "the children, the bands, and I no longer visit the plaza."[35]

If the plaza had once facilitated the private interests of families and office workers on their lunch breaks, it had also served the official interests of the federal government. Critics of Serra's sculpture articulated a nationalist ideal of public spaces—one that liberals in recent years have increasingly ceded to conservatives—dominated by the pageantry and symbolism of the state. The hearing itself became an opportunity for government officials to reassert their symbolic authority over their own territory, which had been invaded by an elite of artistic outsiders. The committee overseeing the hearing was composed mostly of federal officials. Many judges wore their robes to testify, in a brazen display of their own power. For these officials, *Tilted Arc* threatened the plaza's proper operation in legitimating the authority of government. "We have gone to considerable expense to provide proper identification for the courthouse," Judge Re wrote in 1984, "and to generate respect for its symbol of justice." Re's colleague, Judge Paul P. Rao likewise spoke at the hearing of the plaza's need "to accommodate patriotic and civic activities." Another judge, Bernard Newman, recalled that "thousands" jammed the plaza for the rededication of the federal office building in honor or Senator Jacob K. Javits—a "historic, memorable" event that would be impossible to replicate, given the sculpture's presence. Shirley Paris, a local employee, noted that immigrants coming to the Immigration and Naturalization Service to apply for citizenship confronted "a rusty reminder of totalitarianism," instead of a symbol of "the American spirit." Harry Watson of the New York Bureau of Investigations compared Serra's work to statues of Benjamin Franklin, Horace Greeley, and Nathan Hale in City Hall Park, and added, "if [Hale] saw this 'Tilted Arc' he would say 'what did I give my life up for, if this is what they descend to in these days.'"[36]

Such statements idealized a public space given over to private pleasures (the classic liberal public sphere of individuals seeking what is in their own self-interest) or to ceremonial functions (the public sphere of patriots

35. Letter from Edward D. Re to Ray Kline, 5 November 1984, and testimony of Joseph I. Liebman, in Weyergraf-Serra and Buskirk, *Destruction,* pp. 27, 113; testimony of Donald Nawi in "Public Hearing," p. 79.

36. Letter from Edward D. Re to Ray Kline, 5 November 1984, and testimony of Shirley Paris, in Weyergraf-Serra and Buskirk, *Destruction,* pp. 27, 126; testimony of Judge Paul P. Rao in *Public Art/Public Controversy,* p. 145; testimony of Judge Bernard Newman and Harry Watson in "Public Hearing," pp. 588, 29–30.

mobilized to honor and defend the state). These proper public activities were under siege by the forces of civil disorder—criminals, the homeless, terrorists, graffiti, and garbage—that *Tilted Arc* had attracted to Federal Plaza. "This steel slab has virtually invited further desecration by grafitti artists," one petitioner wrote. Judge Re claimed that installation of the piece exacerbated the plaza's rat and sanitation problems. Judge Gregory Carmen testified that the "depressing and overbearing" work "looks like a subway construction site." "Transients have actually been seen urinating upon it," make the plaza "a place to avoid." In the political context of the early and mid-1980s, when American politicians and the media hammered away at the threat of international terrorism, it is not surprising that the demonology of *Tilted Arc* included charges that associated the work with terrorist violence. Judge Dominick L. DiCarlo was one of many who likened the sculpture to "an anti-terrorist barricade," a comparison that served to place the work beyond the pale of acceptable art for public spaces. The most extraordinary argument of this kind came from Vickie O'Dougherty, a security expert for the Federal Protection and Safety Division of GSA. O'Dougherty charged that the work blocked proper surveillance of the plaza. "From our side of the building we cannot see what goes on near the fountain and in the areas around the fountain." The 120-foot-long steel sculpture would create "a blast wall effect" for terrorists who planted a bomb on its concave side. *Tilted Arc,* she explained, "could vent an explosion both upward and in an angle toward both buildings." It hardly mattered that DiCarlo and O'Dougherty placed Serra's sculpture on opposite sides of the government's war against terrorism—as an "anti-terrorist barricade" and a terrorist gang's "blast wall." The problem with Serra's sculpture for such critics was its association with conflict and violence, which made it unsuitable as a backdrop to the individual or ceremonial activities conservatives deemed appropriate to public spaces.[37]

The rhetoric of national security pervaded the entire *Tilted Arc* debate, as both sides drew on the language and symbolism of the cold war to define the political issues at stake in the sculpture. Serra's defenders spoke of Maya Lin's debt to Serra in her Vietnam Veterans Memorial. His critics countered with another cold war icon: "[I]t looks as though it was ordered up by the KGB to fill a gap in the Berlin Wall." The recurrent refrain that

37. Petition to William J. Diamond, *Tilted Arc* files, Arts and Historic Preservation Program, GSA, Washington, D.C.; letter from Edward D. Re to Ray Kline, 5 November 1984, and testimony of Vickie O'Dougherty, in Weyergraf-Serra and Buskirk, *Destruction,* pp. 28, 117–18; testimony of Judge Dominick L. DiCarlo, in *Public Art/Public Controversy,* p. 141.

Tilted Arc was an "iron curtain"—what Shirley Paris and countless others called "the Berlin Wall of Foley Square"—not only preempted the charge of official censorship made by Serra and his supporters, it also associated the work with the national enemy and linked its sponsors in Washington with liberals who had proven soft on Communism. Petitions against the sculpture constantly made the cold war connection. "For the sake of peace, we should donate it to the USSR. Let the Russians put it outside the Kremlin," wrote one petitioner. Another asked, "Why not send that wall to East Berlin? That piece of art is . . . like a piece of Berlin Wall." James F. Cooper saw the two walls as equally menacing. "For conservatives to believe . . . that they've won the ideological battle by tearing down the Berlin Wall, is to ignore the other, equally important wall at home. Although smaller, *Tilted Arc* is symbolically as important as the Berlin Wall."[38]

In the end, conservatives defined *Tilted Arc* as the very antithesis of American patriotic iconography. A flyer that Diamond's office distributed in Federal Plaza to publicize the March 1985 hearing graphically made this point. Headlined "Speak Out!", it juxtaposed a photograph of *Tilted Arc* with a drawing of a Revolutionary War–era town crier ringing his bell while reading from a piece of paper—perhaps a petition denouncing this latest threat to the people's freedom? Tom Wolfe took this line of argument to its logical conclusion in a July 1986 *Newsweek* article on the "Liberty Weekend" extravaganza surrounding the rededication of the Statue of Liberty. Remarking on the outpouring of public enthusiasm for the monument, Wolfe "began to wonder what would be out in New York Harbor if the Statue of Liberty had been commissioned by the same people who would choose such a monument today." He then listed his version of the assumptions about sculpture shared by "all art experts" today: "No more pedestals"; "No more 'pictures in the air'"; "A sculpture must 'express its gravity'"; "A sculpture must 'express its object-ness.'" As he rattled off his parody of Modernist aesthetics, Wolfe described the successive transformation of Miss Liberty—dethroned from her pedestal, reduced to abstract form, and left to rust—into Serra's sculpture for Federal Plaza. "The creators of the new Liberty are in Luck! It so happens that 'Tilted Arc' itself

38. John McLaughlin, "Arc for Arc's Sake?," in *The Advance,* Staten Island, NY, 18 September 1987; testimony of Shirley Paris, in Weyergraf-Serra and Buskirk, *Destruction,* p. 126; petitions to William J. Diamond, *Tilted Arc* file, Arts and Historic Preservation Program, GSA, Washington, D.C.; James F. Cooper, "The Right Agenda: Recapture the Culture!," *American Arts Quarterly,* Spring–Summer 1990, 4.

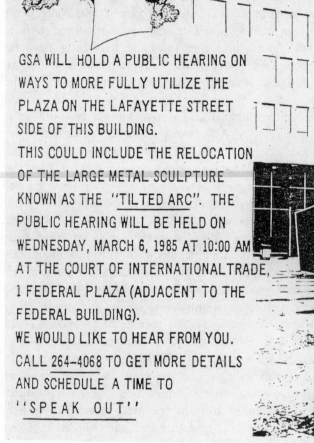

SPEAK OUT!

GSA WILL HOLD A PUBLIC HEARING ON WAYS TO MORE FULLY UTILIZE THE PLAZA ON THE LAFAYETTE STREET SIDE OF THIS BUILDING.
THIS COULD INCLUDE THE RELOCATION OF THE LARGE METAL SCULPTURE KNOWN AS THE "TILTED ARC". THE PUBLIC HEARING WILL BE HELD ON WEDNESDAY, MARCH 6, 1985 AT 10:00 AM AT THE COURT OF INTERNATIONALTRADE, 1 FEDERAL PLAZA (ADJACENT TO THE FEDERAL BUILDING).
WE WOULD LIKE TO HEAR FROM YOU. CALL 264-4068 TO GET MORE DETAILS AND SCHEDULE A TIME TO
"SPEAK OUT"

Flyer distributed by the GSA to announce the March 1985 public hearing on *Tilted Arc*.

is available." With this clever metamorphosis, Wolfe put the finishing touches on a campaign to transform Serra's abstract work into an easily recognizable object of contempt. *Tilted Arc* was not an "anti-environment," as Serra had intended, but an antimonument created by those who loathed the country's image of itself as a tribune of liberty.[39]

Tilted Arc's defenders characterized such arguments as a right-wing effort to privatize the art market, control public conduct, and suppress free speech. Serra described the conservative protest against *Tilted Arc* as "the direct outcome of a cynical Republican cultural policy that only supports art as a commodity." From this perspective, what most infuriated conservatives about the sculpture was its site-specific nature, which precluded its exchange in a traditional art market. The "market-oriented cultural policy of the Reagan administration," Clara Weyergraf-Serra wrote, "wants to suppress all forms of expression which try to circumvent commodity circulation." Douglas Crimp argued that critics of Serra's work envisioned a Foucauldian system of total surveillance and control over activity in public places. Since the destruction of his sculpture, Serra has repeatedly linked the *Tilted Arc* affair to the conservative campaign against NEA funding for exhibits of Robert Mapplethorpe's and Andres Serrano's work. Attempts to deny NEA funding to "obscene" artwork rest on "the assumption of a universal standard" of morality that no longer exists, he argues. "Whose standards are we talking about? Who dictates these standards?" "If government only allocates dollars for certain forms of art and not others, the government abolishes the First Amendment."[40]

It is undeniably the case that a desire to assert property rights over art, a preoccupation with security, and a fear of the troubling content of specific art works all influenced the conservative campaign against *Tilted Arc*. But a focus on the narrowly economic and ideological motives of conservative opponents of *Tilted Arc* obscures the larger cultural issues at stake in the controversy and impedes any understanding of the Right's ability to mobilize sufficient popular support for their cause. The case against *Tilted Arc* was never made solely on legal, economic, or security-related

---

39. Tom Wolfe, "The Copper Goddess," *Newsweek*, 14 July 1986, 35.

40. Richard Serra, "*Tilted Arc* Destroyed," *Art in America*, vol. 77, May 1989, p. 36; Clara Weyergraf-Serra, Preface to Weyergraf-Serra and Martha Buskirk, eds., *Richard Serra's "Tilted Arc"* (Eindhoven: Van Abbemuseum, 1988), p. 13; Richard Serra, "Art and Censorship," *Critical Inquiry* 17 (Spring 1991): 579, 580. See also testimony of Douglas Crimp in Weyergraf-Serra and Buskirk, *Destruction*, p. 74; Crimp, "Serra's Public Sculpture," in *Serra/Sculpture*, p. 55; and Hoffman, "Law for Art's Sake."

grounds. First and foremost, it was made in defense of a particular conception of how public and private spheres ought to be constituted and against imagined intruders who threatened that way of life. The controversy entailed a debate about the good life, a debate about culture in its moral and political—as well as aesthetic—dimensions.

Conservative critics of *Tilted Arc* did not so much advocate a system of total control as they did a vision of the public sphere as a place without significant spontaneity or political argument—in short a public sphere without public opinion. Individuals could make use of Federal Plaza for private, leisure-time activities that had no visible public consequence; otherwise, the function of the area was purely ceremonial. Conservatives invoked, alternately, a pastoral image of a properly policed and depoliticized oasis in lower Manhattan and a more authoritarian vision of government property presided over by state officials. The "refeudalization" of the public sphere that Habermas describes as the outcome of a bureaucratized politics and a consumer culture has as its corollary a shift from public deliberation to the public presentation of power. Public spaces, in the eyes of most conservatives, are places for unanimity, not debate or disagreement. They exist for the display of authority, not the give-and-take of public discussion.[41]

Achieving this end requires that all conflicts over cultural "values" or "subjective" issues be banished from the public realm, and that art objects provoking such conflicts be removed from public spaces. Like liberals who fear that disputes over religious and moral issues will turn politics into civil war, most conservative critics of *Tilted Arc* made distinctions between public and private spheres that essentially privatized culture and turned politics over to value-free administrative procedures. Michael Weyrboff, vice-president of the American Artists Professional League, argued, "In the privacy of our homes we can learn and like anything we like, but we cannot impose some of the ridiculous kind of views on the general public." Given

41. Jurgen Habermas, *The Structural Transformation of the Public Sphere: An Inquiry into a Category of Bourgeois Society,* trans. Thomas Burger (Cambridge: MIT Press, 1989), chap. 6. Habermas believes that the origins of the idea of public opinion derived partly from the coterie of literary and art audiences of eighteenth-century Europe, which constituted themselves as a rational authority separate from the state. Today, conservative politicians seek legitimacy by virtue of their closeness to popular cultural tastes—pork rinds, country and western music, and Hollywood movies—and by their mastery of the technology of mass spectacle.

the absence of a "universal standard by which artistic judgment is made," wrote Herbert London, "one is entrapped by subjectivity." With no way of resolving conflicts in "personal taste," London concluded, taxes should be used "to defend our liberty and not offend public sensibilities." Daniel Katz, a local employee, wrote Diamond, "We have separated our state from active involvement in religion because our wisdom is that the combination of the two is dangerous to freedom. For the same reason we must not let art claim an absolute right to influence the public, under the authority of an agreement with the government." After *Tilted Arc*'s removal, Hilton Kramer made a similar point in an article entitled, "Is Art Above the Laws of Decency?" Government sponsorship of "antisocial" art—including Serra's sculpture and Mapplethorpe's photographs—meant endorsing an unhealthy "attitude toward life" previously restricted to the coterie culture of artistic and sexual radicals.[42]

None of these arguments addressed the political question of how distinctions between public and private culture are to be defined in a democratic society. Just as art administrators cling to professional procedures as a safeguard against public discussion, conservatives search for some "universal standard" beyond politics to order public affairs. Failing to find such a standard in matters of artistic preference, they seek to remove cultural controversies to private life, where they won't interfere with the smooth functioning of public and corporate bureaucracies. If the *Tilted Arc* case demonstrates anything, however, it is just how political the debate over public art actually is, how much it reflects conflicts over the control and use of public spaces, and how these conflicts in turn resonate with deeper disagreements about the ordering of public and private life in modern culture. Such disputes are unlikely to end so long as they are defined in the terms used by artistic professionals and conservative officials, both of whom subscribe to the myth of a unanimous public culture administered according to incontrovertible principles. By denying the possibility of rational resolution of cultural controversies through inclusive democratic discussion, art administrators and conservative policymakers guarantee that

---

42. Testimony of Michael Weyrboff, in "Public Hearing," p. 453; Herbert London, "Let's End Public Funding of Demoralizing Art," *New York Tribune,* 15 August 1985; Daniel Katz to William Diamond, n.d., *Tilted Arc* file, Arts and Historic Preservation Program, GSA, Washington, D.C.; Hilton Kramer, "Is Art Above the Laws of Decency?," *New York Times,* 2 July 1989. See also Hilton Kramer, "A Plaza Taken Hostage," *Times Literary Supplement,* 8 November 1991, p. 25.

such differences will only be resolved through the imposition of force. In the meantime, our collective ability to imagine a truly public culture will remain impoverished.[43]

VI

And what of the phantom public endlessly invoked by supporters and critics of *Tilted Arc*? Conservatives thought they knew all about the public. The public was the silent majority roused from its private routines by the offenses committed by cultural radicals. Tom Wolfe displayed his inimitable gift for patronizing his social inferiors when he described the "Civil Service workers" who gathered at lunchtime in Federal Plaza in the summer of 1981 "to do the usual, which was to have their tuna puffs and diet Shastas," when they first confronted the offending "wall of black steel." John Simon, writing in the *National Review*, championed "the *vox populi*, which, unacquainted with current art criticism, has the honesty and courage to pronounce ugliness offensive." A recurrent device in national media coverage of the controversy involved the juxtaposition of a complex statement by Serra or one of his supporters on the aesthetics of *Tilted Arc* with the earthy comments of employees who hated the work. Despite the occasional references to a potential working-class audience moved by *Tilted Arc*'s radical message, the pro-Serra artists and administrators who spoke at the 1985 public hearing shared a similar view of the public. Hostile to difficult art it could not understand, the public preferred the cheap satisfactions of consumer culture and the nationalist flattery of right-wing politicians.[44]

A very different image of this public emerges from reading the statements that local office workers wrote in the space reserved for additional comments in the petitions the GSA distributed in Federal Plaza on the possible relocation of Serra's work. To be sure, a great deal of ugliness appears in these comments: anti-intellectualism; animus against modern art, indeed art of any kind; and frightening fantasies of violence against Serra and his sculpture. It is not necessary to romanticize the positions advanced in the petitions in order to take seriously the sense of grievance

43. "I think the main reason there is so little genuine public art today," wrote critic Amy Goldin in 1974, "is our disbelief in the reality of the public world." "The Esthetic Ghetto: Some Thoughts About Public Art," *Art in America*, vol. 62, May–June 1974, 34.

44. Tom Wolfe, "The Worship of Art: Notes on the New God," *Harpers*, October 1984, 67; John Simon, "Arc without Covenant," *National Review*, vol. 41, 5 May 1989, 32.

they express. Again and again, petitioners made use of the controversy to address their feeling of powerlessness as federal employees and their resentment at being manipulated by the elite groups fighting over the plaza. "*You* didn't ask for our opinion when *you* put the damned thing in the plaza," one petitioner wrote Diamond, "so why now do *you* want our opinions to solve *your* problems!" "Although I had no say-so in having the 'Tilted Arc' placed in the plaza," wrote another, "I damn sure am against it blocking the beautification of the plaza." Such anger at government officials was matched by hostility toward the perceived presumptuousness of fine art institutions. "Send it up to MOMA," one person wrote, "and let them set it up across 53rd St. Better yet—set it up in front of *their* front doors." And many petitioners, conscious of the way in which the debate turned on the possession of cultural competence, staked a claim to their own competence as art interpreters. They were well aware "that those who support removal of the Arc will be labeled as anti-art, low-brow Philistines," but they made their case against the sculpture anyway, all the while proclaiming their love and knowledge of modern art.[45]

At the public hearing, *Tilted Arc*'s defenders often argued that the sculpture was an irrational target for employees' anger. Art historian Benjamin H. D. Buchloh held that "to defend the prison house architecture of Federal Plaza against the intrusion of Serra's sculpture" was a classic example of what Freud called "identification with the aggressor." Museum director Suzanne Delehanty charged critics of the sculpture with "expressing the nostalgia we all feel for an irretrievable past, for those cities with three-story buildings." Those favoring its relocation were actually venting "the outrage invoked by the architecture of the courthouse itself." Yet the petitions show that very few of the sculpture's critics outside of official circles defended Federal Plaza and its buildings: most believed they were as sterile and alienating as Serra's sculpture implied. "The presence of this junk," one petitioner wrote of *Tilted Arc*, "highlights the gracelessness of most modern government architecture."[46]

What most disturbed many petitioners was their belief that Serra was engaged in a symbolic war with the federal bureaucracy—as represented in the dreary architecture of Federal Plaza—at their expense. These writers

45. Petitions to William J. Diamond in *Tilted Arc* file, Arts and Historic Preservation Program, GSA, Washington, D.C.

46. Testimony of Benjamin H. D. Buchloh and Suzanne Delehanty in Weyergraf-Serra and Buskirk, *Destruction,* pp. 92, 84; petition to William J. Diamond in *Tilted Arc* file, Arts and Historic Preservation Program, GSA, Washington, D.C.

understood the political implications of Serra's work, but they rejected its confrontational stance on the grounds that it aggravated the inhumanity of an already inhospitable space. Such a response was often far more thoughtful than one might guess if one's attention remained riveted to the jockeying of cultural and governmental authorities. "I do not care to be challenged on a daily basis by something designed to be hostile," one person wrote. "With such limited open space in NY City," another wrote, "I believe that this sculpture is totally inappropriate in our plaza. I believe that it is very selfish of the artist to totally occupy public space with his idea of a 'challenge' to that space." "Mr. Serra's sculpture only serves to deface and destroy an already 'unfriendly' public space," another petitioner argued. Such comments suggest that the attempt to expose the political geography of sculptural space that worked so well for Serra in galleries and museums had disastrous consequences in a public space where the divide between human aspirations and bureaucratic power was already painfully evident. "I suppose the Arc is intended to represent the banality and sterility of bureaucracy," one writer noted. "What we need, however, is something to enliven our lives, not something which reinforces the negative aspects of our work lives. The Arc insults us by associating Federal workers with [banality and sterility]." "For several years," another person wrote, "I have commented to friends, acquaintances & associates that even if this piece of rusted metal is supposed to have a 'message' (i.e.—that life in NYC is 'rusted' 'cold' or 'hideous') we do not need constant reminders of that message."[47]

By protesting the ways in which *Tilted Arc* deepened the alienation they already felt in Federal Plaza, petitioners broke out of the confines of both the avant-garde and conservative positions in the debate. They complained about the broken fountain, the jagged cobblestones that made walking in the plaza hazardous, and the dreary offices within the government buildings. "As an employee at 26 Federal Plaza, I am appalled at the working conditions INSIDE the building and I feel that this matter is of more importance than the arc relocation." "I have to walk up and down drab, dimly lit halls," another person wrote, "with dirt and roaches everywhere, in a repetitive search to find a copy machine within a 4-floor radius that works *and* has paper." Several petitioners made the connection between the bleak-

47. Petitions to William J. Diamond in *Tilted Arc* file, Arts and Historic Preservation Program, GSA, Washington, D.C.

ness they confronted every day in the plaza and the authoritarian organization of power within their workplaces. One suggested replacing the sculpture with a "2/3 story (elevated) office complex for the administrative GSA
personnel so that more space can be utilized by the tenants. Also it would
be an aggravation to see the janitorial staff constantly cleaning, polishing,
vacuuming etc only the GSA areas while the rest of the building is treated
shabbily." Many others noted that the sculpture's installation coincided
with the Reagan Administration's layoffs and salary cuts for federal employees. "I remember when this was put up," recalled one person, "there was
a big cut in personnel." "The government can use the money to pay for
the employees they are doing away with it," was one response. "Feed the
hungry, shelter the homeless, restore jobs before you insult us in this way,"
was another. "Also, remove Reagan," demanded another petitioner. Clearly,
the conservative notion that popular mobilization could be limited to a
crusade against the "adversary culture" was mistaken. So was Weyergraf-
Serra's belief that "direct democracy" was aimed only against art. Once the
discussion of public space began, popular grievances erupted that escaped
the terms of conservative cultural politics.[48]

The aesthetic-political position articulated in these petitions might best
be called a "humanistic functionalism." Again and again, petitioners asked
that the plaza "be set aside for people-related activity." The most popular
suggestion was to turn the plaza into a park with trees, flowers, benches,
tables, and food vendors, a place for concerts and art exhibits. Requests
for such "people-related activity" hardly amounted to identification with
the bleak architecture of the surrounding buildings. Such suggestions were
potentially as subversive of the iconography of power expressed in Federal
Plaza as Serra's "anti-environment." Unlike Serra, however, petitioners believed that a participatory ethic should underwrite any redesign of the area.
Even opponents of relocation suggested altering the sculpture to make
Federal Plaza more responsive to the needs and aspirations of its occupants.
"Maybe you could paint it a bright color," was a recurrent suggestion. Many
wrote that *Tilted Arc* "should be made a mural painting." "I feel it should
stay but be 'polished'!!", was another popular request. Others suggested
that holes be cut into the sculpture so as to permit views of Foley Square;
one petitioner proposed placing hanging flowers and wind chimes in the
resulting windows. "Openings at strategic points" in the sculpture would

48. Ibid.

"make it more interesting," one person wrote, "turning it from a cold and bland mass of metal into something enjoyable and useful."[49]

Serra would rightly respond that these alterations, no less than relocation, would entail the destruction of *Tilted Arc*. His supporters among art administrators would also argue, with some justification, that the protection that professional commissioning procedures provide from such popular pressures is indispensable to giving artists free space to experiment with unusual and innovative forms. Professional standards, in their view, provide the context in which debates about the aesthetics of public spaces can take place without fear of intimidation or censorship. The point at issue, however, is that the two elite discourses that dominated the *Tilted Arc* controversy rarely recognized the existence of a popular aesthetic that was as hostile to the official iconography of Federal Plaza as it was to *Tilted Arc*. Blindness to that aesthetic cut short the possibility of a genuine debate about public art from the very start by denying the public the potential for independent, reasoned aesthetic judgment. Conservatives indulged their fantasies of popular rage at the "adversary culture" without bothering to ask if the public shared their idyllic vision of the old Federal Plaza.

Serra and his allies likewise assimilated popular sentiments about public art to the rhetoric of conservative *kulturkampf*. "I should have known," he wrote after the destruction of his sculpture, "that television delivers people, that all public opinion is manipulated opinion." But this assumption of a hegemonic capitalist culture so powerful as to manage the consciousness of the entire public (with the notable exception of avant-garde artists, critics, and art administrators) apparently freed *Tilted Arc's* defenders from the need to inquire about the precise nature of the criticism aimed at the sculpture. Art critic Lucy Lippard made exactly this point in a letter to Diamond protesting relocation. Lippard objected to the removal of the piece as a breach of contract and of faith that would endanger future public arts programs. But she went on to note "that at no time in these lengthy procedings did *anyone* think about consulting with the people who live with the art on a daily basis. Public art is a commitment not only to the artist and the funding source and the owners of the site, but to the people themselves—to the idea of a democratic culture." In its failure to entertain the very "idea of a democratic culture" during the *Tilted Arc* debate, the avant-garde demonstrated the political impoverishment of late Modernism. Unable to countenance public opinion or popular taste, hostile to any

49. Ibid.

understanding of art's relation to other social activities, the avant-garde left itself no defense from powerful critics intolerant of its effrontery.[50]

Indeed, it was the hope for a democratic culture that finally proved so elusive throughout the entire debate about *Tilted Arc*. A few dissident artists and critics were moved by the *Tilted Arc* case to argue for "an aesthetics of collaboration" consonant with the spirit of Lippard's letter. But most of the actors who dominated the events that led to the destruction of the work displayed a debilitating pessimism about the possibility of a truly public art. "What the *Tilted Arc* controversy forces us to consider," Suzi Gablick observes, "is whether art based on pure, content-less freedom —regardless of any relations we have to other people, or any affinity to the community or *any* other consideration except the pursuit of art— can contribute to a sense of the common good." The absence of deliberation on the positive functions of public space forced artists and viewers to choose between affirmations of bureaucratic authority and "antienvironments" that opposed one language of power to another in a gigantic version of Serra's *One Ton Prop*. Despite their differences, both options shared a common premise: democratic debate on a functional aesthetic for public spaces was impossible.[51]

50. Serra, Introduction to Weyergraf-Serra and Buskirk, *Destruction*, p. 10; Lucy Lippard to William J. Diamond, n.d., *Tilted Arc* file, Arts and Historic Preservation Program, GSA, Washington, D.C. One of the terrible ironies of the events leading to the dismantling of *Tilted Arc* was the decision against Serra's legal suit to block relocation on (among other things) First Amendment grounds. The U.S. Court of Appeals ruling against Serra held that "the decision to remove 'Tilted Arc' was not impermissibly content-based." The government's concern with the piece's supposed ugliness was an appropriate "exercise of discretion with respect to the display of its own property," according to the Court. But the judge found "no assertion of facts to indicate that GSA officials understood the sculpture to be expressing any particular idea. . . . Indeed, Serra is unable to identify any particular message conveyed by 'Tilted Arc' that he believes may have led to its removal." That "message" was clear enough to the officials who feared the work's challenge to their authority, but the antipopulist Modernism that guided Serra's aesthetics made it impossible to acknowledge that "any particular idea" was expressed in *Tilted Arc*. *Serra v. United States General Services Administration*, United States Court of Appeals, 2d Circuit, 27 May 1988.

51. Suzi Gablick, "Deconstructing Aesthetics: Toward a Responsible Art," *New Art Examiner*, vol. 16, January 1989, 35. Among other relevant contributions to this alternative position are Anna C. Chave, "Minimalism and the Rhetoric of Power"; Olivia Gude, "An Aesthetics of Collaboration," *Art Journal*, vol. 48, Winter 1989, 321–23; Arthur C. Danto, "*Tilted Arc* and Public Art," and "Public Art and the General Will," in Danto, *The State of the Art*, pp. 95–100, 118–23; and Robert Storr, *Tilted Arc*: Enemy of the People?," *Art in America*, vol. 73, September 1985, 90–97. See also the special issue of *Art Journal*, vol. 48, Winter 1989, devoted to public art. These tentative efforts to define a "collaborative" approach to public art dovetailed with the polemics in the *Village Voice* against *Tilted Arc*. See Gary Indiana, "Debby with Monument: A Dissenting Opinion," *Village Voice*, 16 April 1985, and Schjeldahl, "Artistic Control."

"In order to understand the meaning of artistic products," John Dewey wrote in *Art as Experience,* "we have to forget them for a time, to turn aside from them and have recourse to the ordinary forces and conditions of experience that we do not usually regard as esthetic. We must arrive at the theory of art by means of a detour." A long detour into the terms of

Federal Plaza before and after the removal of *Tilted Arc.* Photos by David Aschkenas (before) and Jennifer Kotter (after).

the debate over *Tilted Arc* locates the meaning of the work in the very "atmosphere of effrontery" it provoked for eight years in Federal Plaza. Today, all that remains of that atmosphere is the scar in the plaza's pavement where the sculpture once stood. The plaza itself has been suitably tranquilized by its official restoration. The fountain remains broken, high winds still rip through the space, but a half-dozen benches and concrete planters break up the blank emptiness of the area and provide an occasional resting spot for employees and homeless people. A bitter defeat for Serra and his allies, the destruction of *Tilted Arc* was no victory for "the public," despite the claims made on its behalf at the rededication ceremony for the plaza. For if one believes that a genuine public thrives on democratic controversy, then it follows that only a commitment to such controversy can foster challenging public art—including acts of effrontery like *Tilted Arc*. To imagine that public requires another detour, far from the avant-garde and conservative elites fighting over Federal Plaza, to "the ordinary forces and conditions of experience."[52]

52. John Dewey, *Art as Experience* (New York: Paragon Books, 1939), p. 4.

Contributors

Casey Nelson Blake teaches American history at Indiana University. He is the author of *Beloved Community: The Cultural Criticism of Randolph Bourne, Van Wyck Brooks, Waldo Frank, and Lewis Mumford* (1990). He is at work on a book on the politics of public art in twentieth-century America.

Lisabeth Cohen is associate professor of history at New York University. She is the author of *Making a New Deal: Industrial Workers in Chicago, 1919–1939*, which won the Bancroft Prize in 1991. She is at work on a book, "A Consumer's Republic: The Politics of Consumption in Postwar America," which builds on her essay in this volume.

Richard Wightman Fox is professor of history and director of the American Studies Program at Boston University. He is the author of *Reinhold Niebuhr: A Biography* (1986) and the co-editor, with T. J. Jackson Lears, of *The Culture of Consumption* (1983). He is at work on a cultural history of liberal Protestantism in America, including a longer study of the Beecher-Tilton affair.

Karen Halttunen is professor of history at the University of California at Davis. She is the author of *Confidence Men and Painted Women: A Study of Middle-Class Culture in America, 1830–1870* (1982), and is at work on a study of murder and the Gothic imagination in American culture.

T. J. Jackson Lears is professor of history Rutgers University. His *No Place of Grace: Antimodernism and the Transformation of American Culture, 1880–1920* (1981) was nominated for a National Book Critics Circle award. In addition, he is the author of numerous scholarly articles and co-editor (with Richard Wightman Fox) of *The Culture of Consumption* (1983), and is currently at work on a book on advertising and American culture.

Joan Shelley Rubin is associate professor of American studies and history at the State University of New York at Brockport. She is the author of *Constance Rourke and American Culture* (1980) and *The Making of Middlebrow Culture* (1992).

Michael L. Smith taught at Yale University and Williams College before joining the faculty of the Department of History of the University of California at Davis in 1986. He is the author of *Pacific Visions: California Scientists and the Environment, 1850–1915* (1988), and has published numerous articles on technology and advanced industrial culture in the United States.

Robert B. Westbrook teaches American history at the University of Rochester. He is the author of *John Dewey and American Democracy* (1991) and numerous essays on American cultural and intellectual history. His contribution to this volume draws on research for "Why We Fought," a work-in-progress on American conceptions of political obligation during World War II.

Christopher P. Wilson is professor of English and American studies at Boston College. His most recent book is *White Collar Fictions: Class and Social Representation in American Literature, 1885–1925* (1992).